Ho

By Jamie R. Smolen, MD

Library of Congress Cataloging-in-Publication Data
    Smolen, Jamie R.
    Hooked / Jamie R. Smolen.
        p. cm.
    ISBN 978-1-937240-01-1 (pbk.)
    1. Teenagers--Drug use. 2. Drug abuse--Prevention. 3. Drug addicts--Rehabilitation. 4. Drug abuse--Treatment. I. Title.

    HV5824.Y68S653 2011
    362.290835--dc23

2011028688

Published by
Casa de Snapdragon Publishing LLC
12901 Bryce Avenue, NE
Albuquerque, NM 87112
http://www.casadesnapdragon.com
20111109

Printed in the United States of America

To JoAnn

Because of you, my eyes wake to incredible beauty every morning;

Because of you, my heart dances to the beat of a warm and tender love song;

Because of you, my mind is free and smiles with Big Wonderful Dreams;

Because of you, all my dreams come true;

Because of you, my life is rich and getting richer, full and getting fuller,

happy and getting happier;

Because of you, I am content and know that the first and last blessing

I will ever need is YOU.

CONTENTS

Preface.. iii

Prologue.. v

Chapter 1: *The First Pill* 1

Chapter 2: *The New Priority*.. 8

Chapter 3: *Any Price at All* 16

Chapter 4: *Sidney Redux* 24

Chapter 5: *Precious Jewels* 28

Chapter 6: *Your Life Depends On It Now* 34

Chapter 7: *This Party Should Last Forever* 38

Chapter 8: *It Takes $$$ to Keep the Party Going*........................... 41

Chapter 9: *Upping the Ante*... 49

Chapter 10: *I'll Never Do That Again* 56

Chapter 11: *Drugs Are Bad—You Know That*................................. 65

Chapter 12: *Pills Are Worth Fighting For*.. 70

Chapter 13: *Keeping Me Alive*.. 77

Chapter 14: *I Didn't Mean for This to Happen* 83

Chapter 15: *The Specialists* 88

Chapter 16: *You'll Eventually Run Out of Something* 95

Chapter 17: *The Fallout* 99

Chapter 18: *Maintaining the Trade Agreement*............................. 105

Chapter 19: *I'm Not a Drug Addict*.. 111

Chapter 20: *Jeffrey*... 117

Chapter 21: *The Rush* 122

Chapter 22: *My Son is Gone, but You Get to Go Home*............... 127

Chapter 23: *Get Me Out of Here*... 130

Chapter 24: *Play Now, Pay Later* 137

Chapter 25: *Gone Again* 142

Chapter 26: *I Didn't Know What I Didn't Know*........................... 147

Chapter 27: *Could I Be Addicted?* 157

Chapter 28: *The Way to the Winner's Circle*.................................. 162

Chapter 29: *Recovery Begins with Honesty*.................................... 166

Chapter 30: *The Loser's Life*.. 173

Chapter 31: *Drugs Are a Tricky Thing*.. 181

Chapter 32: *Journaling*.. 188

Chapter 33: *Your Money or Your Life* 192

Chapter 34: *High Powers Come in All Shapes and Sizes* 197

Chapter 35: *At the End of My Rope*.. 204

Chapter 36: *Learning Lessons* 213
Chapter 37: *The Bruise Brothers* 220
Chapter 38: *A Purpose for Living* 227
Chapter 39: *Welcome Home* 235
Chapter 40: *Addiction in Your Dreams* 241
Chapter 41: *Phone Calls and Messages* 250
Chapter 42: *All Types of Messages* 255
Chapter 43: *Love Someone as Much as You Know How* 264
Chapter 44: *Loosening Up with Jeffrey* 270
Chapter 45: *The First Meeting* 281
Chapter 46: *Messengers* 289
Chapter 47: *Debriefing* 299
Chapter 48: *Different* 306
Chapter 49: *Visiting Dr. Stone* 312
Chapter 50: *Drug Testing* 320
Chapter 51: *Finding Myself* 326
Chapter 52: *Recovery Angel* 334
Chapter 53: *Spiritual Ink* 340
Chapter 54: *Heaven is Being Perfect* 347
Chapter 55: *My Name is George Oliver Danbury* 357
Chapter 56: *Alan's Story* 365
Chapter 57: *The Medallion Story* 371
Chapter 58: *Love Will Set Me Free* 379
Chapter 59: *Hearts Don't See Ugly* 386
Epilogue 391
Acknowledgments 394
About the Author 397

PREFACE

This is a story about the grand illusion that drugs can remove the pain for a less-than-attractive teenager whose life is filled with self-loathing, loneliness, rejection, and humiliating persecution by his peers. It's about the belief that a pill can remodel him into a socially acceptable young man who is self-confident, accepted, and loved.

This is a story about addiction.

When I first decided to write about addiction, my intention was to compose something short—a booklet that I could distribute wherever I was speaking in public. Addictions of all kinds have fascinated me, and fighting them has been my passion for the past nineteen years. In the 1990s I fought to win my own life back after I had lost it to the disease of alcoholism and I knew firsthand the immense, destructive force of addiction. More important, I knew the even greater and unlimited power of recovery. I have always been an avid reader of self-help literature and a practitioner of many recommendations that have excited me into believing I could be, have, and do anything I desired. The incredible results of my efforts in alcohol recovery have proved that to be true over and over again. In my work with patients, I have shared this message candidly and without shame; I try to show those who lack hope that anything is possible. This book is another version of that message.

I have learned a lot over the years about the power of addiction. It lures you in with ecstatic extremes of pleasure before attaching like a parasite, draining the life energy from your body, mind, and spirit. I learned these truths from my own addiction, and they were verified by my many years of experience as a physician who specializes in addiction psychiatry. I know firsthand that addiction begins like a tempting flirtation and it promises something wonderful; just ask any addict to describe the best high he or she has ever had. But once a drug takes you hostage, a potent and destructive force is unleashed and that force has no conscience and no mercy. That is the power that took over my life. I wanted to share my personal story and professional understanding of that insidious, destructive power in an effort to save others from the downward spiral that life becomes when one is addicted to a substance.

As I tried to write my short booklet, I realized that the most effective way to illustrate how addiction really feels was to tell a story about a teenager who gets hooked on painkillers. Sadly, this is a common addiction in my practice, one that has reached alarming and epidemic proportions. At times, the accounts and descriptions may seem unbelievable; I assure you that as a professional who has treated addicts during medical emergencies, every medical detail has happened.

This is a cautionary tale told from the viewpoint of a sixteen-year-old boy named Buddy, who details what drug use is like. You'll feel what Buddy feels, from the euphoria he experiences the first time he gets high to the despair that swallows him when survival seems hopelessly impossible. Buddy is willing to take unfathomable risks to "be happy," even when those risks carry a very high price. Some readers who have already taken the path of addiction will be familiar with Buddy's experience. In this story, Buddy is introduced to frequently prescribed painkillers, habit-forming narcotics known by their commercial names: Lortab, Roxicodone, and OxyContin. Tiny molecules of these drugs attach to the pleasure receptors in the addicted brain and instantly create a delightfully satisfying experience. It's called "getting high," and it is what keeps a first-time user like Buddy coming back for more.

For other readers, the descriptions that follow may seem exaggerated and fantastic. Buddy's story is meant to be a warning to teens and adults who smugly believe "It can't happen to me," because it can, or "I can control this," because they cannot. And yet, there is always hope, and that is why I felt compelled to write this story. Buddy struggles—with pills, with addiction, with himself—but in the end, he finds the path to recovery and attains his sobriety. Like the young subject of my story, I was able to take advantage of the tremendous outpouring of support and guidance offered by those already on the path, and I was restored to someone who could finally look in the mirror and understand the healing touch of forgiveness, acceptance, friendship, and love.

To anyone who flirts with drug use, intending to get high and escape the stress of life, or who suffers the pain of addiction: I dedicate this story to you. I hope you will be ready and willing when help arrives and say "yes" to sober living. You deserve a wonderful life, and as Buddy learns, there are only winners in recovery. You've always been perfect, whole, and complete.

PROLOGUE

I'm only sixteen years old and I'm already addicted to prescription painkillers. That may be hard to believe, but it's true. I thought it would take years of hard-core drug abuse to turn someone into an addict; it only took me a few days to get hooked and into serious trouble. That may seem impossible, but it's not. That's the reason I'm telling my story.

Many kids my age are curious about experimenting with drugs. I wasn't one of them. I was a recluse and kept to myself at school. I hated the isolation, but it was better than being made fun of, which happened a lot when I was a kid. So when I was handed my first painkiller, it was as though the whole world opened up and invited me to join the party. I had been a reject for so long that I was ready for any shortcut to happiness. I just took that pill without hesitation and instantly hoped for the best. I was surrounded by classmates who were having fun, and for the first time in my life I saw a way to be accepted. I liked how that first pill made me feel. Then I wanted another. When the pills wore off, all I could think about was how to get more. Soon, that's all I wanted. The classmates no longer mattered, only the pills. That's what I call hooked.

Getting unhooked was the hardest thing I've ever done. The odds of staying clean are not very good—for anybody. But I did it, and today I'm celebrating three months of sobriety. That may not seem like much but, when you've been used to getting high, you can't imagine living without it. Every day you're on a desperate mission to find money to pay for it. So three months for me, without a pill, seems like a miracle.

I did it by joining a sober recovery group. Every one of us has abused painkillers and gotten into trouble. We meet once a week to talk about addiction and how to beat it. I learned that addiction is a disease, not a disgrace. It's treatable—as long as I stay away from pills and anyone who has them. The fourteen people in my group have helped me understand that my disease wants to get high at my expense. Now I am convinced that it's possible to be happy without feeding my addiction, and that's worth a lot to me.

It's a tradition in the group to tell your addiction story after at least one month clean. That's when the group really gets to know you a lot better. Later on tonight, at our meeting, it's my turn. This is the story I'm going to tell them.

CHAPTER 1

The First Pill

I was not a typical teenager, since I was too ugly to be typical. Not just homely, but pimple ugly. I had the kind of acne that came back after every type of treatment, and my mom made me try them all. She thought if my skin was clear, I wouldn't get picked on. She was wrong; my classmates were mean.

I can't remember a time when I ever really fit in anywhere . . . and I didn't want to fit in anyway. I preferred to be left alone and ignored. My mother had other ideas, though. When I was younger, she went to great lengths to stuff this square peg into every round hole she could. She arranged play dates and signed me up for sports. She thought if I went to summer camp, I'd make friends, because sooner or later somebody had to like me. Instead, I got wedgies. It was torture, and I hated her for that.

Mom eventually backed off. I was a geeky, skinny, scrawny nerd who lived a miserable and dejected existence. I was a prime target for anyone who could show me a way to be happy.

"Buddy, come over here."

I looked up and saw the new girl. She was surrounded by a group of kids I knew from school. I had seen her before, but I didn't know her name. I was walking home from the corner where the bus dumped everyone who lived in the development. I was always the last one off the bus because getting noticed made me nervous. I heard her call my name, but I just kept walking with my head down. The new girl waved to get my attention, but I pretended not to see her.

She had transferred into my school during the middle of the semester as a senior. I had seen her studying me in the hallways, which made me feel like some kind of biology specimen. I wondered why she kept looking at me, because she was beautiful without even trying, and I was too ugly to look at. Plus, I was only a tenth-grader, so what could she possibly find interesting about me?

I had nothing to lose, so one day I decided to stare right back when she looked at me. If she could look at me for her reasons, I should be able to look at her for mine. And I did. My reason was crazy: I imagined that she cared about me and wanted to meet me. She had smiled at me the day before, and I thought she'd winked. Maybe she had just blinked.

Her attention freaked me out, but something inside told me to follow her.

Her every move made my hands clammy and my face heat up, so I stopped. I knew I had no business getting my hopes up that someone so beautiful might be interested in me.

But today I was walking home and she was calling my name.

"Buddy, wait up. I want to talk to you."

I looked up just enough to see her break away from the group and skip toward me. Her blonde ponytail swayed from side to side. She wore a baseball cap that accentuated her perfect nose, and the pale green fabric speckled with tiny green frogs made her eyes look green, too.

She was tall, with long, athletic legs. She was in great shape. I let her catch up to me. I was hoping she would be as kind as she was pretty, but I was prepared for anything. I kept my eyes focused on the sidewalk in front of me, but tried to sneak a glance at her ass. She stood there smiling.

Her teeth were perfect. Of course they were.

"I've seen you at school. My name is Sidney."

I looked at her for another split second and quickly lowered my head. She was way too attractive. I didn't speak. I couldn't.

"You know," she said, "I've been kinda curious about you. I've asked around, but nobody has much to say, except that you keep to yourself."

I raised my head just enough to steal another quick glance, and this time I became captivated by her smile. Her voice was kind, which made her even more irresistible.

"I think the kids at school have treated you badly," she continued, her silky voice beginning to calm my nerves. "So, I thought I'd introduce myself. Maybe you'll give me a chance to show you how nice I can be. What do you say?"

Why would you pick the ugliest kid in school to be nice to? The thought almost made it out of my mouth. I tried to think of the worst reasons why someone as pretty as Sidney would ever approach *me*. She had to be setting me up for something embarrassing.

"You don't say much, do you?" she asked, her voice as soothing as if she was speaking to a skittish puppy.

I nodded my head and shrugged my shoulders, but I said nothing.

"We're all going to have a little fun," Sidney continued, undaunted by my lack of response. "Why don't you join us? I think you'll like it."

I looked at the group of kids she'd been with and then back at Sidney. I knew I should walk away, but she was so nice to me, and people were almost never nice to me.

"Okay, lead the way." My voice was barely a whisper.

As we got closer to the kids who were waiting for Sidney, several of them stopped talking to each other and just stared at us. I pulled up short, and Sidney grabbed my arm.

"Oh, no you don't," she cajoled. "You can do this. Stay next to me and you'll be all right."

I wanted to bolt. I needed to talk about this.

I turned around so I didn't have to face the other kids. I was nervous, so I kept my voice low enough that only Sidney could hear me.

"You seem all right, but I know these kids don't like me."

I pulled on Sidney's arm until we were a few more steps away from the group. They just stared at us as though we were some kind of sideshow.

My voice sounded anxious, even to me. "This is a bad idea. I don't belong here. I'd better go."

"Come on, Buddy," Sidney persuaded as she started to nudge me back toward the group. "I promise you nothing terrible will happen. Give me a chance and I can show you a good time."

"What are you talking about?" I asked. "Have you taken a good look at my face? Do you know what these kids think of me? You've made a big mistake."

I was beginning to get upset with her for putting me in this situation, but before I could take off, she pulled me toward the group.

"Okay, everybody, stop staring," Sidney ordered, sounding as though she was directing traffic. "Buddy's my guest, so let's make him feel welcome. I have enough pills for everybody. The treat's on me."

As she issued her commands in a sing-song voice, Sidney held up a brown plastic prescription bottle and shook it, causing the pills inside to rattle around. I stood there with a dumb, confused look on my face. I wondered why she was showing everyone a prescription bottle of pills.

"Ever heard of Tabs?" she asked as she turned her attention back to me. "It's short for Lortabs. They're painkillers," she said. "We love 'em."

I expected to be the brunt of a practical joke any second, so most of my attention was focused on making sure I was aware of everyone's movements. But the part of me that was paying attention to Sidney had no idea why any of them wanted a painkiller. What was there to love about them if you weren't in pain?

The group swarmed around her eagerly as she opened the bottle and started passing out the pills. It was like feeding time at a zoo. That took their attention off me. Maybe this wasn't going to be so bad after all. When Sidney reached me, she announced "Now it's your turn. Take one."

She held a white pill in her outstretched hand. It certainly looked harmless, almost like a vitamin.

I was confused. "What's this for? Is that why you brought me over here? To take a pill?" I looked around at everyone else. They had each swallowed theirs and chased it with a swig from a bottle of water. They kept on talking and laughing. It looked like they were having fun, so I felt safe and wondered, for the first time, *could I have fun, too?*

Sidney took the pill out of my hand, snapped it in half with her fingers, and put it gently into my mouth. She had the most adorable look on her face. I don't know if it was because I was under her spell, but I didn't resist. I do know I was foolish to take a pill I knew nothing about. She handed me the bottle of water.

"Enough with the questions, already. Swallow it and get a little buzz going."

I wasn't in any pain and had no clue what effect a painkiller would have, but I didn't want to look stupid, so I chugged what was left in the bottle. Everyone looked happy and Sidney looked so pleased with me that I didn't care anymore. She patted me on the head.

"Good boy," she said.

She was so freaking cute. I think I would have swallowed dirt if she had asked me to.

"Give it a few minutes," she said. "Even though you only a get half a pill for starters, that's all you need to loosen you right up."

Turning away from me, Sidney threw her arm around a guy I recognized from my history class. He had taken a few steps away from the others, but stopped short when he heard Sidney call to him.

"Wait up, Jack. I want to make sure you don't forget who's taking care of you, here."

"Not for a minute," he replied, and they exchanged hugs and a few whispers.

"Text me tomorrow," Sidney said and waved her cell phone at him as he walked away. As light on her feet as a ballet dancer, she turned and came back toward me with a playful look on her face.

"Are you having fun yet?" she asked.

I opened my mouth to answer her, but before I could say a word, Sidney put her frog hat on my head and pulled it down over my eyes. I just knew it made me look stupid. Everyone in the group was watching and they started laughing. Sidney laughed the hardest. I mentally kicked myself for letting my guard down, since I knew something like this was coming. I reached for the hat, but before I could pull it off, Sidney removed it.

"You're a good sport, Buddy boy."

She continued laughing and suddenly this all seemed silly to me, too, just carefree and goofy. Nobody was being mean. I couldn't be mad, so I laughed along. They all took turns putting the hat on each other and clowning around. For the first time in my life, I was happy and felt like I belonged here. These pills made that possible. They were awesome.

"Come on, Sidney, it's time to break out the Roxys. We've waited long enough," whined one of the girls in the group. As soon as the other four heard her say the word, they swarmed her and began to beg eagerly. Sidney raised her hands with a motion for them to back off.

"Whoa. Just a minute, Guys. The Tabs were freebies. Anyone wanting seconds has to ask me nicely. Anyone wanting Blues will have to do even better."

The group moaned a collective response. I figured Roxys and Blues were one and the same, and probably another kind of painkiller to get high on. Sidney obviously had some and knew how special they were. I imagined that Roxys were either stronger or more fun to take than Tabs. I was learning fast and couldn't wait to see one.

Sidney produced another pill bottle and twisted the cap. I heard it snap and pop as the lid sprang off. I was fascinated to see the group draw closer to her, their eyes wide and mouths slack and open as the round, pale blue pills tumbled out into her hand.

"Back up!" Sidney barked. They obeyed and widened the circle. Sidney started handing out the blue pills.

I was doing just fine. I didn't need another pill. Not yet, anyway. I was relaxed and energized at the same time. More important, even though I was standing away from the group, I didn't feel like an outcast or someone who should be made fun of. I felt normal . . . and I owed it all to Tabs and Sidney.

I was glad she had brought me over here, but I wasn't sure what I was supposed to do next.

I felt Sidney press against me. "I'm back. Did you miss me?"

I could feel the heat of her breath on my neck and smell how clean and fresh her skin was. As I thought about how much I liked her, I began to feel more awkward and uneasy again. I wanted to impress her, somehow. Maybe I needed another pill after all. I was lost in my thoughts, but suddenly Sidney made it clear that she was tired of waiting for my answer.

"You know, Buddy," she scolded as she took a step back to size me up. "It's a simple enough question."

I paused, trying to think of the right thing to say. I was nervous and wanted to stop being so stuck inside myself.

"Maybe I did and maybe I didn't." I was hoping I sounded playful and mischievous, like Sidney.

She continued flirtatiously, "You like to keep a girl guessing, don't you?" She waved her index finger back and forth like a windshield wiper and shot me a very suggestive grin. "Naughty, naughty."

She was magical. I wasn't going to wait for another pill to help me say something even more daring.

I took a step closer to her and said, "Speaking of naughty, I caught you looking at me enough times at school. What's that all about? Does my ugliness fascinate you so much that you just can't keep your eyes off of me?"

Sidney looked a bit taken aback with my cockiness, but I didn't really care. I was sick and tired of caring so much about what other people thought.

"I check everybody out," she continued. "You're no exception. I've never seen anyone who looks as freakin' unhappy as you. That's why I brought you over here to take a pill. A few minutes ago you were smiling and the Tab was doing you some good. Why are you spoiling that now?"

"I'm not," I said. "I'm feeling it. And remember, this was your idea, not mine." I didn't know pills were going to affect me like this. Actually, I liked the new me. I wondered what another pill would do.

I started smiling. I couldn't help it. I felt really free to speak my mind. But I wondered how smart it was to be opening up to someone so beautiful and popular. I was afraid I was getting too personal and a little aggressive. If I said too much, she might find something to make fun of and not give me another pill.

"Buddy," she said, "Go to a shrink to talk about your face. Not me. But if it's pills you want, then I got what you need. Now, let's get back to having a good time."

I got her message loud and clear. She was here to take pills and play with her friends. I wanted to be one of those friends. I wasn't sure if she really liked me and wanted me to be happy, but the look on her face told me this conversation was getting too serious.

I let my smile take over again, and Sidney smiled back.

"You know, Buddy, I take even stronger pills than Tabs all the time."

"Really," I said. "What kind of pills? Those blue ones?"

"How do you know about Blues?" She looked surprised.

"I don't. You brought it up and everybody went crazy. What are they, something special?"

"They're just the best. My all-time favorites," she replied, beaming.

"Are they painkillers, too?" I asked.

"They're Roxicodone. Much better than Tabs. Everybody wants them," she said.

"Can I have one?"

"You're not going to get that lucky today," she scolded. "I'm only giving out Tabs."

"When can I get one?"

Sidney's face lit up. She had an adorable smile.

"You really want to try one of those Blues, don't you? I have to admit, I'm surprised that you want to move so fast."

"What's wrong with that?"

"You're not ready for it. These babies can knock your head back and put you on the ground."

"Whoa! Is that supposed to be fun?"

"Maybe. It depends on what you call fun. But let's not rush you into it."

"Now I really want one." I was desperate to see if my interest in Blues made her more interested in me.

"Easy does it, Buddy. For now, take another Tab, and let's see what happens."

She popped the top off the prescription bottle, and another Tab fell out into her hand. With a devilish look on her face, she handed the other half pill to me. As I grabbed it, she said, "There's plenty more where this came from. I've got connections."

She spun on her toes, took a few steps away from me, and seemed to be instantly encircled by her friends. I was really impressed by Sidney. She was not only great looking but she had plenty of pills. I was beginning to wonder how it was so easy for her to get so many, but I decided what mattered was her willingness to give them away and how good it was to be on her list.

CHAPTER 2

The New Priority

Once Sidney made it clear that our conversation was finished, I looked around and tried to decide what I should do next. One of the girls was standing by herself a few feet away, looking a little left out. Still feeling liberated by the Tab, I walked over to her and tried to be friendly. She offered me her bottle of water.

"I think Tabs are great, don't you?" She pointed at the pill I was holding.

"These pills are pure fun," I answered.

"You're Buddy, right? Hi, my name's Julie." She was kinda cute, with freckles and a pink T-shirt that read *Girls just wanna* . . .

"Nice to meet you," I said. I extended my hand and she shook it. I knew it was a little queer to shake hands, but I didn't know what else to do.

"This is my first time with pills," I continued quickly, trying to cover my embarrassment. "It's unbelievable how good I feel. I'm only taking half a Tab at a time, and it's giving me a bunch of energy. I know it sounds weird, but my mind is crystal clear or smarter or something."

"Exactly," Julie agreed, excitement creeping into her voice. "If I could take these all the time, I might even try harder in school. Imagine *me* getting all As; that would freak my parents out. I've never gotten anything better than a B." She gave me a crooked smile that melted me.

"You look like someone who's already smart," I said.

"Oh, really?" She laughed. "I had you fooled."

"It's the glasses."

"I hate these glasses," she said. "I should be wearing contacts."

"I think you look great in glasses."

She reached for my hand and held it for a few seconds.

"You're sweet, Buddy," she said.

Her attention made me feel like I was like everyone else, a normal kid; I was on a roll and wanted to roll more. I decided to jump in with both feet.

"You may find this hard to believe, but I've never done this before."

"Done what?" Julie looked confused.

"Talk to a girl like this," I explained. "I'm really running my mouth off, too. I just want to keep talking."

"It's the Tabs."

"Tell me about it," I was feeling spunky and sassy now. All at once, a million words were bouncing off the walls of my mind. I started shuffling my feet and drumming my fingers in midair.

I blurted out, "What do girls just wanna do?"

I knew my courage was coming from the amazing feeling the Tabs were giving me, but I couldn't stop myself. I finally felt like someone who mattered, someone with clear skin and a face worth looking at. Julie waved a finger at me and winked.

"Nice move, Buddy. You think you're ready to know what girls really wanna do?"

"Of course I do. Do you think I've been living in a cave away from civilization all my life?"

"You're a clever boy . . . and funny." She had a teasing laugh.

I smirked and huffed on my fingernails. I was feeling cool . . . way cool.

"We may as well live it up, Buddy. Getting high doesn't last long enough, so let's make every minute a blast."

We continued our witty and playful conversation, which became sillier with every minute. I felt fantastic. I was actually flirting, and I had no idea how I was doing it. The words just came out naturally. In my book, Tabs were sensational. They gave me the courage to talk to pretty girls. I wanted a year's supply.

I pointed at Julie's T-shirt and said, "Okay, let me guess what it means. I think girls just wanna get high."

That was lame, but I didn't care. We both laughed like I'd said something incredibly funny.

When the laughter started to die down, Julie pulled her T-shirt away from her chest and purred, "Girls just wanna have sex. Didn't you know that?"

I could feel my pimply face turning red. No girl had ever mentioned the "S" word to me before. Now I was trapped. I didn't know how to flirt this one out.

She stared at me, obviously waiting for a response. I stammered and hesitated, afraid I'd waited too long to pull off being confident.

"Of . . . of course I . . . I knew that girls just wanted to have s . . . sex. Sex is my favorite subject."

Her smile turned from seductive to sweet. She let go of her stretched-out T-shirt.

"It's good to know how much you like sex, Buddy . . . just in case."

I must have looked stunned, because she grabbed both of my shoulders and shook me, laughing again. "I was only kidding about sex. What kind of girl do you think I am?"

"A . . . a good one. Of course," I stammered. I knew I sounded like a bumbling idiot.

Julie's expression suddenly changed. "Gotta go, Buddy. It was really nice to meet you. Hope you're around when we do this again. See ya later." And she walked away without so much as a backward glance.

Our conversation was over before I could think of something amusing and memorable to say. But being with Julie had been awesome while it lasted. I wanted to have another chance to be with a girl and see if I could do better. I wasn't exactly sure what I was supposed to do, but I'd had a little taste, and I liked it. I just needed more Tabs, and I could get right back at it.

As I stood there thinking about the next time I'd talk to Julie and how entertaining and maybe comical I'd be, I was shoved from behind. Nearly losing my balance, I recovered as the sound of Sidney's sarcastic voice filled the air.

"What's the matter, Buddy, Tabs a little too strong for you?"

She looked right at me, and there was meanness in her eyes. It would take a lot more than a shove from her to humiliate me. I'd had plenty of practice being humiliated and embarrassed at school. Every day was open season for target practice on nerds. I had bullet holes to prove it. This time, I wanted to stay loose.

"No, they're not too strong for me. As a matter of fact, I could easily handle another, and then we'd see who gets pushed around," I warned her, feeling brave enough to stare at her magnificent face with what I hoped was a menacing look on mine. I felt like the Cowardly Lion after a stiff dose of courage.

Sidney looked upset and slugged me in the arm.

"Don't get your undies all bunched up. If I didn't like you, I wouldn't have done that. Ask any of the guys. I'm just playing around. It's what I do after I've had a few pills."

I wasn't sure how to take Sidney. I knew I was out of my league.

As I stood there thinking about how to respond to the beautiful Sidney, two big athletic arms grabbed her by the waist, lifted her off the ground, and swung her up onto massive shoulders. Sidney protested in that way girls do when they don't really mean you should stop, and she demanded to be put back down. I was actually relieved to be rid of her for a minute so I could think. She'd said she was only playing around when she pushed me, but her mood had changed very quickly from friendly to agitated. She'd blamed it on the pills, but that didn't make sense to me. No one else was acting like that.

I was trying to make up my mind what to do next, when the big guy dropped her down in front of me. She was bright and cheerful again. She kissed the boy who gave her the ride; I was jealous, but tried to act as though I didn't care. She already had a powerful effect on me, and I felt sucked in by her charm.

"Who was that guy, your boyfriend?"

Her laugh sounded more like a snicker. "Boyfriend? Him? No way. If he had two brain cells to rub together, he'd start a fire."

She watched me as though she expected me to laugh, but I didn't.

"What about you," she asked. "You and Julie going to hook up?"

Now I did laugh.

"Are you kidding? I probably have more than two brain cells, but I couldn't start a fire, no matter how much rubbing I did." As soon as the words were out of my mouth, I realized how stupid they sounded. God, what a retard I was!

After an awkward moment of silence, Sidney smiled.

"Don't give up so easily. Julie was in a good mood today. You should have followed her home. Maybe you woulda gotten lucky."

"What do you mean, lucky?" We were back to the "S" word. Only this time, I was going to be ready to talk about it, like a man.

"She likes the pills," Sidney replied. "And I bet she would do just about anything to get a few," she finished with a wink. "You know what I mean, don't you?"

"Of course I do." I tried to make my voice sound strong and deep. "It's all over her T-shirt. I couldn't miss it." I knew I was holding my own in this conversation, and I wasn't embarrassed anymore. That was a first for me. I loved the feeling of confidence Tabs gave me.

Sidney reached in her pocket and pulled out the brown plastic pharmacy bottle. She held it up with the label facing me.

"Julie would love these. She asked me for one."

"What are they?"

"Blues," she answered as she shook one into her hand.

"Finally, I get to see one. "So these are better than Tabs?"

"Hell, yeah."

"I expected a huge pill," I said. "This is so small. What's the deal? Tabs gave me plenty of energy. What does this do, blow your head off?"

Sidney looked at me like I was retarded.

"Don't try to sound like you know about pills. It's ridiculous. Beginners like you should stick to Tabs. You don't need any more energy than that. And besides, aren't you having fun?"

I nodded.

"Okay. Since you asked, I'll explain a few things." Sidney was back to being patient. "For a while, Tabs should be perfect for you. But you'll get used to them, just like everyone else does, and they won't pack much of a punch. Then you'll need five to get high."

I tried to act like I understood what she was talking about, but I was clueless.

"So, do you want to learn a thing or two about pills and get up to speed with the rest of us, or do you want to go back into your lonely shell and hide?"

"You're right" I answered, feeling the sting of her words. "I need to know this stuff."

"Okay then, Roxys are a lot stronger than Tabs. If you want to impress Julie or anybody else, bring some of these along. Every girl loves Roxys. And once you take one, every girl will love you."

She had a mocking tone in her voice that I didn't like, but I wasn't going to let it bother me. I was getting a valuable education about painkillers and girls. That was worth a little bit more discomfort.

I studied the blue pill in her hand. Sidney made it sound like the greatest thing ever.

"Can I have one?"

I knew I sounded like I was begging, but I didn't care. I wanted one. I had to find out what I was missing and what I could get if I had one.

She put the pill inside the bottle, sealed it shut, and stuffed it back in her pocket.

"No, you cannot have one."

Now she was making fun of me. I must have sounded desperate, but I didn't care.

"I don't just hand these out, you know. They don't grow on the Roxicodone tree in my back yard. I have to arrange to meet with all my suppliers and that takes a few hours of my time."

"Suppliers?" As soon as the word was out of my mouth, I realized I'd made a mistake; the look on her face made it clear she thought of me as an uninformed adolescent who asked too many annoying questions.

"Listen, Buddy, keep things simple for yourself. You like Tabs, right?"

"Yeah. They're perfect." I felt my face light up as I said it.

"Then my job is to make you happy," Sidney purred as she took my hand, and we walked away from the group, side by side.

I was puzzled by her sudden show of affection. I started to have crazy thoughts about being her boyfriend. For a few seconds, I actually felt handsome. I knew that kind of thinking was impossible without Tabs. I wanted to be convinced that a girl as cute as Sidney could like me. I had even started to like me. I decided that called for another Tab, just to make everything even better.

I was still daydreaming when I heard her ask, "So, is it a deal? I'm going to be the only one to take care of you, right?"

She looked into my eyes and I wondered if I had a chance with her. I felt special. I wanted this moment to last forever. My throat was tight when I spoke.

"Sidney, I hope you don't mind me saying this, but . . . I think you're…"

"Amazing?" She interrupted and batted her eyes. "I know. Everybody says that. I can't help it."

I was back to being awkward and fumbling with my words, but I had to know.

"Why did you pick me to come over here? Nobody picks me. I know I'm a weirdo, but you're not treating me like that. What's this all about . . . really?"

As soon as I asked I regretted it.

But Sidney didn't miss a beat. "We all deserve to have fun, even guys like you."

Before I could react to her words, she made a *shush*ing sound and kissed two of her fingers, then pressed them on my lips. The gesture made me short of breath. I didn't know if she was going to do more, or if I was supposed to make the next move. I was frozen scared.

Her next words thawed me right out, though. "Buddy, you've been a good sport. I brought you over here because I was curious about you. I wanted to see what you'd be like after a couple of Tabs, and I was right. You're way more cool. I bet with Tabs you could get a date, even with Julie."

Why would she bring up Julie after holding my hand and kissing my lips with her fingers? I was falling for her, so I said the most brainless thing.

"What about us?"

There was no sympathy in Sidney's expression. She was colder now.

"We had our fun, Buddy. There isn't going to be any 'us.' This is strictly business."

The wake-up call was alarming. It took me awhile to fully understand what had happened. I was probably not the only boy she had done this to. Sidney set the bait, and I took it. I didn't have a chance with her and never would. I was stupid to have thought that I might.

Yet somehow, I wasn't really that broken up about it. The Tabs took care of that.

And just then, Sidney held up the brown plastic pharmacy bottle, three-quarters full of pills. Two of them tumbled out into her hand. "You know, Tabs are popular with guys like you. They'll pay five dollars for each one. And when you're ready to be serious about getting high, you'll switch to Blues, and for God's sake, don't snort a whole one on your first try."

I made a face; I couldn't imagine inhaling a pill through my nostrils.

"That's crazy," I objected. "If Blues are as good as you say, why would anyone want to do something so dumb when all you have to do is swallow them? Tabs work just fine that way, for me."

"Trust me. When you want to get high in a hurry or if you haven't got many pills, you'll remember my words and then you'll do it. We all did. But don't ever snort a Tab. It'll burn your nose and make it run. Stick to Blues. And since you're so curious, I'll give you another tip." She took one out and held it in the flat of her hand.

"There are a few different brands of Blues. They're all 30 milligrams but the ones marked A215s are easier to handle when you get started. See right here." She showed me the letter A and three numbers carved into the pill.

"You can break 'em in half or even quarters with just your fingers. The Blues with an M stamped on them have a slightly tougher shell to crack. So remember, just crush up a quarter pill for starters, then roll a dollar bill or cut a straw down to size and go for it. A Roxy in the nose goes right to the brain. A Roxy in the stomach takes way too long to make you happy."

"I don't think I'm going to snort anything," I argued. "If you ever give me a Blue I'll take it, but for now, two Tabs are perfect."

"I like a man who knows what he wants," she volleyed back. "I'll set you up with the Blues when I think you're ready. There's no rush. You can take it nice and easy with these and just enjoy the ride."

She held up the bottle of Tabs and shook them until they rattled like a baby's toy.

Her phone chirped, and she stopped to read a text message.

"Somebody wants to have fun," she said, and the mischief was back in her voice.

I watched as she dropped two Tabs into my hand and then closed my fingers around the pills.

"These are for later. When you want more, I'll get with you at school. You deserve a real good time from now on." She winked, then turned and walked away.

I looked at the pills in my hand as I replayed the past hour in my mind. My life had been a mess. I was uptight day after day, my stomach twisted in a knot, and I was lonely and unhappy. I felt like I would be that way forever . . . until Sidney suddenly came along. It didn't matter whether or not she really cared about me. I just wanted her to care about giving me pills. I could easily get used to having more fun with those. A lot more fun.

On that day, when I took my first Tab, I was just having a good time. Unfortunately for me, I quickly decided that I couldn't have a good time without them. Fun was long overdue in my life, and I wanted more of it. Getting high soon became my new priority. That afternoon I decided it was going to be my first order of business every day. Finally my life could stop sucking. Tabs were going to make everything better every single day. And that meant one thing: I needed a supply of pills. I needed Sidney.

At that moment I didn't know much about Tabs, or narcotics in general. Drugs hadn't been part of my world, and I was such a loner and a loser that I honestly had no clue that I could get hooked. I was unaware that addiction had already been activated after I'd taken only two half pills. I had no idea that it was about to take my life over and smash it like a wrecking ball. I had no idea that addiction could destroy my soul. Like every other kid who just "tries" pills, I was having a blast, and that's all that mattered to me.

CHAPTER 3

Any Price at All

The party broke up as soon as Sidney left, so I headed home. There were some disappointed faces as the others walked away, but there was a smile on my face. I couldn't help it. The serious, boring side of me was gone. Tabs were simply the greatest.

It only took me five minutes to get home from the bus stop. As soon as I walked through the door I heard the familiar, "Buddy, is that you?"

I usually went right up to my room when I got home. Mom and I hardly saw each other outside of mealtime. Over the years she had gradually adjusted to my preference for solitude and stopped badgering me with relentless and probing questions about where I'd been and what I'd done. But today I called out, "Hey, Mom."

She was reading a book in the living room. She looked up over her glasses and stared at me, her mouth opened slightly in surprise. "Hey to you, too."

I stood there and grinned boldly. She'd never seen me do *that* before, I was pretty sure. She looked a little stunned, then tilted her head with a puzzled expression on her face.

"What gives?"

"What do you mean?" I asked back, trying not to smirk.

"You're talking to me . . . and you're smiling. You never smile. Did something happen today?"

"What do you think happened?" I was making her work for this. I wanted to hear what she'd say.

"I don't know. You're not the Buddy who left for school this morning. Usually you don't say two words to anyone." She patted the space on the couch next to her.

I moved confidently across the floor with my shoulders square and my head straight up. I sat down next to her on the couch and started bragging.

"I met a girl. No, I take that back. She met me."

Mom dropped her book and took off her glasses.

"Girl? What girl?"

"She's pretty new at school. Her name is Sidney."

Mom looked surprised.

"It's not a biggy. It was easy. I don't know why I waited so long." I laid it on thick and I was having a blast. I felt free to just say whatever I wanted, and now that topic happened to be girls.

Mom started beaming, and I could tell she was enjoying this moment. I'm sure that, in spite of my homeliness, she hoped that some girl would find me appealing and I would instinctively know what to do. I knew she was happy that I was talking to her . . . about anything.

"Sidney who?" she asked. "What is she like? How old is she? Is she in your grade?"

I opened my mouth to answer, but the questions just kept coming. "What does she look like? Is she pretty?"

"Since you ask: she's drop-dead gorgeous."

"Come on . . . don't kid me like that."

"I kid you not. She's blonde, super tall, very popular, and extremely intelligent. How about that for a catch?" I was showing off, but I couldn't stop myself.

Mom was about ready to burst. I wondered how she could seriously think that her pimply-faced son could be attracted to someone so gorgeous.

"She introduced herself after school today and brought me over to meet some of her friends. One was Jack and another was Julie. Everybody stood around talking. It was all right. But Sidney was the best. She knows how to have a great time."

I was pulling her chain while I cruised along in a good mood. I was almost arrogant enough to tell her the truth: that her son took pills and had an absolute blast, and his life as a loser was over. But I was smart to keep my mouth shut. I knew I'd gone overboard with way too much information, so I excused myself and headed for my room. Meanwhile, my mom kept shouting questions to my retreating back.

"Well, when do I get to meet Sidney? What does she like to eat? I'll plan a meal and you can invite her over."

If I don't stop her soon, she'll be renting the banquet room at the country club and ordering a wedding cake, I thought. I headed back down a couple of stairs and stuck my head over the railing. "Whoa, Mom, slow down. Sidney and I just met, so don't get too crazy here."

By then, she had a romantic look on her face. "I think it's awesome. I'm so happy for you. Just give me plenty of time to prepare a nice welcome when you bring her home."

It dawned on me that Tabs had not only made me run my mouth off, but that I'd given Mom the impression that Sidney was destined to be my girl. I wondered what would happen if I handed my mom a Tab and said, "This is why I'm smiling and talking. It had nothing to do with Sidney or Julie or Jack, or any human being, including you. It's a pill that moves the clouds out of the way and lets the sunshine in."

On second thought, I had already said too much and would probably regret it.

Mom kept yelling as I stood at the top of the stairs.

"Where are you going? I've been waiting years for you to say more than ten words in a row. Now you meet a nice girl who's gorgeous. You can't take off yet. Get back here."

"That's all you're getting," I insisted. "I'm heading to my room."

I swaggered down the hall with a smile plastered on my face. The Tabs had to remain a secret. My mom would never approve of her sonny boy taking prescription painkillers to finally be happy.

"I'm not done with you," she yelled up the stairs as I disappeared into my bedroom.

I sat down and reviewed my options. I had two more pills in my pocket. I could feel them waiting there to grant me my wishes. I was tempted to take them right now. But I also considered the advantage in waiting. I had already had a blast, so I decided to save the pills for tomorrow and spend the time now planning my strategy. I wanted to become something I had never been before: happy at school.

I turned on the TV and started watching reruns. I had seen all the shows a million times before, but they were fun all over again, thanks to Tabs. But after a couple of hours went by, a dreary feeling slowly came over me. The programs became more and more tiresome and tedious. I knew what was happening and I got upset. The bleakness of my life had returned as the Tabs wore off. I felt like a slug.

At dinner I sat in stony silence, ignoring my mother's probing questions. She wanted to know what happened to my playful mood. My father and younger brother ignored both of us. I just ate a few bites and excused myself, like I did every night. I was back to being quiet, sullen, and unfriendly. I was relieved that my mother did not follow me into my room to ask for an explanation. She knew better than to disturb me when I was in a bad mood.

Alone again in my room, I toyed with the idea of taking another Tab. I was desperate to feel happy again, to turn back into that lively kid who was talkative and sociable. But I didn't give in. I watched more TV and just stared at those two incredible pills until I was tired enough to go to sleep.

In the morning, I still felt like my everyday, unhappy self. I walked into the bathroom to clean up, stood in front of the mirror, and took a longer than usual look at my body. It was pale and anorexic. Until then, I hadn't cared that I was skinny and scrawny. I knew my body wasn't any better than my face, and I was a human turn-off. But if I was going to take Tabs and blend in with the other kids, I needed to at least look healthier than I did right now. I decided to eat breakfast.

I popped a Tab in my mouth and chased it with a swig of water. Then I thought about yesterday and how long it took to feel awesome. So I took the second pill before leaving the bathroom, knowing that would do the trick, and I couldn't wait. I ate a bowl of cereal before grabbing my backpack and heading for the front door. The bus was due in about thirty minutes. Mom stepped out of the laundry room and planted herself directly in my path.

"Wait up, Buddy. You don't have to rush out so early. You have some explaining to do. You caught me by surprise yesterday." Her eyes flashed as she looked at me. Her hand was on the doorknob, and it was pretty obvious that she wasn't going to let me pass.

"Like, for instance, you came home with a big smile and told me about a nice girl and some new friends. Then you took off and left me hanging. At dinner you were back to being gloomy and wouldn't say a word. What happened? Why did you change back to the old you?"

I forced myself to smile. This morning's Tab hadn't kicked in yet.

"Mom, yesterday was really neat for me. I learned a few important things about how to feel good. Unfortunately, it didn't last long enough. Today is going to be even better. You'll see."

She stood there just looking at me. I could tell she was trying to decide how to respond. I kissed her on the cheek. That disarmed her long enough to get me out the door.

"'Bye, Mom," I said, and I didn't turn around when I closed the door.

As I headed off toward the bus stop, I decided to take a longer route through the neighborhood. I wanted the Tab to be up to speed before I got on the bus. As I walked, I imagined how proud my mother was going to be, having a son who was just like everyone else. As I approached the bus stop, I felt warm and full of life. What I liked the most was the feeling that came over me of being handsome. It was as though my face had been scrubbed clean. I felt so untroubled and carefree.

I saw some of the kids from yesterday, kids who had taken Sidney's Tabs. They were talking to each other and didn't notice me. I wanted somebody to say "hi" and check me out. I was on top of the world, and I wanted them to notice. I looked right at them, trying to make eye contact, but they ignored me. But I wasn't going to give up that easily.

When I got on the bus, I turned and looked directly at the two girls engrossed in gossip who sat behind me. I wanted to say something . . . anything, just to get a conversation started.

"Hello," was all that came out. *What a loser I am*, I thought.

Hundreds of other thoughts streamed through my brain, but I was feeling the pressure to speak up. I needed a bit more courage; all I could do was stare at them uncomfortably.

The girls looked at me and then at each other. One of them sneered at me, clicked her tongue, and said, "Do you mind? We're talking here."

I turned back around to face the front of the bus. Why were they acting like that? They should have remembered me from yesterday. We all had a good time. Sidney introduced me. They laughed when she put the green hat on my head. I was one of them. Or were they just polite when they got their pills?

So what if they wouldn't acknowledge me. I let the embarrassment go as quickly as I felt it. I didn't have time for that nonsense. I was starting to feel the Tab jack me up and I wanted to do something daring to make an even bigger and better impression. Do something they would never forget, like kissing one of them. I even fantasized that the other girl would be jealous and demand to be kissed. What a hoot.

I was feeling gutsy and loose, something I've never been. I wanted to make my move and show them a thing or two. By then my mind had speeded up and a surge of energy raced through my legs; I couldn't stop moving them. Then I got itchy, which made me need to scratch at my face, my shoulders, and my chest. It had to be the Tab, but I didn't care. I wanted to have some fun.

The day before, Sidney had been filled with mischief and I liked her that way. Maybe that's what these girls wanted; a little mischief might score some points. I could feel my confidence increasing. Looking back, I realize I was actually pretty arrogant, thinking I had become irresistible and was doing them a favor. I spun around fast and took them by surprise.

"Hello, again. Remember me from yesterday? Sidney's friend, Buddy. In case you're wondering, I'm not shy anymore, like I used to be."

They were startled, then quickly looked annoyed. I kept talking. I had to. I believed I had the most impressive thoughts and all my words were gifts that just poured out of my mouth. I couldn't shut up.

"I know what you're thinking: This kid doesn't usually say very much. Heck, let's be honest. I haven't said anything in years. Well, today all that changes, because I just took two Tabs. I wish I had more. I'd give you some, and we could have a little party."

One of them smiled and let out a cute giggle, and then her friend did the same thing. I decided they liked me . . . at least they looked like they did.

The prettier one covered her mouth with her hand to smother the surprise in her voice. "Oh . . . my . . . *God*. You're really high, aren't you?"

Her friend chimed in, "I can't believe it. You're going to school like that? You could get in so much trouble if you get caught."

"That's right," I said. "So promise me you won't tell. Okay?"

They looked at each other, then at me, and then both nodded their heads in agreement. I decided to push ahead. "That brings me to what's more important. I'm available, you know. Any time you like. Night or day. Just call me and I'll be there."

I couldn't believe what I was saying. Some part of me thought I was charming, grown up, and cool. The other part of me knew that what I was saying was corny, brainless, and stupid. But again, I didn't care. I felt ten feet tall and bulletproof. If these two girls rejected me, I'd just find someone else. I was unstoppable and fearless.

I kept talking faster and louder, until my words were all messed up. One of the girls tried several times to interrupt me, but I kept rambling.

"Before we reach our destination, and, of course, that's school, but we already knew that, I want to provide you both with an unforgettable chance to get to know me by giving me your phone numbers, which happen to be seven digits that I could easily memorize if you will be so kind as to tell me right now. Okay?"

I paused to take a deep breath. One of the girls, I don't remember which one, blurted out, "Leave us alone! You're not funny anymore. You're pathetic, and there aren't enough Tabs to change that."

We'd arrived at school while I was giving my soliloquy. The bus door opened and both of the girls bolted out of the seat. I just sat there thinking of what I should have said to get their numbers. I hoped I could find them in school and ask one more time. I was clueless about how ridiculous I had been. Soon the bus was empty and I was staring at the driver, who motioned toward the door. "Hurry up, kid. Get off. I got another load to pick up."

I stumbled off the bus and followed the crowd through the front door of the school. I changed my mind about the girls. I wasn't going to chase after them. They dumped me. It was their loss. I was going to turn some other heads. As I headed toward homeroom, I spotted someone else from yesterday afternoon's Tab party.

I tapped him on the shoulder, and in my best nonchalant voice said, "Hey, bro, it's Buddy. Remember me? We got high together yesterday."

He looked at me like I had something contagious. He tried to pull away from me, but I grabbed some of his shirt and pulled him back.

"Come on, Man," I whined. "Yesterday we were doing Tabs and having a ball. Remember? You gave Sidney the piggyback ride."

He tore my hand from his shirt and brushed the area that I had crumpled.

"Listen, Buddy," he snarled. "It wasn't my idea to give you Tabs. We all had a few laughs and it's over. Stay out of my face or I'll kick the crap out of you."

He turned and grabbed the hand of a girl who had also been at the Tab party. As they walked away he said something to her and she glanced back at me. I'll never forget the look on her face, like she'd caught a whiff of rotting road kill.

I was still jacked up on the Tabs, but I wasn't having fun, anymore. What a waste to spend all this energy and brilliant thinking on a bad mood that felt like a soaking wet blanket. I couldn't snap out of it. Then it hit me like a cold slap on the face. What was I trying to prove? Tabs hadn't changed me a bit and everybody knew it, including me. I stood by my locker and waited until the hallway cleared. I just wanted to be invisible again. I heard someone calling my name and I cringed. I couldn't take one more insulting remark. My life was so much easier when nobody cared.

"Buddy, what's the matter?" It was Sidney.

"Buddy, are you okay? I heard what happened on the bus."

Her voice sounded sweet and sexy. But did she really care? How could she? She was prom-queen material. I wanted her to see me high on Tabs and tell me how cool I was. Instead, I felt defeated.

"You missed all the fun," I answered sarcastically.

"Listen," she said. "Don't let them bother you. Those girls on the bus are idiots. They won't get any more Tabs from me."

That didn't make me feel any better. I wasn't even going to mention the fullback who wanted to kick the crap out of me.

"Look, Sidney," I said, "What happened wasn't a big deal. Long before you came to town, these jerks were getting their jollies being mean—today was nothing, 'cuz usually they are much worse. So I don't think I need any of your help or sympathy. What little confidence Tabs gave me is gone."

Sidney held out the open palm of her left hand and clicked a pen in her right hand.

"What's your number," she asked, sounding very businesslike. "I'm going to check on you later."

"Why bother?" I shrugged.

"Because I'm not done trying to help you out. I still have a few pills you haven't tried yet. I do little side jobs."

"Side jobs?"

"I sell pills. That's what fixes broken hearts. Not me. It's the pills."

Everything she'd done the day before finally made sense. She was setting me up to buy pills from her; Sidney wanted me to be her next customer. I was catching on fast.

I was convinced now more than ever that pills could fix a lot more than broken hearts. I imagined that with a little more practice and the right pills, I could learn to control myself and say all the right things at the right time. Better yet, I just needed to find the right people to be around, like kids who wanted to get high and stay high. They'd always be happy. I could probably talk any way I wanted around them.

"Buddy, what's your number? Give it to me." Sidney became more demanding.

I rattled off the seven digits, and she scrawled them on her skin.

"I gotta go now, but I'll call you later," she said. "Don't worry, I'll take good care of you. Count on it."

I stood there in the empty hallway after Sidney slipped into a nearby classroom. I thought about what had just happened: I was added to her list. I was important and I could live with the reason why. Sidney was a drug dealer. One very hot-looking drug dealer. I couldn't wait for my phone to ring. I had a cell phone, but I'd never used it, not even once. Mom said it would come in handy when I needed it most and I had a feeling she was going to be right.

I was late for class. I was supposed to have had an awesome day at school feeling energized and handsome, but the morning had gone totally wrong. Tabs made me high, but that wasn't enough to stay happy. Now I was feeling weary and I wanted to be back in my bedroom with the door locked. No. Come to think of it, I'd rather be even higher and hanging around with somebody who liked me that way.

The rest of the day dragged on in slow motion. I was late for each class, and my head felt like it was in a thick foggy haze. I kept my head down and my mouth shut. Nobody noticed. All I wanted was to get through this day and get back home to my room where I could think.

I wanted to be that new and exciting person I had become both times I'd taken Tabs. Sidney had the supply, but she expected to be paid. I remember her telling me that beginners were willing to pay five dollars apiece for a Tab. That was crazy. She must have been kidding. Where was I going to get money like that? I had no idea, but I sure needed one . . . fast.

CHAPTER 4

Sidney Redux

I sat in the front seat looking straight ahead on the bus ride home. Today, I wanted to be the first one off. Nobody said a word to me. I was invisible again, the way I liked it.

When I walked in the door, my mother was doing laundry and didn't hear me come in. When I didn't go out of my way to say hi, she knew I wasn't in a good mood, as usual. If she tried to check on me later, I didn't want to know about it; I hoped my closed door was enough to make her change her mind. I couldn't face her yet.

Three hours later, I suffered through dinner and got through all of Mom's lame questions with one word answers. I escaped from the dinner table as quickly as I could. Mom looked frustrated and kept bringing up Sidney, asking if something bad had happened at school. I said no, but it must have been obvious from my behavior and my posture that I was lying.

I felt like a real loser as I escaped back to my room. I had to figure this out; if I was going to keep taking Tabs, I had to find a way to make this work. Sure, I wanted to have fun, but I also wanted to belong like everybody else. That wasn't too much to ask, was it?

I lay down on my bed and looked at the ceiling. Suddenly, the reason Tabs had become so important was obvious: there was nothing special about me. Who was I kidding? If I was going to meet a girl, or act like I wasn't a pathetic loser, I needed a pill. I wasn't going to be satisfied fitting in for just a few hours here and there. I had to find a way to fit in for the rest of my life. I couldn't stand being this way much longer. Tabs were my only hope.

My cell phone started ringing. I jumped, because I had almost forgotten that I had one. The only time it ever rang was when my mom called to tell me something. The embarrassing ringtone was the one the phone came with, and it had to go.

"Hello?" I answered tentatively.

"What's happening, Buddy? You miss me?" Sidney's voice sounded refreshing and feisty.

"Hey, Sidney. What's up?" I hoped my voice didn't give away the fact that I had never had a phone call from a girl before.

"Nothin' much," she said. "I'm just checking on you."

I chuckled nervously and said, "I sure could use a Tab about now."

"Buddy, it's like this. Guys like you need an edge. You know what I mean?"

"Yeah. I think I get it," I said. But I wasn't sure what she was referring to. I didn't want to sound stupid by asking, so I waited to hear what she'd say next.

"I've got the edge right here in this little brown plastic bottle. And you can have it any time you want. As a matter of fact, let's meet tomorrow after school. And bring your spare change."

"Spare change?"

"Buddy, let me spell it out for you. Geez, you're a tad slow catching on. It's called M-O-N-E-Y." She spit out each letter as though I were too retarded to understand the meaning of spare change. But I knew what she meant. She was going to sell me pills; it was time to start buying them. I made sure my voice sounded casual before I answered.

"Money. Sure, I get it. I'll have some cash with me tomorrow."

Her last words were abrupt, yet she still managed to sound incredibly sexy. "Bring as much as you can, if you expect to get what you need." There was no good-bye, just a dial tone on the other end.

I didn't mind having to pay for the Tabs. Julie had said she planned to do the same and I guessed other kids were doing it, too. I couldn't blame Sidney for wanting to make a buck or two. I wished I could buy ten Tabs. I remembered the twenty-dollar bill my aunt had given me for my birthday; I'd thrown it in my desk drawer months ago.

There was no way Sidney was going to charge me five dollars apiece. She liked me and promised she would *take good care of me.* That meant I'd be her best customer and best customers got special rates. Once I got my hands on those pills I could crawl out of my shell again and stay that way for quite a while.

The next morning I was back to my usual routine. Mom wordlessly handed me a Pop Tart; she knew I wouldn't eat anything else and she figured it was better than letting me leave on an empty stomach. She didn't follow me to the front door, which was a relief to me. I felt a little guilty that I was always such a disappointment to her.

I spent the day going through the motions of being a student, but I kept looking around for Sidney. I wanted those pills. But it wasn't until I was walking home after school that she appeared. She was right where she'd been two days before when she'd called out to me, only this time she was standing next to her sporty red Sebring convertible and texting on her cell phone. I watched her thumbs dance on the keypad. As I got closer she smiled at me, but she looked like she was all business. "Did you bring it?" she asked.

My stomach did a flip-flop. I was excited to see her and excited about the pills, but now I felt more like a customer than a classmate or friend. I stumbled over my words and could only answer, "Uh . . . sure . . . the cash. I brought it."

"Show me."

I retrieved a crumpled up twenty-dollar bill and held it out to her like a small child offers a flower. Her mouth screwed up into a sneer and the coolness in her voice surprised me. "How many did you expect to buy with this? I told you my going rate is five apiece. I thought you were ready for some action."

I stood there feeling like a little kid being scolded. I thought twenty dollars was a lot of money, but she scoffed at it. I felt embarrassed because I didn't know anything about buying pills and I was already letting her down. I was afraid she would take off and leave me empty-handed. I would die if that happened.

"I'm sorry, Sidney," I said in my most apologetic voice. "You're right; I should have known better and brought more money."

She looked irritated as she yanked the car door open. She lifted the lid on the center console and I could see brown prescription bottles and plastic baggies full of pills. She spun around and said in a degrading tone of voice, "This isn't candy, you know. You get what you pay for. I'm selling drugs here, not ice cream."

I just wanted to shrivel up and disappear. How could I have been so stupid? Sidney possessed the one thing that had made me happy for the first time in years. I saw a future for myself. I could have friends, girls, and who knows what else. Did I really think she was going to just give them away? I wanted to be back in my room and never come out again.

Sidney was holding a bottle of Tabs. She shoved it toward my face and I flinched. "Geez, could you be a little more nervous?"

As I recoiled, she suddenly softened and reached out to coax me back. I timidly stepped closer. I wanted those pills.

"Okay, Buddy, take it easy. We'll work something out, okay?"

"Okay."

"I'm going to give you a break today. So stop looking like I'm not going to give you anything."

"I'm sorry. I'm new at this. I didn't know what to expect. I thought . . . maybe . . . being my first time . . . you know."

"I get it." She cut me off; she had a cold look on her face. "I know you're just getting started with pills, so here's one of my simple rules: I'm not going to come running every time you've got five dollars to buy a Tab. I'm too busy for that."

I wished I had two hundred dollars to spend. She took the cap off and poured out five pills; I just stared at them. As excited as I was about the power they held, I was also painfully aware that they would only last me a day or two. Before I could blink, she took the twenty and said, "The fifth one's free, because I expect you to make up for it on the next purchase. Won't you, Buddy?"

"I promise you I'll buy a lot more next time. I've got more money at home."

"I believe you," she said. "There's no doubt in my mind."

She turned her back to me and got in her car. She turned the key and the engine roared to life and then settled into a purr. Sidney lowered the driver's side window and barely managed a "catch you later" before speeding off.

I felt the pounding of my heart slow down as she disappeared in the distance. I wanted to kick myself for not being prepared to do business. I didn't want to make her mad ever again. Next time, I was going have money, as much as I could get my hands on. I was going to be a good customer. I was going to turn myself into something better than the pimply nerd I was. Now that I had Tabs, I was the new me again.

CHAPTER 5

Precious Jewels

I was now in possession of five fantastic Tabs. I felt my energy level increase even before I took one. I was so excited about getting my confidence back that I just popped a pill into my mouth and started to chew it. It was bitter and nasty without any water to wash it down, but I managed to swallow it. I now knew that Tabs had magical powers and were about to make my dreams come true.

But I had another thought: how much was this going to cost me? Sidney was in the business of selling pills, not in the business of making me happy. That was my job and now I had to be able to pay the price. A little voice in my head spoke up. "And you will, Buddy. Any price at all."

I looked around and realized that everybody had cleared out from the bus stop while Sidney and I had been talking. It was just me, alone again. I wondered how long it would be before I'd feel something happening. I was more than a little impatient.

When the drug kicked in, my body felt more alive and ready for action. Then my mind began to speed up. Any leftover thoughts about being ugly or ordinary vanished. The ideas that fired through my brain fascinated me to no end. Each one was more interesting than the one before; I thought about ways to talk to girls, buying some cool clothes, and even beefing up my body with weight-lifting. All these thoughts were speeding through my mind; it was like having a million gifts to unwrap at Christmas . . . all at once.

I was feeling pretty good by the time I arrived home and not prepared to face my mom. "Hi," I tossed out as I walked right past her, heading for the fridge. My mom followed me into the kitchen and watched me pull out the fixings for a sandwich, something I never did after school. Her eyes were glued on me; I felt like every move I made was being inventoried.

"What's going on?" she asked.

I was humming tunelessly. I didn't answer right away because I was concentrating so hard on building a sandwich with layers of meat, lettuce, tomato, pickle, and a glob of mayonnaise. I pressed it all together so it could fit in my mouth. I looked at her with what I knew was a goofy expression and said, "I'm making a sandwich. Wanna bite?" I stuffed it into my mouth, bit off a huge chunk, and started to chew.

"You know what I mean." Mom was not going to be sidetracked. "It's great to see you smiling, hungry enough to devour a huge sandwich, and happy enough to hum . . . but I don't get it. You're not the same son who left for school this morning. What's gotten into you? You were this way yesterday and then turned gloomy in a matter of hours. Try explaining that, if you don't mind."

She was right. How was I going to get away with that? I needed to convince her that I was changing into a happier version of me. But to make it work for the long term, I would need a daily supply of Tabs and I didn't have enough pills or money to pull that off. That grim reality was killing my high, and it sucked royally. I had to get her off my case so I could at least enjoy what was left of the terrific rush.

"Well, I guess Sidney has more of a good effect on me than I expected. I woke up this morning feeling bummed out, like I usually do. I'm not going to talk to anybody when I'm like that, not even you. I just want to be left alone. Don't get me wrong; you know I love you, and Dad and Junior, too. It's a beautiful thing to be part of such a wonderful family. Don't you agree?" I was running my mouth off again and nonsense was pouring out. I was trying to say something about Sidney and I started yapping about loving my family. I needed to get a grip here.

My mind was moving along at a good clip. I was preoccupied with all the cool thoughts streaming through my head, and I paid less attention to my mother. And even when I did, it was hard to take her seriously.

I suddenly heard my mother's voice, and she sounded annoyed. "Buddy. Buddy! Are you listening to me? I'm tired of having to repeat myself."

"What? What do you want?"

"Finish telling me about Sidney. Are the two of you getting to know each other better? What's she like? When will I meet her?"

"Oh . . . right . . . Sidney. Well, she's not my girlfriend. But she likes me and does special things for me."

"What kind of special things? You aren't . . ."

"Mom! Please! She's a decent girl. Where is your mind going?"

"Why are you laughing so much? Did I say something funny?"

She wasn't funny, but I was loosened up and could not take her seriously. I wanted to take a Tab right in front of her and say, *I just swallowed some magic. In a few minutes you won't believe your eyes. Your son, the dud, is going to disappear and you'll see Prince Charming on a charging horse.*

My mind felt like it was ripping through the gears of a race car. I was jolted back to our conversation when a firm hand gripped my arm.

"Buddy! I'm not kidding. I want some answers."

"Okay, okay. Sidney. You want to know what's so special about Sidney. Well . . . she's nice to me. I don't know why. We must have just the perfect blend of chemistry. You know . . . pheromones."

"Pheromones?"

I thought I was witty. Couldn't she see that?

"That's right. Nature's horny hormones, just for us kids."

"Buddy! What's gotten into you?"

I took another gigantic bite of my sandwich. Mom looked bewildered.

"I've gotten into me, don't you just love it?"

She shook her head and squinted at me.

"I'm not sure yet. You're so different now. But at least you're happy and that's a big improvement. If Sidney's the reason why, then I'm grateful. Lord knows how hard I try."

Junior walked into the kitchen. He's my ten-year-old brother who's always in overdrive. I think it's the Dove Dark Chocolates that are constantly smudged into brown goo at the corners of his mouth. Mom keeps a well-stocked bowl on our coffee table. That afternoon, he was so rambunctious that my mom's attention shifted to him.

"Junior, no more chocolate for you. It will spoil your dinner." Junior was unwrapping another one and Mom was intent on stopping him.

The distraction was perfect for my exit. I took the rest of my sandwich and patted my goofy brother on the head as I walked past him on my way upstairs. That was also something I had never done. It was another giveaway that I was not the same kid who had spent the last sixteen years living here.

By the time I reached the top of the stairs, Mom was finished with Junior and had turned her attention to my father, who must have overheard everything while watching TV in the living room. They're boring people who have nothing interesting to say. But this time their exchange surprised me.

"Harry, what do you think? You heard what your son said. He's happy. And it's obvious that he is, I'll give him that much. But he's weird happy and I'm not buying that bit about the girl, Sidney. It's all too nicely wrapped for my taste." She paused for a second, I guess to see what my dad would say. I stood on the landing and held my breath.

"So, answer me, Harry. Do you think he's on something?" I just about lost my balance.

My dad must have hit the pause button on the remote so he wouldn't miss any *Jeopardy* questions, because the TV suddenly went silent.

"Do you mean like taking drugs?"

"Yes. Do you think it can't happen to Buddy?" Mom shot back. "Look how he's acting, all giddy and bringing up a girl, of all things. Of course I mean drugs."

"Okay, okay. Settle down, Karen. Let's look at it logically. Our son is a shy, nerdy kid who hasn't even had alcohol or tobacco touch his lips. And you think he's a druggie with a girlfriend?" I silently applauded my dad's common sense.

"I don't know. What do you think?" I could hear the doubt in her voice.

"Impossible," he muttered.

Mom sounded thoughtful as she said, "I guess you're right. He's an innocent, naïve boy who is going through a rough time at school. I should be glad that he's finally having a good day. God knows if or when that will happen again. I don't think he'd know what to do with a drug if you put it right under his nose."

They both chuckled and I heard *Jeopardy* come back on TV. I think my parents had finally learned to accept me as the son who would always be different. I intended to use that to my advantage and see what I could get away with, now that Tabs were improving my personality. I hurried back and grabbed a bottle of water out of the fridge and headed for the privacy of my room.

I loved being there. It was a sanctuary, a place where whoever and whatever I was could come out of hiding. My head was still racing and I was looking forward to more fantastic thoughts as I took out the four Tabs and laid them on the bed. I looked at the pills and imagined what more they could do for me. Thoughts like that seemed harmless and they made me feel so much better about everything. It wasn't long before I wanted to take another one; I wanted to feel even more incredible. And then I wondered, *What would happen if I took them all at once? Would that be a blast or what?*

I was kind of afraid to do it. Besides, I wanted to make the Tabs last. They had me under a spell. There was nothing more valuable in my life than those pills.

I started having paranoid thoughts about my parents standing right outside my door and snooping. The TV was still on, but they could have already tiptoed up the stairs and be waiting out there to storm into my room and catch me red-handed with the pills. I reminded myself that my mom never came in my room uninvited. She didn't even make my bed. I had a strict rule forbidding any entry.

I couldn't help it. Paranoia got the better of me and I had to peek into the hallway to prove that it was empty. Once I was satisfied that I had privacy, I knew I couldn't wait any longer. I snatched a Tab and swallowed it with a gulp of water. I listened for footsteps, because now I had the biggest secret of my life to protect. My parents could never find out what I was doing. They wouldn't understand, and they'd probably jump to conclusions and say something like, "Anyone who needs pain pills to be happy must have a problem."

They'd be dead wrong, and I was going to prove it. I'd seen movies about painkillers. I knew they were narcotics and some people got addicted to them. Some people even turned into junkies. Those were not happy people. They were out of control. I was different. Tabs made me smile and feel like living. Besides, addiction brought out the worst in people, but Tabs brought out the best in me. They wiped the ugly pimples off my face and made the world a place where I belonged. Anything that helped me that much could never be bad. Ever.

I was using simple logic. I had never seen an addict in real life, but I had a clear picture of the agony they went through as they desperately tried to get drugs and how sick they were when they didn't have any. I wasn't like that and would never become that way. That meant I could keep taking Tabs, as many as I needed and as many as I wanted, as long as I did it just to be happy. The question was, how much would it cost me and could I afford it? I answered myself: *Price is no object. I will do what it takes to get the money.*

Just thinking that way made me realize that Tabs had sharpened my senses along with my intellect. I knew exactly how good they were for me. The second Tab brought on a warm sensation flowing through the middle of my body like a wrap-around heating pad. My clear thinking got even clearer and I welcomed lots of ideas that made sense. It was as though the reason I was shy, nervous, and awkward was a vise grip squeezing my brain. Tab loosened the grip and my brain expanded, suddenly filling with confidence.

And the energy—there was lots of it. Some part of my body was in constant motion. I just needed a way to keep busy and use all that energy on something worthwhile. As crazy as it sounds now, I sat there and thought about maybe mowing the yard or cleaning the garage or something, just because it was so hard to sit still. Wow, bad idea! That would have really made my parents suspicious.

I wondered what 100 Tabs could do for me. The rush would probably be so spectacular that it would spoil me forever. I couldn't think of a better word to describe it. *Rush* was perfect and a totally brand-new experience for me. Then I realized I only had three more left and I had to make sure to use each one carefully and get my money's worth.

I was jumpy and started pacing. *What should I do? What should I do? What should I do?* I kept asking myself. I realized that I couldn't get my racing mind to downshift. I needed something to do, anything. I walked to my closet because I had a ridiculous urge to organize it. I took everything off the shelves and threw it on my bed. I was grabbing hangers of pants and shirts and couldn't wait to color coordinate them when I hung them back up. I put everything back on the shelves and made it look neater than ever. *That was awesome,* I thought. *Look what I've accomplished.* I was convinced once again that Tabs were the bomb, so I took another one. "What's next?" I asked aloud. "I have to keep busy."

I jumped right into emptying the desk drawers onto the bed and sorting through the pencils, pens, stapler, erasers, paper clips, and other junk. It seemed so important to put it all back in perfect order. I put my headphones on and blasted some music. Tabs enabled me to do anything I wanted and, at the same time, it was washing all the ugly out of my soul, like an all-purpose cleaner: miraculous, powerful, perfect. And I loved it.

I continued to feel like an accelerating locomotive, and I needed to pace around the room in circles. There was a rhythm to my steps and I could swear it was the same as my heartbeat. It all felt so good and I wanted it to feel better. *Push the envelope,* I thought. *Take another one.*

After the fourth Tab, I was prancing around the room and acting cocky. My mind was working at a blazing speed and I felt smarter. I decided I was going to get educated about all the different pills I could take. I wanted to discover which ones gave me the edge that Sidney spoke about and how many I would need to take. I was fed up with being a loser. I tried to imagine how smart I could actually become, maybe even brilliant or exceptionally talented. I wanted to be anything but a nerd and a geek.

CHAPTER 6
Your Life Depends On It Now

I am having trouble recalling every single detail of what happened next, but I vividly recall puking. Before that, I do remember all the energy draining out of me. I became sluggish and just felt bad all over, especially my head and my stomach. I think I got hot, then sweaty, and then I had that awful salty taste before I heaved. There was no time for the bathroom. The wastebasket was close enough. Then I staggered to bed. I just wanted to sleep and be left alone. I couldn't think anymore, so there was no way I was going to figure out what went wrong and why being high had come crashing to a screeching halt.

As I woke up, everything from my neck down felt like a wad of dough. My mouth was dry and my tongue felt like it was coated with sand. I desperately wanted a drink of water. My vision was blurred and I tried to focus on the digital clock display: I think it was about eight. I didn't even know if it was AM or PM. I didn't even care.

I tried to remember more of what happened. I knew things had started out great with the first two Tabs. But after that, it felt like my memories were being fractured by a sledgehammer. My reward for taking Tabs was feeling like some part of my brain was shattered. My mind was crippled and I revisited the same bleak and barren place of cruelty and suffering that I was so familiar with. The ride with the pills had come to an end all too soon and my life still sucked. I assumed I had a good time getting high, but I wasn't any better now that it was over. I was sick as a dog. My brain was sore just trying to figure out what had happened.

I tried to sit up, but I was lightheaded and dizzy. I flopped back on the mattress and crushed the pillow around my head. I needed something pleasant to think about, so I pictured Sidney, tall, blonde, and beautiful, saying, "Bring more money and I'll take good care of you." She obviously knew that pills would make me feel awesome, but did she also know that they can make you feel worse than ever? I had to figure out how to do it right and feel good all the time. That required Sidney and cash. She was going to be my connection, my tutor and my key to happiness. I had to find a way to pay for all this. The quality of my life depended on it, and it wasn't cheap.

I squeezed the pillow tighter around my head in my frustration. As I fought to keep my mind focused, I realized I was hearing a dull banging sound. I loosened my grip and heard a muffled voice yelling, "Open this door!" Now I was really annoyed. I unfolded the pillow to expose one ear and heard my mom clobbering the door. With a groan I rolled over and heard her voice, angry and scared at the same time. She kept spitting out questions: "Are you okay? Why won't you open the door? What's the matter with you?"

I got up and wobbled a bit; my body was sluggish and as inflexible as cold clay. As I reached for the door, I realized that I had wedged a chair under the knob. In what seemed like the same continuous movement, I removed the chair and Mom bolted into the room. She grabbed me by the shoulders and peered frantically into my eyes, searching for clues about my lack of response. Her yelling hurt my eardrums.

"I kept calling you for dinner and you wouldn't come, so we just ate without you. Then I got worried when you didn't come down at all. I don't care about your privacy rule. When you won't answer the door, I know something's definitely wrong. So . . . what's going on? What were you doing in here that you have to keep so secret?"

She scanned the room for an explanation and looked back into my unfocused eyes. Then she sniffed the air while making a face that detected something rancid.

"What's that smell? Did you throw up in here? You look awful. What's the matter with you?"

I was caught off-guard and unprepared. I tried hard not to panic. The best my foggy brain could come up with was, "It's my stomach. I just don't feel good."

She walked around the bed and lifted my wastebasket, holding it outstretched. "Couldn't you at least make it to the bathroom?"

I decided to resort to what had always worked in the past. I acted helpless and needy, like a wounded animal, hoping to draw her sympathy.

"I tried, but it happened so fast. I'm sorry for the mess. I'm really sick."

She put the basket down, folded me into her arms and squeezed me tight. As she kissed my forehead, she said, "I'll take care of you."

I nodded and moaned theatrically.

"Okay, I'll get some Tylenol and Pepto," she said.

Good move, I thought. As she left with the basket, I fell back down onto my bed and then yelled to her for a bottle of water. I felt like I'd caught a big break. I wondered what she would think if she knew that her son, the social weirdo, was doing some Jekyll-and-Hyde thing with Tabs.

She returned and walked through the door with the air of someone who had a nursing degree. "Here, takes these. Thank goodness tomorrow is Saturday so you can stay home and rest."

I swallowed her medicine and guzzled the water. I felt like a sick child being kept home from school, and I loved it. Mom touched my forehead and announced, "Good, no fever."

She turned and looked at me, her face glowing with the assurance of a job well done. "Call me if you need me."

What I really needed was to figure out how many Tabs I took and why did I get so sick. I wasn't sure if I was supposed to be alarmed about that, or did everybody do the same thing with pills? I had a lot more to learn, but right now I was totally exhausted, and I wanted to give my brain a rest.

I woke up when the morning light broke through the window and my head was pounding. Each throb was excruciating. I felt like all the liquid had left my body, leaving me so dehydrated that I would snap like a dry twig. I needed a gallon of water. When I stood up, my feet hurt and each step felt heavy and slow. As I walked past the closet, I did a double take. It was impeccably organized. Now it was easier to remember the exhilarating stream of energy that fueled the cleaning frenzy. *The desk too,* I remembered. *It's just as immaculate.*

As I walked to the bathroom, I felt weak and wrung out. My muscles were stiff and sore. My head felt like there was wreckage inside with scattered nuts, bolts, and screws that had come loose. It was painful just to think and I tried to take it all in stride, like a man with a hangover after tying one on. I actually believed that a Tab could clear the cobwebs and I wondered if I had any left.

I stood at the sink and stared at the medicine cabinet until it dawned on me: My mom kept it stocked with pills for her aches and pains. I swung the door open and, sure enough, there were brown plastic bottles with my mom's name on the labels. I picked each one up to read the contents, hoping to hit the jackpot. *Roxicodone 30 milligram* got my attention. Immediately, my brain started to wake up and get excited. *Do you realize what you've got here, Buddy?* it seemed to say.

These must have been the same Roxys Sidney had mentioned. I hoped they were the strongest ones made, the kind that would repair what I had done to myself by taking so many Tabs, and give me a chance to try it again. I quickly popped the lid to the Roxicodone and took one out. It was light blue and round. I studied its markings. On one side it read A215, on the other side the pill was scored. These were the ones that Sidney preferred, the easily breakable ones. I popped one into my mouth and chased it down with a cup of water from the sink. I drank four more cups to wash the cotton out of my mouth and then brushed the scummy puke taste off my tongue with toothpaste.

I felt better instantly. Sidney said that was impossible, yet it was happening to me right now, before the pill even dissolved in my stomach. I was amazed and believed that Roxys were going to work even bigger miracles than Tabs had. Sidney said they were going to *knock my head back*. I didn't think that could happen if I swallowed just one pill. Even I could figure out that much.

I noticed my headache was easing up and I could think and even concentrate without much difficulty. I couldn't wait to see what else Roxys would change for the better. I needed to be sharp and intelligent about my next move. Mom's original prescription was for sixty pills; I counted forty-two left in the bottle. These were obviously the pills Mom took for the arthritic pain in her knee. I remember hearing her telling my father two weeks ago that the Prednisone she took for inflammation had brought down the swelling. She was better now and maybe she wouldn't need any more Roxys.

That meant I should get all the leftovers. I intended to take possession of those beauties and I imagined how much fun was in my future. The more I looked at them, the more precious they became. I treated them like glittering gemstones. I shook the bottle and watched them dance inside. As long as Mom's knee was comfortable, the Roxicodone would sit on the shelf for years and pass the expiration date. I was going to make sure that expiration didn't happen.

Now that I had the pills, I needed a foolproof way to take them without getting caught. I was relieved that the fog had lifted from my brain so I could come up with an ingenious answer. All I had to do was replace the pills with some look-alikes. Actually I didn't have to be fussy. Mom would never check because, from the outside, the bottle would appear to be nearly full. What a perfect idea.

I looked in the mirror and saw something evil staring back. It was my own reflection. I was holding up the bottle of Blues and smiling. The look on my face was smug as I told my reflection, "They're mine, all mine." What the mirror couldn't reflect, and I didn't realize until months later, was how wretched my soul had become. I turned and walked confidently out of the bathroom, muttering, "Let's party . . . harder" as I thought selfishly of doing one thing . . . pleasing myself.

CHAPTER 7

This Party Should Last Forever

I was holding three Roxys as I scampered toward my room. The smell of coffee got my attention. Mom was up, and I didn't want to be disturbed. I yelled down from the top of the stairs, "Hey, Mom. It's me."

"Good morning," she called back from the kitchen. "How are you feeling? I can have breakfast ready in a jiffy. What would you like to eat? I can make pancakes, eggs, sausage . . ."

"Mom, stop with the menu. I don't feel well enough to eat anything."

"Do you want me to have a look at you?"

I could tell by the sound of her voice that she was getting closer.

"Mom, you don't need to come upstairs," I yelled. "I can take care of myself. I still have some of the medicine you brought me yesterday. That should do it. I'm going back to bed."

She stopped at the bottom of the stairs and gazed up at me, taking a longer-than-usual look. As she studied me, I figured she was trying to make her best maternal diagnosis.

"Okay, Honey. I think it's a twenty-four-hour bug. After a little more rest you should be fine. You're on your own. Dad is running errands and Junior's gone next door to a birthday party. I'm going shopping. Try to eat something when your stomach feels better."

She disappeared into the downstairs bathroom and I dashed back to my room. All I wanted to do was feel the "better" feeling I'd had with Tabs, not the sick feeling from swallowing too many. I learned a lot from taking Tabs and I needed to apply that to Roxicodone. I needed to be careful so I could get high and be happy again . . . no more puking. I remembered Sidney's warning about how potent Roxys were. As I sat at my desk and put the pills on top of my notebook, I had a thought. *They can't be that strong; my mom takes them and I've never seen her high.*

I felt better about that. I had taken one pill already and had three to go. The directions on the prescription bottle said one every six hours as needed for pain. That's four in one day. Heck, if I took what I removed from the bottle that would be the perfect amount. I knew I was safe with that many. I could only be happier, not sicker.

Then I thought about it some more. Suppose I wanted them to last longer? They'd have to be stronger, so I could take half as much. Sidney mentioned one way to step up their potency. At the time, snorting them had seemed unthinkable. Now it was worth considering. She wouldn't have pointed it out if it wasn't such a great idea and that meant everybody must be doing it. Therefore, it had to be worth it. I had to try it.

I wondered what that would feel like. Sidney said it would be fast-acting. I hadn't gotten high from the first Roxy yet and I was anxious to make something happen. Sidney had warned me not to take more than a quarter of a pill on my first try. I thought she was just babying me. She didn't believe I could possibly handle more than that, because I was a scrawny weakling. Little did she know I had already handled four Tabs. So I decided to snap the pill in half with my fingers. The two pieces looked tiny. How could something so small do anything?

The only thing on my desk that I could use to crush it was my wooden ruler. I pressed down on the half piece of pill, and it crumbled easily. I used the edge of the ruler to sweep the particles close together. Then I smiled and spread a thin line, pretending it was powdered cocaine, just like in the movies. I removed a dollar bill from my wallet and rolled it. Junkies did this, but it felt innocent, not like a dirty despicable habit.

I grew more excited by the second. It was so easy. I thought there had to be something else I needed to do first, but there wasn't. *What are you waiting for? Lean over and snort it,* I thought.

I placed the rolled-up dollar bill in my nostril. It felt weird holding it there. I instinctively blocked the other nostril. I paused before I snorted, closing my eyes and preparing for the surprise of my life.

Instantly, I felt the powder hit the back of my throat and I coughed. It left a likable taste in my mouth that I couldn't describe. My nose started to itch something fierce and I kept rubbing it until the itch spread all over my face. This was happening fast, all right. I used both hands to scratch my face and it felt good. At the same time, a nice warm, soothing calm took over and I was in heaven. So this was a Roxy. Everybody's favorite and mine too. I put on a mellow smile and thought, *I could do this forever.*

If half of a pill could make me feel this good, I knew the pills I had left were going to be a real treat. *What should I do now?* I wondered. I kept drumming my fingers on the desktop. I grabbed the ruler and moved the pills around on my note book, just killing time, waiting for the next surprise. It had only been a few minutes, but I was growing impatient. Being mellow was awesome but I wanted more than that.

Sure enough, I got it. The energy burst that kicked in was made to order. I stood up and suddenly felt like exercising, something I never did, but it was either that or pace the room. I definitely wasn't going to leave the room and get caught. So I hit the floor and did push-ups. They were easy. After that came sit-ups, deep-knee bends, and jumping jacks. I wasn't even winded. *But are you happy? Not yet.*

I'd gone on a neatness rampage the day before and there was nothing left to do in my room. I needed a way to use up the energy. I threw myself back onto the bed and stared at the ceiling fan; its droning motor spun the blades. I needed amusement. My cell phone came alive with a text message. I wanted it to be from the one person who could make my heart beat in my throat. I read the message.

I want 2 c u 2day. Brng $$$. I hv pils u lyk. Sidney

CHAPTER 8

It Takes $$$ to Keep the Party Going

Sidney was just what I needed to chase away my dull, ho-hum existence. I wished I could get my hands on her. Attractive was really too bland a word for Sidney. She was hot, and I could care less if she teased me all day long with winks and hand-blown kisses. She could play me for the world's biggest fool — I would gladly take all she dished out just to have her pay attention to me. But then again, if it came to choosing between Sidney and the pills, I would take the buzz any day.

Whatever variety of pills she had to sell, I wasn't ready to buy. I had inherited a generous supply of Mom's unused Roxicodone. There was no rush and besides, there was no money for me to make a purchase. Just the same, someday I wanted to try all the different pills she had.

Before I typed my answer, I made a trip to the bathroom to inspect my treasure. I just liked looking at the pills, touching them and counting them. I would rather have them with me always. At the time, I didn't know that by wanting to check and recheck my supply, I was behaving like someone who was hooked.

When I opened the medicine cabinet, I gasped. The bottle had been moved; it was on the other side of the prednisone. I grabbed it and pried off the lid with fumbling hands. I was petrified just thinking of how many Roxys would be missing and how few would be left for me. I dumped the pills out and started counting. Only thirty-six left, but that wasn't the worst part. Knowing that Mom might take more was the problem. Why did her pain have to return? I did *not* want to share my Roxicodone.

I did the math; I panicked at the thought that, singlehandedly, she might take the rest of the pills in one week. If I stole too many, she would know immediately. I had to do some serious thinking. I removed six pills and inspected what was left to see if the smaller quantity was obvious. I was convinced that she wouldn't notice, but decided not to risk taking any more. Now I needed to plan ahead.

I walked back to my room and typed my answer, **Yes, I'm interested.**

Sidney answered back in seconds and gave me no choice but to meet in less than one hour at the bus stop. The dollar signs kept crawling around in my head. I didn't have any $$$. I needed a brilliant idea to get some, and fast, but I was coming up blank.

I glanced over at the Roxicodone on the desk. If Tabs were food for intelligent thinking then Roxicodone would probably turn me into a genius. I wanted it to be razor-sharp and fast.

I ground up the other half a Roxy and snorted it. The cough, the itch, and the taste returned and I liked it even more this time. I imagined what the Roxy was doing in my brain, probably tripping all the pleasure circuits into the on position. I welcomed the warm cozy feeling again, with a new twist. I could feel the powder in my nose clumping into a glob and sliding into the back of my throat. And I liked that, too. I don't know why I wasn't completely satisfied, but I found myself wanting a rush of brilliant ideas, not just more energy. "I'm in a hurry here," I called out loud, as though Roxicodone could hear me and would instantly solve my money problem.

For five minutes, I circled around my room, then out in the hall, then up and down the stairs. I had to keep moving while I waited for the fresh ideas about getting my hands on a big chunk of money. My next purchase had to be enough to last at least a couple of weeks.

As the minutes ticked by, I didn't allow myself to enjoy the high. Everything was perfect except one thing: the solution. I kept looking over at the two pills that were left on the notebook. I put them in my pocket, then patted the outside, feeling eight tablets very securely nestled there. After a few more minutes, I couldn't take it any longer. I took one out and snorted the whole pill.

I can handle this, I thought. So far I'm doing fine; I don't think I'm going to be sick. Snorting pills has to be safer than swallowing them. Maybe if they didn't go into your stomach you couldn't get sick. Wow, that would be neat.

The only difference between snorting a whole pill and the partial one was the bigger glob that made its way into my throat. That, I liked. The coughing and itching were just second nature by this third time. I wanted to be a pro at this. The warm feeling returned, but I didn't get laid back. My energy was still up from the last pill and, in a matter of minutes, it just ramped up even more.

Finally, I got what I wanted. My head felt like a bright light had been turned on inside. The smarter part of my brain was being activated. The feeling was sensational. I was sure I had snorted the perfect amount . . . somehow I felt safe as my brain picked up speed and was heading into overdrive. The incredible ideas flooded in; thinking had never been so easy for me and the answer, when it came, was just so obvious. My mom kept rainy-day money. Lots of it. We depended on her savings when Dad was out of work. She was always emphasizing the importance of sacrifice and prudent saving. I remembered her showing me a stack of twenties that she'd stockpiled.

"Where does she keep it?" I wondered aloud. She never showed me the hiding place, only the money, but it couldn't be that hard to find.

I headed for the bedroom door feeling happy at last. I playfully skipped down the hall and raced to the bottom of the stairs and into the kitchen. I could hear myself talking out loud, repeating my words. "Let's find the money. Here money, money. I'm going to find you." I sounded silly and ridiculous, but I couldn't stop talking like that as I began my search.

I was back to having fun again. In fact, I think I was happier than I had ever been. I felt awesome and I didn't care if I spent the rest of my life in my bedroom, as long as I had enough Roxicodone to keep me company.

I started opening cabinets and checking every plastic container. "Empty. Empty. Empty," I muttered, disappointed but not about to give up my search. I just kept opening cabinet doors, one after the other. By the time I'd finished, the place looked like it had been ransacked.

In the far corner of the last cabinet I found the stash. A cookie jar held the prize. Now I knew why Mom had purchased a second one years ago: this one had turned into a piggy bank.

I pulled it out, clutched it tightly, opened it, and I could literally smell the money. There were hundreds of bills folded and crammed into that jar—mostly twenties, some even in bundles held together with rubber bands. As I removed a fistful of bills, I heard the garage door opening.

I froze in terror. I was clenching a wad of twenty-dollar bills. Two of the bills slipped from my grasp and fell to the floor. I forced the rest of the money back into the cookie jar and pushed down hard on the lid. First I heard the car door open and then the trunk. That was a welcome sound, because it meant Mom had come home with groceries and I had a little more time.

I returned the jar to the cabinet and suddenly realized there were mixing bowls and storage containers strewn all over the kitchen.

Mom was yelling from the garage. "Buddy, if you're up, will you please come and help? My knee is killing me."

I was in a real panic now. *I'll never get this place cleaned up in time.* My heart was pounding hard. Like a wild man, I threw containers into cabinets without any concern for where they belonged or how they were stacked.

As soon as I'd slammed the last cabinet door closed, I turned toward the door that would take me out to the garage; I knew I'd better be out there helping Mom, not standing around in the kitchen when she came in. As I stepped into the garage, I greeted her, intending only to ask what she wanted me to carry. Instead, a nonsensical stream of words poured out practically nonstop. "Let me give you a hand. I'm really handy…with my hands. Boy, what a pair of hands."

I tried to get busy, hoping that would shut me up. I reached into the trunk to retrieve a few bags of groceries and, as I turned back toward the house, I lost my balance and fell into the wall. I lay there stunned for a moment, tangled up with torn bags, crushed loaves of bread, and broken eggs dripping on me. The whole thing just seemed too funny and I started to laugh.

Lucky for me, Mom was already in the house unpacking the first load she'd brought in. I was able to get back on my feet before she returned. Of course, she couldn't help but notice the crushed food and torn paper bags. I tried to explain, but whatever I said, I must have said at least three times. Mom got a queer look on her face.

"Buddy! Can't you do a simple thing like carry groceries? Look at all those broken eggs! It's a mess, and you're going to clean it up. And why are you laughing? There's nothing funny about this."

I scooped up a handful of egg yolks and shells and mashed them back into the carton. Mom gave me a look and grabbed more grocery bags from the trunk.

"Sorry about that. It's no yolk, I'm really clumsy. I guess the yolk's on me. You can take a yolk, can't you?"

I walked past as she stared at me. I wanted to shut up so badly, but I couldn't.

"What's the matter with you?" Mom sounded really concerned as she followed me. "You're saying the dumbest things over and over again. What's gotten into you?"

"I'm all right," I answered quickly, making a conscious effort to get serious.

My mom looked frustrated. "You kids. I can't figure you out. I never acted like that." She put the groceries on the counter and turned toward me.

Mom's eyes darted past me to the floor and, as she caught sight of the two twenties I'd dropped, she looked surprised. She bent down and snatched up the two bills, tucking them into a compartment of her purse.

"I should be more careful with my money," she said. "God knows what you would have wasted this on if you'd found it first. Which reminds me: the checkout boy at the market, who's about your age, had a ring in his nose. It was disgusting. Don't ever let me catch you getting your body pierced. That would break my heart. You can do just about anything else, but not that."

I watched my precious twenties disappear; nothing was funny anymore. My opportunity to get my hands on some cash was gone and, man, did that suck.

An unexpected wave of nausea filled my mouth with salty saliva. Beads of sweat quickly broke out across my forehead. I was dizzy, too. I had to keep swallowing so I wouldn't puke. The room was going in and out of focus. I needed to get to the bathroom—in a hurry. As soon as I got there, I collapsed onto my knees and vomited into the toilet. I was sweating profusely; I kept retching with an empty stomach.

Mom had followed me. "I knew something was wrong with you. But you're not supposed to be sick again today. I don't understand it."

She wet a facecloth, knelt beside me with a puzzled look, and started swabbing my face. I feared it was blatantly obvious that I was sick from taking way too many painkillers and my mom would soon figure that out. All she had to do was put the pieces together: a sixteen-year-old who'd come home the day before in a great, talkative mood that ended abruptly and the next day he was acting silly and talking repetitious nonsense just before turning pale and praying to the porcelain god for mercy. The combination should have been a dead giveaway.

I wanted to drum up as much sympathy as I could to cover my tracks. But as I look back on that day and that disgusting scene, what I really remember was thinking that another Roxicodone might have settled my stomach and cleared my head.

As much as I preferred to avoid it, I allowed Mom to cradle me in her arms. I tried hard to look pathetic, but I was pretty sure I didn't need to act too hard. I felt pretty pathetic.

"Whatever you've got is really nasty. I'll get the Pepto."

Cold sweat soaked through my shirt. I was as sick as a dog and barely able to whimper. I took the Pepto-Bismol my mom brought back, just to humor her. I knew I didn't have a problem that Pepto-Bismol was going to fix. I had learned something new about Roxicodone: It can also make you puke. But why? I'd only had three.

As the waves of nausea and dizziness subsided, I got off the floor and felt very tired. I wanted to lie down. It was just like the Tabs. I'd done it again. What had gone wrong?

Mom followed behind me as I made my way up the stairs and into my room. I collapsed onto the bed. I didn't want to move a muscle.

Once she was satisfied that I was tucked in, Mom tried to hustle but was obviously favoring her arthritic knee as she headed down to the kitchen. I turned over and spotted the scene of the crime; a ruler, notebook with flecks of white powder on the cover, and the rolled dollar bill. I tried to hurry, but my head spun when I stood up. I brushed everything into the top desk drawer as Mom returned with a tray with tea and toast. I grabbed a stick of gum and then slammed the drawer.

"What are you doing out of bed?"

"Nothing."

"You're sweating again and your color's bad."

"I was looking for some gum. My mouth tastes like you-know-what."

"Get back into bed. This will fix it."

She snatched the gum from my hand, then perched on the edge of the bed and made me sip and nibble. I seemed to be dodging one bullet after another.

"I still can't understand why you got sick two days in a row. There's nothing else wrong with you, is there?"

"No. I'll be fine."

"Well, you just needed some good ol' TLC. I bet you'll be all right by tomorrow. And don't worry about the mess in the garage; I'll clean it up for you." She combed my hair with her fingers as she cooed. I let her soothing voice wash over me as I rejoiced inside that there was not going to be an interrogation. My secret was still safe.

I tried to imagine what Mom would have done if she knew I had been snorting drugs, her drugs. I wasn't sure which would have been worse—her anger or her heartbreak. I decided I really didn't want to think about either one and it would be better for me if I could get her out of my room. I still had problems to solve.

The alert of an incoming text message on my cell phone startled my mother. She lunged across my bed and grabbed the phone before I could.

"I'll get it; I don't want anyone to bother you." She looked at the text display and seemed as amused as she was confused. "Oh my, what's all this mean?"

It had to be Sidney, who was waiting for me and probably getting more pissed off by the minute. I looked at my clock and realized I was already five minutes late. Sidney was tracking me down. Mom studied the message.

"I think I can read some of this. Let's see. You are late. Don't P me off. That P must mean . . ."

"Give me that," I ordered, and Mom looked surprised. I grabbed the phone out of her hands and quickly read the message Sidney had sent: **U R L8. Dnt P me off. Lst chnc. U hv 5 mins to gt ur butt ovr here.** Sidney's abbreviations spelled out a stern warning: "You're late, don't piss me off. This is your last chance. You have five minutes to get your butt over here."

I could feel the beads of sweat as they formed on my forehead. My nerves felt like a steel cable strung too tight.

"What's going on here? Who sent you that? What are you late for and why is that getting someone po'd? I want to read the rest of it. Hand it over."

I deleted what was on the screen just before she snatched the phone.

"Why did you do that? You're in trouble, aren't you? Is it Sidney? Did she get mad at you? Is this your first tiff?"

I was so grateful that Mom had come to the most obvious conclusion. I took a deep breath and let out a heavy, groaning sigh. "Sidney doesn't like being stood up. I was supposed to be there by now. I hope she can forgive me. I really need that girl."

Mom touched a few keys, trying to bring the message back on the screen. "I've got to learn how to use these things."

I wished I could teleport to the bus stop in time to buy the pills and stay on Sidney's good side. Without those pills I had no chance of ever being happy. Those words were worse than sentencing me to a life in prison.

"So will you teach me how to retrieve that message? I want to read the rest of it. Maybe I can help you and Sidney stay together."

"You can. I can text her back and tell her I'm on my way." I watched carefully to see if she was going to let me go save my relationship with Sidney.

Mom stood up and stomped a foot on the floor. She meant business and she wanted me to know it. "You are *not* to leave this house in the condition you're in. Sidney will just have to wait. If she's a nice girl, she'll understand, even if I have to speak to her myself. I can explain it woman to woman. She won't be mad at you after that."

It was pointless to argue, and I knew it. "You're right. She'll get over it. You know what's best. Anyway, I'm beat. I can talk to her tomorrow and explain everything."

Mom's face softened, and she leaned over to plant a kiss on my forehead. "Okay, Sweetie. It's time you got your rest. I'll be right down the hall if you need me." The bed shook a little as she got up, then moved toward the door, turned out the light and closed the door quietly behind her.

The second I heard the door click, I fired a text back to Sidney with an excuse about having to stay home to babysit my brother. That excuse was dumber than a dog eating homework, but it was the best I could come up with in ten seconds. She answered back almost immediately. I read her response and let out a sigh of relief, but the stay of execution came with a price.

Dum xcuse. We do bznz aftr skool on mon.

I stared at the message in despair and disbelief. Even if I'd managed to get the two twenties my mom picked up, I could only have afforded to buy eight measly pills. Nothing was turning out the way I'd planned.

Once again I had tried to have a nice little party, this time with Roxicodone, and ended up making a spectacle of myself and puking. Somewhere, somehow, something had gone wrong. The first pill I'd taken with Sidney had been awesome, but since then, the pills had messed me up more than they had helped me out. I wanted good things to happen when I took pills. They were my only chance, my only hope. I had to learn how to make them do the trick, to work perfectly every time.

I needed to solve this problem. I needed to be smarter about taking pills. Maybe after some rest the answer would come; then tomorrow I would get more pills and do it right.

CHAPTER 9

Upping the Ante

I had already come up with a plan that seemed foolproof. Mom had plenty of money. All I needed was a handful of twenties, which she wouldn't miss. She never counted the cash; I was sure of it. She just kept stuffing it in the jar, so that night as I lay in bed, I thought about how smart that plan still was and I decided to see it through. I set the alarm so the next morning I'd wake up before everybody else.

When the alarm went off I was greeted by a dull ache that consumed my head. My body felt sore inside and out. I desperately wanted water. My mouth felt like the dryness was baked on. This was no way to start my day.

I listened to the stillness of the house; everybody was asleep. I tiptoed down the stairs and chugged a refreshing bottle of water in the kitchen. I was moving slow but carrying out my mission to get the money and buy a new lease on life. I planned on buying enough pills to keep me happy for more than a week.

I found the jar in the same place I had returned it to yesterday afternoon. It still felt heavy with cash. I extracted two hundred dollars in twenties. It was hard to resist taking a lot more. Mom was never going to miss any of it as long as the jar always looked full, and I was going to separate some of the wads of bills and fluff them up to give that appearance. My plan was ridiculously easy.

I wasn't going to chance taking any more Roxys before I headed out for school. I wanted to experiment later, alone in my room, until I got the dose right. Before I left, I put the seven Roxys I had stolen from Mom into my desk drawer. There was no need to hide them, since she obeyed the hands-off policy for my stuff. But, feeling like a thief, I found a box of paper clips and tossed them inside, just in case.

Once I got to school, my day went straight downhill, though. I didn't see Sidney anywhere and I was worried that she'd skipped. That would mean no additional pills and more dejection and gloom. I hated being at school; I wasn't interested in learning anything I had no use for. I thought I already knew more than enough. I was going to keep my life simple. Pills made me happy. Being brainy didn't. Besides, what good was any amount of knowledge if you couldn't use it to make a friend? I'd rather party with a Roxy and call that my friend. Now that I had Mom's stash, I intended to finance one heck of a good time—at least while the money lasted. Knowledge couldn't buy that kind of fun. Book smarts wouldn't clear up my pimples, but pills could make my dreams come true—I'd already had enough proof of that to know how great my life was going to be.

I watched the hours tick by minute by minute until school was finally over. It was almost as unbearable as waiting for someone to volunteer an answer in class. Nobody knew how smart I was. I knew about a lot of different things that really didn't matter, so I kept my intelligence a secret. I'd rather act dumb and be considered stupid—at least that way, I wouldn't be labeled an ugly genius.

Once school let out, I bolted through the exit door and jogged to the football field, but Sidney was nowhere to be seen. I was early and kept pacing and checking my watch. My mind was racing so fast, I thought my brain would overheat. I couldn't stand waiting another minute. I kept touching the twenty-dollar bills in my pocket, just to make sure they were still there. Thirty minutes went by before the alert on my phone signaled a text message.

Its ur trn 2 w8. Hw duz it feel?

After what felt like an eternity, I finally saw Sidney walking toward me. She wore a white T-shirt with a huge red heart on it that accentuated her breasts. In the middle of the heart were two fluffy little dogs standing on their hind legs, kissing each other on the lips. Underneath the heart was a caption that read *Puppy Love Really Turns Me On*. Her baseball hat was a matching red with white lettering that read *Down Boy*. Man, she was hot! As she got closer, she broke into a trot, and her face lit up with a cheerleader's smile. When she was close enough for me to touch her, she tossed a baggie of pills in the air, spun around in a complete circle, and caught it as though she was doing a cheerleading drill. She was showing off and I loved it.

"You must really want these. I can tell," Sidney purred as she waved the baggy in front of my face.

She looked cocky, sassy, and stuck up. That's the kind of confidence I knew I could get from the pills I was about to buy.

"You're my kind of customer, Buddy boy." Her tone was seductive and, even though I knew it was an act, I was still mesmerized by her.

"Let's make a deal. I've got what you want if you've got what I want. Impress me with some money, Mr. Big Spender." And then she winked.

I would have seriously considered giving up my life on the spot if she'd offered me a kiss just then. I still wanted her attention so badly, I was willing to stand there and risk humiliation. I fanned out the twenties and heard a throaty, purring sound of approval as Sidney moved in closer to take them.

"Well, look who's got a bankroll." She grabbed the bills and started counting them, her expression all business again.

I couldn't speak or swallow. Sidney smelled of coconut and vanilla; a luscious combination of expensive creams and scented lotions evaporated off her skin. I was intoxicated by her fragrance and, for the moment, it was better than all the pills in that bag. I fantasized again about consuming her as a deliciously sinful treat, but I knew she was totally off-limits. I was only a customer, and an ugly one at that.

I stood there like a clueless fool. She toyed with me like a cat with a ball of string. I just didn't know how to play Sidney's game. She held the baggie of pills so close to my eyes that I had to pull my head back to focus.

Sidney rubbed her stomach while licking and smacking her lips. "Mmmmmmmm," was the only sound she made. I just stood there staring at her, afraid I might do or say something stupid.

"Do you know what these are?" she finally asked me as she took one out of the baggie.

I nodded yes, but she could have been selling me SweetTarts or Smarties; I couldn't tell the difference at first glance. Looking closer, I could see it was greenish, grayish-blue and slightly smaller than an aspirin tablet. I inspected the pill like an appraising buyer. The corners of her mouth twitched, but she managed to keep a straight face. I was at Sidney's mercy, and she knew it.

"Babycakes, this is an Oxy eighty."

I wanted desperately to impress her, so I said, "Of course it is. I've already snorted some Roxys. I can handle that."

The way her eyes opened wide convinced me that this was probably more potent than the 30 milligram Roxicodone I had been stealing from my mom. Plus, eighty sounded like a whole lot more fun than thirty.

"Roxys?" Her face morphed into meanness as she withdrew the baggie of pills. "You bought Roxys from somebody else?"

"Of course not. Those were my mom's. She had Roxy thirties." I hoped that was how to say it.

Sidney exaggerated the pucker of her lips. "Wow . . . such a big shot.

"I think I know what I'm doing. And you were right. They're great." My confidence was building.

"Really?"

"I want those pills in the baggie. How much are they?"

Sidney snorted. "Maybe you're not as ready as you think you are."

"What do you mean?" I was getting a little nervous. She was about to discover my ignorance and lack of experience. Why wouldn't she just sell me the pills so I could go?

"These pills are coated. I bet you didn't know that, did you?"

I didn't know what that meant, but I was sure it was important, and I wanted to shrink and disappear.

"Oh, that's all right." She seemed to get some sort of sick pleasure in making me look foolish. "I can't expect you to know everything so quickly."

"Okay, you win. What's so important about the coating? Is it bitter or something?"

"No, Sweetie. You have to clean it off. Here, let me show you."

She put the pill in her mouth and I could tell her tongue was busy wetting it with saliva. I wondered how it tasted. She removed it from her mouth, folded the bottom edge of her T-shirt over the pill, and rubbed it dry. It was white without the coating.

"Now it's ready to become powder. Follow me."

She took me over to the bleachers and proceeded to take out a wavy strip of metal with parallel slots running the entire length of it.

"What's that?"

She took out a small mirror, placed it on the bleacher and laid her plastic school ID next to it.

"This is my kit."

"Kit?" I asked. "You mean for drugs?"

She closed her eyes and shook her head in disgust. "Of course. Geez, you're slow. If you want to snort an eighty, you need to turn it into powder. I like to call this baby my cheese machine."

"Blues are easy to crush with a school ID. Oxys crush into big pieces, so you've got to shred them if you want to snort them. Now check this out."

The wavy metal thing was a hose clamp that she placed on top of the mirror and started to slide the Oxy 80 back and forth, grating it like a small piece of cheese, turning it into something that looked like fluffy white flakes. The pill was scraped over the sharp edges of the slots.

"When you straighten the clamp, make sure to leave some wavy bumps so the powder can fall through onto the mirror."

Ah, so that's how it's done. I was riveted by her every move.

"You can also use a dollar bill. Just fold it over the pill and smash it with the end of a lighter or a school ID."

She used her school ID to plow the powder around on the mirror until she had it gathered into a two-inch line."

"Perfect. Now it's ready."

She took out a straw that was the length of my little finger, a narrow glass tube, and a hollowed-out ink pen. The cartridge had been removed from the pen, and she had sawed a piece off the narrow end to make the opening wider.

"All of these work really well. Keep them clean and throw the straw away after a while. It can grow bacteria and mess your nose up."

She really wanted me to get this right. I was too embarrassed to tell her what I had already done with Mom's Roxys and the fiasco I'd caused.

"Watch this." Sidney lined up the straw to the edge of the powder and snorted it gracefully. She made it look elegant and I wanted to do it the same way.

She immediately rubbed her nose and scratched her face like I'd done, only she was cuter.

I could tell when that rush of warmth arrived just by watching her expression. Sidney swiveled her head around as though distributing the Oxy 80 into various compartments of her brain for greater effect.

"Ooo, that's nice." Her eyes were closed. The expression she wore reminded me of paintings I'd seen of angels winging their way to heaven.

Her eyes were glassy and much bluer. I watched as her pupils got smaller and smaller. Everything about her seemed to be at peace until she spoke again.

"There you have it, Buddy, snorting for dummies. Without my handy demonstration, you would have crushed the Oxy, coating and all, and created a messy waste of good money."

I was tongue-tied around her; all I could say was, "How much for the pills?" I could hear the nervousness in my voice as I asked the question.

Sidney reached into the baggie and extracted another pill. She held it up between her thumb and forefinger as though it was an expensive gemstone as she gave me a chance to examine it.

"These are strong, Little Fella. You better be careful."

Her voice was playful again. I didn't know which Sidney to expect from one sentence to the next: lighthearted, teasing, or insensitive. Regardless, I wanted to feel as good as she obviously did and as soon as possible. I heard the word "strong" and figured that meant my next party was going to last longer. Sidney's words did not register as a warning. They didn't register at all. I was in a hurry to throw the cash and run somewhere to get high, but she wouldn't take my money . . . not just yet.

"You're lucky: that pill I just did put me in a good mood. Today they're only forty apiece. After this, you'll have to pay fifty dollars a pill." She took five pills out of the bag, placed them in my hand, and looked into my eyes. The dreaminess was gone.

"These are for the big boys, so go easy, Tiger. I got a feeling you can't wait to snort some of this." She handed me the reshaped hose clamp and the cut-down straw. "I carry extras for my new customers. File the pill right on top of your notebook, but don't use the whole pill. That'll knock you out. Just do a little bit until you get used to it. Make a line out of the powder like I showed you. I'll call you later and you can tell me all about it."

I just stood there as she walked away; I was spellbound by the pills in my palm. I may have started out weak and vulnerable that morning, but now I was standing tall and feeling mighty because I had five Oxy 80s, at forty bucks a pop. As I debated whether to swallow or snort, I thought about the fastest way to be happy again . . . and that meant only one thing. I hurriedly laid four pills on the bleacher and began licking the coating off the fifth one just like Sidney showed me. I dried it with my T-shirt and placed the hose clamp on my notebook. I put the remaining pills in my pocket.

How much of this should I do? I replayed my experiences swallowing Tabs and snorting Roxys and decided to start small again. I scraped the Oxy back and forth about ten times until a quarter of the pill was shaved off. It wasn't much. I used my school ID to push it all together and snorted it with the straw. Nothin' to it.

I was hoping the surprise from an 80 kicking in was going to be the best yet and I wasn't disappointed. Everything felt familiar as soon as the powder landed on back of my throat. I enjoyed rubbing my nose and scratching my face, just because I knew I'd hit the jackpot. Then came the comfy warmth and next the energy burst, just like the doctor ordered.

This was perfection, a feeling so good that it could only be reserved for rock stars who were being chased by screaming girls throwing panties. I had been initiated into the Oxy Club. It was exclusive: only those who could hold their own were given entry. I looked around the football field; I was the only person there. I took off in a sprint, pretending to cradle a football in the crook of my arm, pushing away from would-be tacklers. I was the hometown hero. The MVP. I danced around the goalpost in a touchdown celebration, a roaring crowd chanting my name. This was fantasy. This was fun. I had to admit to myself, "This is why I use drugs. There's nothing else like it in my dull, boring world."

I jogged back to the bleachers and my kit. I loved saying it. "My very own kit." I felt like I was nice and high and wanted a little more of a good thing, so I grated another quarter of the 80. Then I wondered, *What am I stopping for? I'm not going to stand here out in the open and do up a quarter at a time. Sidney snorted a whole pill and she looked fine. Now it's my turn to man up.*

I shredded the rest of the pill and quickly snorted it. It tasted different than a Blue, more like medicine should taste. My acquired taste. I said out loud to no one in particular, "If I don't make it through today, tomorrow will never get here." Then I laughed. It wasn't a funny *ha ha* laugh. It sounded sinister and ghoulish to me.

My answering thought was, What if there is no tomorrow, how would you spend the rest of today? Getting higher . . . of course.

To me, this was sensible thinking. After all, I wanted to have even more fun just being myself. I took out another pill, shaved it, lined it up, and *bam*, I snorted it. I wanted to feel like Superman, indestructible and admired by all.

Time stood still the moment that cloud of powder hit my nasal passages. I remember the itch, the taste, and standing in one place getting numb all over. My arms dangled by my side and my legs turned to rubber. I felt totally helpless just before I went down. My face smashed into the turf, but my brain didn't register any pain. I had done it again and I had to call it what it was: an overdose. It was not a mistake. It was stupidity mixed with a compulsion to feed something that could not be satisfied.

I didn't know then that opioids can cause severe respiratory depression and death. I was unable to take a deep-enough breath to save my life. My muscles were too weak. I started to feel cold. My arms and legs felt like they were bound with duct tape. My eyes were open, but everything was a blur, except for the one thing that was just inches from my nose: a pair of cheerleader sneakers. Even then, when I was seconds away from plunging into darkness, it didn't occur to me that without help, I was about to die a preventable death. All I could think about was how happy I was that Sidney had returned to be with me.

CHAPTER 10

I'll Never Do That Again

There I was, facedown near the bleachers with OxyContin 80 turning out all the lights. I could almost see the neurons in my brain and they were running low on electrical impulses. I needed a jump-start. My mind was barely capable of thought, but I comprehended enough to know I was still alive.

I could hear Sidney's voice from far away, as though she was yelling my name through a lake of mud. She slapped my face, then she pounded her fist on my chest, right over my heart. She probably could have broken a cinder block with the force she used to hammer me. I just stared up at the sky, seeing nothing.

Funny thing about an overdose: I saw myself there on the ground, but it was very peaceful to watch. If you've ever had an out-of-body experience, you know what I mean. The whole scene was vividly clear, as though I was watching a movie about someone else, some other loser who'd made a fool of himself.

Sidney told me later that my pupils were constricted down to the size of pin holes and my breathing stopped. I began to turn blue, first my lips and then my face, until every inch of my body had lost its color.

Sidney called 911 and sounded more annoyed than worried or frightened. "I need an ambulance. Hurry. This kid is passed out and he's not breathing. I think he may have OD'd." Sidney paused to listen to the 911 operator's instructions, then put down the phone. Like a pro who had done so a thousand times before, she began to give me mouth-to-mouth and cardiopulmonary resuscitation. Frothy stuff started to foam out of my mouth, but, except for a muttered "Gross," Sidney didn't do or say anything. She just kept blowing into my mouth and pushing on my sternum with all her weight.

After she'd been going back and forth for a while, breathing and pushing, breathing and pushing, she paused and said, "Come on, you dumb, stupid idiot. Wake up and breathe. I hate this. It's disgusting."

She wiped her mouth and went back to work. She never quit. Not once. She gagged a bit and looked like she was close to puking, but she didn't give up. I, on the other hand, continued to lay there like a slab of meat.

Once the paramedics arrived, they took over the CPR. Sidney jumped up, spit a few times, and asked for water to gargle and rinse with.

One of the paramedics pointed, "In the back of the truck. Help yourself."

Sidney grabbed a bottle, then walked back and watched them work on me for a while.

"He's disgusting," she announced to them. "Do you see those pimples on his lip? I touched those with my mouth. Are they going to make me sick? I mean, look at them, all ooey and gooey. Are they infected?"

The paramedics ignored her and kept up the CPR. I still wasn't responding, though.

"He's not moving any air and his pulse is slow and weak. Pupils are pinpoint. He's in respiratory arrest. "

One of them yelled out to Sidney. "Is he juiced up on Oxys?"

She drank water and wiped her mouth slowly before answering.

"How should I know? Probably. What else could it be? Can't you tell?"

As they rolled their eyes, one said, "Let's tube him and get the Narcan."

There was a flurry of motion as I was intubated and an intravenous line was started.

The next words out of Sidney's mouth could have melted butter. "I've heard about this happening to other kids. Taking too many pills to get high. You'd think he'd know better if this was his first time."

The two paramedics looked at each other and shook their heads in unison. "Narcan's in."

I could smell Sidney close to me as I heard her ask, "What's that stuff for?"

One of the men kept mechanically inflating my lungs. "It's used to counteract the depression of the cardiac and central nervous systems caused by the narcotics he took."

Within seconds my torso bucked, my legs kicked haphazardly, and my head lurched with a violent, twisting motion.

"Atta boy. Time to wake up and face the music. Mommy and Daddy aren't going to like what you did." The two men looked at each other with approving looks. They had brought another one back from the brink of oblivion.

When the Narcan hit me, I had the sensation that every muscle in my body was knotted up in a charley horse. All of my bones began to ache right down to the marrow. I opened my eyes, but I couldn't focus on what was happening. I felt the tube in my throat and started to gag. But just as suddenly as I'd responded to the antidote, I went limp and was paralyzed again. I couldn't open my eyes, but I was conscious enough to hear the conversation around me.

"Well, what do you know. He's a heavy hitter. Pop open another Narcan."

"Four milligrams in. That should be plenty. He couldn't have taken that much."

I recall my eyelids started to flutter, and then my body bucked and lurched in spasms. My eyes shot open, and I was terrified because I was retching and biting down on the breathing tube; I felt like I was suffocating. I reached up frantically to pull it out. I could hear other voices now, people gathering around and whispering to each other. Someone asked if I was going to be okay.

"I think he's ready to spit this tube out. I'm deflating the cuff and extubating."

"Go ahead. His pulse is ninety-five and BP is one-ten over eighty-eight. Color is good. Pupils are dilating and reactive to light." I could hear the paramedics talking to each other, but I couldn't get their attention.

"Kid, settle down. Don't fight this tube. It's coming out. Get ready to take a nice deep breath."

I kept thrashing my head until the tube was removed. Then I gasped for a lungful of air. My throat felt raw and irritated, making me cough up bloody phlegm. The paramedic wiped it away with gauze pads.

"You're gonna be all right, Kid. Just keep breathing."

"Let's pack up and move him."

As I was being lifted into the back of the truck, the paramedic outside signaled for Sidney to come close enough for me to hear every word. "You're probably a nice girl. Why did you let your friend do a stupid thing like this?"

"Not me," she denied.

"I don't believe you. I bet you're the one who gave him the drugs."

"No way," Sidney snapped back emphatically.

"This poor dummy snorted enough Oxys to stop his breathing. He's going to pull through, but it could have turned out differently, a lot differently."

Sidney's answer was loud and angry. I knew she'd gone out of her way to save my life, and I thought that meant she really did care about me, so hearing her next words really hurt me.

"Don't blame me," she snarled. "I was just walking by and found him gasping for air. When I turned him over and saw his ugly, zitty face, I could have bolted and he would have been another OD. But nooooo," Sidney continued melodramatically, "I stayed and called 911. I kept him alive for you guys to do your job. I put my mouth on that disgusting mess. So don't dump any guilt on me. He'd be better off dead, anyway. I didn't do him any favors. Look at him. He's a loser."

I see now that if I'd just been paying attention, I would have understood sooner what was really going on. Sidney finally showed her true colors and I was hurt by what I heard her say; I hadn't really understood how little she cared about me.

The paramedic answered Sidney just before he closed the door to the ambulance. I wish I could have been sitting up to watch her reaction.

"I know you're lying. I'm betting he's one of your customers. Is this how you like to make a buck? Don't you have a conscience? Just for the record, what's your name?"

There was no answer. The door slammed shut and we were on the move with the siren blaring.

The paramedic who was driving yelled back to his partner, "Somebody knows that girl's name. She's trouble. Kids like this one have no clue what they're dealing with. And she could care less."

As I think back on that comment, I realize now that rescue teams talk about the young people who overdose on Blues, Oxys and Roxys. It's funny how the drug names on the street are catchy and cute. That makes those drugs sound friendly, like delicious and harmless candy.

Once I was in the emergency room, there was a flurry of activity. Nurses hooked me up to machines to monitor my heart and blood pressure while a bag of clear liquid dripped through my IV tubing. I was fully awake and breathing more easily with just an occasional cough. When they were finished, a doctor came into the room and gave several orders to the nurses.

"I'm Dr. Bailey. Was it Oxys that you took?"

I mumbled, "Yes."

"How many?" He spoke deliberately, aiming his voice at his clipboard, his eyes watching the pen streak across the page as he wrote.

"Two."

"Two of what?" When I didn't answer immediately, he quickly grew impatient.

"Come on, I haven't got all day."

"I snorted two 80s."

"What else? Zannys? Blues? Somas? Heroin? Coke?" Only his lips moved as the words knifed through the air.

"Nothing else."

"Your parents are on the way. You took too many pills and stopped breathing. The paramedics inserted a tube in your throat and gave you Narcan to reverse the effects of the Oxys." He sounded like a technician who plodded through the tedious routine of his job the same way, day after day. I felt like a medical inconvenience rather than someone deserving compassion, understanding, and respect.

I didn't like his attitude. I could breathe. The aches and pains were gone and my mind was quickly sharpening up. I wasn't feeling nearly so scared, but with my parents on the way, I intended to act ashamed of what I had done.

"Doctor, am I going to be okay?"

The doctor put his clipboard down, ignored my question, and used the stethoscope that was draped around his neck. "Breath is clear top to bottom and on both sides. Pupils are midrange, equal and reacting." He nodded to the nurse who stood nearby writing down his comments, then turned his attention back to me. "Tell me your name, Kid."

I don't know why I hesitated to tell him my name. I knew why I was there: it was the pills, the Oxy 80s. They'd put my lights out. I didn't need an answer to my question. I focused on the idea that my parents were on the way; I had to think of what I'd tell them.

I was silent so long the doctor asked the question again.

"Well, what's your name, Kid?"

"Buddy," I said with a stronger voice. "Buddy Danforth."

Our eyes locked. His looked cold, distant, and judgmental.

"Okay . . . Buddy. Your face is new around here. Was this your first time?"

"Yes, sir."

"I thought so." His voice stiffened even more. "You just wanted to get high, right? Like all the other kids in this town. Only this time, you screwed up and it nearly cost you your life. Thanks to rapid response and Narcan, you're going to go home with mommy and daddy without as much as a scratch. What really fries me is when one of you kids walks out of here and starts snorting pills in the parking lot. Nobody wants to stop. Nobody smartens up. Everybody's careless and expects us to be there on the double when they stop breathing. We can work miracles, but we're always saving addicts who won't stop. What about you, Buddy? Did we waste our time on you, too?"

I thought to myself, *What a jerk*. He's not talking about me and I'm not going to bother to tell him that I'm in it for the fun. I just have to make sure that it's all fun next time. I had no idea I was going to stop breathing. I don't know what kind of kids have been rolling in here, but I won't be back. I've got a brain, and a good one, too. I was just a little too eager to have too much of a good time, that's all.

"Doc, I want to thank you for all you've done. I'm sorry about what happened." I hoped I sounded sincere in case he reported this to my parents. "I don't care what other kids do. This was the first and last time for me, I can guarantee that. This really scared the crap out of me. But I'm fine now. So, where are my folks? I'm ready to go home."

The doctor stood with his arms crossed over his chest, looking down at me where I sat on the gurney. Actually, he glared at me and I was pretty sure he wanted to knock some sense into me.

"Okay, kid, you get an Academy Award for that performance. Trust me, I've heard it all and I'm not buying a word of it. I bet you're going back for another hit as soon as you can get your pants on."

A nurse had stopped my IV and was preparing to remove the catheter. The doctor motioned her aside and pulled the catheter out himself, and he didn't even pretend to be gentle. It was meant to hurt.

"There you go," he said as he slapped an adhesive bandage over the tiny hole in my hand. "Now, let me tell you a bit more about what happened to you. It might help change your mind about snorting opioids."

I tried to look sincere. I didn't want to come across as a wise guy. I was already in enough trouble without making an enemy of this doctor.

As I opened my mouth to declare once again that I was done with pills, the doctor turned around abruptly toward a commotion in the hallway. The most obvious sound was the piercing voice I recognized. I peered around the doctor to see Mom pushing people aside as she rushed toward me.

"My baby," she wailed. "What happened to my baby?" She almost knocked the doctor over in her haste to hug me. She held me tight for a moment, then stepped back and looked into my eyes.

"He's going to be okay, Doctor, isn't he? Tell me there's nothing wrong with him." Her eyes never left mine. She began to cry as her hands cradled my face.

"I'm fine, Mom," I assured her. "Doc says everything's okay."

She stepped aside and I could see my father standing in the doorway. I figured he wasn't going to say a word until we got home. Mom was the family's mouthpiece and Dad was used to giving her center stage. The doctor saw my dad at the same time I did and motioned to him to join us.

The doctor looked at my mother first, then at my father, and then back at Mom. "Did you know your son was taking drugs?"

Mom wailed again and fresh tears streamed down her cheeks. She grabbed my dad for support.

"He took one of the most powerful and dangerous narcotics called oxycodone; they are known as Oxys on the street, short for OxyContin, the brand name. It's a prescribed opioid, a painkiller. It's meant to be swallowed, but kids snort it because it gets them high real fast. They enjoy the high so much that they overdose by accident. The drug depresses respiration and sometimes breathing stops completely. In that case, they usually vomit, and some of it seeps into the lungs causing a nasty pneumonia, even death."

I didn't have to look at my mom to know she was listening intently. She always did when it came to medical problems. She'd stopped crying out loud, and I risked sneaking a peek at her to gauge her reaction. If looks could kill, hers would have caused a mass extinction; she was glaring at me with a mixture of confusion, disgust, and revulsion I had never seen before.

"I don't know how long your son has been using these drugs, but the chemical effect has been reversed with a drug called Narcan. It's an opioid blocker. As you can see, it worked quite well. Your son was found unconscious in full respiratory arrest. Paramedics at the scene injected the Narcan and kept inflating his lungs with an endotracheal tube until he could breathe on his own. He needed a double dose of Narcan. That means he did some serious oxycodone. If he's been taking them for a while, he'll probably have cravings and go back to using real soon. You might want to consider some kind of addiction treatment program. There are all kinds. Residential is the most effective, but it's also expensive. Look on the Internet. There's plenty of information about opiate dependence and lots of advertisements for good, reputable treatment centers."

The doctor continued. He was looking at me now, but the information and the warning were for all of us.

"Those two OxyContin 80s stopped your breathing. I'll bet you're a beginner and didn't know any better. You almost killed yourself, trying to have a good time."

My mother shuddered and looked like she might faint. My dad stood on the other side of the gurney and started to walk over to her. She put up a stiff arm, signaling him to stop, and he threw up his hands with a frustrated look. She cleared her throat and took a sip of water the nurse had brought.

The doctor returned his attention to my parents.

"Some girl, probably one of his classmates, found him and called 911. She did a good job of keeping him alive with CPR until the paramedics arrived. They worked hard and fast to bring him back." The doctor turned back to me, and I could see him struggling to control his own anger. "You were damned lucky to make it. We've already sent three kids your age to the morgue this past month. It's crazy what's going on with these drugs."

I raised my hand and everybody turned my way. I was trying to be polite. It didn't take a rocket scientist to know I was in for it, so I gave my parents my best apologetic look.

"Mom . . . Dad . . . I just started this yesterday. Sidney gave me a couple pills. I didn't know what I was doing. I wanted to try them. I'll never do that again, I promise you."

I tried to look innocent and naïve. I wanted them to believe that I was easily duped. Mom, at least, knew what an outsider I was, so I hoped she would decide I had tried drugs from an immature curiosity to feel good or fit in. I wanted her to let me off with minimal punishment.

And while I was calculating all of this, my party brain was telling me that Oxys rock. I knew I'd been in too much of a hurry to get high. I still had three pills left. I was going to have to slow down and be more careful from now on.

The doctor's voice interrupted my thoughts.

"Listen, I've been in the emergency-room business for enough years. I've probably heard more than a thousand teenagers face their parents with excuses that either made me angry or made me burst out laughing. I don't know what to make of your son and his attempt at sincerity." He paused to let that sink in as he looked back and forth between my parents. "You have to be the final judges on whether or not he will keep his word. In my experience, that seldom happens. These drugs are so addictive that kids will lie to the Pope to get their hands on a few more pills."

The doctor grabbed a clipboard and signed a few of the pages, then continued.

"Obviously your son is not asking for help. He's convinced that since he won't ever touch the stuff again, there's no need for it. I disagree. I think that once a young person like your son has a taste of opioids, he can't get enough, even at the risk of overdosing again. Keep that in mind as you talk to your son. He may be full of surprises. Kids will promise you anything, but they'll lie, cheat and steal behind your back. Your jewelry will turn up in a pawn shop just to get him money for drugs. You mark my words. And that's why he needs help. Unfortunately, he probably won't accept it, even if it is offered."

The doctor paused, looked at each of us to see if his message had gotten through, then shook his head and sighed.

"Good luck. You can all go now. The nurse will take you through the paperwork."

While my parents sat at the computer station with the nurse to sign my discharge forms, the doctor took the opportunity to speak with me privately. He leaned toward me until our faces were nearly touching and the look on his face made me nervous. He spoke softly so no one but I could hear him.

"Buddy, I know what's going on inside that reptilian brain of yours. You think you dodged the big one here. But you didn't. It's waiting out in the parking lot, doing an extra set of crunches and pushups just for you. You won't see it coming and it will hit so fast you won't have time to blink before your plug is pulled . . . again. Get what I'm saying . . . Pal. You have more BS than you have brains. I don't want to see you here again, unless you need stitches or a cast. If you're lucky, you'll hit bottom without killing yourself. And if you're really lucky, you'll see the light while you're down there. Now get your scrawny carcass out of here and keep your nose out of the dope."

My parents returned with several folded papers, probably the typical generic instructions on what to do if I had complications at home. When I stood up, the room spun and the lights dimmed for a few seconds. My dad grabbed both my shoulders, but I shrugged him off and tried to act tough.

"Are you okay, Buddy?"

I chuckled. "Yeah, of course. I just got up too fast. I'm fine now. Let's go. Lead the way."

My feet felt like sponges with each step I took. I wobbled a bit and, at one point, I thought I was going to throw up. I broke out in a sweat and had to stop and take deep breaths.

Mom put a hand on my forehead, the universal way that mothers monitor their offspring for all illnesses. "Honey, you look pale. Maybe we should go back in."

"No way," I snapped. "Let me sit down for a minute, then I'll be good to go."

I sat down on a bench just outside the entrance. There was a warm breeze blowing and it was just the stimulation I needed. By the time Dad pulled the car around, I was able to climb in without assistance.

I had never been so happy to be going home. And that doctor was wrong. It was not waiting for me out in the parking lot doing crunches and pushups. I don't what it was supposed to be, but it wasn't there. Nice try, doc. I was in control of this and now that I knew my limits, I was ready to party without the risk of seeing that guy again.

Mom sat in the back seat with me. I was sprawled across the seat with my head in her lap and she stroked my hair as I pretended to sleep. I was pretty sure I had succeeded in softening Mom. Now I had to figure out how to keep things going my way, because I wasn't done with drugs yet.

CHAPTER 11

Drugs Are Bad—You Know That

Mom gently shook me to wake me up as my father pulled into the driveway. I was briefly disoriented but quickly snapped back to the reality that a barrage of questions was coming and I needed to have answers ready ... fast.

Dad sat down at the kitchen table and motioned for us to gather around. I wasn't too worried about him. He is a wimpy kind of guy. I expected his usual namby-pamby parental nonsense. I sat in my usual chair between my parents.

"Son, I know there are temptations out there in the teenage world and lots of peer pressure to try things like drugs."

I rolled my eyes. I figured this was going to be more painful than the lecture I'd had to listen to for Sexual Awareness Day at school.

"When I was your age, I went to a party, the kind that parents aren't supposed to know about. It was a wild one, a real doozy. I'm not bragging or anything, but I saw some things that would have made your hair curl. Someone rolled a marijuana cigarette and lit it up. It was passed around and eventually offered to me. I kept looking at it and someone said, 'Hey, Man, get with it. Don't let this stuff burn off, smoke it.' So I did. I took a toke off that roach."

"Dear, where exactly are you going with this? Buddy nearly lost his life on the football field. He didn't experiment with some harmless pot."

Dad did what I expected: he cleared his throat nervously, looked at his watch, and started fumbling in his pockets for some keys or loose coins to jangle.

"You're absolutely right, Honey. I should get to the point. I just wanted our son to know that I still remember some of the drug lingo, so we can communicate. I even inhaled some reefer and got high. But I was able to stop right then and there and never touched it again. Why? Because I knew it would be bad for me. I didn't want to become a druggie. I had willpower and Buddy does, too. Son, you aren't like the others. Don't let it happen again. You are better than that."

I looked at the floor and studied the designs in the tile. If I took one look at him I was going to burst out laughing and probably ruin my chances of ever leaving the house again.

Then it was Mom's turn. I expected her to come at me with both barrels loaded. Instead, she took aim for my dad.

"Is that it? Your advice is to have him exert his almighty willpower over drugs? Drugs that are so popular that kids are dying left and right and still can't get enough? Is that all the wisdom you have after raising a son and being a teenager yourself?"

My father looked like he had been hit by a stun gun that rendered him paralyzed and speechless.

"I thought so," Mom snorted. "Now, it's my turn. Step aside."

My father did what he always did when my mom got involved: he put up his hands in mock surrender. "I don't know why I even bother. I'm going upstairs."

My mother made no protest as he left the room. I had no use for him either, but I dreaded being in my mom's sights when she only had me for a target.

"Buddy," she said, her voice biting and unsympathetic. "You have disappointed and infuriated me with this stunt you pulled. I didn't see it coming and what I have learned is practically inconceivable. I can't believe you took those painkillers just for the thrill of it. I am trying hard to figure out what a responsible parent should do here. Part of me wants to punish you for scaring the hell out of us. The other part wants to protect you from any bad influences or temptations to use drugs of any kind. It's not fair. You're not grown up enough. Other kids your age have more experience living in this fast paced world. You're a just a little behind and … innocently vulnerable."

Her facial expressions morphed through fear, anger, and tearful relief. I had never seen her display so much emotion about me. She obviously cared, but it seemed to be too late for her to make up for all of her parenting mistakes. In my mind, she was responsible for co-creating the loneliest kid in the world.

She dabbed her watering eyes with tissue and blew her nose. After a few more sniffles, she was again composed.

"When they called us from the ER, we were just sitting here having coffee and watching TV. A minute later we were in a state of shock. This couldn't be our son. There must be some mistake. We raced to the hospital, praying that you would be alive. We assumed the worst but were hoping that they got to you in time and you would pull through. We were told that you had taken so much of this OxyContin drug that you stopped breathing. We were expecting a brain-damaged son. It devastated us."

She just looked at me. I knew she wanted eye contact and some suitable reaction, but my face was rigid and expressionless. She raised her voice as loud as I have ever heard it.

"Did you hear me, Mister? We were trying to prepare to either bury you or bring home a vegetable. How do you think that felt? Can you answer me?"

She moved her face close to mine and stared at me. That was her way of demanding a reply. It was time for me to let her know that I didn't appreciate her Devoted-Mother-of-the-Year routine. I had been to the edge of extinction and back. I felt stronger and ready to speak up for myself. Roxys and Oxys gave me a voice I'd never had before and I was going to put it to good use.

"Mom, I get it, okay? Isn't it good enough that I pulled through? Maybe you should try to understand what it's like living in my head and why I needed pills. I want you to know that I don't for one second regret what I did. After I took those pills, for a few minutes I felt all the weight of being ugly and a loser just lift off my shoulders. It was the most fun I have ever had. I admit I overdid it and that was dangerous and maybe even dumb, but at least I tried to find a way to stop feeling so shitty all the time."

The anger on my mother's face melted away and she looked at me with a hint of understanding and a trace of sympathy. That was progress and I wanted to push on for more. After all, I was going to keep using and I didn't want her to know that. I wanted an ally, not a bitter enemy. So I lied.

"I promise I won't be that foolish ever again. I didn't want to die, I swear."

I made my move to score some points and leaned over to hug my mom. I think she ate it up. In the end, I was pretty sure she had a greater need to protect me than to punish me. I went through the motions and, by the way she reacted, I figured she thought I was giving her the real thing.

She started crying and hugged me again. I knew she was trying to make an emotional connection, trying to appeal to the child she'd had such high hopes for years ago.

"You know," she began confessionally, "I wasn't always such a conservative. I was in high school, too. I smoked pot with your father. He won't tell you the truth, but we did a reckless thing or two for fun. I know exactly what you mean when you mention how thrilling it was. I felt loose and carefree, but I never lost control. I knew the fun would come to an end and I wouldn't miss it. And I haven't." I was surprised that she admitted to smoking pot and liking it. I filed that little tidbit away in case I might use the information at a later time.

"We love you and only want the best for you," Mom continued. "We tried to be good parents, but you didn't make it any easier for us. We sacrificed a lot trying to make you happy, but that didn't work. You were always gloomy. I don't know where we went wrong, but I'll take the blame. In return, I think you owe us some respect."

"Respect! For what?"

"Don't use that tone on me, young man! I'm sure word of this has already gotten out and we're prepared to deal with that, as long as I know you're done with drugs. We had our fun, but we quit while it was still innocent. Your kind of fun was dangerous, but we want a good ending. So just say good-bye to it like we did. Okay?"

She finished her speech and had a pleading look on her face that made me feel very uncomfortable.

I knew I couldn't keep the earnest, obedient look on my face much longer. I wanted this lecture to end, so I had to pretend to be contrite. But inside I was thinking: *You have no idea what it's like to be hated and tormented by the popular kids. They have everything: the best bodies, the best grades, the best athletic prowess, and the best fun. The world is on their side. You don't know what it's like to wake up a loser and go to bed an even bigger one. I am either ignored or picked on—all day, every day. The only reason Sidney wanted to get close to me was to get me hooked on the freebie pills and then bleed me for as much money as I could steal from the cookie jar. And I don't care about your little pot episode. I'm changing who I am, thanks to Oxys.* For me, the twenty-four-hour-loser clock kept ticking and the shame only stopped one pill at a time. So I wanted my mom to shut up. And thankfully she did, but not before getting in the last word.

"We want you to make us proud. You have so much going for you. Drugs are bad . . . you know that."

As lame as that statement was, I realized that I was no longer in any serious trouble and was way ahead of the game. Before she could get another word out, I put my finger on her lips and dismissed her by saying what she would never expect but probably always dreamt of hearing.

"You're right, Mom. I should listen to you more often. I love you."

Her arms flew around my neck. "Oh, Honey!"

I endured the clench for five agonizing seconds, then squirmed out of it and ended the lecture. "I'm exhausted. Good night."

Two steps out of the kitchen, Mom called me back.

"Your notebook and school ID. You must have dropped them when you were...."

Her voice trailed off and was barely audible, probably as she was reminded of what I was doing on the football field and consumed by disbelief. I snatched both out of her hand, remembering the pills I had shredded on top of the notebook. Maybe I wasn't going to snort a pill as soon as I got to my room, but I knew it would be soon enough.

I exited the kitchen without another word, plodded up to my room, and collapsed on the bed. My body felt like I had taken a beating and I was tired. But not too tired to think about what had happened. My notebook and school

ID had been returned, but not my Oxys nor my kit. Of course they wouldn't be. So who made off with them? The paramedics? No way. Sidney? Most definitely. She screwed me. But I wasn't empty handed. I had seven Roxys in my drawer. Didn't I? I had to see them. As much as I just wanted to pull the covers over my head and sleep like a hibernating animal, I had to get up and check. Until then I grew more nervous by the second.

I jumped out of bed and almost lunged for the paper clip box, even looking over my shoulder to make sure the bedroom door was shut and no footsteps were approaching. It was uncomfortable being paranoid like that, but I couldn't help it. I guess some part of me knew this was illegal and, I suppose, immoral. I made sure that kind of dumb thinking didn't last long. These pills were strictly recreational.

I opened the box and shook out the pills, counting and examining them. *All there.* I was immediately tempted to take one. That quickly grew into an irresistible urge. *Wait,* I thought. *If you take one now you'll be up all night. Don't waste it.* Immediately I put them back in the drawer and felt so proud. What self control I had. Drug addicts couldn't do that. I had nothing to worry about. Obviously, I had proven that I could take them or leave them. *Rather impressive.*

An obnoxious ringtone grabbed my attention. The screen lighting up made it easy to find the phone in the dark. The text was from Sidney.

Savd ur butt. U wer blu. calld 911. T%k ur pills. U cn buy bak.

I stared at the message. I was livid. As I lay helpless on the football field, Sidney had taken advantage of me. She ripped me off and took what was rightfully mine. She was a thief of the worst kind. When she'd found me turning blue, she must have decided I was on death's door and had no further use for pills. She'd kept me alive until the paramedics arrived, and I suppose she felt that it was justifiable payment for services rendered. Now that I pulled through, she wanted to double dip and sell the merchandise back to me.

I wasn't going to be swindled again. I wanted to calculate my next move and plot my revenge, but I needed sleep the most. I was going to have to wait until morning to make another withdrawal from the cookie jar. I knew that getting high again was just a handful of cash away. The quandary was how to get my pills back and, even more importantly, teaching Sidney a lesson. I was going to delight in finding some way to even the score. I just didn't know how I'd do it . . . yet.

CHAPTER 12

Pills Are Worth Fighting For

I slept surprisingly well that night, and felt refreshed and ready for my mission. It was easy to be up an hour earlier than my parents; I was excited to get on with the business of robbing the bank. I emptied out two hundred dollars' worth of twenties and the cookie jar was still loaded to the brim.

On the way back to my room I paused, remembering that I had no kit. If I was going to be well-prepared to snort whatever drug was snortable, I needed supplies. I turned down the hallway that opened into the garage and rummaged through the tool cabinet. Just my luck, two hose clamps were mixed amongst a disorganized pile of assorted hardware. I grabbed one and bent it until it was shaped like Sidney's. Next, I retrieved a straw from the kitchen and cut it into two pieces about three inches each. I couldn't think of any place in the house where I could find a small mirror so I took a flat dish the size of my hand, something for after dinner mints, that was kept with Mom's china. It had a shiny silver finish and was perfect. Up in my room, I put my new kit in my back pack.

I showered, dressed, and thought about how much I needed to fortify myself for the showdown with Sidney. *Take a Roxy, but only swallow it. That should be plenty.* I didn't want to blow lunch or run my mouth off with nonsense in front of Sidney. It was time to be bold and confident. I took two pills out of the box in my drawer, one for now and one just in case. I would do some serious snorting later, when this matter was settled in my favor.

I walked into the kitchen with a clean, scrubbed look. I wanted Mom to think that I was still the new and improved version of myself, the son who would never touch a pain pill, even if my leg were broken in three places.

I held back my excitement and mumbled a subdued good morning.

"How are you feeling? You look better than I expected. I thought you'd need a day off to get those drugs out of your system." Mom studied me carefully as she served my breakfast.

I didn't answer, but proceeded to scarf down some scrambled eggs, bacon, toast and juice. I downed the Roxy when Mom wasn't looking. Everything tasted good. As I finished the last bite, I decided to pick up where I'd left off with Mom yesterday and score a few more points of trust.

"Mom, yesterday was some kind of turning point for me. A wake-up call, I guess. Don't get me wrong; I'm not gonna run for class president or try out for sports, but I *am* a little different. Maybe you'll notice, maybe you won't, but I know I'm not the same." Before she could say anything, I grabbed my book bag off the floor and pushed my chair away from the table. "I gotta go."

She ran after me as I walked out of the kitchen, and as I reached the front door, she put her hand on the knob to keep me from opening it.

"Buddy, yesterday was one hell of a nightmare. I want you to know that even though I gave up years ago trying to plan out your life, I haven't stopped caring. I should have tried harder to be the kind of mother you might have wanted. It probably seems like it's too late to try again, but I hope it isn't."

There was a dead, uncomfortable silence. For the first time I could remember, my mom didn't know what to say.

"I don't mean to be so sappy," she finally finished. "Okay, off you go."

Before I could move, she pecked me on the cheek and said in a syrupy voice, "I love you, Buddy."

"Mom. You know what I told you about that."

"I couldn't help it. I want to make it up to you."

I suddenly reminded myself about my objective to score brownie points.

"Okay," I cautioned. "But go slow. I'm not used to this." She waited until I was well outside the door and yelled, "See you later. Have a safe day."

I headed down the sidewalk and turned around to see that she was standing in the front yard watching me until I was out of sight. I felt really guilty at that moment, like a massive tumor of shame and failure was growing right around my heart and smothering it. I was a loser, cursed with self-loathing made worse by my mother's tender touch. I desperately needed to find Sidney, get my pills back, and end this feeling once and for all.

Thinking about pills and getting high was just what I needed to shake off the disgraceful side of me. Sidney was going to meet someone she wouldn't recognize, someone who would attack from her blind side. I intended to not just get even, but definitely get ahead. This loser was going to take a stand, at least long enough to get what I wanted. More pills. More pleasure. And more relief from my painful, sucky life.

In other words, I was going to have to pretend to be something I wasn't. I hoped that she wouldn't call my bluff. In reality, there was no way I could outsmart someone like Sidney.

Once I finally arrived at school, I bounded up the steps to the second floor and headed straight for Sidney's locker. She was standing around with her friends; she looked gorgeous, stuck up, and important. She was definitely the center of attention and I wondered how that had happened so fast. She had just transferred here six weeks ago.

I wedged through the circle of her playmates and fanned out $200 like I was a big spender.

"You're not getting any of this until you give me what I already paid for," I announced with more bravado than I felt. I wanted Sidney to believe that I meant business and was a force to be reckoned with. I was done with being dull, boring, and commonplace, but I was still just making it up as I went along.

I got my answer when she took off her baseball cap; she swatted me over the head with it and said, "Not here, you idiot."

For a moment, I stood there feeling like a fool. I flashed on the days when I cowered in the gym showers as towels were snapped across my rear end. I needed to toughen up in a hurry or Sidney would eat me alive. It was time to channel my inner Clint Eastwood.

I decided I wasn't going to let her insult bother me and said loud enough for all of her friends to hear, "I want my pills back. The ones you stole while I was nearly dead. I know I have you to thank for the mouth-to-mouth that kept me alive. If I'd had one last wish it would have been to die in your arms the same way, a thousand times over."

The other kids laughed. Was I being funny or embarrassing myself? I didn't care. I wanted more pills, not pals. Sidney looked angry and I felt more equally matched. But first and foremost, she was a business woman and I was sure she wanted my cash.

Sidney composed herself instantly. She put her hat back on and looked at me through eyes that no longer reflected a pathetic loser. When she spoke, I heard a smidgen of respect in her voice.

"Okay, Buddy. Meet me at the back parking lot of the mall." She didn't have to say after school.

I walked away first, leaving her there to answer questions about the geek who was flashing a bouquet of twenty-dollar bills. I was pretty sure I'd damaged her reputation with my accusations that she was a drug-dealing rip-off artist. On top of that, Sidney now had become renowned for using her luscious mouth to revive my dying lips. No amount of explaining was going to get her off that meat hook.

I was edgy and wound up for the rest of the day. I cut school an hour early so I could head for the mall. Once I was there, I paced back and forth on the sidewalk, rehearsing what I was going to say when Sidney arrived.

She was right on time—not a minute early or late. Her car rolled past me and she headed for the corner of the parking lot without so much as a snobbish glance. As she swung her tanned legs out of the red Sebring convertible, my body immediately reacted to her breathtaking beauty and fantastic body. She stood glaring at me, looking more prepared for a photo shoot than a drug deal. I stared at her and for a moment I wasn't interested in pills.

We approached each other and Sidney spoke first. She jabbed her finger — hard — into my chest. I knew I was being prodded into a showdown. I backed up as she continued jabbing me.

"I lied to you on the phone," she said. "You were dead when I found you; stone-cold dead. I did CPR on you. I'm sorry now that I brought you back to life. I wasn't even thinking; I just did it because of my days as a lifeguard. You owe me big time and I expect you to be paying for a long while, Buddy-boy."

My chest was getting sore from the jabbing. I grabbed her finger and bent it backward just far enough to surprise her. She pulled her hand away and flexed her finger several times. I rubbed my sternum as I thought about Sidney's description of what had happened. I didn't want to admit that I almost terminated myself in a reckless attempt to be happy.

She was still talking when I started to pay attention again.

"And another thing: I took those pills from you because you're a beginner. You're either too stupid or too cocky for your own good. I warned you about the Oxy 80s. Did you think I was kidding? Tabs are nothing compared to them. I've got a business to run and a reputation to uphold."

Sidney's venomous words just kept coming at me. "Your death is not the kind of advertising I need, especially since my friends all know that I pushed you into the big leagues. And you had to go and get totally dusted your first time with an 80. You're pitiful and dangerous."

I stepped closer and fanned out the twenties.

"I've heard enough. I want my Oxys back — the ones I already paid for — and five more."

Sidney just sneered at me.

"You're lucky you're getting anything. I don't think you could mess yourself up too badly with Tabs," she said condescendingly, "Or at least, not kill yourself. You can have them for the going rate, five apiece." Her breath smelled like mint gum and Marlboros.

"No deal. I'm not settling for anything less than the best."

"Suit yourself. But you're the one who's gonna walk away empty-handed. Me, I get to keep it all, including what I salvaged yesterday. It's my fee for saving your life and for the case of mouthwash and the facial cleanser I needed to buy as disinfectant."

She started to move toward her car, but after a few strides she turned back and screwed her face into something wretched.

"You know, I don't want to sell to losers anymore. You don't deserve to get high. Any buzz is wasted on you. I don't want your money. I don't want your eyes looking at any part of me. I feel grimy and disgusting whenever you do that. I should have done you a favor and left you for dead."

As Sidney walked away, all I could see was someone stomping on my dreams. I wanted another blast of Oxy and I wanted all the dreams it could make come true. To Sidney, pills were a product to sell and something to make me beg for. To me, the pills were the eliminators of misery and the creators of a life worth living. They were important enough to fight for.

I quickly moved to block her way back to her car, which was still running. She was a supreme bitch and I wasn't going to take any more crap from her.

"Clear out, Loser," she snarled as she tried to get around me, but without even thinking, I pushed her aside and jumped behind the wheel of her car.

The tires screeched, spun, and smoked as I exited the parking lot. I felt exhilarated and dangerous. I filled the car with profanities about Sidney and the way she treated me. Then I cursed myself for not having stood up to her, face-to-face. No matter. I had her car and now I wanted her pills. I expected she had them stashed in the console. My eyes darted from the road to the console and back again, as I searched for that magic treasure.

Three baggies were there, each with about fifty pills. I'd hit the jackpot. I felt a big rush of energy and I could see the speedometer hitting eighty miles per hour as I got onto the highway. I floored the accelerator; the car was doing 100, easily. But even that felt too slow for me and I wanted to get off the road and start taking pills. I took the next exit and searched for a secluded spot. I needed some place to be alone and figure out my next move.

I finally pulled into a new housing development and went down a dirt road where there was no construction. It was perfectly private. I sat back and tried to calm my breathing, but my heart was tripping so hard, it felt like a bowling tournament inside my chest. I got out and walked around the car, still holding all three bags of pills. I had made a gigantic big score. I had all the marbles now and I was ready to get the party started.

I had Blues, 80s and some pills shaped like rectangular bars. It said Zannys on the bag. I decided I didn't want to snort anything just yet, because that had gotten me into trouble the day before. Now I was smarter, not a beginner anymore. I made sure to bring a bottle of water from school, for just that reason, and took my first Blue. The pill from that morning had worn off over two hours ago.

I walked around waiting, expecting to liven up and feel high any minute. The wait seemed to last forever, but when I looked at my watch, I realized only five minutes had passed. *Who are you kidding? You know what to do.*

I studied the contents of the baggies more closely. There were labels on each one: Roxys, Oxys and Zannys. I hadn't heard of Zannys before, but if Sidney was dealing them, they were probably another kind of painkiller. But they looked different from the other two. *What the hell*, I thought, *just one of something won't hurt*, so I swallowed a Zanny. I figured that taking two or more could potentially be trouble. Besides, the Roxy hadn't kicked in yet . . . and I was curious.

While I continued to wait for the party in my head to start, I imagined being alone with all the pills on a deserted island. That would be the end of my misery and everyone who caused it. My mind started down that path, but was interrupted by the smooth, warm feeling that came over me as the pills kicked in. It didn't matter anymore how long it had taken; I wasn't paying attention to anything but getting high.

I licked and cleaned off an 80 next. I set up the kit on the hood of the car and shaved the whole pill and used my ID to scrape it into a nice fluffy line of snow. My brain was firing on all cylinders. I felt supercharged and ready to think fast and move even faster. I could barely keep my feet in one place. I wasn't sure how much of the 80 I snorted. As my thoughts flew by, I may have told myself to snort only half, for safety. Then I probably boasted that I had survived two whole 80s and maybe I spouted *losers never win and winners never lose*.

I do recall feeling a rhythm that flowed through my whole body. I began to dance and I laughed at the thought that it probably looked more like some funky white-boy shuffle. I didn't care, though; the pills were doing their job and I felt like a superhero, a caped crusader, fearless and respected. I continued dancing and crucifying the lyrics of a song, until I noticed that my head was either growing bigger, or my body was getting smaller; it was hard to tell. I could feel the drug buzz in every neuron of my brain and I was convinced that I was immeasurably smarter than I'd been before. I was a genius and I wanted to rent out my intellect for incredible sums of money ... or maybe I'd keep it and win the Nobel Prize.

But the feeling didn't last long; I was stunned when disappointment started to set in. How was that possible? I was getting bored with my own brilliance. It was beginning to feel tedious to be me. I swallowed another Zanny and quickly grabbed a Roxy. I crushed it with my ID card and probably mixed it in with what was left on the plate from the 80. Things were just a bit blurred together and I remember pieces but not the whole sequence of what I was doing. I recall thinking that Zannys were mellow and sneaky, like being walloped with a velvet hammer. And then I wondered what good a hammer made of velvet would be. I was happy to be laughing again, certain that I was clever and funny—just what I needed.

I started thinking again about Sidney and about how obnoxious she was. She'd called me a loser, but she was the loser now. I had her drugs and her car. *How's that for a loser?* I was suddenly overtaken by generosity. I wanted to share this magnificent batch of drugs with the world. I even wanted to bring them back to Sidney and thank her for the use of her car.

Without knowing how I'd gotten there, I found myself back behind the wheel. I started up the engine and revved it like a NASCAR driver. Looking back, there's a hole in my memory about what I did with the rest of the pills and my kit. I was so messed up, I might have taken more pills. But if I did, I have no idea how I was able to drive. I took off spewing gravel, in a cloud of dust, while the CD player blasted and the subwoofer rumbled in the car.

Back on the highway, I wondered why the other cars were standing still. The driver of every car honked at me as I went by. It was weird. In the rearview mirror, I watched as a car touched my bumper. I just drove faster, and the car stayed with me. I knew that was dangerous and I wanted to be safe, so I pushed the gas pedal to the floor. But the car just kept up with me, and I couldn't stop watching the amazing colorful lights on its roof. I was having a blast—Sidney's car had to be the best ride I'd ever had. It was so easy to handle, and I was just gliding along with a light show that was better than fireworks.

I stopped watching the show in my rearview mirror for a moment, and looked forward to see a tanker truck closing in fast. That's when I saw the painted sign that read FLAMMABLE. My mind froze with one final thought: this time I'm not coming back. From somewhere faraway I heard myself scream, "Nooo. . . !"

CHAPTER 13

Keeping Me Alive

The next ten days of my life went by without me. Of course I was there, but I was locked inside a place where nothing seemed to happen for long periods of time. As I think back on it, the situation was reminiscent of watching a seedling grow. No matter how long I would stare and stare and wait and wait, nothing moved. The tiny plant didn't seem to do anything while I was watching. And yet, it was growing, ever so slowly. So, I suppose to someone watching me lying there in the intensive care unit, it was pretty much the same thing; I was motionless for long stretches of time. But inside my unconscious body I was alive and waiting to wake up and move.

My brain was injured and it was too dangerous to let me thrash around deliriously, so I was put to sleep in a medically-induced coma. I felt like I was wrapped in pitch-black darkness. The sounds of air being filtered and blown into a swirl around my face kept me company. Every day, I was kept in a stupor by what I called the "cloud of mist." It soaked through my body and it was like being in a water-filled isolation chamber; I felt submerged and disoriented.

Now and then, I heard a voice that was melodic and sweet, like an angel calling my name and asking me to squeeze her hand. When I did, she rewarded me with a pat on the arm and encouraged me. Then the mist would return and I would sink back to the bottom of the chamber where my lungs were artificially inflated.

There was a large tube passing through my mouth and down my throat. I couldn't swallow. I couldn't breathe on my own. The air I needed was delivered with a mechanical, rhythmic precision. The work of keeping me alive was done by a nameless *entity* that I came to know quite well, since I was totally dependent on it. I had complete faith that it would never get tired of pumping life into me. I was completely helpless, yet I felt safe. There was no pain. There were no problems. I was not a loser in this place.

Sometimes, I tried to reach up from the bottom of the water chamber and break through the surface. And when the mist would evaporate, I heard the strangest sounds. Some were comforting, and some were annoying and unstoppable. Other voices visited my body while I was in the chamber and only spoke to one another, not to me. They used an unfamiliar language of words like hematocrit, cerebral contusion, and potassium bolus. None of it made sense to me, and I felt as though I must be swirling around in a medical text book.

Things happened to me when the mist retreated. No longer in a complete stupor, I was keenly aware of a multitude of sensations like poking, prodding, lifting, and puncturing. A malodorous stench became noticeable, and on some level I knew it came from my own body. I wanted desperately to wake up and have my life back.

When the mist was turned off for the last time, the mechanical *entity* went away. All of its pumping and inflating and life-giving purpose stopped, and the humming of its motor went silent. The water in the chamber drained away and light poured in. Its orange glow turned to a painful brightness that might have blinded me if I could have opened my eyes . . . but I couldn't.

The angel's voice came close to my ear. "It's time to breathe. Take a deep breath, Buddy, you can do it. Take a nice deep breath. There's a tube in your throat and we want to take it out. But you have to help us."

There was still some mist circulating through my brain; I began to feel a terrifying, suffocating panic. I had no coordination. I had forgotten how to breathe on my own. I wanted someone to help me, to at least turn the *entity* back on to save my life. But there was no assistance.

The angel kept pleading with me to breathe. I inhaled as deeply as a drowning man and the sensation was like a blowtorch scorching my insides. That agony was immediately followed by a flood of air that was cool, rich, and delicious.

"Atta boy," the angel said as she patted my arm. "The respiratory therapist is going to take this big ol' nasty tube out of your throat."

I coughed hard as the tube was withdrawn, and it was enough stimulation to make me finally open my eyes. The first thing I saw was a long plastic instrument; it made a sucking sound from the holes in its tip.

"Welcome back Buddy," the angel said and I could hear the smile on her face. "Don't try to talk yet. Just take some nice deep breaths while I listen to your lungs."

I obeyed.

"You're a bit juicy back there. I'm going to put this in your mouth and suction the phlegm and mucus." I gagged and coughed as she used the suction device.

My eyes were watery and blurred. I couldn't make out her face, but she had to be beautiful with that voice. She placed an oxygen mask over my nose and mouth, and it dawned on me that my angel was a nurse, and I must be in a hospital.

I became more alert, but I labored to form each thought. I had no idea what I was doing in the hospital. It was mysterious and scary and I was afraid to start asking questions. I didn't have to be able to think clearly to realize that my body was not right, because it hurt all over.

The nurse took a damp cloth and wiped my gooey eyelids. As I kept blinking, she swabbed the goo away. My vision cleared, and I could finally see my angel. She smiled at me when she noticed me watching every move she made. Her smile was warm and reassuring. With another cloth, she wiped away the crust that had accumulated at the corners of my mouth. It felt good to be cleaned up. She put the facecloth down.

"Buddy, you're in the intensive care unit at the hospital. I'm your nurse, Joyce. You've been in a car accident, but you're going to be okay. You have quite a few injuries, but the doctors will tell you more about those later. The tube we took out of your throat was there to help you breathe. You were on life support. I'm sure you have a lot of questions, but let's take it slow."

My mouth was parched and I couldn't speak. I tried to signal for some water.

"I have these flavored sponges to moisten and clean your mouth," she explained, picking up a white stick that had a green sponge on the tip. "You shouldn't be trying to swallow anything yet. We have a feeding tube running through your nose into your stomach. You've injured your head and we've kept you in a coma for the past ten days for your own safety." My mind was still too clouded to care much about a coma.

I felt very sluggish and could barely move; it was as though I was made of thick molasses. I tried to lift my head, but I was immediately stopped by something pressing on my chest. I twisted my head to look down at my chest, and I saw a brace of some kind; rods, straps, and other unidentifiable components extended from my neck to my hips.

I overheard the nurse talking on the phone. She sounded very excited.

"Yes, he's awake, but hasn't spoken yet. I'm sure he will by the time you get here."

I tried to figure out who she was talking to, but my head hurt whenever I tried to concentrate. My brain felt black and blue. Each thought made my eyeballs feel like they were expanding and too tight for their sockets. I couldn't move much, but I needed to do some exploring for answers. I lifted my head as far as I could until I felt too dizzy to go any higher. The first thing I saw past the brace was several metallic pins passing through my shin bone from one side to the other. I was skewered. The pins were attached to some kind of high-tech gadgetry.

It dawned on me that my leg had been broken, probably shattered, and those pins were holding all the bone fragments in place. I tried to remember the car accident the nurse said I'd been in, but nothing came back to me.

I was getting nervous, but I had to know the extent of my injuries. I put my hand under my hospital gown and ran it across my stomach. Right down the center was something that felt like a miniature railroad track. They were surgical staples, about nine-inches worth. My belly had been cut open. Something bad happened in there . . . but what?

A little farther down was the next surprise. My penis had a flexible rubber tube running right down the shaft. *Of course*, I thought. *How else was my bladder going to empty?* I couldn't resist tugging on it, but it stung a bit on the tip. It must have been anchored in there, so I left it alone.

I tried wiggling around in bed to see if I could move at all. As I did, a red-hot poker pierced my chest. I touched it and felt a thick bandage. *What the . . . ?* I wondered, and I started to pull it off. Joyce quickly grabbed my hand.

"Don't ever touch that again if you want to live."

I froze at the words, afraid to even breathe.

"You fractured several ribs and punctured your lung, and it collapsed," Joyce lectured. "We reinflated it with a chest tube. The tube was removed this morning before you woke up. There is still a big hole there and it needs to heal shut or it will leak."

My head was throbbing. I was having trouble understanding all of this, but I knew that if any of it was my fault, there would be hell to pay. An even worse thought: I had to face my parents. And I didn't even know what I was going to have to apologize for. I just hoped that I didn't have to say I was sorry for killing someone. Maybe waking up hadn't been such a good idea after all.

My brain hurt. I must have had quite the concussion. I desperately tried to remember what had happened to me. If I had a fractured leg, busted ribs, a punctured lung, internal injuries, and a big-enough clout over the head to require a medically induced coma, then what in the world had hit me—a freight train?

I lay there for a long time, trying to sort everything out. A tanker truck flashed into my thoughts, followed by a flood of embarrassment and shame. I began to put the pieces together and, as I remembered more of what had happened, I longed for the mist to take me back to the bottom of the pool where I could hide. I finally remembered what had caused the accident: I had partnered up with the trio of Oxy, Roxy, and Zanny. I had done it again.

I could see me, the pills, the car, and the truck, a big tanker truck that crushed me like a fly under a swatter. And now I would have to face the music or perhaps a firing squad; I was pretty sure my parents were at the other end of that phone call Joyce had made. I didn't want the mist and the chamber. Bring me pills and plenty of them.

Nurse Joyce charged into the room. She was almost breathless.

"They're on their way. I bet you can't wait to see them." She clapped her hands with excitement.

"They have been here every day. For the first week, your mom just wouldn't leave. She kept holding your hand and talking to you, even played your favorite CDs. She's such a dear thing. It would have killed her if you hadn't made it. She spoke with all the doctors and wanted to know all the lab results. She really loves you."

My parents were coming and they weren't packing any good news. Being alive had become a curse instead of a blessing.

I forced myself to whisper loud enough for Joyce to hear.

"I don't want to see them. Losers don't deserve parents. They don't deserve anything. I'd rather be dead."

Joyce lowered my bedrail and gave a long sigh. She looked like the kind of mom who all the kids in the neighborhood would bring their problems to. She didn't panic when I said "dead." She had probably heard it before. She just remained calm. I thought about how my life might have turned out better if my mother had been more like her. I imagined growing up happy and doing what I enjoyed, instead of being forced to try out for sports and endure play dates. In my mind, happy children aren't losers and never become that way, no matter how much they're picked on. At that moment, I wanted to shift the responsibility for my failures onto my mother's shoulders. It was her fault that I wished I were dead. I didn't want to face her.

Joyce didn't say anything; she just picked up the sponge on a stick and rubbed my teeth and gums. It had a citrus, tangy flavor and I wanted to bite the sponge off and chew it.

"Easy, Buddy, that's enough for now. You'll get some food as soon as you can pass the swallow test."

I kept waiting for the lecture about the priceless value of life. Joyce might wait until the end of her shift to deliver the message. Then she could go home and tell her family over dinner what an honorable and miraculous thing she had done today. "I helped some brainless, dimwitted sixteen-year-old freaky kid who couldn't say no to drugs, see the light." That would, of course, be her lead-in to reminding her children that when you get involved with pills, the only outcomes are misery, pain, and suffering until the finality of death. So if I died, she'd have an even better lesson to teach.

But I was wrong. Joyce stayed right there. She took a deep breath and put a firm, skilled hand on my shoulder.

"I heard what you said." That surprised me, because I hadn't realized I was muttering out loud. "I'm not shocked, either. I know all the details and, if I were you, I might want to make myself evaporate, too. I don't know how you're going to face this. All I know is that you can. It's your choice. I'm not going to BS you with all the reasons why you should be grateful to be alive and how this can be a new beginning. I used to do that with kids who pulled through and they told me where to stick it. And they were right."

She wasn't pushy like my mom and I was willing to listen politely while she spoke.

"I do know someone who will at least hear you out. He's the kind of person I would want to talk to if I were in your position. He won't judge you. I've already sent for him; he should be here in a little while. He's a psychiatrist, and his name is Dr. Stone."

Great, I thought. *A shrink. Someone to pick my brain, or what's left of it. He would have to be weird. That's a prerequisite.* I imagined him to be just like a psychiatrist I had seen in an old black and white movie. He had a mangy grey beard and smoked a pipe constantly. He worked in an insane asylum asking all the patients about their childhood hang-ups. I don't why, but I remember him telling everybody they had a "neurosis" and needed "analysis." I was sure he was crazy, too, because he was always nervous and had a peculiar facial twitch. That's all I could think about when she mentioned Dr. Stone. I pictured him as someone with an impressive vocabulary to hide the fact that he wasn't that smart. I figured they would probably send me someone who needed more analysis than I did. I wasn't going to waste my time as he stumbled through an interview with me, a teenager whose life he could never understand. I doubted there were any textbooks written about losers like me that he would have read. This was going to be a total waste.

On second thought, maybe not. I could mentally wrestle with him, purely for the sake of my own entertainment. Better yet, I could dispose of him in two minutes and he could tell his colleagues how he had met his match at the hands of a sixteen-year-old geek. You know what would really make it fun? A few pills, then I could embarrass him with my sharp-witted intellect. If only I had some.

CHAPTER 14

I Didn't Mean for This to Happen

With nothing else to do while stuck on my back, I stared at a million tiny holes in the white ceiling tiles. That made it easier to rehearse the evasive answers I was going to give the psychiatrist. I prepared myself for trick questions. Now that my brain was working again and most of the blank patches of amnesia were gone, the only hours unaccounted for were post-impact.

I remembered all the details about meeting Sidney, feeling thoroughly insulted, and stealing her car and pills as an act of revenge. That had been followed by the best pill-popping and snorting party I could have ever hoped for. I had bags of the good stuff. I certainly could have done without crunching into a tanker, but barreling down the interstate at 120 miles per hour was a total blast that had put some hair on my chest. Hitting that tanker truck hadn't been cool; I must have been tangled up in the wreckage and a nightmare for the paramedics to pry loose. But I had manned up that day and it was worth it.

My trip down memory lane was interrupted by my mom's sudden appearance. She stood at the end of my bed, her hands over her mouth and tears in her eyes. For a moment, she was as still as a statue. Then her arms flew up, and she made a beeline for me, coming around to the side of the bed. She embraced me cautiously, trying not to disturb any of the contraptions connected to my body. The smile plastered on her face was an exaggerated one.

"You woke up . . . finally. I'm so happy. I have been praying so hard."

My mom's sympathy didn't last long, though. After the hug, the kiss on the forehead, a stroke of her hand through my hair, and a pinch of my cheek, she morphed into a lethal weapon. Gone was the woman who wanted to change her ways and make up for her child-rearing mistakes.

"Have you any idea what you put us through day after day, not knowing if you were going to live or die? The doctors told us that your chances were slim. You had surgeries, broken bones, a punctured lung, ruptured spleen, and transfusions. Oh, and let's not forget about your brain. Your brain was so swollen that they were ready to drill a hole in your skull to let the pressure out. Thank God they didn't have to! We watched you every day; you were just lying there, with a breathing machine keeping you alive. You had tubes all over the place. You wouldn't wake up. The doctors kept telling us not to get our hopes up."

Her expression turned to one of exasperation and she fanned her face with her hand.

"You make me so mad! I don't know what to do with you. Why did you have to do this? You stole a car and totaled it. The car was so badly crushed they couldn't get you out for over an hour. They used the Jaws of Life and needed a helicopter to get you here in time. You died twice and they brought you back. You'd better start thanking a lot of people."

I could feel the heat coming off her skin as her face came closer to mine with each sentence. Her voice got louder, and while I was tempted to tell her to back off or keep it down, I didn't dare; I let her continue with the tongue-lashing.

"The officer who followed you said you wouldn't stop. He had his lights on and was blasting his siren, but you were on some joyride, just oblivious. Other witnesses said you nearly collided with several cars. You were weaving in and out of traffic on the highway and you were going almost one hundred-and-twenty miles per hour. What was *wrong* with you?"

I tried to moisten my mouth, but I had no saliva. I blinked a few times and hoped I looked like I was collecting my thoughts. I was only trying conjure up an excuse that would bail me out. My brain felt useless.

I began slowly, accentuating how difficult it was to talk. "Mom, I was driving some kid's car and it was fast—too fast, and I lost control."

She put on her I-wasn't-born-yesterday face and responded with intimidating sarcasm. "Try again and remember that I know about the stolen car, which by the way is a felony and you're probably going to be arrested for that little trick. I also know about the bags of pills and how much was in your system. You must have been out of your mind on drugs."

I felt a twinge of guilt; Mom looked so upset and heartbroken.

"How could you do this? Do you expect me to believe you were inexperienced and took too many pills? Another innocent mistake? Is that what you call 'just experimenting'? I want to know what happened this time and you'd better be honest for a change." She turned away from me and headed for the door, then pivoted angrily and finished, "I'm going to get a drink of water. You'd better not bullshit me when I get back."

I knew I should be coming up with a good story, but I couldn't clear the fog from my brain. All I could think about was the possibility of getting arrested for what I had done. A loser like me would be defenseless in prison; I'd seen the movies of scrawny kids harassed and preyed upon by tattooed, muscle-bound sociopaths. It occurred to me that I might need a good lawyer and a merciful judge.

When my mom reappeared, she didn't look any calmer. This time, she pulled up a chair and sat ramrod straight, looking stern and determined to get my confession. She opened the interrogation like a seasoned detective.

"Start talking and don't leave anything out or I'll know you're lying or covering up."

I picked at the sheets nervously, twisting and twirling them in my fingers. My mom began to look impatient and alternated between scowling and biting her lip. I knew I'd better start somewhere.

"Well, I didn't mean for any of this to happen. I was just trying to have some fun."

I was afraid Mom was going to leap into the bed with me. She dug her fingers into the seat of the chair and stared through me with lie-detector eyes. But I wasn't giving up on this story so quickly. I needed to blame someone.

"It was that girl's fault," I said. "She gave me the pills. I was only going to take a few, but these drugs were different, stronger. I didn't know what I was doing. I just wanted to try them out. She never told me I could get so messed up. How was I supposed to know?"

My mom tapped my hand. "Stop playing with those sheets. It's driving me crazy."

I let go of them and hoped she was ready to give up now, but she gestured for me to keep talking.

"I started out with just one pill, and then I took more. They made me feel so good. I couldn't help it. I guess I took too many." I tried to look pathetic and innocent. I looked up through my lashes to gauge her reaction.

She stood up slowly. It was obvious that she was working hard to hold back her anger.

"That's all you can say? You're unbelievable. You pass out and stop breathing. The doctor saves your life. Then you promise it will never happen again, yet you go right back out the next day and nearly kill yourself and who knows how many other people. You steal a car and turn it into a heap of scrap metal and you almost do the same thing to your body. Explain that, Mister."

This was a losing proposition—Mom versus Buddy. It was a slam dunk. I decided to cut my losses and raise the white flag. I hoped the change in tactics would work.

"Okay, you win. I can't do anything right, not even drugs. I knew the girl who gave them to me. It was Sidney and she insulted me. She kept taunting me about being such an ugly loser. She was the one who did CPR and saved my life on the football field. She told me later that I would have been better off if she'd left me for dead. That infuriated me—big time—and I wanted to get even, so I took her car. I was gonna bring it back." I tried to end with just a little whine in my voice.

That was my best shot. If she didn't buy it, I had nothing else to sell. Besides, she wouldn't disown me. Moms never did that. She was going to have to forgive me some day. And I could wait. Rejection was something I was familiar with, and it was less painful as the years went by. I could take a little more, as long as the Roxys came along for the ride.

Besides, as far as the pills went, I wasn't a beginner anymore and I'd learned my limits. I'd literally had a crash course in what could go wrong when you took prescription drugs and I learned a valuable lesson. The price was a little steep: coma, broken ribs, punctured lung. But I knew if I was careful in the future, I'd be able to take drugs, have fun, and stay alive. I was quite proud of my accomplishment.

I lost track of what my mother said in response while I was busy congratulating myself; I can easily drift off like that when someone is talking to me. Once I dialed back in, though, I was pretty sure I'd won that round. Apparently, the scalding attack was over and she had simmered down. She was back at the side of my bed, holding my hand in both of hers. She raised it gently to her lips and kissed it; I was stupefied. How could she be done with the tongue lashing so quickly and move directly into loving me? She didn't even demand an apology or a promise to swear off drugs. Maybe she had really changed; I wondered if I was going to be able to find ways to take advantage of her. I could put up with a kiss now and them. Heck, I could even kiss her back if it helped to regain her trust that much faster.

"I can't stay mad at you," Mom said, a soft smile on her lips. "I love you too much for that. If these drugs are as irresistible as you say they are, then I don't expect you to be able to stop on your own. I'm not going to be some naive parent who thinks her kid can't end up in a coffin from an overdose. I don't know what it will take to resist those pills, but somebody does. And I will do whatever it takes to get you help. Just tell me that you want the same thing, too."

I looked into her eyes, and I really believed she wanted the best for me. She might not see me as a weirdo outcast or think I was creepy, but I did. Thank goodness I only felt a twinge of guilt for lying to her, because for now I was going to tell her what she wanted to hear. It was the best way to get into her good graces. So I took her hand in mine, kissed it, and said with as much remorse as I could muster, "I am so sorry for all the trouble I have caused you. You deserve a better son than I am."

My grip on her hand got tighter and I tried to sound even more convincing.

"I will do whatever you say. I'm done with drugs. I don't think you will have to worry about me. After this lesson, I'd have to be crazy to ever use drugs again."

Mom almost beamed, she looked so happy.

"I'm so proud of you Buddy... aren't you, Dear?"

My father stood at the foot of the bed, hands in his pockets, obliviously rocking back and forth. He seemed to be caught off guard by the question. He cleared his throat. "Of course we are. Very proud."

The rocking stopped and he jingled the change in his pockets. "Son, using pills is bad for you. I thought we made that perfectly clear. If we could give up smoking you-know-what. . . ." He pinched his index finger and thumb up to his lips, like he was holding a marijuana joint and pretended to inhale. "You can make this nonsense stop. We're confident that you...."

Mom grabbed her purse and tugged on my father's arm hard enough to interrupt his train of thought.

"That's fine, dear. Let's go, so Buddy can rest."

First she called to the nearest nurse and told her to take good care of me. Then I watched them walk out of the room; Mom's step seemed lighter, as though her heavy burden had disappeared. I thanked my lucky stars for a mom who had a heart that I could wrap around my finger.

All I needed now was to heal and get out of there. Life wasn't a curse after all; it was just something that needed adjusting. And now I knew how to do that. I was much smarter. I knew a lot more about taking drugs and I would keep on doing it until I got it right. Pills made everything perfect.

CHAPTER 15

The Specialists

I had been in a medically induced coma for ten days while a large group of doctors and nurses cheated death on my behalf. They called it a traumatic brain injury and apparently I made a miraculous recovery. On the eleventh day, I was disconnected from a ventilating machine, and by noontime I was allowed to eat the hospital's version of roast beef, mashed potatoes, peas, and apple pie.

I was starving. In those previous ten days, my only source of nutrition, if you want to call it that, had been fed through a narrow tube passing from my nose into my stomach. A steady stream of brown murky liquid was my breakfast, lunch and dinner. I probably lost ten or fifteen pounds that I couldn't spare. When my honest-to-goodness lunch arrived that day, I was starving and savored every mouthful as though I were tasting food for the first time. As I finished the last bite, I marveled at how wonderful it was to have a full belly.

I was half-asleep when Joyce, my nurse, came to take away my lunch tray.

"I can see how tired how are," she said. "That's pretty typical after being on the ventilator for so long. Today will probably be your worst day, then your energy ought to return pretty quickly. You'll have to put up with a lot of doctors checking you each day. It won't matter if you're asleep. They're going to wake you up and do their thing. In the meantime, I have to remove your urinary catheter."

I swallowed nervously, realizing immediately that she was going to do some business with my penis. Until now, it had been a very private and sensitive organ that I preferred to keep in the dark. It was not meant to be looked upon by the curious eyes of another human, male or female. I could accept whatever had to be done for medical reasons—while I was unconscious. But being exposed while awake was pretty scary.

She returned with latex gloves and a syringe. I could only imagine what she was about to do with that syringe.

"This is going to hurt. I know it," I moaned, hoping to gain her sympathy. If I could have squirmed away from her, I would have moved as far away as possible.

She laughed as she deliberately drew the syringe back and forth, showing me how easily she could make the plunger glide.

"Buddy, I want you to know that I have seen every size and shape of a man's privacy that God created with His sense of humor. Yours won't win any contest, so let's get on with this."

I cupped both hands over myself. "Can't this wait? What's the hurry? Leave the catheter in for a while."

Joyce pushed my hands aside. I knew I couldn't buy any more time. I winced and braced for the worst.

"First, I'm deflating the balloon on the tip of the catheter that holds it in place so it won't slide out of the bladder." She used the syringe for that part.

She smiled like a nurse about to give a very painful shot of antibiotics. "This may sting a little bit."

As she started to pull on the catheter, I held my breath and felt a surge of burning pain. My eyes flew open just in time to see two feet of tubing make an exit. She dangled the catheter so I could see how long it was. It didn't seem possible that so much could fit inside of me.

"That's all there is to it. We're done. You can relax now. It won't hurt again until you have to pee. That's when you'll feel the razor blades and broken glass."

Again Joyce laughed as she put everything in a biological waste container and snapped off her gloves like a surgeon.

I covered myself with the hospital gown. The burning pain was starting to ease up. I heard what she said about the pain I was in for and made up my mind that I would never urinate again. I would just hold it.

Joyce brought over a quart-size Styrofoam cup of ice water with a straw and placed it on my bedside table. "Get busy drinking. It doesn't hurt so much when your urine is diluted."

I looked at the cup. "What's the hurry?"

She fluffed up my pillow and tousled my hair.

"I was only kidding. I couldn't help it. The look on your face was priceless. Did you really think about razor blades and broken glass shooting out your penis?"

I let out a nervous laugh, pretending that I knew all along that she'd been joking, but I didn't trust her completely. I still thought it would feel like hot molten wax coursing through my plumbing when the time came for me to empty my bladder.

Joyce walked out of the room. I started drinking the water; in an hour or so, I would have the answer.

I settled back and suddenly felt exhausted. I wasn't sure if it was from having a full belly after ten days on a liquid diet or from being scared out of my wits by Joyce and the razor blade story. The day had already been too stressful and I had no idea how many different doctors would be stopping by to check on me. I figured any minute they were going to start filing in one by one leaving me no chance of taking a nap. So I just closed my eyes and waited.

The lung doctor was the first to arrive. He was a portly man in a white coat that was missing a button where his belly was the widest. He looked weary and well into his sixties. His eyes were sad and he examined me like a mechanic. He told me I had several broken ribs that had caused my lung to collapse and that I'd been drowning in about a half-gallon of blood. He also said my oxygen level was about the lowest he had ever seen in anyone who still survived.

He finally finished his examination. As he turned to leave, he nearly collided with the neurosurgeon, who let out a corny, weird laugh that seemed to come out of his nose. He examined me, then carefully explained that my spine was broken; the twelfth thoracic vertebral body was fractured. Fragments of bone came dangerously close to my spinal cord. He told me I was a miracle; instead of shopping for a wheelchair, I should be out of the back brace in about three months and good as new. I knew I should be grateful for that news, but somehow, having a broken back kind of sucked right then.

Next, a gigantic man who was well over six-foot-five walked in. His hands were bigger than ping-pong paddles and he had a mouthful of white teeth. He spouted words like the spray from a surfacing whale. He proceeded to describe my tibial fracture in minute detail: compound, comminuted, angulated, shortened, and bleeding profusely. As he described the procedures he'd performed, he made gestures as though he had Black and Decker power tools and was working on an expensive length of wood.

"So I ran a few pins through your leg, above and below the fracture. I put on an external fixation device, this rigging right here." He grabbed onto the fixator and lifted my leg like it was a pretzel stick. I held my breath in anticipation, but there was no pain.

"Works perfectly every time; should have the pins out in the next three months. Until then, it's crutches for you, my friend."

He turned and left the room so swiftly that there was a back draft from his huge frame. He didn't give me any chance for questions or feedback; I was just a shattered shin bone to him. All he could do was admire his work, but that was okay with me.

I only had time for another generous drink of water before a woman of about forty, dressed in blue surgical scrubs, approached my bed. She didn't make eye contact, but lifted my hospital gown and started kneading my abdomen like bread dough. She spoke with military precision as she described removing my spleen, which had been torn by my broken ribs.

"You're a tough one, sport. The incision is healed up nicely so my work is done here. I'm going take your staples out and replace them with steri-strips. This won't hurt a bit."

I could feel a stinging and ripping sensation as each staple was hurriedly yanked from my tender abdomen. Before I could utter a groan of protest she was speeding away with a marching gait and perfect posture.

I had no idea that surgeons were so detached and mechanical. I felt as though I was just another project that had to be checked on. By the time the last surgeon left, I was in a sweat, because all that activity was just plain painful. I wanted to be left alone with my head under the covers. But no, the nurse strolled in to take her turn. At least she was nicer this time; she gently stroked my arm.

"He's here reading your chart," she announced, and I wondered who she was talking about. "Now, just tell him the truth. He's going to get it out of you one way or another. He's the very best psychiatrist we have. He can help you. Good luck."

"You told me I needed my rest. Can't you see how tired I am? Tell him to come back later." But my plea fell on deaf ears.

I couldn't see him, but I knew he was out there at the nursing station. I had been so busy with all those other doctors that I hadn't had time to rehearse, but no matter. I was going to stay sharp and think fast. This was going to be fun. It was me versus the shrink. I wanted his best shot.

At that same moment, I suddenly had the urge to pee. I laughed to myself at the irony: I needed to empty my bladder and Dr. Stone wanted to empty my head.

I was on my back and it seemed impossible to get things flowing into the hand-held urinal. I wondered if my bladder could burst from being overinflated. I kept trying and pushing hard until a few drops came out. Gradually the stream picked up and I felt the most wonderful relief imaginable. There was no pain. I hoped I'd be as successful with the shrink.

Dr. Stone didn't impress me when he walked in. I expected him to have a beard saturated with the heavy odor of expensive pipe smoke. I thought he'd be wearing a rumpled tweed jacket with elbow patches. To my surprise, he was a broad-chested six-footer with just a sprinkling of gray hair, no beard, and a trim waistline. How could he avoid being paunchy when all he did every day was sit in his oversize leather chair and listen to hysterical women? I could just imagine them sprawled on his couch, sniffling into one tissue after another as he nodded his approval.

I sized him up. Psychiatrists like him were probably well-trained to hide their true feelings. They were experts in expressing empathy and pretending to care. I'm sure he was very professional about fooling every patient—for two hundred dollars an hour. Either he was a mastermind or a supreme rip-off artist. I would be the judge of which one.

He carried in a chair and sat down right beside the bed, a bit too close for my comfort. His appearance caught me a little off guard. The man was probably in his late fifties and he wore stylish glasses and a short-sleeve golf shirt. He had an athletic look about him, like he worked out at the gym. I quickly decided he was a narcissist, all full of himself and how good he looked. I was going to enjoy this mental chess match and I planned on winning.

He settled into the chair and gave me a disarming smile. Go ahead and pretend you're all warm and compassionate, I thought. You'll lose anyway, because nobody wins against a loser like me who has nothing to lose.

"I'm Dr. Stone, a psychiatrist. You look a lot better than the description in your chart. Glad to have you back with us." He gave me a slight smile. "How are you feeling today?"

Oh, this was going to be so easy. He was leading with the "feeling" question. I blocked his pathetic jab and countered with one of my own.

"How does it *look* like I feel?"

His face didn't lose its polite, friendly expression.

"Like someone who's not too happy."

I curled my top lip into a sneer. *I'm not going to retreat like some geek,* I thought.

"I don't need to talk to a shrink. I'm not crazy. You're wasting your time. Why don't you just go have a cup of coffee and bill me for your time."

The smile disappeared, but he didn't flinch.

"What happened that day . . . before the accident?"

The room got very quiet. We were in a standoff. He sat quietly nestled in his chair and looked like he wouldn't budge for an earthquake. I don't know why, but some of my anger melted away and I started having second thoughts about talking to him. What harm would it do?

I decided to let him take a nibble. He wouldn't know what was true and what was a pile of crap. That would be amusing to watch.

"Okay," I began, drawing in a long breath. "It went like this: I rear-ended a tanker truck and got hurt."

We looked at each other for a full minute before he moved. He shifted in his chair and crossed his legs.

"Tell me about the drugs."

I suddenly felt like I was a piece of meat on a butcher's block, ready for carving.

"I read about the baggies of Roxys, Oxys, and Zannys that were found in the car. What were you doing with all those pills?"

I thought that psychiatrists were supposed to stay behind some invisible line and not rattle their patients. He seemed to be taking aim for a kill shot.

"Whoa, Doc, that's not a shrink question," I objected, hoping to distract him. "You're more like a cop. I'm not sure I want to keep talking to you without an attorney present." I wanted to make sure he knew that even geeks and nerds were not all scaredy-cat weaklings.

He pushed on the bridge of his glasses and blinked a few times. I wondered if perhaps I had made him just a tiny bit nervous.

He didn't sound nervous, though. "Let me take a stab at this. I bet you recently discovered that painkillers were a lot of fun. They made you feel like the Energizer Bunny with a sense of humor and good looks. Whether you ate them or snorted them, those pills gave you the ride of your life."

He studied me for a moment to see how I reacted; I tried hard to keep a stone face.

"Now that we're working from that basic set of facts," Dr. Stone continued, "Why don't you take it from there and lead me down the path to this glorious outcome. It's not every day that your body dies twice and you end up in the disaster repair shop."

I decided he knew the game I was playing, but I didn't know his angle. It was time to send out a probe of my own.

"Okay, Doc, score a point for you. But why should I tell you anything? You, who couldn't understand what I've been through. Let's just leave it like this: my wild and costly experiment with drugs caused me to burn out fast and furious. Now I'm in plenty of trouble and I don't need you to add to it."

Dr. Stone sat up taller and straighter in the chair, but he somehow still managed to look relaxed.

"Telling me what happened gives you a chance to make a connection with me. Once I understand what you've been going through, you won't feel so alone. I am pretty certain that right now you are dangling from a thin branch that is about to break, with no safety net in sight."

His words painted a vivid picture. I could see myself holding onto a branch at the edge of a high, rocky cliff; there were pounding waves below. The branch was bending and I had a sense of impending doom. I made myself snap back to reality. Time was in short supply and I quickly needed some answers. What was I going to do? Shut up and send him away or talk to him? I decided to take a tiny risk.

"I don't like to talk about myself. Nobody cares to know me. That's the way I like it, so don't get me started. You won't like what you hear."

The doctor jotted some notes on a pad. When he spoke again, his tone was cordial, as though he had downshifted into a slower, easier gear.

"I'm going to stop writing now. I want to concentrate just on you and listen to your story. Please tell me anything you believe I should know to understand you better."

I had been paying close attention to his every move; I couldn't detect any obvious weaknesses to take advantage of. Maybe I misjudged him prematurely. Perhaps he really did care about his patients. I gave it a little more thought and was tempted to try him out; maybe tell him a few things about myself and see where it went.

I took a deep breath, then let out a long sigh. I began speaking slowly, this time without all the bravado.

"I really don't know where to begin."

CHAPTER 16

You'll Eventually Run Out of Something

Doctor Stone rubbed his hands together before interlocking his fingers. He looked like he was deep in thought about his next move.

"Buddy, why don't you try this? Tell me about the first pill you took. Why did that seem like such a good idea?"

The question put me a little more at ease, because I knew exactly why I did it.

"Well, Doc, I was standing around doing nothing with some kids from school. One of them, a girl named Sidney, started talking about Lortabs, and they sounded good . . . real good. She offered me a pill, and I decided to try one. In no time, I felt brand new."

This wasn't so bad. So far, I was telling him the truth and I was curious to find out what a psychiatrist did with information like that.

I continued. "After one pill, my factory defects were gone. For a few hours, I wasn't a loser. I was comfortable in my own skin, and Sidney was nice to me. She had a real pretty smile and winked at me. I wanted more of that. It happened so easily."

He had been listening intently and then asked, "What happened when the pill wore off?"

I distinctly remember how deflated I felt when the Lortab high faded away. I became irritated by his question and remarked rudely, "What do you think? Life sucked all over again."

Those words hung in the air and we were both quiet and still. The only sound in the room was the hiss of an automatic blood-pressure cuff inflating and deflating on my arm. Those words uncovered some of the painful truth about me and I found myself retreating instead of telling him anything private that I might be sensitive about.

"So, you see, Doc, Lortabs were the ticket, the stuff that got me going good. Then Sidney gave me a few more pills to take home and I thought she'd hook me up with a couple of 'tabs' here and there, just to get high and kick back."

I was keeping our conversation on the lighter side—until the doctor leaned in on me, hard and fast. He interrupted me by waving his index finger like a windshield wiper.

"No, you didn't." The words cut the air like a scalpel.

"You didn't expect to take them just for kicks. You were counting on

Lortabs to make the loser in you disappear. After years of rejection, you finally had some legitimate hope of no longer being, well, you. What could be better? How could you resist an opportunity like that?"

I realized I had underestimated this man's insight. "You got me there, Doc. Right again."

"This isn't a game. I didn't come here to 'get' you."

He watched me as my expression turned from playful to serious.

"Okay, Doc, I'll give it to you straight. I wanted more of the magic locked up in those pills and Sidney had the supply. But I didn't expect her to turn from flirty friend into an unscrupulous drug dealer. It was all a set-up. She knew how good I was going to feel and that I would do anything, short of selling a kidney, to get my hands on a steady supply. Do you know how much those puppies cost? Actually, I didn't really care, because I found an easy source of cash. Nothing was going to wipe the smile off of my face ever again."

Dr. Stone nodded with approval. "Buddy, tell me more about the experience you had with the pills. What else happened?"

"Well, that first day, I swallowed a Lortab and had a blast. Then Sidney sold me five and I got wasted before throwing up. I remember going wild arranging my closet. Then I found my mom's Blues and got right into snorting them. That was an even bigger blast, and of course, more puking."

"Really." He seemed to know what I was talking about.

"Yeah. And I wanted to do it again. As soon as I could."

"Then it must have been good."

"In a weird way, it was. That may sound insane, but I know I'm not, and I wasn't at the time."

His eyes narrowed into slits. "Go on," he said.

"Afterward, my strategy was to find a way to keep a supply on hand. It was supposed to be great. I didn't see any bad until now."

Dr. Stone let out a deep sigh, as though he'd been holding his breath the entire time I was speaking.

"Buddy, do you see how you were played? You don't get anything free from a pill when you're using it to repair some weakness in your mind. Sometime in your past, you were programmed to think loser thoughts. Lortabs and Blues only stopped the flow for a few hours. They never put the machine out of business. They can make you dumb and blind. Before you know it, you've taken too many pills and made bad choices. You're not the only one who's been fooled like this. Get in the line; it's a long one."

He was definitely crafty. He sounded like he had spent a lot of time crawling around in the mind of an addict, but that didn't have anything to do with me, because I wasn't one. I wasn't ready to agree with his position that painkillers were bad for me. Granted, I made a few beginner mistakes, trying to arrive at the perfect amount for me. Except for that, I'd had the best time of my life . . . before the crash. I just had to learn the secret of timing and learn how to mix the pills together safely. This was an art and a science. I wasn't going to give up on it.

I knew I wasn't going to convince the doctor to buy into my logic. I needed a different approach. I decided to agree with him and see where that got me.

"Okay, Doc, you made your point. I think I got the message. I'm done with it. No more pills. You sold me. Am I ready to graduate now?" I looked over at the blood pressure monitor and waited for his answer.

"Do you expect me to believe that you intend to walk out of this hospital and live in the real world without another pill? I've heard some great performances, but that one needs work. Buddy, I'm not here to stop you from using. You have every right to take pills if you want to, but I prefer to devote my time to someone who is ready to quit—and my friend, you aren't even close. Some people have to take the elevator deep down into the basement before it hits the bottom of the pit. I think you have a few more floors left before you run out of cable. I don't know how many pills that will take, how many cars you have to wreck, or how many times you'll end up behind bars. But you're still looking for another bull to ride. And just a little word of advice: they get meaner each time you climb on."

The doctor stood up and moved the chair back into the corner of the room. He clicked his pen, put it in his pocket, then looked at his cell phone for messages. I figured I'd been dismissed.

"If it's the shortcut to pleasure you want, the pills will deliver the goods for just so long. Sooner, not later, you will run out of pills, out of money, or out of your mind. There's no other way this is going to end. It's bad when you run out of money, because you quickly run out of pills, and then you run head on into opioid withdrawal. It's another kind of hell that you can't imagine. You haven't had to curl up into a ball of sweat, drizzle diarrhea down your leg, and heave your guts until you blow a hernia . . . yet. And that's on a good day. So maybe when you're having one of those good days, you might find some use for me after all. My phone rings every day with requests to help dope-sick people. I'll leave you my card. When you're all knotted up with cramps, you'd better hope I have an opening in my schedule."

Dr. Stone picked up my chart as he walked out of the room. I could barely hear him talking to the nurse, but he was facing me and I was a pretty good lip-reader.

"He's an addict who won't quit. He wants to ride the wild beast a few more times. This kid was knocked around long before he took his first pill. He thinks drugs are the only way he can win and he won't surrender. He doesn't realize that victory comes to those who give up the fight. He'll have to figure out that there is a sober way to enjoy life. When he's ready to work with me, I can help him to believe that. Until then, I see no reason to come back."

I wasn't sure how to take his remarks. I felt like he'd taken a supreme dump on me. Shrinks weren't supposed to do that, were they? I also thought about how well I played the game, matching him move for move. He didn't checkmate me. My king is still on the board. Well, good riddance.

But within seconds, I was dissecting our conversation. He'd tried to get me to confess that I was some kind of junky. What a wrong assumption, and based upon what evidence? Maybe I was driving out of control when I was out of my mind, but who wouldn't be, with the all the drugs I took? But an addict? No way. I didn't even understand what he was talking about. Dope-sick? What was that? I bet Sidney had never been dope-sick. Look at her, a perfect human specimen. So why should I worry about having a problem?

Besides, pills weren't the problem. Taking too many, that was the problem. I knew where I'd made my mistake. I wouldn't be so impatient next time. I'd just take one pill and give it a chance to take effect. Then I'd take another and wait a little longer. That way, I'd be fine. I might have been a loser in the past, but I was never going to lose again. Roxys, Oxys, and Zannys were still my best friends.

CHAPTER 17

The Fallout

"So, how did it go with Dr. Stone?"

Joyce's twelve-hour shift was nearly over. She looked weary and ready to go home. Why had she bothered to ask, since she already knew the answer.

"I beat him at his own game. He gave me his best shot and I took it. He won't be back, because there is no reason to have him back. He tried to convince me that I was a dope-head. I bet he was one himself, wasn't he? That's why he's on this crusade. He needs some new recruits for his band of losers. Well, I'm not in the business anymore. I turned in my membership card. He was good, though. Almost had me."

It felt good to gloat. I loved the smell of victory in the sterile air of an antiseptic hospital.

My nurse placed a pitcher of ice water on the bedside table. When I reached for it, my arm got tangled in the cardiac monitor wires. Annoyed, I started to pull at them.

"I can't stand these things. When are you going to take them off?"

"Not tonight." She checked each one to make sure it was properly connected. "You were just taken off the ventilator. I don't expect a problem. But while you're in the ICU you have to be monitored."

When she was finished with the wires, she got a little rough straightening out my sheets.

"I have a thing or two to say about your remarks."

"Should I brace myself for this?"

"Enough with the fresh mouth, okay? You may think you got away with something today, but take a good look at the condition you're in. Your busted carcass doesn't have *brilliant* written all over it. The odds of being able to walk out of here were pretty bleak on the day you arrived. You're going to heal and get another shot at life, and for what?"

I was exhausted and not in the mood for another lecture. I was rude when I interrupted her . . . I intended to be.

"Now, wait a minute. Try trading places with me for a day and see how you like it. Do you know that some of my classmates go out of their way to avoid getting too close to me in the halls at school? I hear things about myself that I am too embarrassed to say in front of you. By comparison, being called *geek* and *nerd* is something I am fond of, in a sick way."

This was a sensitive subject that I never talked to anyone about, not even my parents. Yet, there I was opening up to a stranger. I could feel the heat rising in my face.

"A Lortab changed all of that. For a few hours, I could actually carry on a conversation with the same people who treated me like a freak. I sounded intelligent, and they listened like I was somebody. Lortab spelled *friend* in my dictionary and I figured if I took an OxyContin, maybe I could get up enough courage to ask someone out. If you were this 'busted carcass,' which would you choose when you get out of here: Dr. Stone's traveling show or a chance for a date?"

Joyce just stared at me. I think she was dumbfounded by my cockiness; I had become a sarcastic wise ass. I wanted the nurse to feel my anger and pain. My need for revenge was still driving me to hate even the kindest of people. I knew that only pills could keep it from killing me or someone else.

She tried again. "No matter what you've been through in your life—and I suppose it's been pretty bad at times—you will never find the answer in any drug. But kids these days seem to think they will. We work hard to keep them alive up here in the ICU after they've had their fun and games. I took care of a kid your age who licked the Fentanyl off a pain patch. He passed out, because he was already loaded up on alcohol, Xanax, and marijuana."

She didn't seem weary any longer. She was animated as she told the story.

"He was standing on the edge of a swimming pool at the time and fell in. He took a deep breath and the patch lodged in his throat when he hit the water. You can imagine how challenging it was for the rescue team to figure out what had actually happened. They didn't even think to look for a pain patch in his throat where it didn't belong. It wasn't until they went to intubate him that they saw it and knew what they were dealing with. Even after the antidote was administered, he barely made it here. We were able to save him with the same technique that was used on you."

She pointed at the mechanical ventilation machine. "This is a lifesaver. Those pills are stealing the life from kids like you and you can't see it. To you, it's just playtime. For us, it's terrifying pressure each time we have to save one of you. We can't afford to make a mistake after you've taken your concoction of drugs. Being unconscious and not breathing is a little bit more difficult to fix than you can comprehend. It's getting harder and harder to find the combination that brings you guys back from the brink of death. And after we do, Dr. Stone is there in the trenches trying to figure out why you keep doing the same stupid thing, and he works to guide your poisoned brains back to reality."

She was passionate, all right. But to me, she was just droning on. I found it tedious to keep listening.

"Dr. Stone fights for the impossible for one reason: because he thinks you're all worth saving. He's not, as you said, a traveling show. But he *is* looking for teenagers to recruit for the cause of recovery. You kids are dying off at a faster rate than ever before and all in the name of pleasure. Well, Dr. Stone is trying to put a stop to that, one life at a time.

If you'd been ready and willing to listen, he would have stayed and delivered the message that has changed people for the better. And he intends to keep doing that, no matter what. Your addiction is no match for what he has to offer. That's the kind of man I would follow if I were you. It's your choice. I hope you make the right one."

Joyce completed the last sentence with the finality of a great speech, picked up her coat from the back of a chair, and disappeared down the hall. *Nicely done*, I thought. I had to admit, I was impressed with her zeal.

I thought about the idiot who licked the Fentanyl gel off the pain patch and then inhaled it into his throat before choking. By comparison, at least I was able to drive at breakneck speed through a maze of cars on the Interstate. That took talent and I would have delivered the car back to Sidney in one piece if that tanker truck had been handled by a better driver.

It had been a long day, but I was living proof of an amazing neurological comeback. My brain felt exhilarated by the challenge of dueling with Dr. Stone. I believed I was nearly restored to perfect working order. I concluded that pills weren't the problem. I was getting smarter and wiser by the second. As soon as I could get my hands on some Roxicodone, I would be living the good life once again.

The night nurse arrived. I decided hospital living was definitely improving: I had a bed bath, a hair wash, and brushed my teeth. After a good night's sleep, courtesy of a sleeping pill, I woke to my first real breakfast in weeks: eggs, bacon, home fries, and orange juice. The morning nurse engaged in some playful small talk while she went about her work, which finally included disconnecting me from the cardiac monitor. She was pleasant to have as my nurse, especially because she avoided the subject of the crash and drugs. I felt like a common, ordinary patient, the kind I wanted to be.

The physical therapist arrived midmorning, looking like a fitness instructor who had been carved from a block of granite. He was probably five-foot-ten and two-hundred-and-thirty pounds. He looked to be 99 percent fat-free. He moved with energetic precision, as though he was intentionally burning the maximum number of calories for each pound of muscle mass.

"Good morning, Buddy," he said in a loud, intimidating voice. "My name is Rodney. You can call me Rod. Today you get vertical, my friend. The doctor left orders for you to learn how to ambulate with a walker, non-weight bearing, and then progress to crutches as tolerated. I was going to wait until you got transferred downstairs to the orthopedic floor, but I had some free time, so let's fire it up, shall we?"

He moved fast, grabbing me by the front and rear of the back brace and effortlessly sitting me up. I was completely powerless and felt like a sack of potatoes in his hands. He swung my legs over the edge of the bed, and a nauseating dizziness filled my head as the blood drained out of my brain.

"Whoa there, Buddy, looks like we moved you a bit too fast for comfort."

Geez, do you think it might be my gray-green skin that gives it away? I thought. But I didn't say a word for fear I'd puke.

"Let's put you back down until you get your bearings."

The room got dim and my vision blurred. I felt like I was spinning. Rod reached for the wastebasket in case I tossed up breakfast. "Take some deep breaths," he instructed.

I broke out in a cold sweat. "What happened?" I asked.

"Your blood pressure crashed. You've been lying in this bed for too long and couldn't adjust to sitting up."

He knew this would happen, I thought. He wanted to make the geek throw up. He's just like the others, amusing himself at my expense. "Let's take that a little slower next time," I answered, clenching my teeth.

"Okay, Sport, nice and easy."

That time, I was able to sit up and get my feet to touch the floor. The nausea did not return, but I was overwhelmed by the pain that spread over nearly every square inch of my body.

"Hey, Man, stop!" I shouted. "That hurts all over. My back is killing me, and my lung feels like it's being ripped open by those broken ribs. Get the nurse."

He called out as instructed, and she hustled in.

"What's wrong?" she asked, scanning my body urgently.

"I'm in excruciating pain is what's wrong. Should you guys be moving me like this? I've got broken bones all over the place. This must be dangerous. Call my doctor." By now I was livid. Who did they think they were, treating me like this?

The nurse touched my arm gently.

"Don't worry. You're safe. The doctors looked at all of your X-rays before they gave the orders to get you up. You can do this. Nothing will go wrong, trust me."

The pain started to lessen, so she must have been right. My sense of panic went away and I was sure that I could have carried on with the physical therapy, but they didn't know that. So I decided see how much sympathy I could get and what medication came with the sympathy.

"Could I please have something for the pain," I moaned. "Then I'll do whatever you want me to."

The nurse examined the back brace and all the pins stabilizing my leg. Everything was exactly as it should be. My moaning must have worked. She gritted her teeth.

"Of course this hurts, you poor thing. Let me get you a shot to stop the pain."

Rodney looked at his watch, calculating the time left before he had to move on to the next patient. The nurse returned with a syringe. She called it Dilaudid, when I asked. She injected the full load into my intravenous line. In seconds, a balmy, beautiful sensation spread through every cell of my body. I quietly thanked whoever created that drug, as a warm glow gave way to an awesome tranquility.

Rodney was probably no stranger to his patient being over-medicated and spoke up. "This guy is no good to me like this. He's ready for a nap."

He laid me down on the bed and grunted with frustration. His comment was directed at the nurse.

"I'll be back later and next time, go a little lighter on the juice."

I silently and wholeheartedly disagreed. I wanted even more, because I deserved it.

I drifted off into a wonderland of contentment, peace, and harmony. Even the pain felt like a friend I could trust, because just the mention of the word had produced a syringe full of dope. As long as I was in pain, I was entitled to be medicated for it. Therefore, I never wanted the pain to leave me. I could find a way to love my pain if it was going to legitimately and continuously qualify me for narcotics. What better connection was there? I didn't need money or a dealer, just permanent residency in the hospital where I would be served only the best painkillers.

I drifted along in my thoughts for a while, feeling like I'd been given the keys to heaven . . . until I felt an ominous presence and opened my eyes. She was standing there, delicately fingering the hardware that held my leg together. Her voice was deceptively cordial.

"You looked so peaceful; I thought you might have slipped back into a coma again. I heard you had an awful concussion. I'm glad you're not suffering from amnesia. I can tell by your expression that you remember me. I'd say we have a bit of catching up to do, you and I."

Sidney stood next to the bed, smiling her brilliant cheerleader smile.

CHAPTER 18

Maintaining the Trade Agreement

It was astonishing how Sidney's presence could counteract the dreamy effect of any drug. I was suddenly alert enough to pay attention, but I could still feel the soothing embrace of the Dilaudid in the background.

"Isn't it great?" I replied nervously. "No more coma; I'm just messed up with a lot of broken stuff. Doc says I'll be fine. Ought to be out of here in no time."

That was pretty lame, I thought. It wasn't even close to an excuse for what I had done to her car . . . and her pills. She was pretending to read my get-well cards as I babbled on.

"Sidney, what I did was really dumb. I got really mad when all you offered me was Tabs. I wanted Oxys. How could you expect me to settle for anything less? Can you blame me? I had the money. You could have made an easy two hundred bucks and a long-time customer."

Sidney sniffed a few flowers from different bouquets as though she hadn't even heard me. Then suddenly, she twirled to face me. I wondered if I needed to be worrying about my safety.

"You know, you're right. I was too hard on you. I should have realized that losers like you need things real simple. Of course you want Oxys instead of Tabs. You need a higher grade of fuel to run on. I wouldn't want you to stall out in the middle of being bored and all alone. After all the damage you did to yourself in that crash, you're not good for much of anything else. So I'm willing to help you out, provided you can help me out. I told the authorities that I let you take my car for a spin. From now on, you do as I tell you and I won't file any charges. I might even hate you a little less, although I can't forgive you after what you did to my Sebring."

At that point, I no longer felt like her next victim. The loser remarks were more like being hit with marshmallows. I wanted her to keep selling me pills. Shutting off my supply would be a disaster. I was going to do whatever it took to maintain a trade agreement with her.

"Whatever you have in mind, you can count on me. I might even surprise you. I can make a connection with all the other losers who would love to pay you handsomely for a little of your playful teasing and a handful of assorted pills. Offer them Tabs, Roxys, Oxys, and Zannys, and I can have them lined up with plenty of cash. And that's good business."

I think she liked the idea of being a dealer to the school's lackluster minority. We were a bland, dull, and colorless population of mediocrity.

She dropped her designer purse on the tray table and fingered its gold buckle until it fell open. "I bet they're pretty stingy with pain meds here, so I brought a few of your favorites."

My eyes were riveted on the bag. Sidney's hand disappeared inside it and I heard pills chatter in a plastic baggie as she clutched them.

"Don't go ape on me now. I don't want that nurse barging in."

She pulled the baggie out, shielding it from view with her body. "These are for all of your nasty boo-boos."

She made her lips look full and kissable as she said that. It was intoxicating, and I couldn't get enough.

She put the baggie in my hands and I had to tug it out of her grip.

"I purposely didn't bring a kit for you. I don't want you snorting anything but fresh air. If you get messed up on these pills and pull a nine-one-one, the deal's off and you'll never get anything but your worst nightmare from me." Sidney's face was mere inches from mine. If words could be tasted, Sidney's would have been bitter.

"Remember, I may not hurt you directly, 'cuz that would be bad for my reputation. But I do know people who enjoy that sort of thing and they like to keep me happy."

I slipped the baggie of pills under my pillow. As soon as I did, she turned and headed for the door. She looked over her shoulder for one last word.

"Get better fast. I need you out there bringing in new customers. A deal's a deal."

Sidney was gone, and I could breathe again. I had a bag full of happiness, and as payback, all I had to do was improve her profit margin. Me, the former loser, could not only withstand a bone-crushing car accident but was going to deliver customers with cash. She was already showing her gratitude.

I was fast becoming someone I could admire. Things were looking up. I could keep scoring Dilaudid for pain I didn't really have and now I could blend in some Oxys or whatever she put in the bag. This brought the butterflies back and chased my demons away... for good.

My nurse Joyce picked up the phone as she saw Sidney leave my room. She told whoever was on the other end that I would be ready after lunch and she was going to go easy on the Dilaudid. I knew what that meant: the good news was a chance to get high; the bad news was physical therapy with Rodney.

"Who was your visitor," Joyce asked when she came in to check on me. "Your girlfriend or a classmate?"

I rolled my eyes. "Any girl who dates me would have to be blind, for starters."

"Oh, come now," Joyce cajoled. "There's somebody for everybody. Your turn will come."

Any conversation that tiptoed around my ugliness was best avoided, in my opinion. Adults lied so as not to hurt my feelings. I knew my face was repulsive. I had no features that are found in attractive people. And I was always keenly aware of how uncomfortable people were in my presence.

"Please don't go there and patronize me. I know what I look like and I've gotten used to being this way. I don't need your pity or your worthless positive affirmations. Do your job and we'll get along just fine."

The poor thing looked stunned and hurt, like I had slapped her across the face.

"Your lunch is here." Her tone had changed from caring to cautious. "It's a grilled chicken sandwich with lettuce, tomato, mayo, and French fries. You also get apple juice and chocolate chip cookies." She looked at me for a response. She didn't get one.

I was hungry and ate most of the meal, but the thought of getting another shot of Dilaudid was much more appetizing. I decided to check the stash and see what I had. At a quick glance I was able to spot Roxys, 80s and Zanny bars. I grabbed the first thing my fingers touched and swallowed it with a gulp of apple juice. It was a Blue. I was going to have some fun.

Joyce returned to inspect my plate. She must have given herself a pep talk, because she was trying to be all cheerful again. That was the perfect opportunity to have her play right into my hands. I asked her to lift my leg to reposition it. As she did, I yelped.

"OWWWWW! That *hurts!* What did you do to me?" I winced to complete the effect.

"Oh my God, I'm so sorry. I don't know what happened. It's not supposed to hurt like that!" Joyce looked concerned and confused.

"But it does. What's wrong with it?"

She inspected the apparatus carefully. "The hardware looks fine to me. Are you sure it hurt that bad?"

"Do you think I'm making this up? It's a broken leg. Of course it hurts."

Joyce dutifully asked, "On a scale of one to ten, ten being the worst pain you could feel, how would rate your pain right now?"

"Do you have a syringe the size of a turkey baster? My pain is much worse than a ten."

"Oh, you kids are always exaggerating."

She was right, I was overdoing it. I toned it down to a tiny bit of wincing, but I made sure I was gripping the bed rails with two sets of white knuckles.

"Okay, I'm convinced," Joyce responded appropriately. "There's no need to suffer through this. I'm sure it's only temporary. Let me get you something to ease the pain."

"If you don't mind, I'll be ever so grateful." *Score one for Buddy.* I'd reverted to the boy-next-door who was always polite and helped bring in the groceries. It worked.

Joyce hurried back with a syringe filled with lollipops and rainbows. I was gritting my teeth and taking shallow breaths. She moved quickly and injected the contents into my IV site.

"The physical therapist may not like this, but I can't let you go to therapy in so much pain. You just came off the ventilator; one more day in bed won't hurt. Here you go, Sweetie."

I watched as the plunger pushed the clear liquid through the IV tubing. I instantly felt warm and a bit giggly. I was on my way to take flying lessons with Peter Pan and Tinker Bell, and Never Never Land was our destination. My head started to feel heavy and sank deep into the pillow. My eyes were closed and vacuum sealed behind the lids. My final thought was about the baggie of pills nestled in a nice safe spot, waiting for my return. I plummeted into an abyss of inky black darkness.

A small point of light appeared. It slowly enlarged and encircled me. A hand appeared holding a gigantic baggie of pills so big that I climbed inside. The pills were huge and I was excited, because there were enough to last me for years. No matter how many I snorted, the supply would never end. I was thrilled—until I fell out of the bag just before it was sealed and taken away. I screamed for the pills to come back. I began to feel a deep penetrating pain between my eyes.

Joyce was pushing hard with the knuckle of her index finger directly above the bridge of my nose.

"Wake up, Buddy. Wake up." My eyes still closed, I seized her hand and frantically cried out, "Give them back to me, Give me the Oxys."

Joyce wiggled out of my grip and stared at me as I became more alert.

"Where are they? I want my pills back."

"Come on now Buddy. Wake up. You're having a nightmare."

I had been startled and now the Dilaudid and Roxicodone were washing away all too soon. Joyce peered at me, searching for answers to questions she hadn't even asked yet.

"Buddy, did I hear you mention Oxys, as in OxyContin?"

I was still brain-fogged but I managed to be coherent enough to ask, "Huh?" the universal teenage response to any question.

"I know you can hear me perfectly well."

I began to panic. Had she already found them? I was getting paranoid; I had to know if my pills were okay.

"I suppose I did. What of it? Don't people say weird stuff when they're having nightmares?" I rubbed my eyes and blinked rapidly until I could focus.

Joyce's face brightened; I was pretty sure she'd bought it. But I had to know for sure. I wanted her out of the room so I could check.

"You screamed out something about pills and Oxys. I bet it was a flashback from the day of the accident. You overdosed on OxyContin, didn't you?"

"Yeah . . . so . . . what of it?"

"My goodness, you got nervous in a hurry. Did something else happen in your dream that you want to talk about? Maybe you were trapped in the wreckage and terrified?"

"I suppose so. I'll be all right. I think I heard your name being called from the room next door."

"You've got good ears. I didn't hear a thing."

"Go ahead. I'll be fine."

"I'll be back in jiffy."

As soon as Joyce turned the corner, I hated having to shake off being high but I had to seriously get my hand under the pillow. There was nothing there. Alarms went off in my head. She'd found them and now she was going to keep them for herself. I dug my hand under the left side of the pillow. My hand touched the baggie, and I breathed a huge sigh of relief. It was sealed tight with all of its tasty contents. But I knew I couldn't leave it there—too much chance that someone other than me would be the next person to find it.

I looked around the room for hiding places; the bedside drawer, a flower arrangement, a gift bag with a teddy bear inside, and a box of chocolates were all possibilities, but I picked the closest one: a jumbo two-pound bag of M&M's. I took out a handful of the candies and put them in a plastic cup I used to drink water from my pitcher. I wiggled the baggie through the M&M's until it rested on the bottom, covered up. Then I looked at the nurses' station to be certain I hadn't been observed.

Joyce had returned to write some notes and Dr. Stone was standing right behind her, looking at another chart. He glanced up and acknowledged me with a tilt of his head. I imagined that he must have been thinking to himself, *One of these days, the pills are going to get you and I want to be around to say "I told you so."*

The drugs had put me in a cocky mood and I held the bag of M&M's, signaling him with an offer to take a few. He declined and pointed at his waistline. I laughed and started eating the ones I'd taken out to hide my real treat, silently daring him to open the bag and see the secret of happiness inside. I was going to keep taking pills anytime I wanted and bring comfort to my own mind.

See you later, Dr. S., I thought. *Come back when your boring life has turned you into a fossil, and maybe I'll show you how to really live.*

CHAPTER 19

I'm Not a Drug Addict

A few hours later, my mom and dad returned for a most tiresome visit. Mom droned on and on. I wanted so badly for her to shut up.

"Honey, everybody's just so thankful that their prayers were answered and you are back from that coma. They want to visit, but I tell them to wait a bit more, I hope you don't mind. Your best friend Jeffrey called today. He misses you at school. I told him to come up tonight. He should be here soon. You look so much better today. I hear you're going to be up walking tomorrow. The nurse said you'll be moving to an orthopedic floor as soon as you do. What I don't understand is why you sent that psychiatrist away. He was just trying to help."

I had to interrupt her nonstop monotony or go mad. At home, I could disappear up to my room. But at the hospital, I was literally her captive audience.

"Mom, enough already," I said. "I'm in pain, you know and you're giving me a headache. I'd like to rest a bit, if you don't mind."

"Okay, but answer me about Dr. Stone. What happened? Didn't you like him? They say he's the best."

Shut up shut up shut up, I thought. I got distracted and started toying with the bag of M&M's, shaking it and making the chocolate-covered candies dance inside. The clickity-clack sound they made was hypnotic. I imagined that the bag was full of Oxys all knocking into each other. I was having a wild and crazy craving; I couldn't wait to be alone and start taking the pills. I held in my hand the solution to all my problems.

"Buddy, snap out of it!"

"What? I'm right here."

"It's rude when you do that. Can't you pay attention? This is important. I want to know why you didn't get along with Dr. Stone."

"Listen. He's a psychiatrist. You know, a crazy-person doctor. I've got nothing crazy to talk about, except my boring, ordinary life."

"Boring until you wrecked that car . . . on drugs. That sounds crazy to me. Right, Honey?" My mother turned to my father for support. Apparently, it was his turn to pour some salt on the wound.

"She's right, Son. We couldn't believe it when they told us that you had drugs in your system. Doing it once was dumb; we thought you'd learned a lesson you'd never forget. How can you lie there and act like this was no big deal? Why do you want to take these drugs? What do they do for you?"

I realized that this was going to be mission impossible. I needed to throw them a bone to gnaw on so they'd leave me alone.

"Mom. Dad. Listen up. I am *not* a drug addict. Those people live in crack houses and other rat-infested places, sticking needles in their arms and shooting up. They are whores, prostitutes, and drug dealers and they're covered in prison tattoos. Do I look like that? Addicts don't go to school and turn in homework on time. They don't write terms papers and stay home on weekends. I didn't want to see Dr. Stone, because that's all he deals with: drug addicts who need a fix. He said so himself. There's nothing wrong with me that can't be taken care of with a little common sense. Sure, I took a few pills. Everybody does. It's no big thing. Those pills were prescriptions. Heck, Mom, you take them too, those Roxicodones for your knee. Are you an addict?"

My mom touched Dad's sleeve and gave it a tug. "He's got a point. I hear that all the kids are trying these pain pills. It gives them some kind of energy. For me, it just gets rid of my pain so I can keep going. They are a godsend. I'd be on the couch without them. I'm not hooked. I only take them when I need to. I don't see how anybody gets hooked. They don't get me high."

"But they got *you* high, Buddy." My dad looked puzzled. "So which is it? Are you hooked, or aren't you?"

I held the M&M's bag in the palm of my hand.

"I am no more addicted to pain pills than I am to what's in this bag. To me, they are just as harmless as this candy. My mistake was taking them on an empty stomach. I wanted to feel that energy thing, just like everybody else." *I can't believe how clever I am*, I silently congratulated myself.

Mom still wasn't sold. "What about when you took pills and stopped breathing? That was no energy boost. What happened there?"

It was time to see how much bull I could roll into one meatball and serve up.

"Mom, that's because the first pills I tried were downers, like sleeping pills. That was stupid, I admit, but the person who gave them to me lied. I thought my energy was going to be turned up, not off. The second time, I was sure I had the right stuff and they worked just fine. I would be okay today if that truck hadn't blown a tire."

I watched her face carefully; she looked like she was sifting through all the evidence in a jury deliberation. I thought I deserved an acquittal.

"I don't understand why you need downers or any kind of energy pill. Why not just grow up the way we did? Isn't that good enough? We were happy. Why can't you be happy, too?"

"Mom, have you taken a good look at me lately? Maybe you don't know this, but I'm not going to make the cover of *People* magazine as this year's Sexiest Man Alive. My pimples have pimples. Girls only talk to me because they want to copy my homework. I don't play sports. My biceps are probably the smallest muscles in my body. I have never been on a date. The only females I have kissed are you and your sisters. Sex is something I will probably learn about in class but never actually get to experience. Geez, after all these years, why are you still wearing rose-colored glasses? Don't you get it yet? The only friend your son is able to make is some other reject. Is that what you call being happy? Would that be good enough for you if you were me?"

It was pretty apparent that Mom was at a loss for words. I kept going; I was on a roll now.

"You're in some kind of time warp. Happiness isn't writing in a diary and gossiping on the phone anymore. Let's play a little catch-up, shall we? Nowadays, kids are having sex before puberty. Nobody even brags about beer and cigarettes; scoring pain pills is what gets you into the action. So, can you blame me for trying? I've been a loser all of my life. At least give me credit for finding a way to make it to the inner circle. Believe me, I only wanted to turn some heads when I took the car and a few pills. I wanted to be cool, not dead."

Mom took a deep breath and exhaled slowly. I knew she was trying to think of the exact right thing to say.

"Honey, you're not that bad," she said. "We love you. You're special in your own way and your day will surely come. You just need time. Your father was on the scrawny side at your age and look how he filled out. And if girls need your homework, you should be flattered. There's a girl for you, too. A lot of pretty girls want a smart man to settle down with. Just be patient."

At least I was winning sympathy votes. I turned it up a notch to see how much more I could get.

"Mom, things are different now, like you wouldn't believe. We don't talk on the phone anymore. We text. My generation is moving fast and we're always looking for something new. We need to be stimulated. Take pills, for example. They're just like vitamins to us and they're everywhere. Everybody's doing it. I'm not going to take them all the time. But now and then, I can't see the harm. I promise you I will only take the ones that give me energy. They wear off in a few hours and everything's back the way it was. You have to trust me on this."

Mom pulled the strap of her purse over her shoulder.

"I don't know. That sounds so innocent and too good to be true. I still think that you kids are doing something wrong here so I, for one, have to say no. I forbid it. No more pills for you. That's my final word." Again, my mother turned to my father for support.

"I agree with your mother, Son. These pills seem like a bad choice to me. I hear nothing but trouble when pills are involved. Look at your own situation: this time you got terribly hurt. I don't know if it was the pills or bad luck with that truck. Just don't take any more and you'll be fine. As for the rest of it, some people just start out slow and then turn out great. I suppose I was like that. And look at me now. I have a good job, your mom, you, and your brother. What more could a man want?"

I wasn't done yet, but I'd have to think about a better way to win this argument. Their idea of adventure was a day at Sea World watching Shamu splash the people who sat too close to the water's edge.

"Look guys, all this debating has worn me out and I am really feeling some pain here. Why don't you go home and let me rest a bit? I'm sure I'll see things your way soon enough. I sure hope it's not too late for you to be open-minded. The world's a fast-moving place and you'd better learn to keep up. That's all I'm doing."

Mom kissed my forehead. Dad gave me a thumbs up. As they walked out hand in hand, I raised my bag of supercharged M&M's in a salute.

This is all I really need to get by, was my thought as I smiled at them.

I was ready to break open the baggie and select a tasty treat. I wasn't sure what was in there. I was hoping for an assortment of Oxys, Roxys and Zannys. I poured the M&M's into my empty plastic water pitcher; making enough noise for my nurse to look up from her writing.

I apologized, then shook the pitcher to make the candy rattle. She looked more annoyed than suspicious. She rose from her chair and walked toward me.

"They're my favorite. I'll be back for a handout, but I need a potty break first." She smiled and took off.

Finally, I had some peace and quiet and a chance for a pill inventory. I pulled out the baggie and rotated it, inspecting it from all angles. I was right. There were 80s, Blues and Zanny bars, at least five of each.

I took a look around for my nurse. She was nowhere in sight. I took out an 80 and swallowed it with a gulp of water and a few M&M's. When I looked up, my nurse was heading straight for me with a look of conviction on her face. I shoved the baggie under the sheets and in between my legs. I moved too fast and left the bag open. The pills escaped and drifted into all the wrong places.

In a moment, she was standing next to me, her posture dominating and intimidating, and she was tapping her foot.

"It's time for you to share some of that good stuff with me. You'll regret it if you don't. So give it up."

I felt a rush of anxiety and a trickle of sweat forming on my forehead, and unfortunately in that unmentionable place. I was nailed.

I put my hand under the sheet and reached for the contraband. She leaned over to whisper in my ear, which seemed pretty strange.

"Give me some right now. I'm addicted, too."

I felt like a mouse in a trap. I bet she hadn't gone to the bathroom at all. She had been keeping a long distance eyeball on me, following Dr. Stone's warning of, "Don't trust this kid. He's going to try something."

Of course she wanted her cut. I should have figured that nurses are victims of addiction. They're around pills and injections all day. The temptation to steal some old geezer's pain medication must be unbearable, especially when the guy's too demented to know he didn't get it. Oh, well. I decided to give her a few and get her off my case. If she were smart, she'd keep her mouth shut.

She tapped her foot again and said, "Well . . . I'm waiting."

I started probing for pills. Her eyes followed my hands to my crotch, and she berated me.

"Stop that. If you have to scratch yourself, wait until I'm gone. Now, are you going to hand over some M&M's or do I help myself? Don't keep a chocoholic waiting too long. I can get pretty irritable, worse than PMS, if you know what I mean."

She was smiling now. False alarm. I pulled my hand out into the open and wiped the sweat off my brow.

"Ah, sure, take all you want. I can get plenty more." I lifted the pitcher full of candy and gladly turned it over to her.

She dug in and came up with a fistful, the excess dropping back into the pitcher. "Thanks. I knew you would be reasonable."

She flashed a smile and started plunking four or five in her mouth at a time.

"Okay," she said, "You can go back to whatever you were doing. I've got my fix."

I let out a huge sigh of relief when she left the room. Then I went about rounding up the rest of the pills and corralling them back into the bag. It took some digging. The Oxy I took was finally helping to release the death grip that was strangling my nervous system. The sweat had stopped and was replaced by just a smidgen of cozy, warm comfort. Roxys were faster. It had to be coating on the pill or maybe it was meant to be slow, like a twelve-hour kind of deal. Roxy fast... Oxy slow...until you suck them through your nose. I had a touch of humor again, finally. Next, I made sure to seal the baggie and lock in the contents. I decided to keep it between my legs; that's the last place anyone would look.

CHAPTER 20

Jeffrey

The swallowed Oxy didn't energize me. Quite the opposite; I felt like I was drifting aimlessly down the river, floating on a raft. My eyes were closed and everything was quiet and serene. I didn't have a care in the world . . . until I heard what sounded like a hollow gourd filled with seeds being shaken near my head. And then his voice brought me back to full alert.

"Hey, Man, you got something else to eat around here?"

It was Jeffrey, my only friend, diving into the M&M's and annoying me with that clattering sound. He was my age, but with half the mental equipment and a bottomless stomach; he was perpetually eating and talking. He had already devoured a fistful of the M&M's and was heading for the box of chocolates. I really wanted to be left alone to enjoy the Oxy. But I was awake and needed to tell Jeffrey to go easy on the candy. I needed it to bribe the nurses.

He loaded three chocolates into his mouth in rapid succession, then closed the lid on the box.

"Look at you, being all high-tech robotic. What's all that metal stuff on your leg for? Does it hurt? Can I touch it?"

Jeffrey was firing questions at me and, at the same time, attempting to touch the pins coming out of my leg. I deflected his hand away from the apparatus with a slap.

"Get away from that, will you? My leg is busted and those pins are drilled right through the bone. And don't touch my back brace. My spine is broken." I decided I'd have a little fun and gross him out with a detailed description of all my injuries and operations. When I finished, Jeffrey just blinked in disbelief.

"All you need is a couple of bolts in your neck and we can hook you up for a jump-start." Jeffrey threw a fake punch at my arm.

"Okay, wise guy. Enough of the Frankenstein crap. This is no joke."

I pressed the head-up button on the bed control so I could get more comfortable and talk to Jeffrey.

"Buddy, come on, Man, tell me what really happened. I heard something about a drug bust in the mall parking lot. Then you stole a car and wham, you bashed a tanker truck. They're calling you Captain Crunch."

He laughed and took a few bunny hops. He was always hyper and in constant motion.

"I saw what was left of your car on the news. It was crumpled, Man. You shoulda died. You were lucky, Bro. Enough of that, what about the drugs? Were you dealing? Why didn't you tell me? Did you get busted?"

If there had been reins attached to Jeffrey's mouth, I would have pulled back hard and shut him up, especially now that I wasn't high.

"Give me a chance to talk, and I'll tell you."

"Okay, OKAY," he said. "Go ahead, talk. Don't let me stop you. I'm ready." Jeffrey stopped talking, but was looking around the room for something else to touch.

"First, I am not a drug dealer. Second, I did not steal the car. Sidney let me take it for a while. She was just here and we're cool again. So cool that she left me a nice get-well gift. A lot better than those chocolates."

"Is this the same Sidney who's popular at school? She's got pills, you know."

"The very same Sidney," I said.

"She is a knockout. They call her Foxy Roxy. You know why? It's because she knows how to tease and how to please. She's an absolute babe. She came here to see you? Man, what have you got that she wants? She hates guys like us."

"Not any more. I'm in. That's what I'm trying to tell you," I said.

"You are the killer dude, Man. What did she bring? I gotta see it. Show me."

Jeffrey was trying to dance a little hip-hop. He was messing it up, but he made me laugh. I never laugh.

I took the baggie of pills out of its hiding place and held it up for him to see. "Here it is."

Jeff jumped back and put his hands up to cover his eyes.

"Tell me I didn't see where you were hiding those."

"They're in a bag, dummy. I had to put these in the safest place I could think of."

"I could've found some place better."

"You can't find yourself half the time."

"Funny. Now tell me what you got and what you're gonna gimme."

I dangled the baggie of pills and told him not to move. He was blocking the nurse's view. "Feast your eyes on these babies."

"Wow!" His eyes lit up. "What do they do? Get you high? Make you wild with the babes? Do you have Viagra in there? Give me one."

Jeffrey has always been fast with the questions but I could never be sure about his intellect. I wondered if it drifted in and out of his brain, like the tide.

"Jeff, I don't have Viagra. Try one of these. It'll blast your head wide open," I offered, making sure the coast was clear. I pulled out a Blue and broke it in half.

"Here, swallow this and give it a few minutes," I urged, "And I'll join you."

Jeff looked a little nervous after he popped the pill into his mouth. I swallowed a whole Blue.

Jeff looked instantly panicked. "Should I sit down? What's going to happen? Can I drive after this? I don't feel anything yet. Should it take this long?"

I began to wonder if I had picked the right "loser" to give it to. "Just wait a minute. Trust me; it's better than anything you've ever done or wished you did."

Soon enough our laughter filled the room. We both looked at the nurse; she smiled, but gave us the sign to keep it down. Jeff sprang up and started bouncing energetically on his feet.

"Man, I want to do something, like push-ups or jumping jacks. Do you think that nurse would mind?"

There was no way to turn Jeffrey off. He was a motor-man. "Don't do anything, you fool. The nurse is gonna come in here and know something's up. Can't you just keep it down and enjoy this?"

He stood up and instantly said, "Give me the other half. This is fantastic."

I said, "No, you're already too hyper. What did I tell you? It's better than being invisible in the girls' locker room."

Jeffrey giggled. "Yeah, that would be cool. Come on, let me have some more."

I put the baggie under the sheets. .

"Don't hide 'em. I want one."

His hand was under the sheets before I could stop him. I grabbed it, but the back brace made it hard for me to hold on tight. He jerked away holding the baggie and uncovered me at the same time.

We both froze as we heard her speak. She was standing in the doorway. It was Sidney. She was back.

"Do you boys need a little privacy? I can draw the curtains and put out the *Do Not Disturb* sign."

She walked right over and snatched the baggie of pills away from us. We couldn't keep our eyes off her. She was so cute and sexy. Jeff and I were gawking so much that at first, I didn't realize I was exposed. I blushed and yanked the sheets up.

"Now I know what all the fuss is about," Sidney continued. "I better hold on to these for safekeeping. You two don't seem to be grown-up enough to handle something of this value." She tossed the baggie inside her jacket and zipped it up.

I did my best to regain some composure. "Jeff, this is Sidney, the girl I was telling you about. I wrecked her car under the truck."

"We're not gay, you know," Jeff acknowledged the introduction. "Buddy was hiding the pills. I wanted another one. Those things are awesome. Are you going to have one? Which ones do you like? Which one should I try next?"

Sidney gave me a look that said he'd better shut up or she was leaving. I pointed to Jeff's mouth and warned, "Just zip it, will you, or you won't get another pill . . . ever."

"Okay, okay, I'm zipping. So, you're Sidney. I've heard a lot about you. All good, of course. It was really nice of you to bring Buddy all these pills. Can we have them back? The pills I mean. We really love these pills. Pills, pills, pills."

The Roxy had Jeffrey repeating himself. I was getting nervous that my nurse would know for sure what we were up to and cause trouble. At least I had it under control. I was a bit jacked up but it was manageable.

"I had a funny feeling you couldn't wait to hand these out," Sidney said to me, ignoring Jeff completely. "That's *my* job, remember? I'm in business for myself. We aren't partners. You, Buddy-boy, need to be on a tighter leash."

Just then, the nurse stepped in to see what was going on. I was sure she would report everyone and everything she saw to Dr. Stone.

"I know you think you're entitled to have fun with your friends, but I think you should cut this visit short. You've had quite a few serious injuries and you need your rest. My shift is over and I have to give a report. I'll see you tomorrow before you go to the orthopedic floor. Remember, you two, only five more minutes."

As soon as she left, I asked Sidney, "Are you going to give the pills back to me? I promise I'll take good care of them. I've only had time for a few. What do you say?"

She opened her jacket to look inside at the baggie and said, "This time I'm going to leave you just one Blue. That way you'll be looking forward to my next visit—tomorrow. Don't forget, I make a living off these babies. I name the price and you'll pay.

"Tell you what I'll do. If you can promise me the cash, I'll front you the 80s for fifty apiece. But because you wrecked my dream car you get one week to pay. If you're late, I don't care if you're back on life support: I'll call my friends to make a collection. A delicate girl like me needs a little muscle to protect her interests. And they aren't as playful as I am. So, think about how many you can afford and maybe I'll throw in a kit to sweeten the deal, no charge."

I was kicking myself for screwing up. An hour ago they were free and now they're outrageous.

"I'll take the 80s if you bring a kit, otherwise I'll do the Blues. I can't believe what I have to pay, but I'll do it. They're worth every penny I can get my hands on."

I'm pretty sure my pimply face gave away my doubts about how I was going to come up with any cash if I was still in the hospital. I had to heal with lightning speed and get home to that cookie jar.

"I think you'd better be sure you can get your hands on everything you'll owe me or don't do the deal."

She pulled out two Blues.

"This is all good for business. One for each of you. What's your name again?" she asked Jeffrey.

Jeffrey was smitten with Sidney. That's probably the only reason he could have stood still staring at her until she snapped her fingers in front of his eyes, then winked at him. It was the same wink she'd hooked me with.

"I'm Jeffrey and you're the greatest, just like these pills. I have a job you know and enough money for ten of those pills and whatever else you got. When does this stuff wear off? Geez, I could talk all day. Did I tell you I have money? Lots of it. This is so cool. Will I ever shut up?"

Jeffrey was too far away for me to punch, so I made a slashing motion across my throat and snarled, "Will you just cut it?"

He paused, but continued to move about the room with a nervous energy. I was sure that Jeffrey was a major liability with Sidney.

Wrong. She put her hand on Jeff's shoulder and began to massage him. He shuddered from the chills she gave him. She put her seductive mouth up to his ear.

"Sugar, you get this one for free and a whole lot more just like it tomorrow. Let's meet after school at the football field. Bring all the money your big hands can carry for a deal of a lifetime."

Jeffrey's lower jaw dropped open, and he was motionless again. "God," he whispered, "you smell good. So tomorrow I bring . . ."

Sidney plopped a finger over his lips and the words halted in his mouth.

"Honey, there's big ears right outside that door in a nursing uniform."

She handed each of us a pill and said good-bye and her hips made an unforgettable exit. We kept staring in the direction she'd departed, long after she was out of sight.

CHAPTER 21

The Rush

We finally stopped staring after Sidney, and looked at each other.

"She is really something," Jeffrey began. "She was almost making out with my ear. I think she likes me. I know I like her. She's really likable."

I felt betrayed. Sidney told me the price, but she didn't do the deal or front me pills. She gave us each one and took off. She was going after Jeff right in front of me? She had to know that would drive me crazy. No kid in his right mind would turn her down. That hurt. Jeff had money and now he had Sidney. I needed Mom's cookie jar to get her back.

Jeff put his pill in his mouth and washed it down with a swig from a soda he'd brought with him. I wondered if he took enough to make him sick. I was jealous enough to hope so. I wasn't going to warn him.

"Here we go again, Buddy," he sang out. "Wanna join me?"

"I will, but I'm going to do something special with mine. First, give me a dollar bill and your school ID, then watch me carefully and don't say a word."

I showed him how to chop up and crush the Blue. I used the back of a greeting card. It wasn't as good as a plate with its raised edges but it was better that my tray table. I had to move fast, because the new nurse was due to pop in and check on me very soon.

"Keep yourself between me and the door and check this out." I rolled the bill and snorted the powder, spot on. Jeff was mesmerized watching me rub my nose and itching face after coughing, as I showed off with a smile.

"Now, that's how it's done if you want to get high really fast."

Jeffrey grabbed the rolled up dollar bill. "That looked nasty. What are you doing that for? Is it fun?"

"It makes you warm and toasty before the energy kicks in. My brain's picking up speed every second. Your Blue is just dissolving. But that half a pill I gave you is already running your mouth off."

Jeffrey couldn't keep his eyes from roaming the room. I wasn't sure how much attention he was paying. "Is that what the deal is? I've got instant motor mouth. It's going and going and going. I want to keep saying 'motor mouth' over and over again. What's with that? I can't stay here much longer. I want to be outside and doing something with all this energy."

I had forgotten how gullible and impulsive Jeffrey could be. Now I wished I hadn't snorted the pill in front of him. I wouldn't put it past him to tell the nurse what we had just done. I needed to get him out of there.

It was too late for that. The nurse came into the room. "Hello, Boys. How's it going?"

Jeff started talking up a storm. I expected him to incriminate himself any minute—and me too. "We're having a great time. Want to join us?"

Before I could stop Jeffrey or make excuses for his behavior, he grabbed the nurse by the hand. "I learned this on *Dancing with the Stars.*"

He managed to get her to twirl around a couple of times. She was instantly caught up in his charming lunacy. I was too nervous to enjoy any of it.

"Okay, Killer," she laughed breathlessly when she broke away. "I can see you've got all the moves, but it's time for you to go and I have to get back to work." She winked at me as if we knew something Jeffrey didn't and she was understanding and sympathetic.

"Should I take dance lessons? What a great idea. I love that mirror-ball trophy. I can name all the winners for the past ten seasons." Jeff was too excited to slow down. He kept rambling about dancing and the nurse took him by the arm and escorted him out of the room.

"Visiting hours are over, Jeffrey. Say good-bye to Buddy and let's have you head for home."

Jeffrey just continued jabbering away as he was escorted down the hall. "Dancing is great exercise. It's aerobic. Who was the best dancer of all time? I bet it was Fred Astaire. No, it was Gene Kelly. No, it was Michael Jackson. I can moon walk. Wanna see?"

I heard his voice until the elevator door closed, then I allowed myself to laugh. He really was funny. Now that he was gone, I was relieved that nobody was in trouble. The nurse returned to my room, shaking her head.

"That guy is too much. He's so hyper. I bet he's got ADD."

"You're probably right," I said. "Actually, I'm sure you're right. Of course you're right. It's got to be ADD."

I chuckled and then clenched my jaw shut to keep any more words from carelessly spewing out. *She must be on to me.*

"It's good to see you laughing, Buddy. I'm sorry I had to break up the party but Jeffery acted like he was just about to get out of hand."

"That's ok," I admitted. "I don't think I could have taken any more of him."

The tension was mounting in my voice as I desperately tried to hold still.

"Well, I hope a good laugh means you're putting this terrible accident behind you. It's time for a speedy recovery."

"You're right about that," I said. Energy was surging wildly through my body and I wanted to leap out of bed and move around.

She smiled kindly, looking oblivious to what was obvious to me.

"Just relax and enjoy the moment. Your friend was very entertaining. But now it's back to work for me. I have to help out in another room, so I'll check on you later."

She went into the room next to mine. I was relieved that she stepped away because I was keyed up and supercharged. I wanted to keep laughing and go wild and crazy, but I had to settle for scratching every itch I could reach. After that, I started drumming my fingers on the tray table, listening to a tune in my head. I closed my eyes and tried to imagine performing on stage to thousands of screaming fans. What a rush.

Then I heard fingers snapping in front of my face and opened my eyes.

"Hello," the nurse said. "Is anybody home? Oh, there you are. That was weird. What happened to you?"

I had no idea how long the nurse was gone. I must have looked like I was in a trance. In reality, I was having the time of my life. The Blue had put me into a mental playground and I couldn't have been more alive. I blinked a few times and inhaled deeply.

"I was just pounding out some rhythm in my head. I use my fingers like a percussion instrument. Pounding…percussion…pounding…percussion."

She grabbed both of my hands. "I get it. I get it. Give it a rest."

I put my hands in my lap and laced my fingers together. I started wiggling my toes instead. It was insane. The energy was dancing all over my body and I was supposed to sit still and chill. I couldn't.

She gave me a strange look. It had to be obvious that I was on something. I had to convince her that I did quirky things to amuse myself.

"Are you all right?" She looked at me carefully. "I don't know what to make of you. A few minutes ago you were laughing and now you look like you just had a double espresso. I hope you haven't been taking pills. You could be arrested right here in this hospital."

There was no way she was getting the truth out of me. "My body is just starting to liven up, that's all. I've been stuck in this bed and I really want to get moving. Can you blame me?"

She put both hands on her hips and looked as though she were trying to detect a lie. I was using every ounce of self-control to speak intelligently while my arms and legs wanted to squirm around, something fierce.

"Seriously, I wouldn't use pills and risk getting arrested or thrown out of here." The nurse took a longer look at me and cradled her chin in her hand.

"I don't know what's getting into me these days. I'm almost ready to believe that all teenagers are on something until proven otherwise. I thought you might be high."

I was. Now I feel like a bad case of the heebie jebbies. I wondered if being a loser made all the fun vanish that much faster and replaced it with too many words in my head with no place to go.

"You know," I said, and immediately knew what I was about to do, insert my foot tightly into a small opening. "I've taken drugs and I don't regret it either. Oxys and Blues, they can really do some good things for the right person at the right time. Look at me, for instance. I've hated Mother Nature for playing a cruel joke on my face. I didn't know how to get even until pills took all my shame away. Then I had my power back; I became somebody. I think that was a good enough reason to take them. Don't you?"

I couldn't believe I said all of that without turning my words into a tossed salad.

The nurse stepped closer, and then pointed her arm in the direction of the adjacent room. Her voice sounded irritated as much as it was disappointed. "I'll give you credit for being honest. Most kids would just lie through their teeth about the lesson they learned from getting caught with drugs. I might even let you score some sympathy points about your looks. But I don't care how good it feels to get high. It's not natural and you're making a big careless mistake."

I was still restless and wasn't in a mood for the lecture I knew was coming. But I was stuck there and had to listen.

"The kid in the next room is probably not going to make it. He won't wake up. He shot a load of heroin, passed out, and choked on his vomit. They found him unconscious with the needle in his arm. That was not a first for him. He'd even met Dr. Stone the last time he was here, but he wouldn't listen and didn't care about anything but getting high and getting by. When you go to the orthopedic floor tomorrow, take a good look at that kid as you pass by his room. The drugs have stolen every ounce of life from him. If he doesn't wake up tomorrow, he'll be unplugged."

I acted like I was paying attention. I didn't want to get into a debate with the nurse about the merits of properly-used drugs for people like me. I wanted to convince the nurse that I was sincerely heeding her warning about the dangers of drugs. By the time she walked out of the room, I wanted her to be satisfied that she had turned me away from the dark side. But I knew better. Drugs have their place in the world. Either you learn how to make them work for you or don't get in the cockpit and attempt to fly.

I thought about the kid in the room next to mine, who'd stuck a needle in his arm. He'd probably gotten greedy and injected too much. I made that mistake by taking too many pills and it busted me up good, with ten days on a machine that kept me alive.

But I was different than him. Even though I was kept in a medically-induced coma for safety purposes, I came to life as soon as the pump was turned off. The kid next door was ready for the angels to make a pick-up and take him to a place where the end of his life is the beginning of nothing. I admit, I was in too much of a hurry to have fun and I took a few too many pills. I was a little too inexperienced for my own good. Now I was smarter and wouldn't make that mistake again. I also had a superior motive: to beat Mother Nature at her own game. I was going to remove ugly from my existence. I was going to take my share of all the good things I deserved. The music of my life was still playing, and Oxys and Blues were going to help me enjoy it. It was over for that brain-dead kid in the next room, but I was just beginning.

CHAPTER 22

My Son Is Gone, but You Get to Go Home

I turned on the TV and kept cycling through the channels. I could only watch a few seconds of this and that, because I kept thinking about the kid next door. *Why did she have to spoil my mood? Two perfectly good Blues gone to waste because she had to tell me about a dying kid.*

I imagined his body being inflated and deflated by a cold heartless machine. He was already dead, for all practical purposes. I became tired trying to think of what lesson I was supposed to learn from this and soon enough I was asleep.

Morning arrived with another parade of doctors making rounds before breakfast and, after I'd finished eating, the nurse returned and told me it was time for my trip to the orthopedic floor. My bed was on wheels and she pushed it out into the hallway.

"I'll be right back," she announced. "I have to use the ladies' room."

As I lay there in the hall, I looked to my left and into the room of the brain-dead kid next door. Around his bed were two adults, probably his mom and dad, who looked to be in their forties. A pretty girl was holding his hand, stroking his hair and crying. I figured she was his girlfriend by the way she was carrying on. A guy I took to be his older brother stood next to her. A doctor stood next to the ventilator that mechanically inflated his lungs with air. I watched the doctor flip an "On" and "Off" switch. There really was no plug to be pulled. The lights on the machine blinked a few times and went dark. The humming noise that signaled air was being pumped into the boy's lungs disappeared. A nurse disconnected the kid's breathing tube from the machine. He was flying solo now. I wondered if he would live or die.

The parents held each other tight and stared at their son. The rise and fall of his chest came to a halt and remained as motionless as if he were already in a casket. His parents each took turns bending over close to his face to say something before kissing him good-bye on the forehead. His brother stood back looking petrified and his girlfriend began to wail.

"No, please, don't let him go. Turn the machine back on. I can't let him go. Please."

She reached for the machine, but the doctor signaled the parents to escort her out of the room. He extended his condolences to the family and shook his head in disappointment and disbelief. *Good acting*, I thought. *I bet he doesn't want to waste any more time there, but he needs to leave the impression that he wishes he could spend the day grieving their loss with them.* As the dead boy's sobbing family exited, they had to maneuver around my bed, which was directly in front of the door. *Where is the nurse?* I wondered. Then it dawned on me: she wasn't on any bathroom break. She'd set me up to see this horror show. The boy's parents stood there and stared at me, surveying my back brace and the multiple pins that skewered my leg.

I must have looked like a poster boy for reckless driving under the influence; the caption would read: *Do you know where your son is and what he's doing? He's probably messed up on drugs and driving your car at breakneck speed.*

I tried to look away without making eye contact, but the mother reached over and grabbed my hand. Her tears dripped onto my arm. Her husband tried to pull her back, but she shoved him away.

"I want to say something to this young man," she said angrily. "I know what happened to you. Your mother told me. She's been keeping me company for a week. We've talked about you and my son, Taylor. You had a lot in common. He started out like you, just wanting to have fun. After a while, we knew he was taking pills, but we didn't do much to stop him. We just warned him that it was going to lead to trouble. He said it was under control and not to worry, that he would be careful." She pointed at his corpse and said, "Do you call that careful?"

She drilled into my eyes with an intimidating look. I refused to blink. I didn't want to be disrespectful but I wasn't going to be a pushover either, just because her son had kicked the bucket. I wanted to tell her to get off my case.

She raised her voice. "I know what happened to you and how bad you got hurt. But you will get to go home with your family. My son is gone. That's not him in there. That's just an empty shell he left behind for me to look at and cry over. Well, I'm done crying. I'm really mad at him for doing this. Now I have to go home and walk by his room every day and see it empty. I have to look at his picture and see him at the same age as I grow old. I have to watch everyone in the family get married, but not him. I have to wonder what would have been if it hadn't been for those damn pills."

Her husband came over and looked at me, his eyes filled with sadness. I imagined he was thinking, *you're next, Pal, if you don't get some help.*

He turned to his wife. "Honey, I think that's enough. Let's go."

She shot an icy glare at him; she wasn't done. I knew I was in store for some lecturing. I figured she wanted to plunge a dagger into the heart of my addiction and extinguish it, since she hadn't been able to save her son.

We held each other's gaze. I was not going to flinch.

"My son didn't care," she continued. "Those pills were his friends. Pretty soon, he couldn't do anything without one. He called them his buddies, always there to give him a lift and brighten his day, he would say. Well, he was wrong. Those pills were just the beginning of a sickness that corrupted him. He was stealing our money and selling our valuables." Her voice seemed to get louder with each sentence.

"And then one day, I walked in on him snorting heroin. He was smug and arrogant without a care in the world. I was heartbroken. He said, 'Chill mom, at least I'm not shooting up. If you ever catch me sticking a needle in my arm, that will be the day that I die.' Was he ever right."

She thrust her arm in the air and shook her fist as though Taylor was still alive to hear her. She glared at me with the angriest look I have ever seen.

"So, is that what you want? Take a good look at him. He didn't just die a few minutes ago when we turned that machine off. He killed himself the very first time he got high on those pills and he didn't even know it. But now *you* know it. Don't let his death be in vain. Make it mean something. He died, but you don't have to," she pleaded.

My nurse finally began pushing my bed down the hall, but that woman's eyes stayed riveted on my face. *So what*, I thought. She wasn't going to take me down and neither were 80s, Blues or Zannys. I wasn't going to be stupid enough to snort heroin or shoot any kind of dope. I'd found the way to turn chemistry into a beautiful thing. Her son was obviously reckless and didn't learn how to pace himself and save some for another day. He bought the one-way ticket to the undertaker. But pills were my liberators, not my captors. They harnessed the energy of the sun and turned it into happiness. I wasn't going to give them up. Taylor could rot in hell or rest in peace—it didn't matter to me. My life wasn't over yet.

CHAPTER 23

Get Me Out of Here

I arrived on the orthopedic floor without anyone taking notice. I liked that.

The ICU nurse said, "This is as far as I go. Take care of yourself, Buddy." She was gone before I could decide if I even wanted to say thank you.

I looked around and watched a lot of busy hospital personnel ignoring me as I lay in my bed in front of the nursing station. I saw my medical records sitting on the counter. They were in two separate three-ring binders, each about two inches thick. *How much could they write about one person?* I wondered.

Suddenly, I was accelerating down the hall. I wondered who was responsible for pushing me so fast. I was maneuvered around one corner after another until I arrived at my room.

I was shocked when I saw who was pushing me. She was built like a Dodge Ram truck, her arms decorated with tattoos of snakes and Chinese symbols. She was enormous, more than six feet tall and heavily built. No wonder she could maneuver my bed so easily. Her muscles were probably developed in a state-of-the-art gym.

Her hair was bleached blond and pulled straight back, smooth and tight. Her uniform was a short-sleeve scrub top and drawstring pants. It was blinding white and operating-room clean. She appeared to be about thirty years old and spoke with a husky voice.

"Welcome to the orthopedic floor. Today you get your lazy, skinny body out of bed, and you walk." When she crossed her arms over her broad chest, they resembled well-fed, overgrown pythons.

"There are a few simple rules to follow here if you want to avoid trouble," she continued. "Number one: Do as you're told and don't whine. No crybabies allowed on my shift. Next: Don't annoy me with questions. Third: You don't get any pain medications, except Tylenol. Last: If I catch you sneaking drugs in here, I will personally break a few more bones in your body—big ones, too."

The last two rules were spelled out from very close range. I could feel pressure waves from each word. There was a fragrance coming from her body that reminded me of an untamed animal. As she leaned closer to slide the tray table over the bed, I noticed physical features about her face that were more masculine than feminine. Her jaw looked like it had been chiseled from a block of granite and was still rough around the edges. Her eyebrows were overgrown, obviously never plucked.

It was going to take a little ingenuity to figure out a way around her military manners. I had to discover if she had a fondness I could exploit, like ultimate cage fighting or power-lifting.

She plopped a pitcher of ice water on the table and tossed the TV controller onto the bed. "I'm calling the physical therapist to get things going here. Don't bother pressing the call button, because I'll be too busy to answer it."

As she walked away, I could feel the floor rumble from her footfalls. Judging by her physique, I figured she could probably bench press more than three hundred pounds.

I realized that my vacation in the ICU was over. This was going to be more like boot camp or doing hard time. What I had to face was unavoidable. I couldn't just walk out of here. I was going to have to either put up a fight or take the punishment. But now, all my experience as a social misfit was going to pay off. If I could take what my classmates dished out, I could deal with the muscle-bound nurse and the physical therapist on steroids.

Just then, as though on cue, the therapist stormed into the room, looked at his watch and started barking orders at me.

"All right, today's the big day. No wimping out on me. I'm going to sit you up like it's the most natural thing to do. Then you are going to stand and bear weight on the good leg and start moving with that walker. Got it?"

This time sitting up was easy. The therapist was in a hurry and hoisted me like a slab of meat until I was standing. The room tilted to the left before spinning counterclockwise. The therapist gave me a stern warning.

"Oh, no, you don't. You're staying up if I have to move your legs myself."

The lights got a little dimmer and my skin was clammy and cool. The therapist splashed ice water on my face and it worked. I was able to follow the command to grip the handlebars of the walker.

"Now, keep your weight off the left foot. Lift the walker and place it ahead of you. That's it. Now brace yourself and lift your right foot and step forward."

My first step was very wobbly, but I made it, which surprised me. The pain was consuming, making me feel weak, and I had to keep pausing to catch my breath. It seemed to take forever to get to the doorway.

"Okay, Sport, let's turn around and go back. You've earned a nice rest in that lounge chair over there. You'll be sore, though. Too bad. Suck it up. You're going down the hall on the next trip. Drink plenty of fluids and eat everything on your plate. You need to grow some muscles."

After what seemed like hours, I finally made it across the room to the chair. He held me under the armpits and lowered me down. The chair tilted back and my leg was automatically supported. I was glad that was over.

The therapist grabbed a clip board, wrote a note, checked his watch, and carried the walker toward the door.

"See you later, Champ. Go easy on the nurses."

I was stiff, weak, and wracked with pain. Thirty minutes later, two orderlies came in and lifted me back into bed. I was too exhausted for any small talk.

My lunch came and went, and I let it go without taking a bite. The pain had eased, but I was overcome by exhaustion and started to doze off.

The sound of a motor and the sensation that the head of my bed was being elevated made me open my eyes. There she was: the mountain of a woman was pressing the controller. "Wake up, Big Fella."

"Hey, wait a minute," I objected. "Give me a break, why don't you? I need to take it easy. I've got broken bones, you know."

She ignored my protests. "I suppose we should get properly introduced. My name is Brenda. I already know yours."

"Well, Brenda, I think you should leave me alone for a few hours."

"No can do. My job is to get you up and out of here. This afternoon, you get to show me how a man with hardware sticking out of his broken leg makes it down the hall and back without stopping."

"This is crazy. You're crazy. You can't do this to me. Get me a real nurse."

She ignored me again. I guess she'd heard all of this complaining before and was immune to it. She lifted me with ease and I was on my feet in seconds. I didn't get dizzy, but the pain was excruciating.

"That wasn't so bad now, was it?" Brenda asked, her voice more than a little patronizing.

I was infuriated and wanted to get her transferred off my case. That would do for starters, but getting some revenge would be much better. I wanted her to suffer, too.

She placed the walker in front of me and said, "You know how to use this thing, so let's get going."

I started moving—slowly. She growled at me.

"That's too slow. This will take all day at that pace. Pick it up, Buddy."

I tried, but the pain shot through me and ricocheted off everything that was broken.

"Oww, ouch! Ouch! This is brutal!" I said. "Can we take a break here before something happens that isn't supposed to? I already did this once today. What's the rush? I got insurance, you know."

I could feel Brenda's hand pressed on my lower back, pushing me faster than I could keep up. I lost my balance, stumbled, and put my weight on the broken leg. The pain seared through the bone like a hot poker.

"What are you stopping for? Can't take a little pain?" She smirked at me.

"I can take a lot more than you think. I was told not to put any weight on my bad leg, which I just did. Maybe something moved in there. You're pushing a little too hard, Sister."

We were thirty feet away from my room and all I wanted was to be back in bed. I could hear the air going in and out of her nostrils like she was a furious animal. She snarled at me.

"Hey, you're the one who got loaded up on dope and trashed your car. Whimpering won't do you any good now. I know for a fact that the pins in your leg are strong enough to drive a Mack truck over. Your doctor is too conservative. You can do twice as much. I suggest you just ignore the pain or this hike is going to get a lot longer."

I was stranded out in the hallway with no option except to keep moving. I dreamed of a morphine injection.

"If I keep walking, you better be right," I said.

She nudged me from behind. I took another step and built up some momentum. Her sarcastic comments were relentless.

"You're so scrawny, it's no wonder you can barely hold yourself up. Why anyone would let their body wither away into something so useless is beyond my comprehension. Do you even weigh a hundred pounds? Start working out with weights, why don't you?"

Brenda had me by the waist, just in case I lost my balance again. Her grip felt like a steel clamp around each kidney. She was coaxing me to keep up the pace she set. When I was three feet from my bed, I completely ran out of steam. I was fed up and I gave up. I let go of the walker. I didn't care anymore. She snatched me and I was suddenly airborne, my limp body dangling as she lowered me safely onto the bed. I was still mad, but I decided to remain silent. She won that round.

Brenda raised the bedrails as she told me, "I went easy on you today. You kids need to learn a thing or two about commitment and discipline. I read your chart and all about that party you had with Oxys, Roxys, and Zannys. God saves a lot of people who should know better but get hooked anyway. It's my job to take care of them when they arrive here in bits and pieces. Now that you're a guest at my party, you have to play by my rules. So get your rest while you can, because I don't take no for an answer. I'll have you skipping rope before you leave here."

The unbearable pain subsided after I'd rested in bed for a few minutes. I nestled my head in the middle of my pillow and expected to fall fast asleep. I figured I deserved it after walking one hundred feet. But I couldn't seem to nod off; instead, Brenda's formidable shape was in my thoughts.

Brenda was big; in fact, I don't think I had ever seen a woman so large. She had to be a genetic freak. No one would want to sculpt themselves into what she had become. She was not attractive. Her facial features were masculine. Compared to her accentuated girth and intimidating muscle, I was a dwarf. As she lowered me onto the bed, she'd been gentle and careful, and then agile as she'd walked out of the room. That baffled me. There was something fascinating and mysterious about her.

Sometime later, I was aroused by the enticing aroma of a cheeseburger and fries; my mom had arrived with my favorite foods.

"Honey, wake up. I brought you something yummy."

I hated being called Honey, as I'd told her a million times. At least she'd brought something I wanted. Mom reached into the bag, pulled out the burger, and unwrapped it. "You must be famished. I heard that you didn't eat lunch today." She salted my fries while she talked.

"You got that right," I said.

I dove into the burger; it was juicy, greasy, and perfect. The fries smelled better than anything on earth. In two minutes, I was licking my fingers and working on the chocolate shake.

Mom looked pleased as she watched me devour the food.

"How did your physical therapy go? I heard you walked out in the hall. Isn't that wonderful?"

I pointed at the door. "That nurse nearly crippled me. She belongs in the Marines or a Nazi concentration camp. She's not a nurse. She has no heart and probably no soul. I can't take anymore. It hurts too much. You have to get me out of here or get rid of her."

Mom cleaned up all the debris from my snack before she answered, and then she said exactly what I expected she'd say. "You're not leaving. These people have jobs to do. Their motto here is 'no pain, no gain.' You should accept that and do your best. Besides, I can't take care of you like this. You need professionals for that. You look pretty good right now. It couldn't have been that bad."

"Did you meet the nurse? Brenda? The one who blocks out the sun when she stands near the window? I think she flosses her teeth with a chainsaw. She made me walk until I collapsed."

My mom smiled and patted me on the hand like I was a good doggy. "I guess that's exactly what you needed. Exercise never hurt anybody. And she's not that bad. She's just well-developed and a bit rough around the edges, but I'm sure she's all nurse. On another subject, did you hear about Taylor, the boy who was next door to you in the ICU?"

"I heard he croaked. What of it?"

She looked surprised and very displeased with me. "What kind of attitude is that? Can't you show a little sympathy? He was just your age and started out with drugs exactly the way you did. Now his mother has to bury him and wonder how he made such a lethal mistake and why she didn't get him some help. I want you to get some help. What do you say about drug treatment? Dr. Stone can come back and talk it over with you. I couldn't bear it if you ended up dead."

If Brenda had walked in right then and told me it was time for a walk, I would have gladly obliged. Anything was better than listening to my mother drone on about drugs, addiction, and rehab.

"Mom, get off it, will you? How many times do I have to tell you that I'm not a drug addict? Those people are craving dope night and day. They walk around like zombies, popping pills and smoking weed, and they have no life. Addicts beg for drugs. It's pathetic. Take a good look at me: I'm not like that. I made a stupid mistake. When are you going to get that straight and shut it down? I'm not going to any rehab and I won't talk to Dr. Stone, so don't send him back. I don't even take pain meds here. I'm done with drugs, so don't worry. Now, do something to get me out of here."

She looked a little more sympathetic after my speech. "I guess time will tell. It's pretty hard to get into trouble in a place like this. But once you're back home, you are on probation. I'm going to be watching you like a hawk. I read on the Internet that kids who use drugs tell the most believable lies and then they'll break your heart over and over again, while the lies keep piling up. I don't want to go down that road with you. Just tell me the truth. I can help you—or at least I can find someone who will."

She touched my hair gently, but I pushed her hand away. She looked wounded by my rejection.

"Mom, getting over these injuries is going to be hard enough. I don't need you badgering me about whether I'm using pills. That kind of aggravation would probably drive me toward them. Do you want that? Because if you do, then keep it up and I can promise you that if I do use drugs again, it will be your fault. It's parents like you who make it so hard. All this pressure. It's no wonder kids use drugs so much, just to deal with these hassles. If that's the way you are going to treat me, I would rather you leave."

Her anger, which I knew had been simmering just below the surface, finally came to an irate boil. "You have no idea what I have sacrificed for you. For years, I devoted my life to being a good mother. I passed up a very different life so I could stay home and raise you. I'm not even going to go there, because you obviously don't think I did such a good job of it. Pardon me for caring so much about your well-being. I stood by your bed for the past two weeks, watching that machine keep you alive. I spoke to every nurse and every doctor around the clock, asking about your condition. I didn't sleep and didn't eat the whole time. I spoke to you while you were in a coma and kept begging you to wake up. You weren't supposed to make it, so I prayed harder than is humanly possible. Here you are, complaining about me hassling you because you took drugs, after you nearly killed yourself. You put me through a living hell. If this is the thanks I get, it's high time I did leave."

I reached out, but it was too late to stop her. She was out the door and I was frustrated. She should have been more sympathetic. She'd been using this tactic for years, trying to get me to fall in line. She wanted to call the shots and have me obey. It hasn't worked yet. But I knew she wouldn't be angry with me for long. She never was.

I felt sorry for myself; just look at the way I turned out. I was nothing to brag about. I lost most of life's battles. She didn't do a very good job preparing me to compete and now she wanted to abandon ship, so I let her go. My lifeboat was arriving soon with a shipment of pills and I could take a little of this and a little of that to break up the clouds and make a whole lot of misery and suffering instantly dissolve. Sidney was coming back. I could feel it in the air.

CHAPTER 24

Play Now, Pay Later

After Mom left, I felt massive physical, mental, and emotional pain. Thinking about how I had endured a lifetime of misery started to tick me off. There was still no end in sight. Pills were my only hope for surviving this madness. I would have given anything for an Oxy 80 or a couple of Blues. I wondered, *what* would *I give for a pill?* The list included any of my vital organs and a first-born child. That game continued for a short while until Jeffrey walked in looking triumphant.

"I got 'em. Take your pick. You want one?"

He was energized with all the action of a pinball bouncing off the bumpers. He had a mischievous glow in his eyes and seemed to crackle when he moved. Seeing him high brought an instant craving for a fix. He showed off a baggie with at least ten pills in it, and was talking loud enough to wake up someone in the morgue.

"Keep it down, will you? How many of these did you take?" I hissed at him.

"Not that many. I feel great."

"Give me those pills and go check outside. I don't trust the nurse around here. She's got eyes all over the place."

Jeff handed me the baggie. I saw 80s and Blues and straws and I could vividly remember everything I liked about snorting them, especially the taste and strangely enough, the globbed-up powder in the back of my throat.

"These are perfect," I said. "Who's out there?"

Jeff glided over to the door like he was on roller skates. He looked into the hall, checked both directions, and said, "Dinner's coming."

It was five o'clock and I was full of cheeseburger and fries.

Jeffrey intercepted the server at the door and took the tray of food, parking it on my table. "Let's have a look-see at your chow."

His nose was nearly touching the roast beef, mashed potatoes, and green beans as he sniffed in the aromas. "You gonna eat this?"

"I'm stuffed. Help yourself."

He quickly started carving meat and shoveling everything into his mouth. He kept talking, muffling and mumbling the words as he gobbled.

"Did you even taste any of that?" I asked.

Jeffrey ignored the question. "Hey, man, I met your nurse, getting off the elevator. Those arms of hers are huge. I bet she could hurt someone real bad. She stopped me, you know, just to check me out. The way she looked at me was creepy. She asked me where I was going in such a hurry. I told her I was coming to see you. She laughed real hard and said you'd be hurting and not to stay too long because she had plans for you tomorrow. Man, she looks like a lady wrestler. I bet she's taking steroids and shaves her face."

"She looks like a man; she has to be," I replied. We laughed and bumped our fists together. "All right, it's time to do one," I said. "I just wish I could get out of this bed without getting in trouble. Yesterday I had a ton of energy and nothing to do. It drove me a little crazy. When the nurse came in my room I couldn't stop shooting my mouth off."

"You, too," Jeff agreed. "Sidney, warned me about that. I kept saying the same thing over and over again. It's the weirdest thing. I'm not nearly so bad right now, or am I that bad? No, I don't think I'm that bad." Then he laughed like a child. "I am that bad, aren't I?"

I nodded. "You're bad."

"I don't care. It's cool."

"Just watch it when that nurse comes around, okay?" I instructed.

I took a Blue out of the bag, putting it on the greeting card. "Gimme your school ID. I'm going to snort one."

He handed me the plastic card.

"Be my lookout."

Jeff hustled to the door and I crushed and chopped up the Blue as fine as I could. I was in a hurry. When it was done, I leaned back, sighed deeply, and stretched out as much as I could with that brace tying me down.

"Ahh...That was nice." I tried to imagine swaying in a hammock on a balmy day, but Jeff started tapping on everything in the room like it belonged to a drum set.

"How many did you take today, Jeff? You're really jumpy."

He wasn't even listening to me; he was focused instead on butchering some street rap lyrics.

"Give it up," I advised. "You really suck at that."

That got his attention. "You know," he said. "Blues are awesome. I can't take a whole one yet. Sidney told me not to. I get too much energy. I already cleaned my room, and the garage. Maybe I'll do your garage. You think your folks will mind? Mine don't mind. Why should they mind? I could go on and on all day, nonstop."

"You're gonna get in trouble doing that. Nobody expects you to clean anything. So watch it."

I was already beginning to feel the first wave of warmth mix in with a slight jolt of energy. Now it was my turn to be careful.

"Oh, I almost forgot. I met Sidney after school. That's how I got these pills. She's got way more. She's going to keep fixing me up. I wanna try them all, don't you?"

We were like two happy kids talking about candy.

"She is so cool—and hot, too. I think she wants me. But what am I supposed to do if she tries something? Do you think she'll try something? What would she try? I haven't tried anything. I need lessons, Man. You have to help me. What if she wants me to get condoms?"

I was not in the mood to coach him on the finer points of romance or love-making. Besides the fact that I was pretty much clueless myself, I was trying to enjoy the Blue with as many brain cells as I could.

Jeffrey kept talking. "Sidney's teaching me how to take the pills. I'm taking half a pill at a time. I eat them. That's what she calls it, 'eating a pill.' Weird huh? And I snorted some. Did you know that a Blue has oxycodone in it and an 80 has oxycodone, only it's supposed to last for hours if you eat it, but you don't really get that high?"

"That's enough," I interrupted. "I figured all that out on my own. That's why I snorted the 80s on the football field. Everything's faster that way."

"You're right about that." Jeff interrupted me. "Sidney knows more about pills than a pharmacist. She told me to be careful and not do anything stupid like snorting up a whole bag of pills. Did you really do that? No wonder you nearly got yourself killed. What's it like being dead and brought back to life?"

"It's dark and cold, Bro. You do not want to go there." He wasn't really listening to me.

I didn't try to shut him up; I just let him ramble on. So far he wasn't out of control.

"Anyway," he said. "A few hours after taking a half a Blue, I can take another. But Sidney said to wait a week before I move up to a whole pill. I shouldn't rush it. Eventually, I'll be able to handle an 80. She wants to help me to do it right. She's great. To make a long story short, I only took two half-pills so far. Pretty good, heh? You want another one?"

I had drifted away into a fantasy, parked on a lawn chair, sipping iced tea and watching the neighbor's eighteen-year-old daughter butter up her body with tanning oil. Her skin was glistening and she saw me peeking. I could read her lips as she looked at my feasting eyes. *You naughty boy.*

Jeffrey chose that moment to speak right into my ear. I was yanked back to the hospital and the starchy, rough sheets.

"I said, 'Are you going to snort another one?'"

I had the baggie in my hand and already lost track of where I had wandered with my thoughts.

"Of course, I want another one," I answered. "These are like candy now. Set one up for me, Bro."

Jeff took out another Blue and I pulverized it. I leaned over the line of powder, ready to snort away, when a finger blocked the end of the straw.

"Ladies first."

Sidney pushed my head away and snorted the Blue with her own straw.

She barely coughed or cleared her throat. She rubbed her nose, looking cute and innocent, like a child. "I told you I'd be back. I brought you some Blues and 80s for your very own. Those are Jeffrey's in the bag. Yours aren't paid for yet. Are you ready to make a deal, Mister Big Shot?"

She wasn't even fazed by that pill. She must be made of the stuff.

I was still in a nice, agreeable mood. "Of course I want some pills. How many can I have on credit?"

Sidney removed a baggie of pills from her purse and shook out five Blues and five Oxy 80s and two Zannys. I imagined all the good moods and fun that were stored in each one, ready to be released, just for me. I felt like a happy leprechaun dancing around my pot of gold.

"I've tossed in two French fries," she said, holding up a Zanny. It was shaped like a tiny bar. I could see the resemblance to a French fry because it was yellow. "They're also called 'coffins' and 'school buses.' The whole package will cost you four hundred. You've got a week to pay up. Is it a deal?"

With those pills, there would be no more ugly thoughts. I could walk around school like a winner, finally fitting in. I had to have those pills at any price.

"Buddy, I'm waiting for your answer."

"It's a deal. I'll have the money. You just keep 'em coming."

She made a cooing sound like a dove. It was beautiful and sinister. She took another Blue out of the bag and handed it to Jeffrey.

"Here, Precious. Mama snorted one of yours and she wants to pay you back."

She handed me my own baggie and spoke with a throaty growl, like a lioness. "I'm going to give you another hose clamp for the 80s. You'll need some plastic for the Blues so I tossed in a customer savings card. If you want the Zanny to hit you in a hurry, chew one up before you swallow or leave it under your tongue. I'll teach you how to parachute some other time. And one last warning, there's enough kick in that bag to have you flying around this room like Harry Potter on a broom. You better not overdose again. If I hear that you needed a jump-start from the Code Blue team, I will personally let every dealer know that you are shut off forever. Got it?"

She tossed the bag, with pills and equipment, on my table.

I picked it up and moved it out of sight, just in case.

"What's this parachute thing you're going to teach me?"

Before answering, I watched her seductively coat her lips with ruby-red gloss. "You parachute a pill by crushing it up and swallowing it, wrapped in a piece of toilet paper."

I nodded my head trying to act cool. "I'm game, let's do it some time." I couldn't think fast enough to realize that a crushed pill in the stomach also gets absorbed faster and goes to work quicker, almost like snorting it. Later, I learned from my friends in recovery that parachuting releases the full impact of a drug as though it were in a rapidly dissolving capsule. For addicts in a hurry to get high, this is better than swallowing all the crumbles, bits and pieces after chewing, which I ended up doing after she left.

Sidney then turned and gave Jeffrey a commanding look. "Jeffrey, let's go. I think he wants to have some fun all by himself."

Jeffrey locked arms with her, and they strolled toward the door. He turned back and said, "I think this could be my night, Bro." He winked at me, and Sidney cuddled up to his shoulder.

Sidney had some parting words, too. "We've got plenty. You'd better make yours last. Bye-bye."

CHAPTER 25

Gone Again

It was peaceful and quiet again, just the way I liked it. I was back in the game with a supply of Blues and 80s and Zannys, and I wanted to get busy having my private party. The Blue I snorted earlier put me in a good mood and I wasn't even restless or fidgety. That meant I was ready for more. *I can handle it, just like Sidney,* I thought.

I took out a Blue before putting the baggie under the sheets. The plastic card was perfect, just like my school ID, for crushing. I had a line of powder ready to go on a greeting card, when a knock on the door changed my anticipation into panic. I had no choice: I blew the powder away, watching it disperse like pollen in the wind.

A nurse walked in. She looked like a new grad, with rosy cheeks and pristine skin. I hated her instantly, because she had ruined everything.

"Hello. May I come in?"

She was squeaky clean and way too polite. I'd ditched the baggie under my sheet. She didn't suspect a thing.

"I wanted to wait until your company left to introduce myself. My name is Wendy. Is there anything you need?"

Now I was fuming. One precious pill was gone, and I wanted her to leave so I could start over. I hoped she would spare me any boring small talk; I wasn't in the mood to hear about a dog or a fiancé.

"I spoke to Brenda at the end of her shift. I hope she wasn't too intense today. She's pretty imposing, and I'm afraid she likes to intimidate the young men."

"Is that what you call it?" I was getting riled up. "She's a beast."

Wendy approached me, remaining calm, as she checked the water level in my pitcher and looked me over, paying more attention to the back brace and fracture pins as a matter of routine.

"Everything looks okay. I'm sorry that you're so upset. Is there anything I can do?"

She seemed to be naturally sweet, and I had to admit she was very pleasing to the eye. I began to feel the tension leave me and I wasn't in such a hurry to get her out of the room.

"You could get Brenda off my case."

Wendy smiled. "That's not going to happen. You'll get used to her. You might get to like her before you leave. She's very protective."

I actually didn't mind Wendy's company. I considered prolonging this by keeping her in my room with small talk, but I decided it was time to get back to my pills.

I looked around the room for effect. "I think I have everything I need: TV, remote, and urinal. I'm set. I'm sure you've got more important things to do, so don't worry about checking on me. I'll probably turn in early after I watch a few shows."

She made a check mark on her clip board and gave me a dimpled smile.

"I'm glad we had this chat. You're a nice boy. I'll be back to peek in on you, but you'll probably be asleep. Gotta run, Sweetie." She hustled out the door, and I heard her enter the room next to mine.

I couldn't help thinking about the meaning of *nice boy*. She said it with the cutest look on her face. She wasn't that much older than me. I took a deep breath and almost got carried away with a foolhardy fantasy. *Don't go there* I thought. *Stick with the pills, they're safe and dependable. Women, on the other hand, are probably too much like Sidney and will always break your heart.*

I brought out the baggie and instantly thought about doing something new with a Zanny. Thanks to Sidney I could do more than swallow a bar so I chewed it up and kept it under my tongue. Before a minute had gone by, I couldn't stand the bitter taste so I swallowed it with water and then ate a few chocolates. *Now what?* I took out the baggie of pills. *Be careful,* I thought. So, I waited and waited and waited. *This is nonsense. I need another pill.*

I didn't know how much longer it was going to take. Five minutes already seemed like forever and I wanted to get high before the nurse came back. I decided not to waste my time on another Zanny and took out another Blue. Crushed up, it looked like such a small amount, so I grabbed an 80. *Now we're talking.*

I quickly shaped the hose clamp into a dome and started grating the 80 after I licked off the coating. The flakes toppled onto the greeting card and I pushed them around, mixing in the Blue, setting up two lines. One more time I thought, *Be careful.* I reassured myself that I had nothing to worry about. I hadn't felt much energy from the first Blue and the Zanny must have been a dud. Nothing was happening and one more Blue probably wouldn't really get me as high as I wanted. The combo with the 80 was bound to do the trick, so I let it fly and snorted all of it.

As I was rubbing my nose and feeling the drugs in my throat, I was so proud of myself. I had accomplished much: hooking up with a dealer, my own baggie of pills, a friend willing to give me his pills, and I was gaining experience by the day. I knew about bars, Blues, 80s, snorting, chewing and parachuting. On top of that I could handle bigger doses which meant I could be much happier. Life was finally good, just the way I wanted it to be. Now all I needed was to get the heck out of the hospital, back to my bedroom.

The warm glow of the drugs began to well up in me until I was completely filled with a total sense of relaxation. I closed my eyes, but at the same time I didn't want to miss any of the wonderful feeling. I had been trying so hard to find the perfect combination of every pill to make me happy. This was demolishing and driving out the last ounce of pain from my ugliness. I wondered if there would be anything left of me when it was over, but I didn't really care. I only wanted the loser in me to win. Was I finally there?

Then a bleak feeling came over me. I was confused. It seemed like I was at the bottom of a deep hole, alone with my darkest thoughts. Snorting pills was supposed to be fun, with the Superman cape included. Instead, I felt like my mind was a deserted ghost town, as though I were on the verge of extinction. *Did I need help?* I hadn't become a winner, after all. I wanted to leave this dark place, even if it meant returning to the way I was.

I don't know how much time passed, encased in pitch blackness, before luminous beings hovered around me. Some were talking, some were touching me, and some were undressing me. They looked like every rendition of angels I'd ever seen. Some had electric hands that were crackling with the force of life. Some were tugging and pulling on me, but in a loving way. Some were waving good-bye, and some were saying hello. I was sure I'd been delivered out of the deep hole directly into heaven. It was spectacular.

And then it was swept away as I heard a voice say, "We lost him."

I yelled out, "I'm right here. Come back!"

The voice spoke again. "I think he's gone, let's call it. What time is it?"

I yelled out, "It's *my* time. Don't give up on me."

And then I was sucked into a tunnel of wind. Blinding light crashed into me from all sides. The luminescent beings were back again, smiling with celebration and relief. A voice beckoned me to open my eyes and told me the coast was clear. The danger had passed. I was safe.

I was greeted by a throng of people. They were medical personnel, not angels. I was naked, I had an IV in my arm, and there was a tube coming out of my mouth. Someone pumped air through it with each squeeze of an inflated rubber bag. Someone else held two paddles with electrical wires attached. I heard beeping and saw lots of syringes and needles scattered around.

A woman had her face close to mine and was trying to get my attention. She spoke slowly, exaggerating the words as though I was hard of hearing. I couldn't talk and the tube in my throat was making me gag, so I grabbed it and pulled it out. Somebody tried to stop me, but I was faster.

My first breath was painful and was followed with a lot of wet coughing. I saw one of the women inject something into the IV and almost immediately I felt more alert. I looked around to get my bearings.

"What's going on here?" I demanded. "What did you do to me? Everything hurts."

A man in a scrub suit stood at the foot of my bed and glared at me for a moment.

"You're alive, Kid, but you shouldn't be. We already know what your favorites are," holding up the baggie with pills. "We assumed you couldn't resist taking too much of everything, so we reversed the overdose with some of our favorites." He held up two empty syringes. "You're going to live to breathe tomorrow's fresh air. But it wouldn't surprise me if you get bounced out of here."

I needed to blink a few times before I could focus and be certain it was him. Dr. Stone was back in my life. He stood there staring at me as he gave Wendy and another nurse the okay to put my brace back on. They logrolled me on my side to fasten the back portion with the front section. He continued to glare at me as they covered me with a gown and pulled up the sheet. I wanted to disappear underneath it. I didn't have any excuses.

Dr. Stone began again, "You could have died, my friend. Wendy found you just in time. You cut it mighty close, Buddy. I had a hunch you'd be trying to get your dealer to bring some pills in, and sure enough, there you were with pinpoint pupils, barely any air moving through your lungs, and a heart rate so slow that I could take a nap between beats. We caught you red-handed."

This man was beginning to annoy me again. "I'm not getting any of this," I protested weakly. "What are you talking about?"

Dr. Stone rolled his eyes in frustration. "Okay, I'll make this very simple. We found your pills and knew you snorted Oxycontin and Roxicodone and whatever you did with the Xanax. That turned your lights out. You stopped breathing and your heart stopped beating. That's called cardiac arrest. Get it?"

His voice had been growing louder and more intense with each sentence. "You were shaking hands with death and we had to work fast. We intubated you, jump-started your heart, and injected Narcan and Flumazenil. That snapped you awake and here we are: you, me and your addiction to drugs. Anything you'd like say?"

I stayed silent and I didn't know what I was going to say to my parents, let alone him.

"No. Then I don't see any medical reason to keep you here, now that you can walk. Expect the hospital administrator to show you out the door tomorrow morning. If you're glad to be alive, you might want to thank a few of the people who gave yours back after you threw it away. My work here is done."

He walked out of the room and I was alone again; everyone had left while Dr. Stone ranted. I noticed some powder left on the greeting card and the straw next to it. The rest of the pills were gone. How many had I taken? I vaguely remembered thinking about being a pathetic loser . . . again. Then it felt like I was being snuffed out and I hated it. Then I could have sworn I saw angels.

The pills were meant to do me a favor; instead, my ticket got punched on a one-way trip to Never Never Land. How could I have screwed up so royally— again? I had to get a lot smarter if I was going to keep the party on the sunny side of the street. I was done getting my butt kicked by pills that were supposed to be friendly and fun.

CHAPTER 26

I Didn't Know What I Didn't Know

I wasn't alone with my thoughts for long. Wendy returned to clean up the last remains of my rescue. The syringes, needles, endotracheal tube, and other bloody objects were packed into special medical-waste containers. The cart that contained the life-saving gear and medication was wheeled out of the room. Wendy removed the bag of fluid dripping into my arm and the tubing that was attached.

"I'm leaving the IV site in place, just in case." She took my blood pressure, measured my pulse and jotted the numbers down. She stared blankly at the page for several seconds longer, as though carefully contemplating her next words.

"We reversed the effects of the pills you took. We had to use the paddles to shock your heart. That's why you're sore. You should be fine, because your heart is young and strong. Now, I have to write my report, and you have a few important things to think about. I suggest you take this very seriously. I know I did."

I felt like I'd hurt her feelings somehow and wanted to say something appropriate. "Wendy, I want you to know that I . . ."

"Save it for later," she interrupted with a hint of disappointment. "You're not ready to explain this to me or yourself. Sleep on it and we'll talk in the morning. Maybe that will help you get ready for Dr. Stone and your parents. I'll be checking on you through the night."

As Wendy left the room, a senior nurse walked in to make her final inspection. She probably had to write a performance report on how this fiasco developed and how it turned out. Even though they saved my life, I was a major liability for the hospital, and liabilities were potential lawsuits.

I caught her attention. "Nurse, what's going to happen now?" I made sure my voice sounded worried and nervous.

She looked calm and unflustered, which I'm sure came with experience. Her tone was professional, and she sounded almost kind.

"Young man, Dr. Stone alerted us to expect something like this overdose. That's why Wendy, your nurse, checked on you so soon after your friends left. Dr. Stone was sure your girlfriend would bring in some drugs. The nurse found you unconscious and going into respiratory arrest. She saw the straw with a white powder residue on it and your bag of pills. You also had pinpoint pupils, which meant at least an opioid overdose. She called a rapid response code."

She poured a glass of water and handed it to me. There was something about her that put me at ease. "Dr. Stone was down the hall when the code was called," she continued. "He was the second responder, started the IV, and administered the Narcan. By then, the rest of the team was there and worked to bring you back. You owe them a big thank-you. No, you owe them your life."

She pulled up a chair and sat down. I could feel a lecture coming.

"You are out of danger and stable now, so there is nothing more to do. We searched the room and didn't find any other drugs. Your parents have been notified. Since you're okay, they won't be coming tonight. They will be here in the morning to meet with the doctors to discuss what to do with you."

Her expression softened as she stopped with the nursing routine, looking instead like a grandmother. "Do you mind telling me why you did this? I just find it so hard to believe you could do something so careless and dangerous."

I didn't want to answer any more questions, but she sat patiently waiting for my explanation. Until then, she had been my ally, but now she wanted to dig into my private and personal thoughts about being an ugly loser. I wasn't going to oblige her.

"I just slipped up," I answered. "I only wanted to get a little buzz going. I've been cooped up here for so long, I felt a little stir-crazy, you know. My friends came and they had pills. I didn't even ask for them. They were high and said 'Come on, try one, you'll like it.' It seemed okay for them, so I thought it would be okay for me. Just for fun, that's all. They left me a few pills, and I took a couple. Wow, were they strong. I must have passed out. It's good someone found me and acted fast. I am so grateful. I definitely will thank everyone who helped."

The nurse gave me a wise look. Her lie detector was turned on, and the needle was in the red zone. She moved her chair a little closer and huffed a bit.

"That's about what I expected you to say. Tomorrow, you won't be able to get away with a story like that, not if you want to stay here. If you level with them, at least they'll hear the truth, and you can work something out. I've been around the block a few times and I've seen nice boys like you wheeled down to the morgue in white bags. It's a tragedy. We do all we can, but you have to help, too. Good luck. Now try to get some sleep. We'll be checking on you tonight."

She finished writing on her clip board, removed her reading glasses, and walked away. I was left in silence. Her comment about nice boys in white bags actually rattled me just a bit. How close had I come? I knew the pills were strong, so why did I take so many, so fast? I felt uneasy. I was in trouble, and I wasn't sure what to do next. I had no clue how to pray, but that seemed like something I should be doing about now. But how does someone pray? Not knowing how to do it made me feel like an even bigger loser, if that was possible.

I thought about the nurse's choice of words; she'd described my actions as "careless and dangerous." I thought about what I'd done and I had to be honest with myself, at least. I'd snorted enough Oxys to send myself into a blackout and I couldn't remember enjoying any of it. Maybe I kept snorting the rest of the pills and pulled up outside of death's door. I thought I was just freeing myself from the bondage of being a loser.

I snorted those pills one after another. I hadn't given any thought to the possible consequences. There should have been a giant alarm going off telling me to stop. But I didn't see anything, I didn't hear anything; I just kept going, totally out of control. What do you call that?

It seemed important to give this more thought. After all, I really was smart enough to know how to snort just enough Oxy to have fun. I didn't need to go crazy and pass out. I don't know why, but my mind flipped this into a different perspective. Maybe snorting OxyContin wasn't very smart, no matter how careful I was.

This was probably the kind of advice Dr. Stone would give. I was baffled. There had to be a way to use Oxys. I was still living a miserable life and wanted to be happy. But how could I use pills without creating problems? It couldn't be that complicated.

I grew tired thinking about all of it and soon fell into a heavy sleep; it was deep and dreamless. At 6:00 AM, it was time to wake up for the new day, and Wendy came in to remove my IV before taking my blood pressure, temperature, and pulse.

"You slept well, especially after all the excitement. How are you feeling?"

I didn't mind the questions this time. Yesterday, I wanted an Oxy so bad that I ended a friendly conversation with her just to be alone with my pills. Today, I saw a young, attractive woman who was probably dedicating herself to helping the sick and suffering and saving those who were dying. She had been nice to me and I was surprised that I wanted to be in a kind and receptive mood.

"I'd like to say I feel fine, but I'm afraid I blew it last night. I did a real dumb thing with those pills."

Wendy stood at the side of my bed and touched my arm in a sympathetic gesture. She was very pretty, with blond hair that was neatly pinned up.

"I think I know why you did what you did."

"You do?" I liked her even more for trying to understand.

"Quite a few teenagers have come through here after doing the same thing. Some of them reached a turning point in their lives after it happened. That's how I know."

I lowered my head and turned away. She raised my chin in the palm of her hand.

"I am grateful that I found you in time."

Wendy held my gaze while she spoke. I imagined her heart was big yet gentle, with no need to feel pity for my stupidity or my complexion. I heard no judgment in her voice and saw only kindness on her face. She made me feel more comfortable. I decided to take a chance with some honesty of my own; I owed her that much.

"I'm a bit shook up about nearly killing myself with a stupid overdose. I really wanted those pills and I couldn't wait to crush them up and snort them. I wanted to feel just right, for a change."

Wendy listened respectfully. Opening up to her was easier than I thought it would be.

"But something went very wrong. I had no idea that OxyContin could make the black hole inside of me even bigger. Instead of being protected from it, I fell right into it. Even while I was unconscious, some part of me was scared and thought I was never coming back to life."

I wondered what she thought. Her expression became very serious. She grabbed a chair, moved closer to my bed, and sat down.

"I know the reason why you took so many pills. My brother taught me. I'm telling you about him because I think it may help. I'm taking a chance that you might be ready to hear this.

"My brother was a drug addict," she began. "Actually, he is a drug addict. He says once an addict, always an addict. Before he got into recovery, he found himself in serious trouble with drugs. He started with marijuana and alcohol, just at weekend parties. He was such fun to be with, always laughing and playing practical jokes. He was doing fine in high school and was headed straight for the top. He tried Lortabs. Everybody tried Lortabs. Heck, even I tried them once or twice, but they did nothing for me. They did something for him, though; I couldn't understand it. He gave up drinking beer and smoking pot, just for those pills. He said they gave him energy and made him high."

I found myself paying attention as she spoke about her brother's addiction. This was a first for me and I realized I cared because she wasn't talking to me, or at me, or about me, but *with* me. She wasn't just there on business. She wasn't even playing nurse. She was pouring something beautiful out of her soul and offering it to me with no strings attached. I wanted to hear what she had to say.

"At first, my brother was using pills just here and there, a couple of pills at a time. Then in college, he got into OxyContin and Roxicodone. Before long, he was snorting them every day and he turned into someone who was real moody, irritable, angry, and looking for arguments, even a fight. He was sarcastic, mean, and nasty when he didn't have them. I could always tell the difference. He would walk into a bathroom with a scowl and a bad attitude and come out all huggy-kissy, and it made me mad, because I knew he'd snorted an Oxy."

I was listening intently. I hoped she wouldn't mind my question, because it was important to me that I know the answer to it.

"It's obvious that your brother was anything but a loser before he started pot, alcohol, and pills. But he went through a radical change once he started using. Was it all because of the Oxys? Do they really have that effect on you if you take them for too long?"

Her eyes sparkled as she looked at me. She was as delicate as she was pretty, and wholesome, too. As I listened to her, I stopped feeling like a loser. She put me at ease. I no longer feared that she would suddenly find me too repulsive to stay.

"When he became addicted, there was only one thing he ever wanted: more OxyContin. He spent his entire day finding ways to get it and that meant getting money to buy it. He never asked me for drugs, but he was always asking me for money. He always said it was for clothes, a date, books, gas, and so on. I knew what it was for, but he was so convincing in his begging.

"I found out he would shoplift," she sighed, "and sell what he stole. He wrote bad checks. He asked everybody for money, my parents the most. He had conned them. They had no idea that their college boy had become a drug addict, until he used their ATM cards and emptied the account, more than five thousand dollars in one week. But that still wasn't enough. I remember him telling me that if I didn't give him money, he was going to be beaten up by drug dealers. I believed him and gave him five hundred dollars. What could I do?"

"I don't know much about addiction, except what I see in the news; you know... crack houses, prostitutes, and junkies. Not college kids," I replied. "This is unbelievable. How could something like that happen to someone like your brother? What happened to him?"

"He stopped using, but he didn't go quietly. He was something like you.

He kept taking more and more pills and looking worse and worse. He wasn't sleeping. He wasn't eating. He was tense, uptight, and anxious. He could snort more than 300mg and claim it didn't faze him. He wanted so desperately to get high. But he said he couldn't, no matter how much he snorted. Those days of getting high were over. But he kept trying. He had a few overdoses, too. That part also reminds me of you. We found him passed out and barely breathing when he took Xanax and Soma on top of the Oxys. He went to the emergency room twice for that and ended up in detox more than once."

I perked up. "Detox. What's that? Sounds important."

"It means detoxify," she said. "My brother needed it, because he had such a high tolerance for pills and he experienced withdrawal when he didn't have any. Over time that is bound to happen, even if you just stick with Lortabs. Eventually, you need a lot more pills to feel any effect. It's called chasing the high. Most addicts move up to something stronger and add alcohol, cocaine, pot, and other things to the mix. That really messes up your brain."

"You seem to know a lot about addiction," I said. "I think I get what addiction is all about. Fortunately, I don't have that problem. My problem is taking too much of a good thing and turning it into a bad thing. That's where I need the education. I appreciate all the time you're spending with me. Do you know anything about that?"

Wendy put her hands on her hips and frowned. She looked like she was about to scold me. "Buddy, I'm not surprised to hear you say that. My brother was just like that until he couldn't take it anymore. He said no matter how hard he tried, he couldn't find a way to be satisfied with the pills he took. They were nothing but trouble for him. He wanted to quit, but he couldn't. He would start to get dope-sick twelve hours after his last pill. I don't have time to explain it all right now, but I can give you something to read that might help. Dr. Stone wrote it for his patients. It might help clear a few things up for you. Let me get it; we always have a copy around."

She left, then returned holding a pamphlet titled *A Lesson on Addiction*. When she handed it to me, I saw the author's name: Andrew Stone, MD.

"Thanks, I'll read it after breakfast," I said, as I watched the plate of scrambled eggs and bacon coming through the door. It smelled delicious.

"Dig in," Wendy said. "I'll be back later."

She was still smiling as she walked out of the room and gave me a good-bye wave. The way she looked at me, I almost felt like my acne had vanished.

Once my breakfast was finished, I picked up the pamphlet. A part of me thought *this doesn't apply to me. Why bother reading it?* Then I thought, *this is no accident. Wendy told you about her brother, and you're just like him. And you're in serious trouble to prove it. So, read it and learn.*

As I read, I learned that when your brain is addicted to pills, those pills do less and less, which makes you want to take more of them. The brain literally gets accustomed to the drug, and a higher dosage is required to get you high. That is known as tolerance. Eventually a potentially dangerous amount of pills is required every time you try to get high. If it were alcohol, you'd need to drink a fifth to get drunk, which is a whole lot more than a couple of shots of Jack Daniels.

The addicted brain, while intoxicated, has a way of convincing you that everything is fine. There is no warning or caution light to make you slow down or stop. For a lot of people, it's full speed ahead, and the outcome is usually bad. Learning that reminded me of my case. When I first met Sidney, I got a little high and it was fun, but the next time I blacked out, which meant I went way past getting a little high. Last night, I was so messed up that I kept feeding myself more pills without knowing I was doing it.

It was just like being in a state of amnesia. I was awake but totally unaware of what I was doing. Any memory of what I did was wiped out. The pamphlet said people are sometimes amazed at the stories their friends will tell about the stupid stuff they did while in that condition. The stuff can be funny, embarrassing, or tragic. People drive home that way and wonder later how they did it. Some find it amusing the day after, but others are terrified to imagine what could have happened when they had no clue what they were doing.

I'd taken OxyContin without any concern for my safety. I was too busy trying to have more fun and I didn't know that a few more would make me lose consciousness and my breathing would stop.

While reading the pamphlet, I realized that Wendy must have studied the subject of addiction. She seemed very bright and I bet she knew the material well enough to teach it. I admired that. I also concluded, from the little time we spent together, that she was going to make the world a better place.

There was more to pills than just getting high and I was beginning to understand what my brain was up to when I took them. There was actually some kind of mechanism that created a compulsion to do it. Knowing that made me wonder if I was going to keep taking pills whether I wanted to or not. Could compulsion control me that much? Why was addiction so disobedient? It seemed that telling it "no" didn't work.

The next part of the pamphlet was titled "Receptors and Neurotransmitters." In Dr. Stone's words, the brain is an amazing organ made of cells called neurons. Each one is equipped with many receptors. These are actually docking sites for each molecule that the brain has to interact with. Every molecule visiting the brain needs a place to park itself for something to happen. Every molecule that attaches to a receptor completes a very tiny circuit, which releases chemical messages and electrical impulses. With opiates, the neurotransmitter dopamine is released and that's what is responsible for getting you high.

Next was the part about tolerance. Dr. Stone called the brain a "smart cookie" in this section. When an addict starts to take too many pills to get high, the brain gets busy making more docking sites. More pills need more docking sites. Without them, an overdose is more likely to be lethal. After a growth spurt of receptors, it is possible for the addict to use a lot more drug and still remain functional. That's why someone can drink and drink and drink and not be falling down drunk; that's called a functional alcoholic. Dr. Stone wrote about some addicts who could take twenty Roxicodone in one day and barely feel it. When that's the case, tolerance compels the addict to take more pills in hopes of getting high. Except for the expense of having to buy more pills, addicts never seem to raise an objection to taking more, at least not until the very end, when taking a lot of pills doesn't work any longer.

When an addict can't seem to get high anymore from their favorite pill, they will definitely "upgrade." That means taking something stronger to bring back the desired effect. An addict who starts out with Lortabs will typically move up to 80s of OxyContin. It is very common for addicts at that stage to create a stronger effect by mixing the pills with alcohol and Xanax. The effect of combining several drugs or substances is addictive and creates a different kind of high. Most of the time, the addict tries to stick with a group of drugs that do the same thing.

Sometimes, addicts will take too much of a drug and will then use another drug to counter the effect. For example, Xanax, a potent sedative, is used frequently to reverse the overstimulation caused by cocaine. Otherwise, the addict can't sleep when the party is over. When an addict wants to drink all night, cocaine is used in combination to lessen the effect of feeling drunk and tired.

I found this all amazing. Reading this section of the pamphlet reminded me that I had said, "Better living through chemistry." I, too, was looking for the perfect blend of drugs to create the feeling I wanted. I had been sure there was a combination of drugs that would deaden all of my misery. Unfortunately, the drugs were deadening a lot more than that.

After a drug gets you high, it is eventually taken out of action by being metabolized and converted into different molecules. Some of those keep the high going, but eventually the entire amount that was taken is deactivated and removed, until the body has cleaned itself back to normal. After all, those molecules aren't natural and the body knows they don't belong there.

The body is always trying to remain in a harmonious state of balance so it can function with the greatest ease. When that balance is disturbed, the body knows exactly how to restore it in the fastest possible way. Every cell wants to remain healthy and cells have a sophisticated mechanism to accomplish that. Quite literally, if we would just leave the cells alone, they would take very good care of us and we would be amazed at how seldom we got sick in the traditional ways.

As I continued reading the pamphlet, I felt it was obvious that I had not yet become dependent on OxyContin. Dr. Stone wrote that when an addict becomes dependent, it is really a physiological phenomenon. Dependence is described as needing a daily fix just to feel normal, or as close as possible to it. Addicts have to supply their brains to avoid withdrawal. It is more important to avoid withdrawal than it is to get high.

By the time addiction is so advanced that withdrawal is experienced, addicts are not getting high anymore: they are just trying to maintain. What upsets them the most is the staggering amount of the drug they must consume each day, just for that purpose. The drugs are costly. Oxys can go for about a dollar a milligram. Wendy told me that her brother had a $200-a-day habit. That's what turned him into a criminal and his family into enablers. They couldn't stop him from using, so they paid for his pills to keep him from getting dope-sick.

The chapter on withdrawal intrigued me the most. I learned that withdrawal can start in a matter of hours if you don't have the drug, because the nervous system has grown too many receptors. Once the opioid molecule has done its job, whether you get high or not, it is removed from the receptor, and the nervous system goes into a state of panic.

Withdrawal is the nervous system's way of taking its revenge on the addict. The nervous system goes into a rage, and the addict ends up with sweating, watery eyes, runny nose, shaking, and aching in every muscle, bone, and joint in the body. When the nervous system goes into overdrive, the body reacts with unbearable anxiety, cramps, diarrhea, nausea, and vomiting. An empty (naked) receptor causes an overstimulated physiological response. This will go on for days, until the empty receptors are removed or quiet down naturally. The entire process takes time. That's when the addict wants to die . . . quickly.

Finally, I got to the part on detoxification, which begins once you stop taking pills (opioids) and withdrawal begins. A medical detox refers to taking prescribed medicines from a doctor that quiet the nervous system. These are usually safer drugs to replace the ones you can't get. At least a good detox will stop you from being dope-sick. I got the impression that addicts frantically seek out this treatment when the withdrawal gets bad enough.

The fastest acting and most comfortable way to detox has been to substitute another opioid. The popular drug for this purpose has been methadone. The newest ones are Subutex and Suboxone. These drugs are a different kind of opioid replacement for oxycodone and make the receptor comfortable again. Stopping withdrawal is a short-term solution, and it buys some time until the treatment for addiction is underway.

After I was done with the pamphlet, I could see all the ways it didn't apply to me. I had learned enough about addiction and wanted to know more about Wendy's brother. What became of his life? More important, was he happy? I wanted her to come back and tell me the rest of his story.

Just in case she asked me later what I thought of the booklet, I made sure to summarize it in my head: Addiction is a condition that always wants more. Initially, you give it more in the pursuit of fun. Then more is needed to make the fun last. Eventually there is no fun anymore. If that's always the outcome, why get started in the first place? It's not that simple. Once you have a taste of the fun, you're hooked. And then it dawned on me. I'd had a taste of pain relief. Pills took away a big chunk of my emotional misery and I got hooked on that. The feeling was too powerful to resist. A car wreck, losing consciousness, and even respiratory arrest weren't enough to stop me.

My thoughts turned back to Wendy. If she were here, I thought she might ask me, "What do you think about it now? Are you or aren't you an addict?" Just saying the word *addict* sounded so ugly. I asked myself, *Could that really have happened to me?* I didn't think it was possible, in part because I was so young. Maybe her brother could get addicted, but not me. Could I?

I expected Wendy would say, "Buddy, look at the evidence. You can't deny it." I also thought about my parents, who were going to be banging the same drum and probably would have Dr. Stone right there with them. Were Wendy and this pamphlet my wake-up call? I wasn't sure just yet. If I was truly having some kind of awakening, what was I supposed to do next?

CHAPTER 27

Could I Be Addicted?

I put the pamphlet down and looked out my window. There was a world out there. A world I wanted to return to, if I could only find a way to feel better about myself.

Wendy returned with sparkling eyes and a very wide smile. She pulled up a chair next to my bed and asked, "Do you want to hear more of the story about my brother?"

Of course I did. I nodded enthusiastically

"The first time I saw my brother in withdrawal, I wanted to rush him to the hospital. He was writhing in horrible pain and kept screaming about how bad it hurt. He was sweating, shaking, puking, and having diarrhea all at once. I couldn't take it. He said he was ready to quit pills, so I took him to a detox center. He needed a lot of different medications to stabilize him and make him comfortable.

"Why didn't they give him methadone or Suboxone?" I asked. I hoped she noticed I had read the pamphlet she'd left and was impressed that I knew the names of those drugs.

"If he'd been given one of those, his withdrawal would have stopped, because they're opioids and a perfect substitute for the pills and heroin. But he was not that fortunate. Instead, they gave him Valium, which is a tranquilizer. My brother was going out of his mind with anxiety and that calmed him down. They gave him clonidine, too, because his blood pressure was too high at 180 over 120 and his pulse was too fast at 125 beats per minute. Clonidine also helped to stop the profuse sweating and some of the shaking."

"What else did he have to take?"

"If you've ever had stomach cramps so bad that you think you're going have to sit on the toilet for a week, then you'll want some Bentyl. If brown water comes pouring out of you so fast that diarrhea is not a strong enough word to describe it, then you want Lomotil. If you're throwing up and all you have left is the lining of your stomach, Phenergan will probably do the job."

"I had no idea it could get that bad," I said.

"That wasn't his first detox, and it wasn't his last, either. After each detox, he vowed that he would never go back to using. It took a week before he could eat and walk around, he was so weak and exhausted. But he still relapsed over and over again. Sometimes it was days later and sometimes it was weeks later.

He couldn't adjust to life without drugs. He claimed the cravings were too strong. His friends always had pills and it didn't take much to talk him into it."

"It sounds pretty awful," I said. "It seems like addiction is as hopeless as having terminal cancer. I can understand why being in withdrawal feels like it's worse than dying. I bet some addicts would rather commit suicide than keep going through that over and over again. I didn't realize I knew so little. I doubt my parents know much, either. I don't think they would want to hear all of this."

Wendy continued. "The real miracle happened when my brother met Dr. Stone. I know you probably don't want to hear about him, but there is something you should know that may change your mind. Dr. Stone came to visit my brother the last time he was in the hospital. He had overdosed again, claiming it was an accident. He snorted heroin, OxyContin, and Xanax, one after another. He was looking for the perfect high; instead, he ended up face down in his friend's bathroom, lying in vomit."

I could see why Wendy's brother had to quit, but I wasn't convinced that I had snorted my last Oxy. It was pretty obvious I wasn't as bad as him.

"By then, we were all fit to be tied and wanted to disown him. The entire family took an oath to never give him any money, bail him out of jail, or do anything that would keep his addiction going. We cried and felt like we'd lost him. He was so lucky that once they revived him all he had was a bad case of pneumonia," Wendy added thoughtfully. "When they pulled the breathing tube out of him and turned the ventilator off, he woke up and looked at me in a different way than ever before. He said, 'Please don't give up. I'll do anything now. I'm ready. I've had it.' I was new here at the hospital, so I asked around. Everybody told me the same thing: ask Dr. Stone to visit him, and he did."

There was that name again. I wanted to know why everyone thought he was so good.

"He came to see me in the ICU," I said. "I wasn't impressed. I think he would have preferred to tie me to a chair and sweat a juicy confession out of me. He tried to get me to crack and tell him that I was a disappointment to my parents and used drugs to cover up all my childhood guilt."

"He's not like that," Wendy said, shaking her head.

"He's worse. He was really boring, so I kicked him out. And just before I did, he made some lame prediction that I would come crawling back to his office, begging for an appointment, when I was cramped up with an accident in my pants. That's not going to happen. And honestly, I wouldn't waste my money on him, even if it did."

Wendy kept her composure, but I could tell she didn't agree with my assessment of the good shrink. Her hands were clasped in a praying position and she spoke carefully.

"I can only speak for my brother and myself. I was there when Dr. Stone met us. I suppose my brother was in a different place than you are. He was receptive and humble for the first time in his life. It was very moving to see him like that. I was so grateful, I cried."

I really didn't want to hear anything more about Dr. Stone, but Wendy had been so nice to me that I let her keep talking.

"Dr. Stone saw my brother and knew by the look on his face and the remorse in his voice that he had endured as much shame and suffering as any human soul was capable of. Dr. Stone came with a spiritual light to show my brother the way out of the darkness he was in. Dr. Stone took his hand and they walked together, in a manner of speaking.

"I can tell by the look on your face," Wendy continued, "that you don't understand spiritual terms and concepts. That's all right. What really happened was that my brother and Dr. Stone made a connection of trust, and it's a bond that remains intact today. My brother is one year sober now, and that is a major milestone for addicts. Most don't ever get that far."

I rolled my eyes. Actually, I still felt the sting of Dr. Stone's remarks and I was angry. After making such a fool of myself with the overdose of OxyContin, I could have used a little sympathy from him. But no, he had to smack me between the eyes and punch me in the gut with his reality check. I don't think he cared how embarrassed I was or he would have done a better job.

My thoughts had wandered away from the conversations. When I realized Wendy was waiting for me to comment, I lashed out.

"Just what exactly did he do that saved your brother? It must have been impressive." The sarcasm dripped off my words.

Wendy sat up straighter. "Being defensive is what got my brother into a relapse. He was so cocky and so sure that anyone trying to help was just going to spoil the party. He knew he wasn't ready to stop taking drugs. There was another deeper level of pain that he hadn't felt yet. As they say, he had a way to go before he hit bottom. It was so painful to watch him go through that and I really thought there was no hope for him, until Dr. Stone showed up. He became my brother's coach . . . trainer, if you like. He taught my brother how to get through a day without any pills, pot, or booze, no matter how much he was hurting."

"That's the part I wanted to hear about," I said. "You mean Stone actually helped your brother when he wanted pills? And he didn't take any?"

"Yup."

"Like, how did he help?" I wanted all the details.

Wendy softened her posture. "He met with my brother every day while he was here. He would listen to my brother tell him all about his life. I guess Dr. Stone got to hear everything that we never knew about him. Some of it must have been pretty grim, bleak, and harsh. To this day, I don't know what my brother told him. It's just between the two of them, confidential. But after that first week, I saw a transformation. My brother wasn't the same young man who had torn his life to shreds and discarded it for garbage."

I couldn't imagine telling Dr. Stone the grim, bleak, and harsh details of my life. I'd rather take them to my grave.

"My brother said once he told Dr. Stone the darkest part of the truth, he knew the doctor would never abandon him. More important, Dr. Stone promised to answer any call for help, night or day, and never question the reason why. My brother felt he would never be judged by Dr. Stone, even if he was guilty.

"The doctor agreed to be available, but there were some conditions. If my brother wanted to recover, he had to be willing to move in the right direction with a sober mind. An addictive mind will always try to wheel and deal. Any addict who is not sober has the potential to harm the one who is trying to help and Dr. Stone warned my brother he'd walk away if that was the case."

I knew Stone planned to have me dismissed from the hospital. But I still couldn't help but wonder if he would treat me like Wendy's brother. Would he give me a second chance? What if he sat with me privately and heard my dark truths? What then? Would he be willing to be my coach? I wasn't sure I wanted to know . . . or even try. There had to be a way to make the right decision.

I asked Wendy, "What would your brother do if he were me right now?"

She looked thoughtful for a moment, and then she suggested, "Why don't you ask him yourself? He works here in the hospital and came on duty at six this morning. I bet he can get free for a few minutes. Will you let me give him a call?"

I agreed to meet and tell him about my overdose last night. I wanted him to know that today I was going to face a firing squad. She started dialing his cell phone and immediately I thought of changing my mind. The pressure was getting to me. A stranger was coming to talk to me about addiction. It seemed like I was surrounded by the topic of addiction and I wanted it to end and leave me alone.

Wendy gave me a thumbs-up gesture as she hung up the phone.

"He's on his way and would love to meet you. He is so dedicated to his work in recovery. He goes to Narcotics Anonymous meetings every single day and his sober-date anniversary was last week. Maybe he'll show you his medallion. I was there when his sponsor gave it to him. I'm so proud of him. He won't be able to stay long, but I'm sure he'll know how to answer your questions."

She bent over with her arms open.

"Whoops. I was going to give you a hug. But your brace is in the way. I'll save it for later when you're standing." And then she held both my hands and embraced them with hers. "This will have to do for now." I didn't know what to say, but for the first time in a long time, I felt warm inside.

CHAPTER 28

The Way to the Winner's Circle

He walked in looking fresh, clean, handsome, healthy, and fit—a college man from head to toe. He was the vision of what I would never be and just looking at him made me want to be back in the stupor of an OxyContin high. At least that didn't hurt.

His sister engulfed him with a tight hug. I could see how much she loved and admired him. "Buddy, I want to introduce you to my special brother, Joe."

His handshake was firm and very athletic. It made me even more uncomfortable.

"Hello, Buddy," he said. "Nice to meet you. I'm glad you're okay."

Wendy started walking toward the door. "I'll leave you two alone. Don't take too long." Joe waved good-bye to her, then pulled up a chair next to me.

"My sister told me what happened in about two sentences and it sounds like we have something in common. What did you take?"

I was surprised to feel genuine warmth and humility from him. I wanted to trust him and tell him the truth. I needed an ally.

"I snorted Roxys and Oxys until I passed out. You know the rest."

He nodded and was gracious enough not to appear to be shocked or impressed.

He said, "We do some very interesting things to get here, don't we? After I overdosed, I remember waking up in a total choking panic, with the breathing tube down my throat. I pulled that thing out as fast as I could. It was gagging me. I shoved it at the nurse and told her where to stick it. I was crude. I feel bad about that now."

We laughed and it felt good.

"What about you?" Joe asked. "What was it like?"

"I swear my tube was a foot long. It must have been touching my toes, it was in so deep. I tried to bite it in half before I yanked it out. You should have seen the look on the doctor's face. I think he was more scared than I was. He thought I'd damaged my vocal cords."

We were laughing to the point of tears. We were medical survivors with incredible war stories that bonded us together. I already felt closer to him than I had been to anyone in my life. I wondered how that was possible.

Once we stopped laughing, Joe's tone of voice got serious. "Well, Buddy, are you ready now? Do you want that overdose to be the last one ever?"

I knew what he was getting at. I wanted the laughter back.

"I don't blame you for not answering," he said. "I completely understand. I didn't want to give up that easily, even when I knew that my chances of having another birthday were slim to none. But I didn't have Dr. Stone's help at the time. Once we met, things got better but not easier. I had to work my tail off. But I'm here to tell you, it was worth it. Recovery is always worth it. *You're* worth it."

He leaned over to give me a friendly squeeze of my shoulder.

"We can show you how to get better. If you don't like the recovery way of life, your misery and pain are fully refundable, anytime you want. Life is good for me, Buddy. It's your turn now. Dr. Stone knows the way. Give him a chance. He's been there and back."

I wasn't expecting Joe to turn into to a replica of Dr. Stone. I thought he was here to cheer me up before I got booted out of this place.

"Hey, what gives? You sound a lot like Dr. Stone."

"I know I do. And I'm glad I do. It's your turn to have something better than what you have now. I can help you. He can help. You have my word. I wouldn't say this if I couldn't back it up. You've been dancing with the devil, my friend, and he will dance you right into an early grave if you don't get out now."

There was something about Joe that was reassuring. I wanted to believe that he had my best interest at heart. I had been putting up so much resistance that it was getting tedious. Maybe it was time for me to shut up and listen to what Dr. Stone had to say. If he was some kind of leader or teacher, what harm could it do to hear him out? I hoped that I hadn't burned the last bridge, because Joe was looking mighty good standing there on the other side. It was a place where maybe I wanted to be, right next to him.

He wrote his phone number on the back of one of my get-well cards.

"Call me anytime, night or day. There are twenty-four hours in a day. Take them one at a time. The crap you have to put up with is more manageable that way. I gotta run, but I'll be around. Think about it. You're closer to doing the right thing than you know."

He left with one final wave and a winner's warm smile. I missed him as soon as he walked out the door. The feeling was strange but nice.

Wendy returned with a pitcher of fresh ice water. "How did it go?" she asked. "Isn't he something? You would never guess that one year ago, he was a total loser. He was sick, flunking out of school, and on the verge of suicide. He was even being hunted down by drug dealers, but now he's a completely new man."

"Is he ever," I said. "He's truly amazing. Thanks for asking him to come. I've never met two people like you. I am trying to get used to being treated so nicely. Life hasn't been too kind to me. I'm not going to bore you with my sad story, but if there was anyone I would pick to listen, it would be either of you."

"Buddy, that's really sad. Not having anyone to talk to, I mean."

"It's not that bad once you get used to it. I had to. One look is all you need to see how much *loser* I have written all over me. Wherever I go, I'm the guy who doesn't belong there. People would rather hold their breath than talk to me. So when you were both so nice, I didn't know what to make of it. It made no sense. At first, I thought you just pitied me, that you were being kind because it's your job, and you probably treat everybody that way. It took some getting used to, but now I want more of that."

I felt like I was exposing my heart with all its vulnerabilities. I didn't realize I was holding my head down until I felt hands cradle my face and lift it up until I was looking into Wendy's eyes. She touched me, pimples and all, without reservation. I could feel the sheer force of her love for another person wiping away my fear, shame, and guilt. I felt clean and I began to believe that I had some value. I belonged right here with her and I felt safe. It was getting easier to talk to her and now I felt like I had things to say.

"I want to thank you for taking so much time to reach out to me," I said. "I have been turning away from anyone who offered to help, mostly because there was nothing but well-deserved criticism being dished out. My parents were the worst, then came Dr. Stone. I think a little kindness might have opened my eyes to see what was going on."

She put her hands on her lap as she sat on the edge of my bed, but didn't say anything.

"Something weird has happened to me this morning," I continued. "I hope it lasts, because my thinking is beginning to make sense. I actually see the way out of at least some of the mess I'm in. For instance, I can see that your brother, the smart college jock, and I, the high-school geek, had different lives, but that didn't matter when it came to OxyContin. We both ended up with an addiction. Addiction didn't play favorites. It took us both down, although I suppose some go faster than others."

Wendy placed her hand on top of mine. It was warm and soft.

"Your brother showed me that I can turn around and go in the right direction any time I want. I can start walking out of the woods now that I know I'm in too deep. And how deep is too deep is up to me to decide."

Her hand on mine felt pure and free of any judgment. She touched an inner part of me that had never been a loser or a geek. If I had any love, that's probably where it would come from and it would be a healing and forgiving kind of love. I wanted to believe that such love existed in everybody, including my parents.

"What about today, Buddy? What path will you walk today? You can leave the loser behind and step further out into the light. You're doing it right now. The way will always be shown to you. Just look for it and believe it's there. The loser in you can't survive when you make winning choices."

I decided right then and there that if I greeted my parents and Dr. Stone like I was a winner, at least I couldn't make matters worse. I was going to have to pretend, but I had to start somewhere.

CHAPTER 29

Recovery Begins with Honesty

Wendy got through to me with simple human kindness, a type of love that was perfectly suited for me. That was going to come in handy once my parents arrived. I expected them to be tough on me after what I had done. I wanted to make a better impression than the last time they'd seen me, so I fixed my hair and brushed my teeth after breakfast.

My mom arrived first; my father was parking the car. If you'd seen the way she looked, you wouldn't have thought she looked like the mother of a boy who nearly died the night before. She looked annoyed and inconvenienced. I tried to look like a winner. I told myself the loser in me had no voice; only the winner was allowed to speak on my behalf. I waited for Mom to speak first.

"Did you know we were coming?" she asked.

"Yes, I was told by the nursing supervisor."

"You really did it this time, didn't you? I thought you were through with drugs. That's what you told us. Doesn't your word mean *anything*?"

Her face contorted as she emphasized the last word; it was painful to look at her. I didn't flinch when she spoke and I tried to look like I was sorry for what I had done.

"I lied to you," I said. "I'm sorry. I wasn't taking this drug thing seriously. I was hooked and didn't know it. I thought I could just have some fun and get high. I didn't mean to cause so much trouble."

Mom walked around my bed, looking exasperated. "I'm not letting you off that easily. We can't live with your lies, young man. 'Sorry' won't cut it, either. You've caused a lot of trouble for this hospital. You're dangerous and they want to discharge you. Your dad and I don't know how to deal with this. We wish we could send you away and let someone else straighten you out." She sat down in the chair next to my bed and stared at me, a cold expression on her face.

"Mom, if you give me a chance, I can explain. I just learned something really important about myself and it may help you understand me better."

"I can't listen to any of that right now," she interrupted, turning away from me. "Where's your father? He needs to have a word with you. He can't believe this is happening. He just keeps saying, 'Our son is a drug addict.' He's heartbroken and disgusted."

My father walked in just then and Mom ordered him to "talk some sense into your son."

My father, who usually didn't have much to say, began by pointing his index finger at me, and he used it to make his points—every one of them—as he lectured, "We have had it with you. One overdose was bad enough. We were scared and confused. We had no idea you were into drugs. You're just a kid. How the hell did that happen? Then you crashed a car and nearly died. We thought for sure that would be the end of taking pills. But you went and had them smuggled into the hospital and then you nearly died *again*. What if they hadn't found you in time? What then? Are we supposed to just let you keep doing this to yourself? Why do you do these drugs? Can't you just be normal?"

He kept talking, never pausing for the answers he was demanding. He kept ranting and raving until my mother interrupted him, saying, "Give him a chance to speak, will you?"

My father cleared his throat, straightened his tie, and backed up a few steps. His crimson complexion began to return to a normal color. He motioned for me to start explaining, but I felt like he was pushing me overboard into shark-infested water. I reminded myself I needed to talk like a winner.

"I don't blame you for being angry with me. I'm angry with myself. I got scared last night, too. I wasn't ready to admit I had a problem, until a nurse talked to me. I met her brother. It turns out he had done the same thing I did, only he didn't stop until he was stealing his parents' money and being chased by drug dealers. He wants to help me stop using drugs. I think I can do it."

I could tell by the looks on their faces that neither one of my parents believed me. I guess I'd lied too many times—I couldn't expect them to believe that this time I really did want to change.

We just looked at each other for a minute and I wondered what to say next.

"I think you're ready to stop using drugs."

Dr. Stone was leaning up against the wall. His presence was a relief—maybe he could help me explain things so my parents would understand.

"Dr. Stone, I want you to meet my mom and dad. Mom and Dad, this is Dr. Stone, the addiction doctor who came to see me in the ICU."

The three adults shook hands while I continued. "It may surprise you to hear me say that I appreciate you coming, Dr. Stone. I know that I caused the hospital a lot of trouble. I expect you to show me the door. I deserve that after what I've done. But before you discharge me, I have something to say."

"I don't think we need to waste this fine doctor's time," my mother interrupted. "You should just apologize and hope that you won't be arrested. You are so selfish. Tell the doctor you're sorry, and let's be done with this. I am already embarrassed enough by you."

Dr. Stone listened to her carefully, a sympathetic expression on his face. "This is no waste of my time. I like to be around when things like this happen, because this is when things change. They either get better or worse. I never want to miss out on the better part. So, young man, you have the floor. Tell us why you think drugs should be eliminated from your diet."

"I want to ask for another chance to work with you, Dr. Stone. I didn't care for you or how you treated addiction when we first met, because I wasn't ready to get on board. Wendy, my nurse, was concerned about me and she called her brother Joe in to meet me. He works here in the hospital. It turns out he's one of your patients and he's been sober for a year. He was really nice and told me what a difference, for the better, you made in his life. He told me about the stupid things he had done; he was actually worse than me when he bottomed out. We have lots in common. We were both losers, but he's not anymore. Today it ends for me, too.

"It's not like me to talk this way. I'll understand if you think that I'm trying to get off easy for my screw-up. I can assure you that's not the case. I swear it." I glanced at my mother; she wore a pained expression on her face. I was not convincing her with any of my sincerity.

Dr. Stone motioned me to continue.

"I don't know if anything like this has ever happened to any of your other patients, but I feel like my mind has shifted. What used to make sense is nonsense now. It's weird, but part of me really doesn't want to do drugs anymore. Is that possible or is that just part of feeling guilty?"

Dr. Stone pulled up a chair and sat down next to me with a smile. "It's incredible that you survived the large quantity of drugs you've taken, Buddy. You didn't know what you were playing with and it nearly cost you your life on two separate occasions. I believe what you're feeling is the beginning of something better for you. I believe you mean what you say, and that's a good start."

It seemed that Dr. Stone had changed, too. He was no longer talking down to me. I respected him for that. Now I was ready to hear what he had to say.

"In a way," he continued, "I'm glad it turned out like this. You had an awakening and became approachable. Your nurse took advantage of that. She gave you hope that you could recover and that turned you in the right direction. The question is, what do you want to do now? You have some choices. You can walk away from the drugs, but they have a way of following you around. When you get sidetracked by problems, the drugs will be all too happy to ask you out on a date. They won't pack up and go away; neither will your friend who brings them—or your dealer."

"All right, I think I've heard enough for now," my father interrupted. "None of what you said proves anything, Son. It's just talk, and that's cheap and in this case, worthless. I don't believe a word of it. You don't go from smuggling in drugs to being Mr. Recovery overnight. I don't think that's possible under these circumstances. So what's it going to be, Doc?" my dad asked, turning to Dr. Stone. "Is he staying, or is he being discharged from this hospital? The nursing supervisor said it's up to you. I don't care either way. I don't trust him here or at home."

"My husband is right," my mother agreed. "Our son is out of control, and I haven't heard anything that makes a believer out of me. I wish he'd agree to be your patient. Maybe you could straighten him out for us."

The thought of becoming Dr. Stone's patient freaked me out, but I tried to appear calm. A voice in my head kept telling me to *shut up, shut up, shut up,* so I did. *Just listen and wait. The answer will come.* I decided to obey. My mouth had already gotten me into enough trouble.

Dr. Stone looked first at my parents, then at me, before he spoke. "You all raise valid concerns. My job is to help someone whose life has been taken over by drugs. And that, my friend, is you. If you want to stay in this hospital, you have to welcome me onto your team. That means we meet every day, maybe twice a day. You have to talk and that includes telling me the story of your life. Nothing withheld. The good, the bad, and the ugly are on the menu. If we can create an alliance, then you have a shot at becoming drug-free and a whole lot more. The only condition is that you have to want it. Before you decide, I need to explain a few things. If it turns out that you aren't ready for what I offer, then you will be released from the hospital and you won't have to see me again."

I looked directly at Dr. Stone and said with conviction, "I'll do it. When do we start?"

My parents looked at each other.

Dr. Stone stood up and walked over to my parents while extending his hand. "I am so glad that the three of you had an opportunity to speak your mind. We're at a crossroads here and I want to help all of you take a step in the right direction. I would like to spend some private time with Buddy so we can build our alliance. For both of you, I understand why you're frustrated, disappointed, and irritated with Buddy. However, he is at a critical turning point and I hope you can give us more time and give him another chance. I think it will be worth it. I think we accomplished a lot here today, believe it or not. The two of you can go home if you like. We're going to be talking for an hour. How about if I call you later and tell you how it turned out?"

My mother shook the doctor's hand, looking like she was about to cry. "We know you're the best and we have faith in you. I hope Buddy cooperates. But if he doesn't, we'll be available to take him home right away." My father didn't even look at me. They disappeared into the hall.

Once he was certain my parents had time to reach the elevator, Dr. Stone turned his attention back to me.

"Listen up, Kid," he snapped. "I have to see a few more patients before I can free up enough time to hear your life story. The physical therapist is outside, itching to get at you and take you for a walk. I'll be back in the next hour." His warm demeanor had vanished and I began to get nervous. What was I letting myself in for?

The therapist brushed by the doctor as he came into the room. "I guess he's staying with us a little longer," Dr. Stone informed him. "I hope it's for all the right reasons."

The therapist charged into the room clapping his hands like he was ready to lead an advanced aerobics class. "Okay, Superstar, let's move that body of yours and see what kind of speed you've got. I want one hundred percent from you—no excuses and no whining."

Getting out of bed was much easier this time. I was able to maneuver with the brace and the hardware on my leg. I was still weak and sore, but I could tell I was getting stronger. I had better coordination and stamina, and I covered twice the distance in half the time with minimal pain. The therapist actually interrupted my workout to explain why I was showing so much improvement.

"Do you know how a weak atrophic muscle begins to grow rapidly after stimulation?"

Even though I kept saying, "No" and "I don't care," he continued making references to muscle and bone physiology throughout the rest of our session. I was not impressed; it was as boring to me as an infomercial on hair removal. I resented his knowledge and his toned body, but then I realized that I was judging him the same way I had been judged. It was time to stop doing that.

Just then I heard Brenda out in the hall. Big Brenda was my nurse for the day. I dreaded seeing her; she would know about the stunt I pulled last night after Jeffrey and Sidney had visited. I wondered why she was taking so long to come in. I was ready for whatever tongue-lashing she was going to inflict; I just wanted the torture to be over.

The knock on the door was far from delicate; it was actually thunderous. Brenda's booming voice caused the small hairs all over my body to rise in unison.

"It's my turn now." Brenda's voice had a chilling sweetness that belonged in a Stephen King movie. She was scaring the crap out of me.

"I heard you played a little game last night after I left and you got the lucky straw." She stood next to the head of my bed, a sadistic glint in her eyes.

"Your friends had all kinds of treats, didn't they? I wish I had been here to catch all of you. That would have made my day. I would have shoved that drug-snorting straw so deep inside your body that it would have taken a surgical team to remove it." I was afraid to say anything for fear of what she might do.

"Your friends are restricted from any further visitation," she said. "If I see them, they'll wish for a quick and painless death. But right now, I'm going to search this room for contraband. I'm going to be thorough, including a few dark places that are probably getting sweaty about now. Nothing is off-limits for me."

I shuddered at the thought of her probing around my private areas. I didn't want to be the subject of her vulgar humor. I raised my hand to stop her. "Wait! I don't have any pills. I think I snorted most of them. Dr. Stone took the rest. I got wasted and you know the rest. That's why I'm done with pills. Dr. Stone is going to help me. You don't need to check me—I'm clean. I swear it."

She kept moving as though I hadn't said a word. She grabbed the frame of my brace and used it to roll me on my side. I felt like a helpless box turtle.

"I know all the hidy holes," she said. "I used to be a prison nurse. Nothing gets by me. My motto is 'Never trust an addict.'" She put on latex gloves, making a snapping sound as she stretched and released the rubber.

"Nurse, I don't think that will be necessary. We checked him last night when he was unconscious. He's clean."

Beads of sweats were forming on my forehead as Dr. Stone winked at me. Brenda let go of her grip on my brace and slapped my rear end briskly, as though it belonged to a disobedient child. She pulled my gown back where it belonged, turned me on my back, and fluffed up my pillow.

"I'm not done with you yet," Brenda warned me. "We still have some unfinished business. You are not going to smack any dope on my shift. The doc gets his turn with you now, but when I come back I'm going to keep searching for your pills. I know they're here somewhere."

I held my breath until she was gone.

Dr. Stone had a smile on his face as he offered, "I should have waited a little longer before coming in. You were about to have the ultimate cavity search. Do I hear a thank-you?"

"You saved my life again. I thought she was really going to do it."

"Me, too. And she won't give up trying, either. She certainly is unique. If I were you, I wouldn't give her any reason to believe that you have a secret stash of pills. Don't even joke about it."

"One question, Doc. Did someone, you know, really check me down there?"

His laughter caught me off guard.

"I'll make you a promise," he said. "You work with me and I'll make sure that she doesn't go any further than looking under your pillow. Deal?"

"Deal."

CHAPTER 30

The Loser's Life

Dr. Stone settled into a chair and looked comfortable enough to watch a great football game on TV.

"Okay, let's begin. I already read a fair amount about what happened the day you came to the hospital. What I want to know is how this all got started. Tell me about the first pill. What made you do it?"

I took a few deep breaths and decided to let the winner do the talking. The loser would only attempt to start a pity party or get defensive and that would be embarrassing. I intended to tell the truth now. Trusting Dr. Stone was my only hope of breaking away from pills.

"Okay, Doc, the first pill was a Lortab. It was great. You know, all the energy cranking through my body. I eventually took enough pills to get high and that's when I discovered how my life should have been. I felt like I could be anyone and do anything. That was the best feeling I ever had."

So far it was easy. He sat there looking at me without blinking.

"I promised myself that when I talked to you today, I would only allow the winner in me to show up. I've been living my life as a loser. I guess I can tell you about the loser while still being the winner, can't I?"

The doctor nodded again. He still hadn't blinked. I wondered if psychiatrists ever blink.

"As the loser, I was pretty messed up in my head all the time. I avoided the other kids. That way, I didn't have to figure out how to behave. You'd think that I would know. But I didn't. I didn't know if anything I did was going to be okay with anyone else. I was afraid to screw up and be rejected."

Dr. Stone rubbed his chin and crossed his legs.

"The pills changed all of that," I continued. "I felt like a different me while I was high. I wasn't ugly and I could talk to girls. I thought I could fit in and be one of them. But it didn't last and you know the rest. I crashed that car and as soon as I came out of the coma, I got loaded up on pills again. I nearly killed myself just trying to have some fun. It's confusing and stupid, I know."

Dr. Stone finally blinked. Then his expression changed and he looked pleased, almost in a proud fatherly way.

"I really don't know what more to tell you. I've never done this before. What do you expect me to say? I mean, since you're a psychiatrist, do you need to analyze me?"

"It's best if you just say what comes into your head," Dr. Stone answered without hesitation. "Don't worry about me trying to analyze any of it. I don't do that sort of thing. If you just keep talking about yourself, I will learn what I need to know. I can form some ideas about your personality and how that affects your decisions and choices. More important, it will tell me a lot about how you think of yourself as a person. From there, I will know how to approach coaching and guiding you in recovery."

I was pretty sure I understood what he was getting at and I knew what I wanted to tell him.

"I am kind of shy most of the time. It makes me nervous when people look at me and expect me to say something. I am pretty okay around the house with my folks and my brother. But at school, if I don't know somebody, I would rather not say anything. I start to tremble inside and my stomach feels like it's twisted and running in circles. I hate school just because of how the other students treat me. I only have one sort-of friend: that's Jeff. I don't like sports of any kind. I suppose I could just play video games, read books, listen to music, and live on the Internet. I take pictures, too. I have a pretty good camera. How was that?"

"Tell me about your parents. How was it growing up with them?"

"I guess they're okay, as parents go. When I was just in first grade my mom took me to Little League soccer. She said I spent too much time in my room and I should get some exercise and make new friends. Soccer was awful. The other kids were way better. I would have been more useful if I had been the water boy. It was embarrassing."

"I can imagine," he said.

"My mom came to the games and would constantly yell at me to hustle. She even spoke to the coach. She told him that the other kids were hogging the ball and that wasn't good sportsmanship. I wanted her to stop interfering. The other moms didn't do things like that. One day I refused to go to the game, and she gave up. There were no more sports after that, thank God."

Dr. Stone removed his glasses and fogged them up before carefully wiping them clean. "What else did your mother do to make you fit in socially?"

"She tried real hard to get me to have friends and mix in with the other kids. My teachers told her I didn't play well with my classmates, that I was quiet and kept to myself. I always tried to stand in the back and keep my head down during a group event. I hated that I was always the last one picked for everything."

Dr. Stone interlocked all of his fingers and placed his hands on his lap. I studied his face carefully to see what sort of reaction he had to what I'd told him so far; he merely look inquisitive.

"What was it like for you to be the misfit of the classroom?"

"My mom kept interfering and my life got even worse. She insisted that the teacher make me do what the other kids were doing. 'He'll outgrow it,' she said. My mom even came to class trying to find playmates for me. When I was really young, she would stand there and say, 'Okay you two, start playing.' The other kid and I would just stare at each other, not knowing how to begin. Eventually, the other kid would pick up a truck and play as though I wasn't there. It didn't get any better when I was older, either. She invited a group of kids to the house and had all sorts of games planned for us. She set the whole thing up and told us what to do, like a game director. The other kids had a blast. When it was my turn to do something, I just stood there feeling awkward and scared. My mom got so frustrated and mad that she even spanked me. She just kept pleading, 'Why won't you play? What's wrong with you?' Then she sent me to my room and took the kids home."

It dawned on me that I was talking up a storm and I didn't feel self-conscious or ugly.

"You're doing very well, Buddy," Dr. Stone encouraged me. "It must have been hard to be pushed like that. Did your mother ever realize what she was doing to you?"

"I don't exactly remember when it started to let up, but it did. I think I was in the fifth grade with Mrs. Johnson. She was the nicest teacher I ever had. She never asked me to do anything or be like the other kids. She was always kind and very complimentary. It worked. I actually began to feel more comfortable being in class. She was my first true friend. I was never embarrassed around her."

"Do you remember what she said?" the doctor asked.

"I sure do. I'll never forget it. She said, 'Be yourself. The world has room for everybody. Some day you will find out where you belong and it will be easy. Because your preferences are different, other kids may not treat you right, because they don't know how.' I remember that word *preferences*. It seemed too big at the time to mean anything and I think she knew I didn't understand it, so she explained it this way: Everybody has the right to seek happiness in their own way. That is their preference. You should eat what tastes good, not what tastes bad. That made so much sense. My life choices became a little simpler for me after that. She said, 'When you do what you like, you like who you become, and you won't have to pretend to be something else.' I decided to just ignore the kids as much as I could. I even ignored my mom. One day she ignored me back and that was okay."

Dr. Stone raised an eyebrow. "Your teacher sounds like a wise woman. I'm impressed. Based on that, I would have expected only a minimum of ugly or bad from that day forward. What happened? What went wrong?"

I paused for a drink of ice water. "This next part is definitely uglier and bad, too. I'm not sure if I want you to know all of me at once."

"I'll be the judge of that. You're doing fine. Keep going."

"Doc, what happened was puberty, pimples, and hormones. When I finished middle school, I had a few zits like everybody else. I took care of them with cleansers and creams and other stuff. My voice was changing. It was kind of too high, then suddenly it changed into croaking. I didn't want to talk. I watched the other kids my age grow up. Guys were shaving, girls started to get curves, and everybody was talking about making out. I had been ignored for so long that there was no way to get back in with the others, even if I'd wanted to. And then the real pimples hit, a huge crop of them. I was so disgusting.

"My mom took me to a pimple specialist, a dermatologist, when I was in high school. He prescribed one thing after another. Most of the pills caused side effects and I felt worse. Finally, I refused any more treatment. The pimples kept coming, one after another, each one bigger than the last one. I couldn't stand it. There was nothing worse than knowing that every eyeball in the room was focused on my face. Every single person who looked at me was wishing they could squeeze one and see it pop and squirt a big, juicy wad of pus. I just knew that's what they were thinking."

As I told my story, I began to have even uglier feelings about myself. It sucked, but I was willing to stay in that dark place for the sake of this interview, if that's where he needed me to go. I hoped he knew what he was doing, because it hurt.

"By that time, Doc, most of the harassment had stopped. Nobody cared about me, and I liked it that way. I felt more invisible and was able to get by. I did the required work at school, nothing great, and the teachers left me alone to focus on more important students. I planned to keep going through the motions until graduation. At some point, Jeff started roaming around me. I don't know why. He liked to talk to everybody and usually he wouldn't shut up or take no for an answer. Everybody else told him to get lost, but I let him tag along. We really didn't do anything. He did most of the talking, and that was how I found out what the others were thinking about me. He liked to snoop and couldn't keep a secret."

The doctor poured himself a cup of ice water from my pitcher and signaled me to keep going.

"I couldn't believe the things they said about me. I was the guy no one would talk to, yet everyone talked about me. The stuff about my pimples wasn't any worse than my own self-criticism. The other stuff was just mean and cruel. It's hard for me to understand how that was so entertaining to everyone. How would you like to be described as a monster? According to them, I was a psycho-freak with schizophrenia, I practiced witchcraft, ate dead animals off the side of the road, listened to satanic rage music backwards, never slept, drank blood like a vampire, and never bathed. Do you want to hear more, or is that enough ugly for you?"

"That got you pretty riled up. Do you need to take a break?" Dr. Stone looked concerned.

I was seething with anger. I thought if I talked about it, the anger would go away. I thought that was how therapy worked.

"No, I don't need a break," I said. "I have more to say about this. Looking back, I know I had a choice. I stuffed it all back in and kept quiet. In my mind, I had to endure my problems like a snake that's been run over by a car. Ever seen one? Until it dies, it will thrash around writhing in pain, trying to get off the road, but it won't make any forward progress. One car after another will drive over it until its dead. Well, I didn't have that luxury. I was that snake, but there was no more traffic coming my way. I had to wait and suffer."

Dr. Stone had stopped blinking again. "It sounds to me like your waiting is over. By complaining and getting it out of your system, you get rid of some of the suffering. I think that's the beginning of a breakthrough. How does it feel?"

I slammed the mattress with my fist. "I'm pissed off because I took so damn long to get this out. I just didn't know how bad it was to hold it in. Now that I feel this rage inside, I want to tear things up. I want to break something or someone. I want to get this bomb out of me and let it explode somewhere."

Dr. Stone leaned forward in his chair. "Listen carefully to me," he said. "This is a moment you can take advantage of. I'm going to teach you an exercise that will help you let go of some anger. First, I want you to ask yourself, *What's bothering me right now*?"

"I'm angry," I said.

"About what?"

"I've been humiliated since I was a kid. Once I got older, pimples made it much worse. People were just cruel and would never let up. I hate them all. I wish I could hurt them somehow."

"For now, we'll have to do the next best thing. I want you to use all your senses to feel what you've just told me. Close your eyes so you can recreate the images and hear the voices that make you so mad. Put yourself there right now."

I followed his instructions. I surrounded myself with images of kids and heard them taunting me, saying the meanest things while making fun of me, the geek.

"Okay. Now let yourself just be there with the whole mess of it. Open your arms and welcome it."

My eyes popped open and I started to object.

"Trust me, this works. Go ahead: welcome it to be here with you. After all, you created it. All of this is inside of you. It wasn't put there by anyone. Nobody has that kind of power. You reacted to someone else's opinion. The pain you felt came from your own interpretation of what other people said about you. What other people thought of you was not the truth, only lies for the sake of their own amusement. You were the one who took them seriously and made them matter. Now, you can welcome the feelings to be here as your creations. They have only become as hurtful as you've allowed them to be. It was always your choice. So just let them be here and see them for what they are—only feelings, nothing more."

In my mind's eye, I was standing in a room filled with the voices of all the people who were mean, nasty, and vicious. It was a very painful place to be and I could feel how evil and vile it was.

"Okay, Buddy, allow those feelings to flow right through you. There is no reason to stop them. They will leave you alone, safe and unharmed. Then ask yourself, could I just let this pain go? In other words, am I capable of letting it go?"

I thought about that. "I should be able to let this go. Shouldn't I? Yes. I definitely think that's possible."

Those feelings were painful. But I became aware of something important: if I could let them go, I must not be attached to them. And since I'd created them, I was free to do as I pleased with them.

"Now, to the best of your ability," Dr. Stone continued, "Would you just let this pain and all you imagine about it, go? And if so, when?"

Something amazing happened once I decided that I wanted no part of that pain. It felt pretty poisonous. I imagined my chest opening up and I could see my heart being choked by everything negative in my life.

"Now reach inside and grab handfuls of the pain and release it. Then, watch it scatter and float away." My eyes were still closed and I tried to do what Dr. Stone instructed. It felt a little silly, but it worked. I really felt like I was getting rid of those poisonous feelings.

Each time, Dr. Stone asked me to give the pain a score on a scale of 1 to 10. He then wanted to know how much was left. He took me through the same process, asking me if I *could* let this go; *would* I let this go and, if so, *when*. Each time, the pain number got smaller and smaller, until it had reduced from ten to two. Then I realized the heavy load around my heart wasn't there. I knew I still had a long way to go, but I felt better. His method worked.

"How did it go?" he asked.

I took a cold drink of water before I spoke. I needed a little more time to collect my thoughts.

"Whatever pain I was stuffing was right there. I could feel it and see it all around my heart. Did you see me grabbing it and letting it go?"

"Yes, I did."

"Right now, if I want to, I can remember what people said about me. But those are only words. What they said isn't who I am. They don't hurt like they used to. I'm telling you, it's true. I'm not making this up so you'll like me. How did you learn that?"

"I met a beautiful man of peace named Hale Dwoskin. He's a brilliant spiritual teacher. I attended a seminar and this is what I learned from him. It is very effective, as well as simple and easy to use. It will work every time if you do it properly."

"Doc, thanks a lot. I think this is going to come in handy. I have a feeling I may not be running out of things to release anytime soon. Now that you taught me, I can do this on my own . . . right?"

"Right. Anytime you want."

"I have to hand it to you, Doc. I never would have figured you for a guy who's into this stuff."

Dr. Stone smiled. "I think that's enough for today. We've both earned a bit of a rest." He stood up to leave. "I want you to know that you can release any and all emotional pain this way. You can replace it with higher energy states, such as courage, acceptance, and peace. I will teach you more next time. For now, relax and take it easy.

"One more thing: your friends are off-limits. I don't want you to see anyone except your parents, staff, and that nurse's brother. I also want you to keep this good feeling going. If you slip back into negative thinking, release it as best you can. Negative thoughts will only lower your energy and weaken you. When you are weaker, you make more mistakes in judgment. I think you get the idea."

I reached out to shake his hand. He held my grip much longer than customary and placed his other hand on top of mine. It felt special to be joined to him that way. It was as though he was leaving some of his spirit behind and it felt like a gift.

He turned to leave. As he walked out the door, he said, "Take good care of a friend of mine."

I wasn't sure what he meant by that. But it sounded important.

CHAPTER 31

Drugs Are a Tricky Thing

By the time Dr. Stone left the room, I needed to lie there in silence. I'd been through an emotional wringer, feeling sad, humiliated, embarrassed, and angry, but now I felt a sense of peace inside. I think the letting-go exercise had something to do with it. I wondered how long the peace would last.

My mind was full of questions, and I looked forward to Dr. Stone coming back to coach me. That could only mean one thing: I was ready to trust him. That was new for me—I usually didn't trust anyone—but it felt good and gave me some relief. It made sense that all along I had been creating my own painful feelings and holding onto them. But I was confused—why would I hold on for so long to something that felt so bad?

I had more questions and no answers. My mind was hungry for something right away. I was excited and wanted to tell somebody what had happened to me. That was odd, because all of my life I'd wanted to be left alone, not because it felt so good, but because it didn't hurt so much.

There was a knock on the door. Dr. Stone had returned.

"I had another thought. You must be loaded with questions by now. I wish I had time to answer them for you. So here's what you can do. Take this notebook and pen, and start writing whatever comes to your mind. You probably have a million thoughts that need to get out. Journaling is the best way to get that started. Some good material will end up on the page and the rest will be the garbage you need to get rid of. Writing makes room for creation. Recovery is a creative way to try out new thoughts. New thoughts can lead to beliefs that you can put to good use. Start writing and keep at it. I'll see you in the morning. Oh, and this is private and confidential. Don't let anyone read it."

The doctor left as swiftly as he'd arrived. In less than a minute there was more knocking. I quickly opened the notebook and pretended to write, hoping to impress him as a model pupil. The notebook was swiped off the table by a thick, tattooed arm.

"What's this all about?"

Brenda fanned the pages and dropped the book. "It's empty," she said.

She scowled at me. "I don't know why, but Dr. Stone has taken a liking to you. He told me to go easy. Sorry pal, that's not my nature. Guys like you only learn the hard way. It's my job to see that you do. I may not be able to search your body, but I will check every nook and cranny in this room. If I find so much as a crumb of dope, I will have the nursing supervisor in here faster than you can swallow your spit."

She laced her fingers together, then snapped all of her joints at once. The sound reminded me of dry branches breaking; I wondered if she was getting ready to hurt me.

She scooped me up in her arms effortlessly, like I was an inflatable toy, and plopped me on the large reclining chair in the corner of the room. She stripped the sheets off the bed and shook them until they billowed in the air. The pillowcase was turned inside out, then she removed the mattress, leaned it up against the wall, and inspected it from all angles. She ran her fingers over all the surfaces of the bed frame before getting on her knees and looking underneath.

"This is clean," Brenda muttered to herself. She sounded disappointed.

She examined the countertops, opened drawers and cabinets, and banged them closed again. "Damn it, there's nothing here." She was getting more irritated. "Where did you hide them? You may as well give it up now."

She went through the plant arrangements before wrestling with the box of chocolates. It was a double-decker my mother had left behind and the bottom layer hadn't been touched. Brenda emptied the entire contents on the table, popped three chocolates into her mouth in rapid succession, then pushed the wrappers and the rest of the chocolates around.

She looked pretty pathetic on this useless mission to find pills. I was amused though, and thought about asking her if she'd like to call in a drug dog. I was afraid she'd smack me, so I kept my mouth shut. Brenda drummed her fingers on the counter top and scanned the room one more time.

"I am satisfied for now. You won't be using any happy pills today." She restored the room back to order and made my bed. "You're on your own," she said. She plopped the pillow back on my bed, then took off.

I was anxious to begin writing in my journal, but that had to wait for a while. First lunch, then two of my doctors took up several hours of the afternoon. But I finally was able to open the front cover of the notebook.

Something was written on the left-hand side.

Every journey begins with the first step. The destination is only a wishful thought. It is not a guarantee. The only certainty is what happens now, in the moment. That is all you've got and will ever have. Use it wisely, and live it fully.
Your friend in recovery, Dr. A. Stone.

That stopped me in my tracks. I swallowed really hard, as though clearing a lump out of my throat. The feelings I had were new and a bit scary. I was grateful and appreciative that Dr. Stone had taken an interest in me.

I had more questions and I needed answers; I wondered if journal writing might reveal something about me that would prove to be interesting or even useful.

I was just getting ready to write when the phone rang and startled me.

"It's me, Jeff. Hey, Buddy, how ya' doin'? Did you have a good time last night? We did. Man, that Sidney, she's a knockout. Just what the doctor ordered." He was laughing. I was pretty sure he was high.

"You got anymore Oxys left; or did you snort them all?" Jeff continued rambling. "Did you ever think we'd be snorting pills? Two guys like us? We're a team, you and me. You never talk and I don't shut up. When do you want me to come over? I got more pills. We can party. I can bring her, too. She's really got a lot of pills. She's got bags of the stuff. Man, we are set for life. My girl will keep us happy for a long time. Hey, is that snake lady slithering around? Watch out for her. She will pull you apart and eat you like a chicken wing."

"Jeff . . . Jeff! Shut up and listen, will you?"

Jeff was finally quiet on the other end.

"You can't come back. Stay away from this place. Do you hear me?"

More silence, and then laughing.

"You're a funny man. What do you mean, stay away? I got a package to deliver. You need more supplies. I got Roxicodone and Zannys. You're gonna sleep good tonight. I can be there in an hour. Find a good hiding place. This is what we've been waiting for. Did you know you can inject this stuff? I haven't done it yet, but it must be awesome. She's got even more goodies to try, like Ritalin and cocaine. You name it. I'm just getting started. There is so much to learn about this. We can do it together. I gotta go, Buddy. See you soon."

He hung up. I dialed back frantically, but the call went straight to voice mail. I knew he never checked his voice mail. I'd been with him when he deleted them; he always said they were old news and not worth listening to.

I began to panic. Jeff was on his way with pills—and trouble. Brenda would certainly intercept him, frisk him, and call the cops. Jeff was already high and he would be arrested if there were any pills on him. Dr. Stone would think I broke my word and think that I'd asked Jeff to smuggle in pills. That would be the end of me. I'd be totally screwed.

As I tried to figure out what to do, a volunteer walked through the door and dropped an envelope on my table. There was no stamp. It hadn't been mailed.

"A friend of yours gave me this an hour ago and asked me to include it in today's mail. Enjoy."

She was gone before I could quiz her. I opened the envelope hesitantly and removed the card. It read, "When life isn't the way you want it to be and gets worse anyway, look inside."

Inside was a picture of two hands pressed together in a praying position. Below them was printed, "Just put your hands together like this and say, *Please help me now.*"

Below that was handwritten, "A phone call usually speeds things up."

It was signed, *Your new recovery friend, Joe,* followed by a phone number.

I picked up the phone and dialed. Another voice message: "If you are hearing this message, I am either on the phone, going to the bathroom, eating something important, or saving someone's life. Please take a number and have a seat in the waiting room." Laughter followed the recording.

I said, "Joe, it's Buddy, I need help. Please call as soon as you get this message. I can't wait."

The last word was barely out of my mouth when the phone was abruptly plucked from my hand and swallowed up by a tight fist, a very large woman's fist.

"I heard that," Brenda snarled. "I knew you'd try something. Can't stay off junk, can you?" She slammed the phone on the table. My lifeline was probably broken. Brenda was breathing hard and had a wild, unruly look on her face.

"So, you need help and you can't wait. Is your dealer packing up a goodie bag just for you?" A low rumbling growl started to vibrate her throat. She sounded like a pit bull getting ready to lunge and bite.

"Did you think I was kidding?" she demanded. "I know your game. I know your kind. I know all about you." She folded her huge arms and began tapping her foot impatiently.

"We'll just wait for your package to arrive and have some handcuffs ready. This should make a nice headline in the newspapers: *Drug Dealer Nabbed in Hospital. Police Crackdown on Teen Source of Pain Killers,* blah blah blah. I don't know if I should call Dr. Stone or just let him find out when it all hits the fan and his new recruit gets thrown to the wolves."

I raised my hands, not knowing what else to do.

"What are you going to do, beg for mercy?"

"Brenda, you've got it all wrong. Give me a chance to explain."

She grabbed my wrist and twisted it into to a submission hold. The pain was searing and my vision darkened for a moment. She let go quickly and laughed.

"You weenies are all alike. Do you think I'm going to listen to your lame excuses? It's time for action."

"I couldn't agree more."

The voice that came from behind her made Brenda stand at attention. The nursing supervisor cruised into the room with her clipboard and quite a bit of momentum. She was all business.

"I thought I would find you two together. I'll take over from here. You have other patients to attend to. Don't worry; he won't get away with anything. Now go."

Brenda did an about-face with military precision and marched out, huffing and puffing. The supervisor stepped closer and put a calming hand on my shoulder.

"She's not used to working at a regular hospital. She's used to taking care of prison inmates. She is very highly qualified and really knows her stuff. She just doesn't know her own strength. I'm sure you're okay, aren't you?"

I shook my wrist; it was sore, but nothing serious. Once again, Brenda had terrorized me. She'd hounded me for being an addict, then she expected a drug dealer to show up with more pills. I needed the nursing supervisor on my side.

"Is there any way you can keep that nurse away from me?" I pleaded. "She belongs in a lumberjack camp. She thinks I have drugs in my room. I swear I don't. But someone might . . ." I hesitated for a moment; I didn't want her to know that Jeff was on his way here with a bag of pills. I could take care of him if I could just get him to shut up and listen. I didn't want to rat on him and get him arrested.

"Um . . . you might think I'm still using, but I'm not," I continued. "I met Dr. Stone and he's helping me. He's pretty cool."

"I will speak with your nurse. I'm quite sure the two of you can work out your differences." The nurse supervisor smiled disarmingly. "She has a certain flare for getting things done her way. I have to admit, patients do show a rapid and dramatic acceleration of their progress whenever she's around. They all express their gratitude on discharge day. I think it's her zeal."

I didn't really care what the other patients had to say about Brenda—she struck me as the type of sadistic person who would enjoy waterboarding if it were a spectator sport. I needed protection from Brenda, but the nursing supervisor was still jabbering away. Trying to recruit her to protect me was going to be a waste of time.

"And remember, drugs are a tricky thing. Even when you have good intentions, they can tempt you into slipping up. Do everything Dr. Stone tells you. And for heaven's sake, don't let anyone with drugs into your room."

She walked away without saying goodbye and I heard her call out to Brenda. It didn't matter what the nursing supervisor said to her about me; Brenda had a one-track mind and was determined to return and clean my clock. I could feel it coming and it felt bad.

I picked up the phone and shook it gently. Something rattled inside, but it came to life with a red light as it started ringing. I answered it. The voice on the other end was charged with excitement.

"Hey, Buddy, what's up? I got your message. It sounded urgent. Are you all right?"

I couldn't believe how lucky I was—Joe got my message, and my phone wasn't terminal.

"Yes, I think so. The nursing supervisor just left and I have a stay of execution. My floor nurse, the one who looks like a fire-breathing dragon, has got it in for me. She used to be a prison nurse. You know what that means, don't you? She probably likes pain. My pain."

Joe chuckled. "I think I know which nurse you mean."

I was too nervous to laugh. "She's the one with the snake tattoo and the body that looks like an oil tanker with legs. She got in my face and accused me of hiding drugs in the room. She wouldn't let up. It started to get a little rough. She tried to unscrew my wrist. I think she would have done it, too, if the nursing supervisor didn't put a stop to it. Joe, I don't think I'm safe here anymore. Can you come up and act like my bodyguard?"

"Sure, Kid. Hang in there. You still have your kneecaps, don't you?"

Before I could say, "Ha ha, very funny," he hung up and walked through the door, cell phone in hand. He was wearing some kind of maintenance uniform. He had a utility belt with hand tools and other equipment attached. He shook my hand with a strong athletic grip, which was very reassuring.

"Seriously, what's the problem? This sounded urgent."

"It's my friend Jeff," I explained. "He's on his way here with more pills. He's not allowed to visit me. He wouldn't listen when I told him to stay away. He's high on pills and he's coming anyway. Nurse Brenda knows he's coming. She set a trap and I'm going to go down with him. She threatened to have the cops here with handcuffs to arrest us both. He just started using. He's harmless, impulsive, and not too bright. He's just trying to have fun. Can you head him off and send him home? We can talk to him later and maybe smarten him up."

"You can count on me, Sport. What's Jeff look like? I'll find him." Joe hitched up his tool belt, which had slid off his hip just from the weight of all the items he was carrying.

I told him how to recognize Jeff and when to expect him. Joe agreed to post himself as a lookout and approach Jeff without drawing attention. Then he made an excellent suggestion.

"Why don't you write a note that introduces me to Jeff?"

"Sure. He'll know my handwriting," I agreed and jotted the note.

Jeff, this is a friend of mine. He is here to warn you. Don't come up to my room. They are on to you and there would be trouble if you come. I want you to know this was a bad mistake. I am not playing around with drugs anymore. I suggest you do the same. I'll call you. The guy who's giving you this letter is someone you can trust.

Joe read it and said, "This should do it. He can't be that stupid."

"I hope he's not too high."

"I'll let you know. I've got to go." He left the room, the tools knocking together and making a lot of assorted noises.

An hour went by before he called. "It's me. It worked. Jeff read your note and was high, but he got the message. He thanked me for stopping him. He said he would call you later."

"Thanks, Man. I owe you big time."

"No, you don't," Joe said. "This is how it works. You'll get the hang of it. Just try feeling grateful for now."

"I think I get it. And I'll do it."

"That's the spirit. You did the right thing, you know. More important, you protected yourself. Addiction will find any crack and pry it open until it gets through. Your friend and his drugs are risky business. Stay away from him. When he's high, he wants a using partner and, since you're his friend, he will call you to join him. Don't for one minute think you can talk him out of it, because you can't. It's best to walk away and be safe. So if he calls, just tell him that you are on a different path. If he wants to hear more, then give him my number. I know what to say. This is how we help each other. I'll see you tomorrow before work."

Before he said good-bye, he told me to write about this in my journal and then get some rest. He sounded sincere and compassionate.

"Take good care of a friend of mine," I told him and I meant it.

CHAPTER 32

Journaling

I opened the notebook, dated the first page, and began to write.

> *This is my first day of writing in this book. I don't know what I will say, so here goes. Today I learned something valuable. I'm in serious trouble with no idea how to get out of it. Along comes Joe, working his way through college here at the hospital. We have a lot in common. He offered to help me stay away from drugs, the main cause for all of my biggest problems. I said yes, and we struck up the beginnings of a friendship.*
>
> *I trust him and I know I made the right decision. Why? Because I have already called him when in desperate need of help, and he said he would take care of it, without any hesitation. I don't deserve this. I can't think of any way to repay him. So, I intend to accept his offer and be thankful. This is a pretty important lesson for me. It feels good, too. I may not be a winner yet, but I am certainly no longer a lonely geeky loser. I am actually creating a better life for myself. That's good enough for right now.*

My favorite nurse, Wendy, walked into the room. She looked great and I felt special.

"Hi, Buddy. I thought I'd come by to see what you're up to. It looks like you're busy with one of Dr. Stone's journal-writing assignments."

She was visiting before her shift started in another hour. She had the kind of inner beauty that showed right through to the outside.

"I just got started, but I keep getting interrupted. I haven't written much."

"I heard about Brenda. She's really got a thing for you."

"A thing?" I mused. "She's brutal. I was minding my own business and she twisted my wrist with some kind of prisoner take-down technique. She stopped just short of breaking it, then called me a weenie."

"She's done that before," Wendy said. "She's always got a good reason to use what she calls a show of force. Anyone with a drug problem needs to be taught a lesson, in her book. I think the nursing supervisor is impressed that Brenda knows all these self-defense moves. I heard them talking about an instructional in-service to teach us how to do them. I think she spent too much time around killers and psychopaths in prison. I'm sorry I didn't ask sooner: are you all right?"

"Of course, I'm all right." I demonstrated how I could move my wrist in all directions.

"I feel like I have a new lease on life. Especially since you found me near death and called in Dr. Stone to bring me back. A lot of good things have happened to me since I overdosed. Your brother became my friend, and Dr. Stone taught me how to let go of some of the pain from my past. Jeff tried to bring in more drugs, but your brother found him and sent him away. I hope the prison nurse is off my case now—and I made my first journal entry. How's that for progress?"

Wendy stepped forward with her arms open wide. "You deserve one of these," she announced as she gingerly hugged me around the neck, taking care not to hit my brace. The soft, clear skin of her cheek made direct contact with the pimples on my face, but she didn't seem to mind. When she let go, I was speechless and taking shallow breaths. I was pretty sure I was blushing. What she did was so spontaneous and loving, my pimples became insignificant. Her perfume lingered on the fabric of my hospital gown. I didn't need OxyContin or any other pills to enjoy myself—and that surprised me.

"I am proud of you, Buddy," Wendy praised with a generous smile on her face. "You have changed so much in such a short time. Doesn't it feel great? Don't you want to stay with this nice clean recovery feeling?"

I would have gladly spent the entire day with her. Nothing had ever felt that good in my life. Getting high on pills was no comparison. The way Wendy made me feel was magical and changed me in the right way forever.

Her visit was over too soon. When she left to begin her shift, my heart sank a bit. She'd hugged me in a way that was more intimate than I could recall ever having been hugged; it was different than being hugged by my mom. At least one person wasn't afraid to get close to me. She made me feel that I could not be harmed as long as she cared. She was trying to be close to me inside, where I lived. She wanted to be with the real *me*. And the real *me* didn't have pimples. My face did. That proved to me that what people see with their eyes is not who I really am. Maybe my body looked repulsive, but I wasn't repulsive.

Maybe Wendy didn't think I was attractive, but she found something about me that she wanted to be near. Her affection for me seemed to have a lifesaving power all its own. All I had to do was allow her to be herself. I didn't resist; I just accepted it. When dinner arrived, I devoured it like it was a last meal. I guess feeling better about my life had given me an appetite. As I licked the last bit of barbecue sauce off each finger, my cell phone rang; it was Jeff.

"Hey, Buddy. How are you doing without any pills? What happened? Why did you change your mind? I had plenty of great stuff. I was going to join you and get buzzed. I met that guy you sent with the note. What's his thing? He told me that you're on some kind of path. What's he talking about? You can't leave me now. We're just getting started. Sidney is here with me now. Hold on, she wants a word."

Sidney's voice was sexy and sultry. "Is that you, Handsome? We wanted to come over and bring you something to clear your sinuses. But you made one of your Boy Scouts send Jeffrey away. That's no way to treat guests. So be it. Jeff and I have each other and you were getting to be a bore. No more goodies for you. Don't bother begging. All I want is my money. Remember, money makes the world go around. Oh, and by the way, I have some friends who will be collecting for me. They would be happy to give you a matching pair of broken legs, free of charge. Enjoy the nice path you're on."

She hung up, leaving me baffled. How was I supposed to get the money? After all the good things that had happened, I was screwed again. I imagined her hit men had no necks and no patience. Even the nurses wouldn't be able to protect me. Hit men always find a way to get in—I knew that from watching movies. I thought I had more time, but now I wasn't sure. I'd seen Sidney yesterday and she said I had a week to pay up. I should have had six more days left. I needed an answer on the money. Where would it come from? I turned to the second page in the journal and began writing.

> I am in trouble. I need money, about four hundred dollars. I have a week to get it or I am going to be visited by men without manners. I am scared. I could ask Mom for her rainy-day money. No, she wouldn't part with any of it. My parents would rather call my bluff or notify the police. They might tell the hospital administrator. I can tell Dr. Stone. I'm starting to panic.

I paused for a moment and took a deep breath before resuming.

> Somehow, there will be a solution. Don't worry. Should I try the releasing technique? No, not right now. All I can think about is how much trouble I got into. I had to have those drugs, didn't I? I remember saying, "No matter what the price, I am willing to pay it." The first time I got high, those pills were worth it. I just wanted to have some fun. Not this. What if I'd known the outcome? Would that have stopped me from using?

The answer came as quickly and decisively as the question. No way. I would not have stopped myself. Nothing was going to change my mind. I wanted the drugs. I was crazy to be that way. Why couldn't I have seen that? What prevented me from doing the smart thing? Now somebody could get hurt—starting with me.

CHAPTER 33

Your Money or Your Life

A shadow spread completely across my bed. Before I could look up from my writing, a cobra-quick hand swiped my notebook away. Brenda's agitated voice stabbed the air.

"Gotcha! I see you've been a busy little beaver, writing your fingers to the bone. Let's see if you're any good. I'm sure you mentioned me in there somewhere."

She fanned all the pages of the notebook and read a few paragraphs. Her eyes widened with a menacing glare.

"This is pathetic. Fifth graders can write better than this. Why don't you stick to squeezing your zits? Losers like you don't win . . . at anything."

I wanted so much to cause her a significant amount of pain. But I had no brilliant ideas. I just lay there waiting for what I knew was coming.

"Oh, I like this entry," she snickered. "'I am in trouble. I need money, about four hundred dollars,'" she read aloud in a sing-song voice. "'I have a week to get it or I am going to be visited by men without manners. I am scared.'"

As she read aloud, Brenda paced like a lion in a cage. I watched as she tore the pages out of the book, folded them, and tucked them in her uniform pocket. She tossed the notebook back on the table. She moved her head in several different directions until I heard cracking sounds from the joints in her neck.

"What about my pages? That's my property. I want them back."

Brenda bent over the bed and looked me straight in the eye.

"You're a weakling. I'm adding these to my collection. I take something from every loser I treat. It's like a trophy. Besides, you need to be taught a lesson. You've had it way too easy around here. As a matter of fact, I think it would do you good to have a couple of goons work you over. That's what you get for playing on credit. It doesn't take long to snort up four hundred dollars' worth, does it, Pal? And now you have to pay. I want a front seat to watch this happen. What a match: Men Without Manners versus Teenie-Weenie Dope Fiend. They're going to squash you like a bug."

She took the torn pages out of her pocket and glanced at them, then waved them in front of my face.

"I had no idea you were so talented. You must be so proud of yourself. Why don't you submit this for publication? I hear they're looking for new material for *Chicken Soup for the Loser's Soul.*"

Brenda let out a sinister laugh. She jammed a very imposing index finger into my collarbone, causing a searing pain that felt electrical—icy and hot all at once. The pain shot into my solar plexus; I couldn't breathe or speak. I couldn't even beg her to stop.

She withdrew her finger and all systems returned to normal within seconds. She held the torn notebook pages up to my nose and crinkled them with the crush of her paw.

"I could have killed you with just ten more pounds of pressure. Don't forget that. I didn't leave a mark. You can't prove a thing. Now that you know I have lethal talents, and somebody's coming to collect on a debt, you might want me to be here during visiting hours . . . for a reasonable fee. Those bag men won't get past me."

Her lip curled slightly; Brenda played the blackmail game very well.

"I don't need up-front money to give you protection. I am a patient woman. I can wait until you get home. I'm sure you can convince mommy and daddy that your life is worth that much cash. Besides, I'm beginning to like taking care of you. You're a good investment. Is it a deal?"

Things had suddenly gone from bad to worse and I wished I could have wiped that smug, cocky look off her face. I willed myself to keep thinking like a winner.

"I don't want your protection," I said. "I'll take my chances and pay up as soon as I get the money. I'm not worried. My folks are good for it. Why don't you leave me alone?"

She rolled her shirt sleeve well above the elbow and flexed her bicep. The veins engorged and stood out like rivers on a map.

"Take a good look, Buddy-boy." She caressed the mound of muscle with her palm. "You need this fortification because you're a pencil-neck geek. Those ham-handed thugs only know one law out there in the jungle: eat or be eaten. You are a puny appetizer for them. They'll take your money and your life. I'll only take your money. Think it over, Prince Charming."

Brenda rolled her sleeve down and covered the slithering python tattoo that she'd exposed. Then she opened up the notebook pages and smoothed them out, using her hand like a rolling pin.

"Here, now that you're my investment, you can have your notes back. There was nothing in there about me anyway. We'll pick this up again tomorrow. Tonight, I'm working my pecs and lats at the gym, just for your extra measure of protection."

The room seemed larger the moment Brenda left it. I didn't know what to think or do next. This was all too complicated. My life was starting to mean more to me and I wanted to be on a clear path—but that was proving to be difficult and painful. By comparison, being a shy, geeky loser had been pretty easy.

But I couldn't let myself think that way. I had survived Brenda's pressure-point threat and turned down her demands for my parents' hard-earned money. I was getting the hang of being more like a winner.

I decided to call my mom and see if I could convince her to pay off my debt. She answered the phone like she didn't have a care in the world.

"Hello?"

"Hi, Mom, it's me."

"Hello, Son. What do you want?" The tone of her voice instantly changed, as though she expected very bad news.

"I met with Dr. Stone today. He's a pretty good guy. He listened to some of my life story and taught me this neat way to let go of stuff that bothers me. I built up a lot of anger since I was a kid. I made a lot of progress today getting over it. I have more to do, but I should be all right."

"Is that all he did?" Mom asked. I think she was hoping for more of a psychiatric breakthrough. I wondered if she thought I should be ready to run for class president by now.

"No, that's not all he did. I wasn't sure if you wanted to hear any of this."

"Of course, I do. I'm paying for this fiasco you got yourself into. Was it really worth it? Taking a few pills to end up like this? Do you know how much this is going to cost us? We will probably have to spend your college tuition." She was not going to spare me any of her sarcasm.

"So, what else did the good doctor do for you today?"

I wanted to rap the phone against the edge of the table and send a loud, penetrating noise through her ear drums. That would have felt better than a full scholarship. But I held my anger in check. "Mom, Dr. Stone is helping me. We made a great connection. He gave me a notebook to do some journal writing. He said it will reveal some inner problems for me to work on. I can do this, Mom. I can change and say goodbye to drugs. And speaking of drugs, I have a little favor to ask you."

I heard the sharp intake of my mom's breath on the other end. I shut my eyes tightly in preparation for the fallout.

"Go on," she said. "What have you done now? Should I bring your father to the phone?"

"No, just you. It's not that bad. I need a few dollars. I owe somebody money for the pills I took the other night."

"You mean to tell me you have to pay for those things?" Her voice got louder. "Don't you get them from your friends for free? Who's been paying for this nasty habit of yours?" She was up an octave now and getting more intense. "How much is a few dollars?" Silence. "Ten?" Silence. "Twenty?" Longer silence. "Fifty?" Eternal silence. "A hundred? What on God's green earth do these pills cost?"

My mouth was so dry, I couldn't even swallow. I closed my eyes and crossed my fingers. "Four hundred." Silence. "Mom . . . Mom. The Oxys cost eighty dollars apiece. I didn't use that many."

"Eighty dollars for one pill!" Now she was screaming. "Are you crazy? Suppose I don't pay. Then what?"

I couldn't tell her about the debt collector.

"I am not going to waste that kind of money on pills. Tell your friend that it was stupid to sell you something you couldn't pay for. It's his loss, not mine."

"Mom."

"What!"

"The person who wants the money is not very nice. She's a drug dealer. And she hired people to collect the money. They sort of don't take no for an answer, if you know what I mean."

"You mean gangsters? That's who you buy pills from, gangsters?"

"No. She's a student at my school. Sidney. Remember the girl I told you about? The one you wanted me to bring home. Well, she's the one who gave me my first pill. I owe her the money. She's the drug dealer. The men she's going to send will be very upset if I don't have it. They'll probably break my good leg."

"That's impossible," she said. "You're in the hospital. Are you trying to get me to give you money to buy more drugs? Hey, wait a minute. Why should I believe you? Of all the lowdown tricks to get drugs and I almost fell for it. I'm so furious, I can't even talk to you." The line went dead.

When something goes from bad to worse, what happens next? Worser? I couldn't believe this was happening. Sidney had lured me into her tangled web. I'd seen a chance for a wonderful life without pain and I couldn't resist. Now I owed her four hundred dollars and, if I didn't pay up fast, I was facing the unthinkable. All I could imagine was the kind of torture that I'd seen in the movies. Could it be any worse than that?

My only source of cash was Mom's cookie jar and she believed I wanted the money for more drugs. I also had a nurse who offered me protection for a fee to be negotiated. There was no place for me to hide and the sand in the hourglass was running out fast. What was I supposed to do?

I was overwhelmed, and I couldn't see a way out. To make matters worse, I was stuck in a brace because of a broken back. I had a shattered leg that was skewered with pins. I was slow and clumsy at best, completely defenseless, and vulnerable. How does a winner deal with that?

I didn't want to give up my life to anything or anyone. It may not have been perfect, but it was mine, and I now knew how it could be fixed, slowly but surely.

The pressure got to me and I began to cry. That was a first. I didn't know much about crying. It was a very strong physical reaction coming from a place of fear and sorrow. I wished more than anything that I could talk to Dr. Stone again. I had more questions. Why was all of this happening? Of course I was scared. Who wouldn't be? I was all alone in a world of hurt and I had no experience on how to make any of it stop. I couldn't even get up and walk out of there. Or could I? I didn't know. I did know this much: Others must have been in this predicament before. Other kids like me who screwed up with pills and were threatened. What did they do? Some of them must have made it through and left the drug life behind. Who protected them? Brenda couldn't be my answer; she was part of the problem.

I would have given anything to be back in my room with video games, music, and a book. I just wanted this nightmare to end.

CHAPTER 34

Higher Powers Come in All Shapes and Sizes

I lay in the dark room, my thoughts a continuous loop of fear that was overwhelming me. I almost jumped out of my skin as the rustle of clothing alerted me to someone entering into my room.

"It's me." I exhaled with relief at the sound of Wendy's voice.

She turned on the small overhead light and I wished she'd give me one of her fantastic hugs. She had a way of making me feel safe from any harm.

Wendy sat on the mattress beside me and placed her hand softly on top of mine. It was gentle and friendly, not sensual. "I wanted to see how you were doing."

"Thanks for coming in," I said. "Right now, I can sure use your company."

She looked into my eyes and all I saw was kindness.

"I had quite a day," I said. "It went from better to worse in a hurry. Earlier today, I thought my serious troubles were over. I couldn't wait to learn more about recovery and start changing my life. Tonight, one phone call scared me so much, I want to get out of here and hide. I don't know what to do."

I felt the full weight of her body settle into the mattress. She gently pushed some hair off my forehead and her fingers felt soothing.

"You've been crying, haven't you?" Wendy asked gently. "I don't know what's wrong, but I'll bet it can be fixed. Trust me. I have been through so much with my brother. Your problems couldn't be any worse. What's got you upset enough to cry?"

She gave me a fresh tissue to blow my nose. I explained about my drug debt and the unsavory collectors who were bound to turn up with a vengeance. Then I told her about Brenda, who hated drug-addicted losers, yet was willing to protect me for an undisclosed fee.

"Listen, Buddy," Wendy offered when I'd finished. "I know you've got problems, big problems. That kind of wreckage isn't easy to clean up. At some point, you have to face it and deal with it as best you can. My brother went through something similar."

All I could think of at the moment were gangsters who would fit me with cement shoes and throw me overboard into the river. I wondered how long I could hold my breath; I hoped I would pass out before drowning. The thought of inhaling water into my lungs terrified me.

"Tell me," I said, "how I am I supposed to deal with a sadistic nurse who likes to inflict pain when nobody's looking, a mother who won't part with a few hundred dollars to save her son's life, and a drug-dealing girl who wants pay-back or my broken body parts?"

Wendy stood up and smoothed the bedcovers while she decided how to answer my question. "You've got me there," she said. "I don't have a solution to your problems. I only know that there are choices you can make that won't make matters worse. When I need help, I use my Higher Power."

"And who might that be?" I was a little snappy with Wendy, because I felt like my back was up against the wall. I was already imagining the worst: I was going to pay for my crimes with my life at the tender age of sixteen.

Wendy paused, waiting for me to pay attention. I think she wanted to be sure I was ready to hear her answer. "Higher Powers come in all shapes and sizes. It's a topic that has been written about for centuries. There are as many Higher Powers as there are people with opinions about them. I like to call my Higher Power the Source. I think of it as the energy of existence. It's all-inclusive; the *It*, the *All*, the *One and Only*. Kind of makes your head spin to think about something you can't imagine, doesn't it?"

I was still upset; her explanation wasn't working for me. "I don't get it, Wendy. You are way over my head with this Higher Power. It sounds like you're trying to talk about God without His permission. My problems aren't going to get fixed by something called the *It*. That's a Stephen King novel. You have to do better than that. This is crunch time for me and I'm wondering if I'll ever get to go on a date or graduate from high school, never mind the other stuff that comes after it."

She looked at her watch and turned to leave. "You're right. That was pretty insensitive of me to expect you to grasp the concept of a Higher Power and then apply it to a problem as serious this. It does take some explaining and a whole lot of understanding before it all makes sense. More important, I want to thank you for opening up and trusting me to listen and care about you. I wish I could do more right now, but I can't; I have to check on other patients. But don't despair, because I'm sure Dr. Stone can talk to you tomorrow about it. It's one of his favorite subjects. Try to get some sleep tonight." Wendy turned the light out again and left the room to resume her rounds.

I was in the dark – literally and figuratively. My life was in shambles and about to get worse and Wendy wanted me to believe that some kind of energy was supposed to fix my problems? I was ignorant on the subject, and I was focused on one thing: survival. I knew I was solely responsible for the mess in my life and I had no idea how to clean it up. Even if I tried to run, there was probably no place to hide.

I tossed and turned through the night, and when the faint grey morning light filled the room, I had lost my confidence. My winning attitude was gone.

Breakfast came earlier than usual; I took a few bites but had no appetite. I decided to try getting up on my own and was surprised how easy it was. My strength had increased and I was able to maneuver around the room. I was really comfortable for the first time. My back, the brace, the leg . . . they all felt amazingly good. I must have been healing rapidly. It was time to ask about going home, so I could get out before the drug money was due.

The physical therapist entered just as I was about to get back into bed. "Good morning Buddy," he said briskly. "It's good to see you up already. Today, I'm going to teach you how to walk with crutches. Because you have stairs at your home, we'll practice on those, too."

My broken leg felt comfortable and secure and I was surprised at how coordinated I was using crutches. By the time we made it to the exercise room, I was walking at a pretty good pace and feeling proud. He took me right over to a box with three steps going up one side and three steps down the other. He sat me in a chair and I watched as he demonstrated how it was done, with the right foot going first on the way up and the crutches going first on the way down. It was my turn next: I was more out of breath than when I was walking on the floor, but I made it slowly to the top of the box and back down again.

"Don't worry, Kid, you're doing fine. If you're staying for another day or so, we'll practice more before you go home. Let's head back to your room."

I had all the proof I needed that I was ready to go home. "You're stronger than you look," the therapist congratulated me. "Keep it up and you'll do fine. I'll recommend you go to outpatient rehab when you're discharged."

As we headed toward my room, we passed my orthopedic doctor who was in the hallway. He asked me to follow him to a room where several other doctors were standing around drinking coffee. He introduced me to them as "the young man who took on a tanker truck at 100 miles per hour." The doctors all looked at me with curiosity. My doctor knew he had a captive audience. He described my injuries in detail and sounded almost giddy as he described how he'd patched me up. "Show them how you can walk, Kid." He pointed down the hall in the direction he wanted me to go and waved his hand.

"Watch this," he said. "He learned this just today." He motioned again with greater emphasis to get me going. I felt like a circus animal about to perform a trick. The other doctors looked impressed as I walked.

"Good job, Kid. You're okay for discharge from my end."

I was pretty proud of myself; not only was I walking, but I'd managed to keep my sarcastic comments to myself. My attitude was definitely improving.

Once I was back in my room, I realized how exhausting my little performance had been. I decided to sit for a while, prop my leg up in the reclining chair, and snooze for a bit.

I woke up to the sound of a commotion in the hallway. Brenda's voice was loud and distinctive and I could hear her arguing with someone. I walked to the door for a look.

There were two men wearing blue coveralls standing next to her. They carried tool kits and one was wheeling a cart. Brenda was poking her finger at one of the men.

"For the last time, that room is off-limits. I don't care what repairs are needed, they can wait." She scowled at them and one of them handed her a work order. "It says right here, lady. Replace leaky oxygen distribution valve."

Brenda shook her head vigorously. "I don't care if it says replace leaky heart valve. If you try to go into that room, you'll both be leaking from a few places that won't be fixable."

"Suit yourself, Ma'am. We got other things to do. If you want us back, you have to put in a new work order. Come on, Charlie, this broad is on steroids."

Brenda turned and walked straight toward me. It was too late to duck and hide. When she arrived at my door, she looked pumped up with victory.

"Hey, Junior, I just saved your butt from those creeps. I can't be fooled that easily. They were as phony as three-dollar bills. They probably had some brutal torture tools in those bags. I'm earning my keep already. You see, Kid: you're not safe unless I'm around. Maybe you should hire me as a private-duty nurse, twenty-four seven."

"I saw you with those guys," I said. "I don't think they were here to collect the money. They couldn't bend copper tubing with their bare hands. Maybe you aren't such a hotshot bodyguard after all."

Brenda got close enough for me to see her fully-dilated pupils. I had seen that look before. "Listen, Punk. When I worked in the can, I learned a thing or two. Prison is a place where you have to be prepared for the unexpected. You have to be on your guard. Anybody can stick you when you're not looking. Just one jab right here with a shiv and your kidney goes down in a hemorrhage."

She jammed her thumb into the flank side of my lower back and a cramping pain instantly shot straight down into my groin. It was gone as soon as she stopped. It was just a demonstration, but her point was well-made.

"I've been around some hardened criminals, Tinker Bell. They don't need teardrop tattoos or gold-plated teeth to be bad or dangerous. They can look like sweet Uncle Louie and be serial killers. They are all a scheming bunch of lowlifes who would sell their mother's wedding ring for cigarettes. I was assigned to the infirmary and I saw the injuries from every beating and serious fight. Those who were damaged the most were child molesters and, of course, the boneless weenies, like you."

I had no clue where she was going with the trials and tribulations of life behind bars. But she was on a roll, so I just let her keep talking.

"You see, the molesters are going to get what's coming to them. We can't stop it as long as they are in the general population. Some call that justice. Then we have the drug addicts. Some of them are a very bad bunch. They can be sociopathic criminal types who would hurt you just for fun. If you got arrested for possession, you'd get probation. If you kept snorting and shooting dope, you'd eventually get caught with a positive drug test and end up behind bars for violating probation. You'd be easy pickings. They'd nail you like it was open season. You wouldn't last an hour in the can."

"Okay, enough, I get your point," I said. "I think I'm ready to get out of here. The orthopedic doc says I can go if everybody else agrees."

She walked over and sat on my bed. Her hands were pressed into the mattress and her arms looked like the marble pillars at the Lincoln Memorial.

"Kid, listen to me. You may not find me attractive, but I have my admirers. You may not like my persuasive methods, but I get the job done. You've been reckless and barreling down the wrong path with major-league drugs. I won't stand for it. While you're here, it's my duty to get you across to the other side. You may be a little sore when you get there, but I don't know any other way. Drugs are the devil's playthings. I want you to leave them alone. You understand? If you use drugs, there's only two ways it will turn out: prison or death. Which one would you prefer? If I think you're high, I'm coming after you and there will only be one of us left standing."

Mercifully, I heard Brenda's name paged over the intercom. She was gone in a flash and I was thankful that all I'd had was a lecture and no new injuries.

I settled down in the recliner. Brenda was quite a presence when she was around and I was happy to enjoy some peace and quiet now that she was gone. I was dozing when my phone began to ring.

"You are more resourceful than I gave you credit for. I won't be stopped. You had your fun at the amusement park. Now you have to pay for the ride—one way or another." Sidney's voice was cold and hard.

"Why are you bugging me for the money so soon? You'll get it. I can't just take a wheelchair to the ATM machine."

"Don't be coy with me. I can have your ticket punched anytime I want. I'm making an example of you. This is good for my reputation and my business. My customers will think long and hard before they try to mess with me."

"Listen, Sidney, you don't have to worry about me. The money is a done deal. I've got it. Give me another day and it's yours."

"You know, Buddy, you have cost me money, time, and a misuse of manpower. At this point, I just want to see you suffer. I almost don't care if I get paid. The pleasure of knowing you got roughed up would almost satisfy me. If Nurse Darth Vader tries to interfere again, she's going down and you will learn the meaning of honoring your debt. It's always fascinating how quickly money appears when my boys arrive. It's like magic. Just a word to the wise, I never send the same team twice. If your nurse plans to spend the night, she better not even blink. Sweet dreams."

I put the phone down and held my head in both hands. This was serious. I had to get out of the hospital and get my hands on some cash. My problem seemed to have no solution. I didn't know what else to do, so I started writing in the journal notebook again.

> *I can walk farther than yesterday. I am much better than I thought possible. Unfortunately, a load of bad news swarmed in on me like buzzards on a carcass. Two guys who looked like the Maytag repair men showed up. I saw them standing in the hall and Brenda intercepted them: she sniffed them out and disposed of them without a fight. I owe her. I thought they were hospital employees.*
>
> *I think Brenda has a lot of experience dealing with bad people. She told me about doing hard time—I have no idea why. Maybe she was trying to scare me. I know one thing: the weaklings in prison probably wish they were dead. I would have no life span in prison. I'd rather be dead anyway.*
>
> *Sidney called. She was irate because her men came back empty-handed. She's not giving up, though, and I don't want to be here when the next guys arrive.*
>
> *My mom is disgusted and convinced that I am a hopeless drug addict. She thinks I would stop at nothing to get money from her to score more pills. She'll never part with any of her cash now.*
>
> *I tried to understand what a Higher Power is all about, but I don't get it. It sounds more like make-believe. I'm not ready to ask something that isn't real to take care of me. That's my job.*
>
> *Why am I bothering to write any of this? I suppose it's because I am still hurting. I should do some releasing. I know it would help, but I don't feel like it. It's not that easy staying on the path. It's times like this when I wish I had something to take the edge off. I*

need a little something to lift the troubles off my back. I want to be safe, alone, and protected from any harm. Does that mean I would take an OxyContin if I had one? I think so . . . I know so. Does that mean that my recovery has worn off? I bet it has. I can't keep it going all by myself. I would rather quit and take the easy way . . . the painless way . . . the loser's way. Why does this have to be so hard?

CHAPTER 35

At the End of My Rope

I slammed the notebook shut and threw my pen toward the door. I was about to toss the notebook in the same direction.

"Hey, wait, I come in peace."

Dr. Stone stood at the door with his hands raised in mock surrender. He bent over to retrieve my pen and brought it back to the table. "Life putting you to the test today?" he asked.

"You might say that, Doc. I have had it up to here with everything. I feel so bad today. I just wrote in this notebook that if I had an Oxy, I'd take it right now. No kidding. I would snort that thing right in front of you. I'm at the end of my rope. Nothing is going right. I want to give up. How does anybody get through this?"

Dr. Stone pulled up a chair and sat down right next to me. His loose, relaxed, and casual manner was exactly the opposite of mine. He opened up a full bottle of water he'd brought with him and made half of it disappear in two swallows. He looked like he was ready to take on the entire world's problems.

He leaned toward me slightly, a serious look on his face. "If you want an OxyContin that much, what's stopping you?"

"Simple. I don't have one."

"So either you pick up the phone and make some arrangements for delivery or you make some arrangements for recovery. Which is it going to be?" He paused for a minute to let that sink in. "If you can't make up your mind, then take the next step and walk me through what will happen if you get a pill."

I didn't exactly follow his logic, but I followed the instructions.

"Okay, let's say I can get Jeff to smuggle in four 80s. Do you want me to tell you what I would do?"

He nodded yes.

"Simple: I would shred one and snort it faster than you can finish that water."

"Then what?"

"I might just relax and let it work. Or I could track down Brenda and tell her off."

"Brenda? What's that all about?"

"She's been on my case since I got here. She's insulting and intimidating. She's sadistic and pokes fun at me. I'd use my superior intelligence to outsmart her somehow and get even. I would love to see her beg for mercy and suffer."

"An Oxy could do all that for you?"

"Yes. And then I would find Wendy and tell her that she is the most beautiful creature on this planet. I wouldn't be afraid if she slapped me and walked away. I would just tell her how much I cared and be ready to give her a kiss if she let me."

"That's ambitious. All that from one Oxy?"

"Well, maybe I would have to snort two before I took her in my arms and kissed her. But there's more. I would tell my mom that she's got me all wrong. I am loveable. I am not a reject. And finally, I would get out of here today."

"Why are you in such a hurry?" Dr. Stone furrowed his brow.

"There's a price on my head—four hundred dollars. I owe money for drugs and I don't have it. Two bone breakers are coming. If I had an Oxy, I could leave immediately, no hesitating. No looking back . . . gone."

Doctor Stone started teasing the label loose from the empty water bottle.

"Do you really think that a little OxyContin can do all that? Don't answer, because you're just going to repeat yourself. Listen. OxyContin is just a molecule. It's hydrogen, carbon, and oxygen atoms all put together. It doesn't do your thinking. It doesn't do your kissing or make any of your injuries heal. It doesn't do anything but sit in your brain on some opioid receptor and release dopamine."

I wished he'd spare me the biochemistry lecture.

"Do you realize that you can release just as much dopamine of your own free will? If you want to create courage, fun, excitement, or love, you don't need OxyContin. You never did. You just need some social training and practice. But once you've mastered the art of happiness, you can create a bunch of it anytime you want. It's like having a natural pharmacy. Do you understand that?"

I was perplexed again. I hoped he wasn't going to try to sell me on some all-purpose Higher Power.

"I don't get it," I said. "I feel so great when I take OxyContin. It's quick and easy. The price I can do without. But I don't see how it's possible to feel good enough without a pill."

Dr. Stone stifled a sigh. "The secret to feeling good is to stop having thoughts that feel so bad. What you create with your mind becomes who you think you are. All repetitive thought eventually turns into a belief. You can't do anything without having a belief to back it up. You can't walk out that door without believing you can put one foot in front of the other. You can't be shy without believing that you don't fit in. You can't believe you are beautiful if you think you are ugly, no matter how many people tell you otherwise. It's all about the power of belief. It's not about the power of OxyContin. OxyContin is not a belief. It is a drug and nothing else."

"I thought OxyContin made it easier to believe in myself."

Dr. Stone pulled his chair a little closer. You see," he continued, "OxyContin is a narcotic. After taking it, you simply stopped feeling how much pain you created in your life. OxyContin never really changed you at all. That's why you needed more and more to keep the truth from coming back to disappoint you. It's time to challenge the beliefs that don't serve you anymore, like believing that you're a shy, geeky loser. OxyContin just covered up those negative feelings. The loser belief is still there waiting for you when the drug wears off. I can teach you once and for all how to get rid of limiting beliefs and create new and improved ones. It just takes practice and time. Eventually you'll get there—I guarantee it."

All this talk about what could happen someday was frustrating me. "Okay, that all sounds nice, but today I've got big troubles. If I'm not going to take an Oxy, then you'd better come up with something. Because I'm in a tunnel that's caving in and I am a long way from getting out alive."

Doctor Stone stopped playing with the water bottle label. "When you get overwhelmed like that, it usually helps to keep it simple. That is why the KISS tool is used in recovery. It means Keep It Simple, Stupid."

"I don't see anything simple about my problems," I argued. "I owe money. There are hit men trying to get past Brenda, who's now my guard dog. My parents are convinced that the payoff money is to feed my drug habit. I have a busted spine and a leg I can't walk on. What part of that can you keep simple for me?"

Dr. Stone took off his glasses and cleaned the lenses. His eyes were kind. "Let's take them one at a time and keep first things first," he said. "When you do that, it is easier to understand the problem without so much fear, panic, and dread. Those emotions lead to suffering and suffering is the greatest force that weakens the mind and spirit. At this point, you need maximum energy in those departments."

I told him to start with the money and the hit men. Those problems made me nervous enough to want to sleep with a baseball bat under my pillow.

"First, always begin with the status of your addiction or, better yet, the status of your recovery. Like it or not, you are addicted. There was nothing social about the way you used drugs. You binged on pills and instead of having the best party of your life, you tried to take out a tanker truck with your body. Agreed?"

He was right. I had no argument there.

"Next, you check in with a simple question: Are you sober right now? Answer?"

I offered a very weak, "Yes."

"Damn right, you are. It's time you began to appreciate the fact that you have chosen to abstain from drugs right this very moment, today. From that vantage point, you can declare sobriety, albeit at a beginner's level. Your spiritual path may not be too enlightened yet, but you are officially drug-free. And for an addict, that's the biggest accomplishment of every single day. There will never be a bigger one."

My sobriety did not impress me. "Why is being drug-free such a big deal?"

"Because addiction plays for keeps. It prevents you from being happy, successful, healthy, sane, or alive. Its only purpose for existence is to get you high, again and again, until you destroy your life in the process. The sooner this all happens, the better. Addiction could care less about your problems. There is a very insidious reason for all of this."

"What's that?" I was still skeptical.

"For addiction to survive and fulfill its destiny, it needs one thing: to be fed whatever it craves. It wants whatever will strengthen its hold on you. It doesn't matter whether that's drugs, booze, food, sex, gambling, or cigarettes. The pleasurable experience must travel though the dopamine circuit in the brain.

"The reason I use the word insidious is because it means cunning and sneaky. Addiction can convince you that what you are doing is justifiable and fun. Addiction is so dangerously subtle that any negative consequences can easily be written off. If you did something you regret, addiction can conveniently make it into a forgotten memory or, better yet, a sincere apology. The infamous line, 'I'm sorry, I'll never do that again,' usually works like a charm—and it's cheap. Then you're back in the game. And that is exactly where addiction wants you. Playing the game to get more, while actually believing it's never enough. You just can't win against addiction as long as you're in the game. And the price you pay for playing keeps getting higher and higher."

"That's a lot to follow, Doc. What's your point?"

"Sorry about that. I can get a little carried away with this stuff. These principles saved my life, so I'm just a bit passionate. My point is that when you are sober or drug-free, you are winning by not playing. And very few are chosen for that. It is an honor and privilege to be drug-free. Being drug-free cannot be bought. It's a gift that is given to those who ask and are willing to do whatever it takes to receive it."

"Slow down, Doc," I interrupted. "I think you said something I can use. Did you say being drug-free is such a big deal because it's a slap in the face of addiction? Maybe it's like getting shot while wearing a bullet-proof vest. When you say 'no' to a drug, it may be painful, but you don't get hurt."

"Not quite. You don't become drug-free because addiction leaves you alone. You become drug-free because something stops it from getting to you."

"What do you mean? Aren't I stopping it?"

"No, we aren't that fortunate. If we could stop our own addictions, a promise would be all we needed and it would be done. In that case, one bad experience would be enough for any of us, and we'd never go back to pat the beast that bit us. But addicts are notorious for getting bitten over and over again. No matter how many times we say 'never again,' we try to tame the beast and make it our friend. Meanwhile, the beast gets hungrier and takes bigger bites. No matter how many bites have been taken, we come back and try it again, certain that it won't happen the next time."

Now he was getting interesting. "If I'm not stopping the addiction by myself, then what is?"

"Good question. I think you might be ready for this. It's something that addiction is no match for. Actually, it is more powerful than addiction itself."

"Doc, are you getting spiritual on me again?"

Dr. Stone sat up straighter in his chair. "This should help you," he answered. "Imagine that addiction is mean and nasty, always looking for a fight anytime you get near it. No matter what, you can't win. You train hard and become faster and stronger with amazing endurance. You try day after day to win, but you get your head handed to you each time you get in the ring. What would you do to keep your head attached?"

"That's a no-brainer," I replied. "Stay out of the ring. Get someone else to fight for you. Retire from the fight business. Yadda yadda."

"That's right. So, if a day comes when you finally want to stop getting high, there can only be one way to make it happen. A power greater than you has to step in and take the punches or you don't get even one day of sobriety. Therefore, what you want is a Higher Power that can take unlimited punches and never get tired or hurt. Addiction would obviously be no match for a Higher Power like that. There is one condition, however."

"I knew there had to be a catch. What do I have to do—donate a kidney, pay dues, and go to church?"

Dr. Stone smiled. "No. It's even easier than that and it's free. To get the full protection from a Higher Power, all you have to do is believe."

"Believe in what? I gave up on the Tooth Fairy, Santa Claus, the Easter Bunny, and God a long time ago."

"You have to believe that it exists."

"I need proof before I believe. What have you got?"

"Me."

"You? How can you be proof?" I thought Dr. Stone must be losing it—how could he be proof of a Higher Power?

"There was a time when addiction found my door and I let it in. It stayed for twenty-five years and wrecked my life. You wouldn't have recognized me, I was that bad."

"Were you an addict or an alcoholic?"

"It doesn't matter. They're both the same; they are only different ways to get high. This isn't the time to tell you my whole story, but it's pretty miraculous. I sacrificed way too much to spend all my free time with my addiction. I was mostly into booze. I drank enough rum to fill an Olympic-size swimming pool. Imagine my poor liver having to detoxify all of that booze, day after day, for twenty-five years. It's a wonder I even have a liver left. I couldn't say no to a drink. I tried to quit many times, but somehow a rum and coke always reappeared. So, how is it possible that a loser like me could be sitting here with you, talking like this and having an incredible life?"

"How? No, don't tell me," I added quickly. "I'll take a stab at it. You reached a point in your life where you couldn't go any lower. You hated yourself and were filled with shame and guilt for being such a failure. You were an embarrassment to your family, your friends, and your profession. Right?"

"Right so far."

"Then you were all alone, with nothing left but your last ounce of pain. And I'll bet you said the magic words: 'I can't take it anymore. I can't stop. I need help.' How's that?"

"Pretty close. For me, it was more like saying, 'Please help me. I don't care who you are. I am ready to surrender. I don't want to fight this any longer. I give up. Whatever you ask, I will do. Just keep me sober today. No booze today.'"

"And that was it? That was all you had to do?" I was skeptical; it sounded a little too simple.

"For that day, yes, that was all I had to do. And my prayer was answered. A power greater than me stepped in and lifted my desire for a drink. I have been sober since June 3rd, 1988. On that day, I began a fantastic journey that has brought me here to be with you. It's time for you to decide if you are ready to believe. I know without a doubt that a Higher Power was responsible for the results of my recovery." Dr. Stone smiled, and he looked so comfortable with himself. I wanted to feel that way, too.

"I can buy into that. You made quite a comeback, didn't you?"

"I did. And you can, too."

"Okay, you sold me. I believe. So, what's next?"

"It's your turn to ask."

"For what?"

"To be taken care of by a power greater than you."

"Right now? Today?"

"For starters, why not ask *my* Higher Power for some help. Mine has plenty of time to spare and loves a challenge. My Higher Power never sleeps, is always on call, never takes a day off, and answers all of my requests. It never steers me wrong and is always helpful and operating in my best interest."

"Whoa. That's too perfect for me. I'll settle for just getting me some money and getting Sidney to call off her thugs."

"It doesn't quite work that way."

"What way? You did pretty well. I'm sure you're rich, with a gorgeous wife, a Mercedes, a boat, and a mansion. I'm not asking for that much."

"This is a beginner's lesson, so it may take a while for all of it to sink in. Try it this way. You can ask for whatever you want, but it is better to accept what you get and be grateful. More important, your number one request is to ask for sobriety. That is always first. Second, you ask for whatever will move your recovery in the right direction. Notice I did not mention money or getting rid of the bad men. When you believe, you will always get what you *need*." Dr. Stone emphasized that word as he said it. "I had trouble at first. But I have seen enough proof over the years and I don't question it anymore. This is the time to start believing that you will be shown the solution to your problems."

"Just like that? I am supposed to believe I will be shown the way. That, if I trust in this Higher Power, I will be taken care of."

"Yes, you will. It's called turning your life and will over to the care of a power that is greater than yourself. I didn't always get what I wanted. But what I got was something I could put to good use, even if it was painful. I won't go into the examples, but I assure you there are more than a few scars on the inside of my soul. More important, each one represents how much stronger and wiser I became, able to deal with even bigger problems over the years. All you have to do is say, 'I believe and I will be grateful for what I receive. Please put the people in my life that I need to help me through this. Amen.'"

"I will, Doc. I got no other choice. That finally makes sense. I knew you could do it. Thanks."

The doctor rose and stretched his arms upward. "I've got a few more stops to make before I go to the office. Take some time right now to review what you remember and write it down in your own words. Read it several times in the next twenty-four hours and then tell someone. Better yet, teach someone. It gets locked into a useful part of your memory that way. Next, keep asking for help from my own Higher Power and pay attention. The answer may come in a completely unexpected way. Once you get the answer, prepare yourself to act. If you are not sure if it's a good idea, ask someone you trust. Two people usually can figure out whether it's worth following or should be discarded."

"Thanks again, Doc. I'll do just that," I said.

I held up the notebook and tapped it so he knew I was serious.

I expected him to walk out the door, but he hesitated. "If you want an easier way to contact my Higher Power, it's better if you start like this. First, stand up."

I was a bit nervous, but I complied with his request.

"Good. Now face me and hold your arms out straight in front of you."

I looked like a robot about to take his first baby steps. Dr. Stone came closer until our noses were nearly touching. He placed his head over my shoulder, put his arms around me and, just like that, we were hugging each other.

"There," he said. "That wasn't so bad, was it? Now just relax and give my spirit a chance to connect with yours in a nice, comfortable human embrace."

Two men hugging should have sent me into a panic, but as he'd drawn me toward him, I'd felt quite the opposite. It felt safe, secure, and natural. His arms gently tightened around my upper back and I did the same with my own. Then he said something I always want to remember.

"Thank you, source of all energy, kindness, compassion, and humility. We are here together, as brothers in sobriety, asking for your help. Listen to our concerns. We don't have the answers, only the questions. Show us the way through our internal guidance or bring others into our lives to lead us away from trouble and into safety and solution. Be here with my friend and comfort him as he yields to you with his belief. Grant him strength to follow your will. Thank you. Amen."

We held each other for another moment, then separated. The feeling of his hug filled me with hope and determination. Our eyes met and I saw a pool of love in the center of his. I felt welcomed and accepted by him and I wanted it to last.

In earth time, that hug had probably lasted ten seconds. In heart time, it was generously longer.

"Did you feel that?" Dr. Stone asked. "Pretty remarkable. That's what we call the heart hug: my heart beating right up against yours. There are no words to describe what it's like when two humans get this close. I bet there was a part of you that was petrified. But then you realized that I came in peace and was reaching out to touch the same part of you that wanted to be united. That, my friend, is the spirit of recovery. The spirit of recovery is a power greater than both of us. It combines with us and then becomes us, yet it is more. So much more. Now, let some of that sink in for a while. I have to go."

I watched as Dr. Stone casually strolled toward the door. He turned as he left the room, holding up his hand to wave. I returned the same gesture, feeling bonded. I wanted to believe that his presence still lingered in some special way, even after he was gone.

The feeling of the hug impressed me the most. It was a sense of protection that engulfed me, a gift of love that made me feel safe from harm. So . . . that's a Higher Power. The doctor's Higher Power. He said I could use his Higher Power for now to take care of me. I could feel it and I intended to ask it for help.

CHAPTER 36

Learning Lessons

I put the journal writing on hold because lunch arrived and I was ready to take a break. Once I had a full belly, I decided a nap would be a better way to lower my stress.

I thought about the doctor's hug as I stretched out and got comfortable. I realized the hug connected with a place inside of me that was peaceful and calm. It was a place without fear and had no physical location. Until then, I had identified my face and the pimples that covered it as ugly things. Whenever I thought of myself as a loser, I blamed my appearance as the reason. When Dr. Stone hugged me, something wonderful in me hugged him back—something I never knew existed. It was a very important part of me. And a part I knew the least about.

These thoughts caught me by surprise. It was good stuff, all right, but where was it coming from? I would never have figured this out on my own. It was as though Dr. Stone was in my head and teaching me. It had to be the Higher Power he left behind.

I found myself smiling and felt grateful, even humble. Those feelings were new to me. I whispered with appreciation, "Thank you, whoever you are," and dozed off.

After my nap, I felt refreshed and energized. I felt brighter somehow, as though drapes had been pulled open to let sunshine stream in on my thoughts.

I decided to take a walk. I was pleased with how much easier it was each time. I handled the crutches well and headed down the hall. I hoped all the doctors would give consent for me to leave the hospital now that I was getting around on my own. As I passed by a charting room, an arm in a white lab coat jutted out and stopped me.

"Just the patient I wanted to find." It was the neurologist. "How are you doing? Any problems I need to know about?"

"I think I'm good to go, Doc."

He motioned toward a nearby examining room. "Let's make sure. This will only take a minute."

I followed him into the room and he helped me onto the exam table. He checked me from head to toe, using a lot of medical terminology during the exam. I wasn't sure if he was trying to impress me or if it was just his own methodical routine.

"How'd I do, Doc? Clear for takeoff?"

"You're not the same young man they wheeled in here. I didn't give that guy very good odds, but you made one heck of an amazing comeback. It's as though you never had a concussion. You must have a special connection with the Almighty. If I were you, I sure would be extremely grateful it turned out this way."

"Was I really that bad, Doc?" I felt like a kid, wanting him to list all the gory details of my injuries. But he didn't.

"It could have been a whole lot worse," he said. "It is a bonus to be so young when you get seriously hurt. It seems like you've healed overnight. All you really have left is that fractured leg and your spine. I'm no bone specialist, but the orthopedic surgeon expects you to have little to no disability when you finish rehab."

"That's great!" It was starting to sink in. I had been crumpled up in a high-speed wreck and was literally walking away from it. He helped me off the exam table and we headed for the door.

"Maybe you had somebody praying for you or maybe somebody up there heard your prayers. Either way, you're a winner."

We were walking down the hall by then; he kept going and I stopped to ponder the idea. Was I really a winner or just lucky? Was there an Almighty or something by a different name? Was it out there looking after me or in here taking care of me? I had more questions.

Before I could think about it any further, the doctor said, "So I'm writing a note giving you neurological clearance for discharge. I'll leave instructions on the chart for your follow-up appointment with me."

He disappeared into the charting room and I headed down the hall, wondering to myself, *a winner . . . or lucky, blessed . . . or a medical miracle? Or is it all the same?*

I arrived back at the room and felt like I had a clean bill of health, even with the pins in my leg and the brace. I think my mind was in a better place, and my body was right there with it, just waiting to finish healing. I decided to rest in the recliner and call home, hoping for a kind voice on the other end.

"I'm glad you called," my mother greeted me. "I just got off the phone with the neurologist. He said that he just completed your assessment and found no abnormalities. Since you no longer require a hospital level of care, you are free to go on his authority, providing you continue your recovery with outpatient physical therapy."

"I'm dying to go home. When you come to get me, bring some pants and scissors so you can cut enough material off for my leg to go through. Bring me an oversized shirt to fit over the back brace. And get here as fast as you can. I don't trust this place."

"I got a phone call from Dr. Stone this morning. He was quite impressed with your session today and believes that you are making a lot of progress. I told him about the money you requested to pay off your drug dealer."

"Well? What did he say?"

"He said that you made a commitment to be sober and drug-free. You even hugged on it. He said the money you owe is a small price to pay for the valuable lesson you learned and that other kids have owed a whole lot more. Drug dealers expect you to pay up and can cause a lot of trouble if you don't. He said we should make you repay our loan, though, with interest."

My knees went weak with relief. I couldn't believe what she was saying.

"Dr. Stone said we should be proud of what you have accomplished in such a short time in your sessions with him. He reassured me that your condition is treatable and it is your desire and intention to learn how to be happy. He is inviting you to join the treatment program at his office. You can start tomorrow and sign the contract when you get there."

Dr. Stone had not only connected with my special inner place, but with my mother's, too. Or did his Higher Power do that? What difference did it make? Mom was back in my corner and she would probably use some cookie-jar money to get rid of Sidney's Bruise Brothers. This spiritual stuff really worked and it was practical, too. I didn't have to lift a finger and the problem was solved.

"Mom, does that mean you'll pay?"

"I am seriously considering it. But before I part with that kind of cash, I want to be sure that you follow up with Dr. Stone after you leave the hospital tomorrow."

"I will. I promise."

"Okay. But I still have to ask: Didn't it seem like a big waste of money to take pills that wore off in a few hours?"

"Mom, please don't start up again. Remember what Dr. Stone told you. Be proud of me. For the first time in my life, I don't feel like an ugly geek. I feel like my inner self is just as good as anyone else. That's what he taught me. That's worth four hundred dollars, wouldn't you say?"

"I could have told you that for free. But I suppose he's right. I need to give you a break. If he can find something about you to believe in, I guess I can, too. Okay, I'll give you the money. But if I catch you with a pill, I'd rather not say what I will do. Just stay away from drugs. Is it a deal?"

I hung up after we said our goodbyes. I felt the need to journal again, so I retrieved the notebook to write down everything that happened. I dated the page and began.

> *In the past few hours, my life has unexpectedly changed so much. Even more important, I have changed for the better. I have had a chance to look back over my life and better understand the reason drugs became so important—even necessary—to deal with the problems that I created. Being ugly and feeling inferior have been two of the primary reasons, or rather excuses, for taking drugs to make me happy.*
>
> *I would never want to relive my life with all its problems. At times, it seemed more like a nightmare. I suppose recovery has something to do with thinking differently about the path I took and how it prepared me for the path I am about to take. Getting smashed up had to be necessary before Dr. Stone and Wendy and Joe could show up and turn my life around. I think Dr. Stone would call it a blessing, something a Higher Power would use to change me. Right now, I'm chuckling at the words flowing right out of my pen. I would never talk like this, yet I'm curious to see what I'll write next. Here goes.*
>
> *I accept that you can't be a nerd unless you act like one, which is exactly what I did for years. I had no choice about being ugly and I realize it's also a matter of opinion. It has been very painful to travel through life that way. I am ready to believe that my true authentic self must be different and better than that. I am sick and tired of being miserable. I want to see how a Higher Power can help me. I want to find out who I really am and what I can become.*

I paused from my writing to eat a few of the remaining chocolates. My thoughts were so radically different than ever before. Gone was the usual self-hatred and lack of interest in life and living. That must be some kind of mental breakthrough. I wondered what a Higher Power had in store for me. Could I really get what I wanted, just for the asking, as long as I believed hard enough? I was too new at all of this to know. So far, it worked. My debt to Sidney was going to get paid off. And shouldn't a Higher Power mean what it implies: something that is capable of doing all things at any time?

I played around with the idea of building my own customized Higher Power. It seemed neat to think of creating a sort of Designer Power to my specifications. I wondered if Dr. Stone did it the same way. I started writing and expected some wild and crazy ideas to surprise me.

> *I want my Higher Power to know everything. Heck, why not go bigger and make it the source of all intelligence. I want it to have the power to make all things happen, not just the good things.*
>
> *I want to communicate with it, so it knows what I am thinking and feeling. It has to know what I like, what I want, and what I don't want. I also want it to have the power to do what it wants, without limitation. Not only that, I want this Power to be everlasting. That's right — Eternal. It can never be turned off.*
>
> *I can see how complicated this is, but if I do it right, it'll be worth it. I have already been a witness to what a Higher Power can do, so I am moving forward and trying to imagine what it should look like. Or should it be invisible? That suits me better, because all I can picture is the cute but hyperkinetic Energizer Bunny beating his drum and going and going and going. That would be too absurd for me. I am not going to pick God, either. Everybody has their own ideas about Him, and I want to stay away from any debates on that subject. I am still in the building process, and I don't know what the finished product is going to look like.*

When I looked at what I had written, it was too extraordinary to have been of my own creation. I was convinced that the ideas, and the words to describe them, could only have come into my mind if a Higher Power existed and put them there. I was being helped. All of this flowed right through me as though I was receiving a transmission from somewhere. It made me wonder about the creation of thought and whether or not any thought was mine and mine alone. I quickly returned to writing in my journal.

> *This too much for me to comprehend. Imagine if I had a book of instructions teaching me how to use the Higher Power I am going to call my own. A book called Higher Powers for Dummies would be perfect. There would be no guesswork; pretty much like having a genie in a bottle and using it wisely. That way, I could ask for a lot of money and learn how to live like a millionaire instead of blowing it all like most people who win the lottery. A book like that would help me receive what I'm ready for. That way, I wouldn't ask for things I can't handle and get frustrated because I never got them.*
>
> *If I get what I ask for, I'll enjoy it because it is meant to be. If I*

am grateful for what I've got, I am more likely to get more to be grateful for. If I complain about not having enough, I am likely to get more of what I don't want, and the complaining will continue . . . that has to be in the Dummies handbook.

Chapter One: Complaining is not only a waste of time, but it just might be a request for more to go wrong in your life, giving you more of a reason to keep complaining until you're an expert at it. Most people complain about something they don't want or something they can't have. For example, I hate being ugly . . . but I don't think my Higher Power is about to change the way I look.

My mind was on a roll. Thoughts were coming easily to me. That kind of thinking was a new kind of fun for me and quite entertaining.

These thoughts just keep coming, so I'm going to keep writing. A Higher Power must be a Creator. It must be responsible for making something that wasn't there before and constantly changing what already exists. It sounds cool, so I want to buy into it, but I don't really get it.

As soon as I wrote that, I watched the answer appear, knowing that it didn't come from me.

I looked at the hardware holding my shattered leg together and asked, "Where did the idea for the pins and fixator come from?" Somebody had to have a thought before they could be designed, manufactured, and used on my body.

So what are thoughts? How are they made and where do they come from? The answer: A thought cannot exist before it exists. So what is it before it exists? It is nothing except the pure potential to become a thought. But, where is this pure potential found?

No answer came to that question. But I had a hunch this pure potential was big stuff, and it was going to be responsible for the existence of more than thoughts; it was probably responsible for everything in the entire universe. An enormous WOW!

Was my Higher Power going to be this pure potential or was my Higher Power going to use this pure potential? Either way, would it mean that both must exist in no particular place since they were no particular things? And what would this no particular place be called . . . no-where?

At the same time I was the recipient of those amazing thoughts, I couldn't imagine ever again wasting my time being a loser or thinking about pimples. It wasn't important anymore. I even wondered if thinking about pimples as much as I did was the main reason why my body kept making them. The flood of ideas was very weird, but so cool. Did other kids have thoughts like this? Were they nerds, too?

I had to be tapped into a Higher Power connection that was way smarter than me. I wasn't sure what to do next, but I wanted more. I put my journal aside and, feeling very relaxed, I decided to close my eyes. It was interesting how I immediately became more aware of my body, especially my breathing. I could feel my chest rising and falling as air went in and out of my lungs; it was something I usually took for granted. With my next breath, it dawned on me that it came on its own. It was as though my body took the breath for me. I didn't have to. And this was happening effortlessly every time I slept. Something other than me was keeping me alive. I had a pretty good idea what that something was. I had been writing about it: it had to be my Higher Power. *Amazing,* I thought. *Absolutely amazing.* I focused on my chest rising and falling with each breath and my mind drifted to the thought of being alive. I thought about life and the zillions of tiny cells that made up my body, each one with its own identity. There was no mini-version of me in any of the cells. I did not personally create a single one. Each individual cell had its own life force and it wasn't me.

I picked up my pen to write more in my notebook.

> These fascinating thoughts don't come from me. They just come through me. I don't understand all of it, but I think I will someday. The part that I do get is a bit mind-blowing. For instance, if I'm not in any of my body parts, then where am I? I didn't get the answer to that question yet, but what I did get was something better: If my body is ugly, and I'm not my body, then I'm not ugly. That would also mean I'm not handsome, either. Nor am I skinny. I'm just me. I exist as life itself. That has to be the true, authentic, one and only me, instead of all the labels I put on myself. Geek . . . nerd . . . ugly . . . loser. Next, I imagine just being life and nothing more than that, with no one to please and no one to disappoint. There are no pressures and no burdens. What a great thing. I am ready to believe that I have a Higher Power who's making all kinds of neat stuff happen. I think I'm ready for life. I should be able to handle it.

CHAPTER 37

The Bruise Brothers

I heard three knocks on the door. Before I could answer, two men walked in, closed the door behind them, and stood side by side looking at me. I knew immediately this was not a social visit. I glanced down at the notebook and saw the words *I have a Higher Power who's making all kind of neat stuff happen,* and I felt like I had just lost the connection.

I was petrified as I looked at the two men, one tall and muscle-bound with a square jaw and hairless arms, the other one short, thin, and jumpy. His neck was scrawny and his Adam's apple was so prominent, it looked like a small elevator car riding up and down as he swallowed. He spoke first.

"Looks like we found the right room. Back brace, broken leg, pimples, and ugly."

The muscular one laughed and said, "Don't leave out deadbeat, stupid, and loser. Anyone who thinks he can use drugs and run a tab on Sidney is either dumb or dumber."

The skinny one looked irritated and unsettled. He took out a comb and pulled it through his thick and shiny black hair.

"Allow me to introduce ourselves," he began as he put the comb back into his shirt pocket. "I am Jake and this is my brother, Elwood. We're collection agents, at your service. You are certainly the Buddy we are looking for. We will be on our way as soon you pay to us the sum of four hundred dollars for the drugs you received courtesy of Sidney, who has hired us."

They didn't pull any guns or knives, so I thought I was safe. They didn't look too smart, either; I was tempted to think that maybe they were just a pair of fools. I figured I didn't need a Higher Power for these guys.

Skinny Jake watched his brother's large, ponderous hand move toward the box of chocolates that still sat on my table.

"Will you hurry up and take those. We're on a mission here."

"Sure thing, Jake," Elwood said just before inhaling three chocolates at once.

"Now go get the money and let's split."

Elwood was wearing a sport coat with a white shirt and tie. Every stitch was stretched at the seams as though he had bulked up thirty pounds since the last time he wore the outfit. His neck veins were distended and his face was scarlet red. He mopped his forehead with his bare hand.

"You're sweating like a pig already," Jake griped. "Loosen that tie before you blow a gasket."

Elwood did so. He walked across the room to where I sat in the recliner.

"Okay, give me the dough." His outstretched hand was the size of a serving platter.

I stared back at him, contemplating how to handle this.

"Come on, Kid, four c-notes."

Jake looked impatient and edgy. He kept checking his watch, tapping his foot, and cracking his knuckles.

Elwood glared at me. "Get it!"

If my Higher Power was supposed to step in, it was long overdue. I had to say something.

"Okay, okay. Take it easy. Sidney told me I had more time. Why are you here so early?"

"Because we wanna be, all right?" Jake was almost growling. "Don't make us wait, kid. Elwood here can get pretty nasty if I let him."

I was nervous. "Please guys. You're gonna get the money. My mother's got it. She'll be here later. Why don't you come back in a couple of hours?"

Elwood started punching his fist into the palm of his other hand as Jake approached me.

"I've heard enough," he said in exasperation. "I'm taking over."

"Please, I don't want any trouble over a few hundred dollars. I promise you'll get it."

I was looking from one to the other; they converged on me so fast, I didn't have a chance to holler for help. A small towel was stuffed in my mouth and sealed shut with duct tape.

"Stand aside," Jake advised his larger brother. "Let me show you how it's done. He has to know you mean business."

Elwood must have known what Jake was about to do, because he clamped my right wrist, which cut off the circulation. I couldn't move a muscle; my fingers went numb as my hand turned blue.

"Okay, Kid, here's how it's going down. You're out of time and we are, too. We came for the money. If you don't have it, we understand. We'll be back another day. However, we want to leave you with a fond remembrance of our time together. We start dainty. One broken finger should do nicely for now."

Looking at Elwood again, Jake said, "Now watch how I do this, because you want to make sure it snaps in half and just doesn't dislocate at the joint."

I was in a panic, and I started to get dizzy. I tried to pull my hand free, but I couldn't budge. I tried to talk through the towel and tape, but my voice was muffled and incomprehensible. So I tried to let my eyes do some talking.

Jake must have been watching for that. "So now you want to talk?"

Elwood began to peel the corner of the duct tape with his free hand.

"No. Don't touch that. We're done talking here."

Jake blew in his hands and rubbed them together like a safe cracker. "The easiest one to break is the index finger. It doesn't wobble around as much as the others and it's long. Pay attention, Brother—you want to break the bone closest to the first knuckle. Push hard and fast like this."

I squeezed my eyes closed and held my breath. Then I heard what sounded like a tree limb snapping, followed by a scream. I opened my eyes and saw the tattoo of a snake connected to a sledgehammer-sized fist pummel Elwood in the jaw. He collapsed onto the floor and was out cold before he landed.

The tree limb was Jake's forearm breaking in half. Brenda tossed him into the corner and told him not to move. He whimpered.

"Buddy, are you all right?" she asked. "I never should have gone on that break. I had a feeling about this. I'm really ticked off."

I rubbed my lips where the duct tape had been. I was trembling all over, and Brenda put a reassuring hand on my shoulder and squeezed gently.

"I somehow knew you needed me. You were pretty lucky, Kid. I know that skinny dude on the floor. He's already done time and he's bad news. The other guy, with the pretend muscles—I've seen him in the gym trying to sell anabolic steroids. I know he's shooting them up. Thinks he's a bodybuilder, the way he poses after a workout. Jake brought him along for his size. But he's a joke. I messed these guys up pretty good, didn't I?" Brenda flexed her bicep into a mountain of meat.

I was relieved . . . and impressed. This was not the same woman who had threatened me with a cavity search. This one cared about me more than any payoff money and I wanted to show my gratitude but that would have to wait. She had work to do.

Elwood was staggering to his feet. She led him over to Jake.

"Because I'm having such a good day, I'm willing to let you bums walk out of here and never come back. Or, I can call the cops and have both of you doing some serious time."

Jake and Elwood looked at each other and headed together for the door.

Jake appeared to be in severe pain. He cradled his broken arm.

"We're not messing with you and Godzilla anymore," Jake said as he caught up with Elwood. "Sidney can do her own dirty work. This is no way to make a buck." Elwood gingerly massaged his jaw as they disappeared out the door.

Brenda methodically checked all the equipment attached to me. "Everything looks okay," she pronounced once she was finished.

I was still trembling from the adrenaline. I was too wired to settle down; I knew Sidney wasn't done with me yet. I was afraid of what she might do next.

Brenda made my bed. "I can see how nervous you are. It's going be all right. I'm on the job; you've got nothing to worry about."

I wanted to believe her, but I couldn't. "Brenda, you knew those guys, didn't you?"

"Kid, I was a prison nurse. I saw the scum of the earth playing their con games. Jake, the skinny one, is a small-time punk. He acts tough and tries to hurt people. He's not very good at it. At least I put him out of commission for a while."

"What about the other one, Elwood?"

"Oh, he's a piece of work. And by the way, they aren't brothers and those aren't their real names. It's a street thing. They renamed themselves when they teamed up and tried to pass themselves off as a reincarnation of the Blues Brothers. Their real names are Cornelius and Walter. I forget their last names. Walter is the big one. He'd rather inject himself with muscle-building drugs than actually lift a dumbbell. The two of them met in prison and they've been attached at the hip ever since. Cornelius has the brains, but only by a slim margin. Walter was stupid enough to sell steroids to an undercover cop."

While she was talking, I saw her in a completely new light. She wasn't evil; she was just driven to play hardball with drug addicts like me. I couldn't be upset about that, and I wanted to show my appreciation for what she had done to rescue me.

"Brenda, I don't blame you for riding me hard and scaring the crap out of me for doing pills and causing trouble. I had you all wrong. Thanks for saving my life. Those guys were going to break my finger. I tried to tell them that my mom was bringing the money, but they wanted to hurt me anyway. You were spectacular and definitely worth whatever you charge."

Brenda stood next to my bed. She looked like a human tower.

"I couldn't let those pukes harm you. Besides, it was fun to hurt some bad guys. I miss it."

An impulse came into my mind that I couldn't resist. "Before I get into bed, can you do me one more favor?"

"Sure, kid. What is it?" The late afternoon sun seemed to soften her features.

I stood directly in front of her and looked at her face-to-face. "I want you to extend both of your arms out straight toward me."

"What for?"

"Just do it," I said. "Trust me."

Her arms looked like two outstretched cranes, and I slipped in between them. I moved in a few more inches until my head made it over her left shoulder. The brace made it a little awkward, but I was actually able to hook my arms around her and pull her toward me. What happened next convinced me that a Higher Power existed and truly cared. Brenda lowered her arms hesitantly and very slowly, as though something hydraulic was controlling them. As they came to rest on my shoulders, they felt like heavy logs. Then she embraced me with a gentle caress. It was so reassuring, even a frightened child would have felt safe. She cradled the entire back of my head in her right hand, then stroked my hair with a soothing tenderness. She began to whisper.

"I didn't know you had this in mind. I love hugs. I just don't get very many, you know, looking like this. I prefer to keep people on the hard side of my life. It's safer there for me. That's where I'm in charge. I don't let my heart go over there. But I've changed my mind about you, so I'm making this exception."

I could hear her release a deep breath with a heavy sigh. "This feels good, doesn't it?"

It was extraordinary and indescribable. I was in the arms of a behemoth of a woman who was tender and I loved it. Me—the ugly geek—not only asking for a hug, but getting one in return from someone who was an enemy less than twenty-four hours ago. This was a miracle.

It felt like she kissed the top of my head. Then she gave me a tighter squeeze. After our bodies parted, there was energy between us that kept me feeling safe and desirable. It felt like a pulling force—alive, but not human. I wasn't sure if my Higher Power had arranged that. If so, then a Higher Power could probably become just about anything, anywhere, anytime, for any reason, a sort of Universal Power. One Power fits all. I liked it.

After she stepped away, I also thought about how Brenda must see herself. She was physically colossal with huge muscles and flamboyant tattoos. She seemed to have a healthy admiration of her appearance, accepting it with confidence and love. She used her well-developed power, speed, and strength to touch the world and experience it. Her true self lived on the inside, a pure force of life and existence.

I realized I was thinking in terms that were in a spiritual realm I did not understand . . . but I needed to, if I was ever going to be at peace. I had come a long way from thinking about pills and pimples. I had found a way to shed some of the loneliness. I had a Higher Power hanging around me and a smart one, too. I wondered if there could be more than one Higher Power, one for each person. Or did we all share the same one? Where had it been all this time? Why was it coming into my life now? More questions, but no answers . . . yet.

Brenda was studying my facial features. Perhaps my pimples no longer disgusted her. She smiled and I smiled back. Then she winked. "You know, you're not half-bad looking. Actually, you remind me of a young Humphrey Bogart. I never noticed that before."

I followed Brenda's lead. "I have to apologize for not looking beyond the obvious—you know, the tattoos and everything else. When we met, you were pretty imposing and not very nice to me. I thought that you were purposely trying to rid the planet of all kids who tried drugs. I was terrified every time you came into my room. I didn't know if you were going to take my temperature or use me for target practice. But I do want you to know that I was only using drugs for a few days. I went down fast. I got lost in the good feeling and couldn't get enough. I was irresponsible, but at the time I didn't care and I didn't know any better. I wanted more drugs and money to pay for them. So, you see, we had each other all wrong. I'm not a druggie. I'm a shy, geeky, nerdy loser. And you are something else." I pronounced the words "something else" with a fondness that meant she impressed me as a person with great virtue and value who would make an honorable and admirable friend.

She grabbed both of my shoulders and sat me back down on the bed. "Take a load off. Your leg must be sore from standing. I have a few things on my mind, too. For one, I put you in the loser tank with the rest of the drugged-out teens who think the world owes them a good time without any penalty minutes. I was too rough with you. I guess I was taking it out on you because you represented all the drug addicts I have ever seen. A bunch of them were doing time at the prison when I worked there and I built up one hell of a resentment. When you came along, I wanted to teach you a lesson. No, I wanted to hurt you, and I compromised my standards and crossed the line. I was dead wrong. Now I'm asking that you forgive me."

"Of course I do," I answered, "but I can't help wondering what kept us from knowing this about each other. Why was it so difficult?"

"I don't know. I had no idea that inside of you I would find a young man trying to grow up and step away from the lies. If I'd just looked long enough, I would have seen that. I want you to know that you are not a geeky, nerdy loser. Not in my mind. Not in my heart. I know a loser when I see one and you aren't even close. As a matter of fact, I think you have a lot of love to give. You are quite tender-hearted and affectionate. When we hugged, I felt more beautiful than I have in a long time."

The future was looking better and brighter. I wanted Brenda to stay.

"You're one heck of a kid. I wish you well. If you ever decide you want to put some meat on those bones, I'll be happy to show you around the gym and get you started. Muscles don't make the man, but they sure do come in handy."

She flexed her body with a few different poses, as though showing off for a camera. Then she laughed and admitted how superficial she knew that was. The deeper meaning of her life was even more obvious to me now. I laughed with her, but tears were starting to form as she rounded the corner and disappeared from view.

I felt humbled by this gentle giant. She had touched me deeply. I had experienced an awakening and emerged with a spirit of kindness, understanding, and acceptance for myself that I shared with her. I had to know her value in friendship to miss her, and the sadness I felt as she walked away revealed to me how much I cared. I intended to keep crossing her path and remain her friend. She was worth it.

CHAPTER 38

A Purpose for Living

I was exhausted; all I wanted to do was take a nap, but my parents were on the way. I thought about what I had just survived. My mind felt too small and insignificant to understand it all. I would not forget what a Higher Power had done for me, nor would I take it for granted.

I pressed the controller button to elevate the head of my bed and lay back to relax. Within the hour, my dinner arrived and I devoured it in less than five minutes. As I swallowed the last bite, I heard Mom enter the room; my dad was right behind her.

"What's that I smell? You had meatloaf, didn't you? Was it as good as mine? You ate it all. It must have been." She walked to the bed and kissed me on the forehead.

I didn't lean away. This time, her affection was okay with me. She had a Higher Power, too; if her Higher Power liked her to kiss, so be it. I was willing to be open to everything and anything.

"Hi, Mom. You missed all the excitement," I said.

"How can meatloaf be that exciting?"

"I meant, those guys were here."

"Guys? What guys? The bad guys who want the money?"

"Yes, those guys. You should have seen them. One was big like a body builder and the other one was a twerp. They tried to break my finger." My mom rolled her eyes and put both hands on her hips.

"You can't fool me. They wouldn't let people like that in here. Besides, you're not even hurt. Your hair isn't even mussed."

I looked around and pointed to the floor.

"Look over there. See that duct tape? It was holding a towel in my mouth so I wouldn't scream. There's the towel right next to it. And look at my lips. See the skin missing? That's from the tape."

She looked at the tape and nudged it with her foot. Then she got right up close to my face and inspected my lips before touching my swollen finger.

"Ouch."

"Is that sore? Oh, I'm sorry. How could they do such a thing? They should be arrested. How did you get them to stop? Do you want us to call the police? Didn't you tell them we were on the way?"

My mother could be very trying. I silently summoned my Higher Power.

"I tried to get them to stop," I said. "But they didn't care whether they got the money today or not. They wanted to break my finger. I thought they came to break my leg."

"These men have to be apprehended. And you have to be protected until they are. This is unbelievable."

"I don't think these particular guys will be back. They sort of got roughed up."

"By you?" my father asked. "Do you mean to tell us you took care of them yourself?"

He sounded a little sarcastic and on the verge of laughing. My mother shot him an icy stare. He shut up.

"I was saved by my nurse," I said. "The one with the big arms and the snake tattoos. She got physical, throwing punches and breaking bones. They were hurting pretty bad when she kicked them out. They won't be back to collect the money, either."

My mother looked at me in disbelief. "Why am I having so much trouble imagining that ever happened?"

"I swear it did. Ask Brenda; she'll tell you."

"Really?"

"We made up, you know. We found something to like about each other. She thinks I'm pretty neat. You should, too."

"You know what would be neat," Dad suggested. "We pay off your drug dealer and you stop using pills."

My mother nodded quickly and added, "I knew you had to come to your senses. I hope you're back the way you were before this whole thing started."

I felt the strength of my conviction starting to build.

"Mom, Dad, I am not the same kid who smashed up that car and my life along with it. I am not the same kid who stayed up in his room hiding from the world. I have what you might call an inner guide. It teaches me things about life. You might say I finally woke up and now I see everything differently. It's a new me, not the old one."

My parents shared the same stunned expression as I continued.

"I found out that there is something pretty good about me, after all. Dr. Stone pointed it out. I'm not ugly or a loser. I'm no longer a kid. That means I've changed the way I think and the way I feel and that's good enough for me. Who knows, maybe someday I'll discover my real purpose for being here. Isn't that the reason for having an inner guide: to carry out the instructions you're given?"

My mom and dad looked astonished. I snapped my fingers to break the trance they seemed to be in. My mom blessed herself with the sign of the cross. I had never seen her do that before.

"I never thought I would ever hear you say anything like that. That was remarkable and incredible. Whatever this inner guide is all about, I'm in favor of it. You aren't the son I knew—you're better. Let's take you home." She kissed my forehead.

My father handed me a small bag filled with clothes. The shorts had one leg split up the side and they easily slipped on. I pulled out a new T-shirt that was packed in the bag. It fit over the back brace and hid it completely. On the T-shirt was a photo of a large Doberman with a snarling expression and long, pointed, gleaming teeth. His eyes seemed to follow whoever was looking at him. He wore a studded collar that looked like barbed wire and an ID tag with the name *Nice Boy* engraved on it. Below the photo was a caption:

If you leave it alone, you won't get hooked
Addiction—Don't Get Started

"It's perfect. That dog is just like addiction. It will bust your chops and eat your lunch." I knew I'd wear that shirt proudly for a long, long time.

My parents gathered up the plants and my notebook. Nurse Wendy came into the room, holding my chart; it was three inches thick. She pulled out several forms.

"Hi, Everybody. I'm just starting my shift, but now it's time to say good-bye. This is your big day. It seems like you have been here forever, but we just got to meet three days ago."

She warmed up the room with the glow from her face. She introduced herself to my parents as the nurse who "found me," but spared us the details about the OxyContin overdose. We all knew what she meant.

She hugged them both like she was having a reunion with old friends. "You have a very special son. He put us through quite a scare, but now he's a changed young man. Buddy, you overcame more and did it in a shorter time that anyone else I can remember."

She touched me on the shoulder before taking my hand. Her eyes gleamed with praise and admiration. "You were a tough case, headed down the wrong path. You thought drugs were the answer to all your problems. We had great talks and finally you were ready to listen. I'm so happy that you've heard the message that drugs never make anything better."

I was paying close attention to Wendy, so I didn't notice her brother Joe walk through door.

"Hello, Buddy. I got here as soon as I heard the awesome news."

"Mom, Dad. This is Joe, Wendy's brother. He knows all about quitting pills. Wendy called him when I needed help and he came right over to put my mind at ease."

Four very important people were watching me as my confidence kept building.

"We both got into the same kind of trouble and he's already turned his life around. Joe's in college, works at the hospital, and has been sober for a year. I want to be done with drugs, too. I want to be happy like Joe and I'm really going to try."

I stood up as Joe gripped my father's hand and gave my mom a bear hug.

"Now it's your turn, Little Brother." His arms were a bit more cautious around my brace but it felt especially good. "Buddy, I've decided to be your sponsor."

"Sponsor?" I had no idea what he was talking about.

"From now on, I will be your recovery coach. I will show you how to live sober. One day at a time. You will learn how to be naturally happy. I will take you to Narcotics Anonymous meetings and get you all the right books to read."

"What are these meetings you're talking about?"

"Don't sweat it," Joe explained. "When we give up drugs, we're all at risk for cravings and slip-ups. Meetings are good protection from addiction. They're where we get together as a group and become stronger individually. We'll go to a meeting every day. I'll introduce you around. It's easy: all you have to do is sit there and listen. Write down your address and I'll pick you up tomorrow at five."

Hearing about meetings made me nervous. My natural instinct was to retreat back into my shy personality and hide behind my ugliness. But I knew if I was going to pull away from that, I needed support.

Joe must have seen the nervousness on my face; he put his arm around me and said confidently, "You can do this. We're all scared the first time. I'll be there with you."

I felt like my Higher Power was speaking directly to me through him. Joe had a way of getting me inspired and ready to go. At that moment, if I had been a football player, I would have wanted the coach to give me a chance to score the winning touchdown.

I turned to my parents. "Looks like I'm joining NA." I may have been a little nervous about it, but I actually couldn't wait to learn more about this meeting place for addicts. I imagined a club house with memberships and a secret handshake.

We all hugged one last time and Wendy went over the discharge instructions. I was told to see the orthopedic and neurology doctors in two weeks, and Dr. Stone left word to have me in his office the next day. I was given some supplies to clean the pinholes with antiseptic. I could remove the back brace and take a shower as long as I didn't twist or bend my spine.

My parents walked out with Joe. I stayed behind to say a private good-bye to Wendy.

She put her hands on both sides of my face and looked deep into my eyes.

"Listen up. You learned a lot in here, but it's crazy out there. You can't do it alone. Nobody can. My brother needed help. Now he wants to help you. Let Dr. Stone work some magic, too. Get as much as you can."

I felt the heat from her hands and smelled a heavenly fragrant lotion.

"Buddy, you've learned a lot about who you really are and who you're not. Never forget it. Nerds and losers don't exist. Remember: their negative thinking only gains power through repetition. That's what brings it to life."

I knew she was telling me something important, but her beauty got more of my attention.

"You may not like the way you look, but your outside is not a reflection of the inside. Your life is not on the outside; it's on the inside and I love that part of you. You should love it, too. It will take good care of you and help you find a place for your outside to live. Not everybody is going to like your outside, but enough people will. They are the ones holding the welcome signs."

She kissed my cheek and I blushed but kept my composure. She walked with me out the door and down the hall toward the elevator where my parents stood waiting.

I didn't know how to say goodbye to someone who meant so much to me. "My folks are waiting for me. Thanks for everything. See ya."

I tried to walk as fast as I could to catch up to them, but Brenda came out of nowhere and stopped me dead in my tracks. Her voice sounded rough, like gravel mixing in a cement truck.

"Come here you little dweeb, I'm not done with you yet."

Brenda did that intentionally, just to run one last shiver up my spine.

"Don't get your skivvies all bunched up. Remember, I'm your guardian angel."

By the time she said *guardian angel,* her voice had softened and I relaxed.

"I stayed overtime, just to see you again and tell you a few things. Your parents are waiting for you in the lobby."

She paused to gather her thoughts and I felt so protected standing next to her.

"Listen, Kid, you piled up some strikes against you over the years. That doesn't matter now. Keep swinging and the hits will come."

She pointed her finger at me for emphasis. "Find people who are through with drugs and have cleaned up their own messes, someone like Wendy's brother. He'll introduce you to people in NA who came up the hard way, real street smart and dependable, like me. Get their phone numbers and call them. They'll show you how to take life seriously and always play to win. And you better do it with your head on straight. If I hear that you've been using drugs again . . ."

My back brace was crooked and it caught her attention. She adjusted one of the straps as she paused her lecture.

"Where was I?" she asked when she'd finished.

"Ready to track me down if I use drugs again."

"Right. Keep your nose out of the junk. You'll do better if you find some of my kind at NA; brothers and sisters from my neck of the woods, with tattoos, leather, and zippers."

She crossed both arms in front of her chest; that made the snakes look enormous and menacing.

"This is what's up front. Pay attention to what your NA friends have inside. Before they got clean, they were probably a little dirty. Maybe they still play in the dirt, but it's good dirt now, and they're not doped up anymore."

I got the message loud and clear. I was going meet her *family* at these NA meetings. They were bound to be interesting characters. I imagined men and women with a very few teeth, lumberjack muscles, and expanding midsections. They would be bikers with tattoos of swords, dragons, skulls, and large-breasted, scantily clad women. I wouldn't be enough meat in the middle of a sandwich for any one of them. I probably wouldn't even understand their language. I wondered, *How are they supposed to help me; the geeky, puny nerd?* Maybe I could get tattooed and blend right in. On second thought, I may need a bodyguard just to go to NA.

Brenda kept talking while I drifted off with my thoughts about tattoos and bikers. She didn't notice, and I was back to paying attention by the time she was ready with her closing remarks.

"I've taken a liking to you, Squirt. I wish I could go with you and be your shadow for a while. You can get swallowed up out there and think you're only in a dark place. So I want you to have this. Keep it with you at all times. It will protect you." She opened her hand. I had never seen anything like it.

"I got this meteor from a lifer in the joint," Brenda explained. "He didn't have much time on the clock. Cancer was eating him away faster than maggots on garbage. He never told me where he got it, only that it was burning up the sky before it hit the earth. I think he was American Indian, or at least part of him was. He spoke a lot about sweat lodges, the great spirits, and smoke."

She placed it in my hand; it seemed to weigh a pound, but it was not much bigger than a walnut. It had a dull, dark chocolate-brown finish. It was oval in shape and the entire surface was rippled with bumps the size of large granules of sand. It was warm and felt alive, but I knew it couldn't be. My Higher Power must have arranged it.

She pulled my attention away from the meteor and said, "There is one last thing we must do to transfer ownership of its power to you."

"What's that?" I asked.

"It's time to show you my kind of hug. As I give you this talisman, you must promise to always keep it in your possession and use it to unlock your true self."

"Now you're talking." I had been dealing with an invisible Higher Power. Now I had something substantial. Something real that my Higher Power could put to good use.

"If I am going to entrust you with this, I have to make sure that you understand how to use it and how it will use you."

I turned it over and studied its contours and markings.

"Brenda, you're getting real serious here. I think I liked you better with all the geeky wisecracks."

She rolled her eyes and bit her lip in frustration. "Don't worry, Cowboy, Brenda's still here, ready to poke someone's eye out if I have to. Just give me a minute, will you. This talisman is a big deal."

"Well, maybe I'm not ready for this thing."

"Oh, you are. I knew it when you put your arms around me. You have potential. Now, you need teaching and guidance. So here's what you do."

She took the talismanic meteor from my hand and pressed it over my heart. She told me that in less than one minute, both our hearts would beat in unison, completely synchronized. The pressure from the talisman was slightly painful on my chest. That gave way to a numb feeling. Then a faint rumbling, almost a vibration, replaced it. Brenda told me to close my eyes. After a few seconds, it felt as though the talisman was beating to the rhythm of my heart. I knew that was impossible, but it sure was freaky.

She drew me in closer until we hugged. "That seals the deal. You are protected now. Remember, this is just a rock from outer space, nothing more. The rest is a rite of passage. I want you to take your life seriously. Stay clean and the path will be shown to you. We will find each other when it's necessary. Now go."

She believed that this rock had special powers, but that was too weird for me. I could accept that it was a symbol of faith and inner guidance. It belonged to a dying man and Brenda had taken it over. It meant a lot to her and now it was my turn to take possession. The best part was connecting with her. I was convinced that our friendship would really come in handy in some incredible way.

As I walked on, the talisman felt solid and stable. I realized that it had survived a journey of a million miles, maybe light years, just to find its way into my life. I turned to wave and say one last thank-you. Brenda looked very imposing, except for one thing: she was wiping tears away from a caring face.

When I reached the lobby, my parents were both snacking. My mother had what was left of a Milky Way and my father popped the last piece of an ice-cream sandwich into his mouth.

"Thought you might like these," Mom offered as she held something out toward me.

It was a family-size bag of M&M's.

She might have a hard time showing it, but I knew my mom loved me. The three of us walked outside and my father jogged away to get the car. As I stood there munching handfuls of the candy, a warm breeze swept past me. The palm trees on the hospital grounds swayed just a little. To the right, I could see boats cruising on the river, and sea birds filled the sky with squawking and fluttering wings. It felt good to be alive and I wanted to live like there was no tomorrow—because there wasn't. Once tomorrow arrived, it was today all over again.

My father pulled up in the car; the front seat was moved back to make room for my extended leg. As we drove toward home, I saw places where I rode my bike, where I'd bought Mom a Christmas gift, and where we'd watched a parade go by. I saw our town theater and remembered a movie that scared me half to death. Even my grammar school playground with its monkey bars and swings represented something meaningful. How was it possible to have such a revived point of view? Maybe it was the talisman. Maybe it was my Higher Power again, gifting me with a new set of eyes to see what I'd never seen before: a purpose in everything.

CHAPTER 39

Welcome Home

The TV was blaring as I walked through the door to our house. My brother was perched on the edge of the couch with the remote in his hand. He was jabbing it toward the screen as he changed the channel every five seconds. Before I could say a word, Mom screamed, "Turn that thing down! There are people with ears in this room." Junior hit the power button and the room went as quiet as a church on Friday night.

"Your brother's home. Come say 'hi' to him."

He took one look at me and said, "Hey, dude. 'Sup?"

His face lit up once he saw the pins and fixator. "Are those things really going through your leg? Does it hurt?"

"No," I chuckled. "I don't feel a thing."

He put his face inches away from my leg.

"The pins hold all the shattered pieces of bone together. You want to see where the pins go into my leg?"

"That's cool. What's that thing on top of your T-shirt? What does it do?"

"It's a back brace. One of the bones of my spine is crushed. This holds my back straight so it'll heal."

After a casual glance at the brace, Junior held up the remote and asked, "Can I watch TV now?"

Mom pulled the remote out of his hand. "Is that how you welcome your brother home? Didn't you miss him?"

He scratched his head as though he was trying to figure out the correct answer to regain possession of the remote. Then he smiled and said, "Of course I did. You wanna play video games?"

"It's after eight," Mom interrupted. "You better go upstairs and get ready for bed. We have some talking to do. I'll tuck you in when we're done."

Junior made childish objections on his way to the upstairs bathroom. A minute later, he leaned over the railing with a Spiderman toothbrush dangling from a foamy white mouth.

"Can I watch TV in your room until you finish talking?"

"No!"

As I sat down on the couch, I saw a plate on the coffee table heaped with chocolate chip cookies—my favorites. I devoured two before Mom and Dad got settled. It was good to be home.

Mom took her seat next to me and offered a glass of milk. "I made those cookies today. Just the way you like them, with extra chocolate chips."

"Thanks, Mom, they're great." I knew she was leading up to something far less pleasant than cookies.

"It's good to have you back, but we haven't gotten over what we went through while you were in a coma. We were chewing our nails off and terrified that any minute you would die or the doctor would say it's time to pull the plug, like that boy who was next to you in the ICU. God, that was awful; those parents lost their precious son."

As much as I wanted to be home, I hated being lectured to. I thought it might be a good time to check in with my Higher Power. *I need your help. Please show some mercy and shut her up.* I don't know if my Higher Power heard my plea, but I decided it was time to diffuse some of the tension in the room.

"Mom and Dad, before you say any more, please just hear me out. Thanks for all your prayers; you really stood by me. That's what pulled me through. I feel pretty guilty about messing up and taking all those drugs. I can't imagine what you must have gone through." I shook my head; I was filled with shame.

"I was too stupid to know how stupid I was. I wouldn't listen to you or the doctor after the first time. And even after I wrecked a car and half my body, I wanted to get high pretty soon after I woke up from the coma."

My parents sat attentively, listening to what I had to say.

"Mom and Dad, you have no idea what that feels like, wanting pills more than anything else. My life sucked with a capital S and I'm ashamed to admit that once I got started, I couldn't say 'no' to drugs. They gave me more excitement than I've ever had."

My mother looked like she was ready to interrupt, but I kept talking.

"I am not going to blame you for any of the reasons why I ruined my life. But I had help, too. Wherever I went, I heard things that I can't repeat in this room. You probably aren't aware of the names I've been called and the cruelty I've been subjected to. I have no clue what possessed people to treat me that way. I wish my name showed up in the dictionary next to the words tall, handsome, athletic, or sexy . . . but those adjectives are reserved for everyone else. Me . . . I feel like a nobody."

It was not going to do my parents any harm to listen as I unloaded some of the anger I had dammed up inside. "I am not just complaining for the sake of complaining. I really want you guys to know what it feels like to be me. At times, it's painful—even excruciating—to live in a world that can be sadistic and vicious. I am trying to find a way to let you in on it, but not dump on you."

"What do you mean?" Mom asked.

"Dr. Stone taught me something important about emotional pain. It's real, but it doesn't have to hurt so much that I suffer. The secret is to stop finding fault; complaining serves no purpose."

"But some things do hurt and suffering is what you have to go through. It's unavoidable," Mom interrupted.

I paused and thought about her comment. "I see it differently. I've been so mad at the world for screwing with me that I filled my life with self-pity and resentment. Now I realize that whatever happens is meant to be or it wouldn't have turned out that way. I can accept the results I get and move on or reject them and be miserable. It's my choice. Either way, life keeps going and takes me along with it. Until recently, I didn't think anybody cared about how bad I felt—including the two of you."

"That's ridiculous for you to say that about us," my dad protested. "Of course, we care. We are good parents. What more do you want?"

I was about to tell them exactly what I wanted when I heard a little voice inside my head. *Be careful what you say. These are your parents and they've sacrificed a lot for you.* It was fascinating; I could have sworn it was my Higher Power warning me to choose my next words wisely. After all, I'd have to live with them and they could make my future better or worse.

"You're right, Dad. That wasn't fair to include you, just because I was mad at the whole world. What was I thinking? You are the only ones who put up with me for my entire life and you deserve a lot more credit than I've given you. I'm sorry about that. If it's okay with you, I'd like you to understand me better. I don't mind sharing my private thoughts, but it's really important for me to know that you won't judge me, no matter what I'm trying to work through. I've got a lot to learn and I expect to make more mistakes. I would rather be honest about my screw-ups, instead of trying to cover them up with lies." My parents looked at each other and then back at me.

"Yes, you can count on us," they answered in unison. Then they looked at each other again.

"Because we love you." My mom pulled a wad of tissue from her purse and covered her face as she began to sob. "I think you never felt loved enough—maybe not at all."

My father put his arm around her shoulders. There was a look on her face that tugged at my heart, a look of shame mixed with pain. Perhaps she really knew what it had been like for me all those years. Perhaps she tried to help more than I knew. Had she felt defeated, giving up on me because I gave up on myself? I wanted to do the next right thing and silently asked my Higher Power before I spoke.

"Mom." I placed my hand tenderly on the back of her neck. Her face was hidden from view. "I'm not sure what to say."

She was trembling and seemed frail and breakable. I wanted to be honest, but I realized that my mom's heart was on the line. She deserved the truth, but slowly.

"Mom. I've never been able to open up and talk like this. I think you're ready to listen to what I have to say and it's time for me to say it."

She reached for my hand, gripping it tightly as she lifted her head to meet my eyes.

"Mom, I'm not sure what love completely feels like. In the past few days, I think I've come close. When I hear you say it, I still can't feel it the way you do. But I know you mean it." She was still holding my hand. That was a good sign.

She blinked and studied my face as though seeing me for the first time, like she was looking at a newborn.

"I have never loved myself," I said. "Heck, I have never even liked myself. Losers never do. I have been playing the loser card all of my life. That's all I've known, up to now."

My mom held her other hand up to signal for a pause. As she gathered her composure, she looked carefully at my face as though she wanted to remember every detail. As I watched her become more absorbed, I noticed how attractive she was, as mothers go; I hadn't been aware of that, ever. Why now? What was changing about me?

She lowered her hand. "Son, you were beautiful to me the day I brought you into this world. My heart looks at you the same way today. I assumed you automatically knew that. I was wrong. You needed to be told and I should have known better. I confess to being way too caught up with things that didn't matter, cleaning up after everyone, doing laundry, preparing meals. I lost sight of what really mattered in raising a family and being a good mom. I'm sorry."

She sniffled and wiped some of the tears from her eyes. "I had no idea your life hurt so much. I want to make up for it somehow. Right now, I am happy to be your mom. I can tell you have changed. I think it's my turn now. I could sure use a hug. What do you say? Shall we give it a try?"

This was a perfect opportunity to break new ground with my mom, a chance to get close and see what happened. I knew this was all part of recovery. I had been selfishly withdrawn for years. Now I was about to share a very intimate act with the woman who brought me into this world and I knew exactly what to do. "Follow my lead," I said.

I asked her to stand up. She was trembling, but not from fear. As I lifted my arms, she copied me. She laced her fingers across my back. I tilted her head toward my left shoulder and guided it gently to rest there. I patted her head soothingly. As we drew closer, it felt as though our spirits were getting acquainted. We swayed from side to side and I closed my eyes, enjoying the gentle rocking. Her trembling subsided and, at one point, I felt united to her in a way that was indescribable.

"Mom," I whispered. "How do you feel?"

She pressed closer. "Special," she answered. "I enjoy sharing our love with each other."

It was definitely a Higher Power moment. We were both feeling the same thing. She called it love. So why couldn't I? It had to be the real deal.

Neither of us was ready to let go and the longer we held on, the more ideas I had about love. My Higher Power was busy teaching me an important lesson.

"Mom, I just thought of something kind of neat that may help us out. Love is forgiving, which is how we made up. It's also for giving, which is what we are doing right now. We forgave each other and we gave with love. It's hard to believe, but I think I'm feeling both of them right now. What about you?"

"I've always known that love is an instrument of peace," she said, "something both of us desperately needed. Now we've both got inner peace and it never felt so good. Thank you for doing this. I don't know what's next, but I think it's going to be better than the way things used to be—for both of us."

Mom showed me that I was loved and always had been. Now, I knew what it felt like: It was powerful and it touched me in an unforgettable way. Love had been there inside of me all along, just like my Higher Power, waiting for me to arrive. I now knew how to give it and receive it. More important, I knew how to create it using a source of power far greater than myself.

As we separated from each other, I felt different: stronger, yet lighter. My mom stopped crying and a warm smile spread across her face. I matched her smile; it felt natural but entirely new.

"I forgot how different you look when you smile," Mom said. "It's been so long. You know, a smile is God's way of fixing any mistakes we think we have. You've been so self-conscious about your appearance that you stopped smiling when you hit puberty."

"It was a lot sooner," I replied. "My smile went into hiding when I realized I was so different from the other kids. I could tell by the way they looked at me. Everything about me was out of place. I began to know what ugly looked like and felt like. It was awful and it was embarrassing. I wanted to run away and hide forever."

Mom placed her hand on my face and it felt like a velvet glove. I could sense her pride, and my fear and shame began to fade away. How could I ever be ugly in her eyes or in her heart?

"Your complexion is not who you are," Mom explained. "This acne is no fault of yours. It's an act of Mother Nature. I think a smile is a good way to deal with it, a nice bright, happy smile. What have you got to lose? It can't make things any worse."

As I began to smile, she said, "That's just the way you looked when you were a toddler. You were so cute and cuddly back then. I just loved you to pieces. I still do."

"I was a happy kid, wasn't I? We had some good times after all. Whatever happened to us?"

"I don't know for sure, but we didn't adjust very well to all the ways our lives changed. I'm not making any more excuses and you shouldn't, either. Pimples are pimples; they're not people. We decide how we want to treat each other. Hugging is a great way to start."

The feeling of satisfaction that filled me was like being stuffed after a hearty meal.

"I'd like to turn in," I said. "I want to sleep undisturbed for once. No nurses, no blood pressures, no temperatures, no blood tests, and no bedpans."

"Don't worry about getting up early tomorrow, it's Sunday and I'm giving you Monday off to see Dr. Stone. You're back at school on Tuesday."

Giving my mom a quick hug and a kiss on her cheek, I turned to my dad, who settled for a handshake and a pat on the shoulder. It was good to be home.

CHAPTER 40

Addiction in Your Dreams

I didn't have pajamas rigged for pins, fixator, and a back brace, so I climbed into bed in the clothes I'd worn home. I was exhausted. My head sank into the pillow and the mattress felt heavenly.

Falling asleep was a breeze, but my dreams revealed my inner conflict. I dreamt vividly about an assortment of human bones. They were being taken apart by a large, shadowy figure and snapped back together like Legos. I could hear clicking as the shadow kept connecting them in ways that didn't match. When the shadow was done, the skeleton was a jumbled mess.

The shadow pulled the bones apart and left them scattered on a table. I saw its beady red eyes, creepy and sinister.

It looked up and saw me spying. It pointed at me as though it were an executioner selecting a victim.

"You're next, you pimple-faced weasel. I'm going to suck the life out of you. You'll be just like every other junkie," it pointed at the pile, "nothing but a dead heap of bones when I'm done with you."

I wanted to run, but I felt like I was frozen in a block of ice. All I could move was my eyeballs. As they darted around the room, I saw three fluorescent blue numbers blinking on the wall: 2-3-0. The shadow reached up and grazed my leg with each attempt to snatch me. I began to hyperventilate. The shriek I let out woke me up.

There was perspiration on my forehead and my body was clammy with moisture. My first thought was, *Where am I?* I looked around. The desk light was still on. I spotted the clock, furniture, TV, and the poster of Albert Einstein. His hair was frizzed and his tongue was sticking out. I was in my bedroom. I was back home and safe—for now.

My breathing slowed down and the fear subsided. I thought about what the dream meant and, although I was not a master interpreter of dreams, I decided that one was pretty obvious. The shadowy man was addiction, coming back to finish me off and claim my life and soul. I was safe as long as I stayed on the recovery path. I was glad it was just a dream.

I had expected to sleep all night. It was only 2:30 AM and I felt wide awake.

Nature was calling, so I headed for the bathroom. Once there, it hit me fast and hard, even before I had a chance to pee. I remembered the Roxys I had stolen and snorted. I closed my eyes tight and shook my head, thinking that I could erase the memory of getting high with Mom's pills. It didn't work. When I was finished at the toilet, I washed my hands and couldn't help staring at the cabinet door. *They are in there,* I thought. And then I remembered the stash I hid in the paper clip box in my desk drawer. *I want to see them, just to look at them and leave them alone, that's all. What harm could it do? Shouldn't I test myself and see if my Higher Power is all that it's cracked up to be?*

I opened the cabinet door carefully. The brown plastic bottle was perched there. Mom hadn't even thought to hide them. Was that going to turn into a mistake or was I going to shut the door and walk away, sober and proud? I hesitated for a second before grabbing the bottle and rattling the pills inside. Suddenly, I felt a surge of sensations; I could feel the powder in my nose and taste it in my throat. It all came back: the warm, itchy energy that put a smile on my face and some swagger in my attitude about everything. It was the fastest way to be big and tall. Now I had to have a look-see.

The white lid popped off with a familiar sound. Peering into the bottle, I saw the Roxys and I felt like they were begging me to crush them and send them on their way to my brain. I turned the bottle over and four tumbled out into the palm of my hand; I put three of them down on the counter and held one up.

"I want to do this," I said to myself. There was no caution light flashing to slow me down, think it over, or change my mind. I was ready to go and felt I had already gone too far to turn back. I was going to make this happen. It was time to play and I had hours before anybody was due to get up. I poured a glass of water and made the pill disappear with one swallow.

I stood there drumming my fingers on the countertop, wondering who else was out there awake in the middle of the night, doing exactly the same thing. After swallowing a pill, we wait for something to happen. After snorting a pill, we don't have to. I drummed my fingers some more. I hated waiting.

I recapped the bottle and looked at the bottom of it. It was nice and flat; suitable for use as a crusher. I remember being in this much of a hurry to get high after hijacking Sidney's Sebring. I'd swallowed and snorted one after another that time, now I was ready to do it again. I pulverized all three Roxys on the counter. I wasn't even going to bother with a straw. I bet I could get the powder up my nose, right off the countertop. As I bent over with my nostril just a few millimeters above the powder, I heard a voice. It sounded as though it spoke directly into my ear.

"Stop what you're doing."

I jerked my head up and did a quick three-sixty. I was alone and the door was closed. I was paranoid and poked my head out the door to look up and down the hall. Nobody was up. *Forget about it,* I thought. *Hurry up and do it, already.*

I tried again, but I felt a force holding me back and I couldn't get my head anywhere near the Roxys.

"Get away from that."

The voice was not mine. It was a man's and very menacing, which started to irritate me because there was no one there. There had to be something weird going on in my head and I had no time for that. I wanted to snort the Roxys and put a smile on my face.

Out of sheer frustration and for no logical reason, I asked, "Who are you?"

"Who do you think I am? Your fairy godmother?"

I don't know why I wasn't shocked enough to run out of the bathroom. Instead I stood there curiously annoyed. Something was talking to me, plain as day. And I was talking back. I needed answers or a straightjacket. I looked around the room one more time and threw up my hands. "Are you in here somewhere?"

My leg was getting tired just standing there so I sat down on the lid of the toilet seat and leaned my crutches against the wall. "Okay, if you're not going to answer that question, how about this one: Who are you?"

Silence. "I give up. This is nonsense. You're nobody and I'm not crazy." I looked over at the powder and wanted to give it another try. I reached for the crutches and stood up.

"You're not crazy and this isn't nonsense. This is a business call, Dimwit. I'm your Higher Power." The voice was a little louder this time.

No way, I thought. *I didn't create any talking Higher Power and I'm not going to stand in my bathroom and talk to myself.* I maneuvered back to the powder and, as I bent over for a snort, it was all blown away into a tiny cloud of dust. Gone.

"I told you not to do that, Knucklehead."

That got my attention. Not only had I lost my favorite treat, but I was now willing to consider the impossible: a visitation from my Higher Power. I didn't know if I should be honored, afraid, or ticked off. I decided to cautiously engage this entity. After all, if it was really my Higher Power, it was all knowing and all powerful and could do anything it damn-well pleased, even vaporize me. I couldn't help chuckling to myself at the thought of disappearing, too.

"Okay, you convinced me. What gives? Did you just come here to blow away my Roxys and teach me another boring lesson in recovery?" I had no idea why I chose to be sarcastic. This was the ultimate spiritual force of all the universe and I should have been in awe and not a wise guy.

"So what's the big deal? Am I supposed to show my appreciation for saving my life after that spectacular crash? Do you want me to give you credit for summoning Brenda to bust up those thugs? Come on, Man, what do you want from me, an apology for trying to snort a couple pills?" I waited for an answer, but there was nothing but silence.

When the voice finally spoke, it was more emphatic and sounded like an aggravated Al Pacino. "You petitioned me for help. Remember? I didn't break my rule of silence just to hear myself talk. It was your idea, inviting me to join up with you."

"Join up with me?"

I couldn't get used to talking to what I couldn't see. It was hard to take this seriously. *And yet,* I thought, *I asked my Higher Power for help several times in the past two days and now He's here.*

"I am giving you one more chance and then I am leaving you alone. Think long and hard about these words. Drug-free. Sobriety. Forgiving—one word. For Giving—two words. Love. Any of them ring a bell, Simpleton?"

He was right. I had accepted those conditions as a miraculous gift. What went wrong with me? I looked at the bottle of Roxys and I felt like addiction had taken over my mind again. I wanted to get high and live an easier life. At that moment, I had no practical use for sobriety, or love, or anything besides having some long-overdue fun.

"Go ahead. Pick it up. Tell me what a *pimple-faced loser* sees inside."

I lifted it off the counter and tilted the opening towards me. I could have sworn all the pills had beady, red eyes.

"How about these words? 'I'm going to suck the life out of you.'" Then it hit me. I felt panic start to build as a menacing laugh ominously swarmed around me. I started to feel ice cold and trembled; the Roxys flew out of the bottle across the counter.

"You're the shadowy man from my dream, aren't you? This is all about the Roxys, isn't it? I swallowed one and now you're going to take what's left of my soul."

I gripped my crutches and pivoted toward the door, ready to make my exit before the shrouded figure appeared for real. I was scared enough to believe it was about to happen. Al Pacino's voice returned.

"Gotcha, didn't I? Thought I was the Boogieman, come to get you? I know all about your dream. I made it happen. You need dreams like that if you're going to be serious about recovery and you, my friend, are not. So that's why I'm here."

I caught my breath as the icy fear melted and turned my legs rubbery. I needed to sit down again.

"Stay on your feet, Buddy. You'll be all right. Now pick up those pills, put them in the bottle, and then get the pills from your bedroom and put them all back on the shelf."

I was still speechless.

"You're not going to get an easy ride from me if you want recovery. It's tough, but I'm even tougher. You get no breaks, understand? You signed on to do what it takes. Start doing it and I'll watch your back. Stop doing it and I won't be back."

I did as I was told. Once the Roxys were back in the cabinet, I returned to my room, thinking about what happened and pondering what He said. I couldn't believe how quickly addiction had nearly caused me to snort some Roxicodone. I had been saved again and, gratefully, there was no shadowy man to snuff me out. But, now I had a supreme hard-ass for a Higher Power. As I sat on the bed and looked up at the Einstein poster, the reality of his tongue sticking out at me had new meaning.

I was finally convinced that my Higher Power was for real and, if I truly wanted recovery, He was going to be on my case. I wondered why it was so difficult to say, "Of course, I'll do whatever it takes." Why did that seem like punishment just for being an addict? I didn't ask for this. Did He have to be so pushy? I imagined Dr. Stone telling me it would be worth it; that I would find a way—how had he said it? —to be naturally happy. At least I had a Higher Power with a voice. That should make it a little easier, but it was going to take some getting used to. "So now what?" I asked.

"I didn't put you on this earth just so you could get wasted on drugs with reckless abandon. You've got a bright enough mind for me to work with. But if I'm going to help you turn your life around, I want you to put it to good use, not squander it up here in this room watching reruns."

It sounded like my Higher Power wanted me to be *all that I could be*. That didn't seem like much fun. I didn't want to be enlisted in the Army nor did I need another parent. I already had two and I wasn't too thrilled with how they'd helped me get through the past sixteen years. This one was worse.

I had to be honest with myself, though. He did catch me trying to feed my addiction once again. I had to decide: either I wanted to be sober, with all the trimmings, or I could try to make it through life with an ugly face and no friends. As I thought about it, images of Joe, Wendy, and Brenda converged in my head and had the effect of snapping me out of my pathetic negativity. Of course I wanted what they had. And I was going to do whatever it took to get it, even if it meant taking instructions from the toughest coach on the planet, my Higher Power. I wanted to be sober. An apology was in order, and I hoped one might settle Him down.

"I'm sorry," I said, not sure what direction to face while I was talking to Him. "You caught me going crazy for those pills in there. That was total insanity. I really didn't expect my addiction to do that to me again. Not after all I had been through trying to change for the better. Once I saw that Roxy bottle, I attacked it like a fish after bait: I couldn't resist. I would have snorted all the pills. God knows what would have happened if I had. I suppose I should say thanks, but isn't that your job? To stop me? Anyway, I guess you're pretty handy to have around."

"Even I, who does not judge, will accept your apology. Humility is good. Now for a little lesson about insanity." The voice was a little gentler. "It's doing the same thing over and over and expecting a different outcome. That's what addiction is. Every time you take pills, you can't just stop after a little fun. Instead, you take more, even when you tell yourself not to. Ah, but the next time will be different. You won't take so many, you'll make them last longer; after all, they aren't cheap. And so on and so on, the insanity continues. Well, it's my job to restore your sanity, otherwise you won't stop."

I had to admit I was impressed. He made sense. "You're good," I said.

"I better be. Your life's at stake. If I don't do my job right, addiction will take advantage of you; the world won't get to see the masterpiece you really are."

"Masterpiece? You need to have your eyes examined."

"That's enough for now. You're tired. Get some sleep. I'll stand watch."

I let my crutches drop to the floor and slid under the covers, maneuvering more easily, even with a broken back and a skewered leg. As I drifted off to sleep, I heard one last comment.

"This time, you're going to get it, if I have to work a miracle." That sounded stern but reassuring. A miracle. For me?

The morning sun flooded my bedroom. My brother kept jabbing me in the arm with his finger.

"Wake up, Man. Wake up. Breakfast is ready." He jumped off the bed and hoisted a crutch up to his shoulder and aimed it at me like a rifle.

"I've got him in my sights, Captain. Ready to fire when you give the order, Sir. This dirt bag is going down. He's history. Pow! Pow!" He provided the sound effects of a discharging weapon. I pretended to be mortally wounded.

"I'm hit! My leg! Medic!"

Junior dropped the rifle and switched roles. "I'm here, Soldier. I have to stop the bleeding if I'm going to save your leg. Don't move." He jumped off the bed, retrieving a belt from the closet and a ruler from my desk.

"Bite down on this, Soldier," Junior ordered, sliding the ruler between my teeth. "The tourniquet has to be tight." I pretended to bite down on it with all my might.

"Be tough, Soldier, you have to take the pain. I'm out of medicine." Junior tightened the belt, and I hammed it up for dramatic effect.

"I'm not going to make it, Doc. I'm hit bad."

"Hang in there, Soldier."

"You gotta get a message to my wife."

He lowered his ear as my voice grew faint.

"What is it? What do you want me to tell her?"

I was gasping; my eyes wide open with fear. "Tell her . . . tell her . . . that I . . . love her."

I went limp, and Junior paused as he tried to decide his next move. He pressed his fingers on my eyelids to close them.

"Rest in peace, Soldier. You'll get a medal for this."

The performance was over. Junior undid the belt saying, "That was cool. You die real good."

"Thanks," I said, remembering that I needed more humility.

"Let's go. Breakfast is ready."

He left the room at breakneck speed and yelled, "We're on our way, Mom. Start the pancakes. I'm going to pour my own syrup. I want a can of whipped cream to make a happy face."

I headed to the bathroom, feeling stiff for the first few steps. I did my thing, flushed the toilet, and got everything ready to brush my teeth. The cabinet door was open and there they were: the Roxys. I glanced down at the fine granules of powder that were still on the countertop and swept them away with my hand. It was no dream. I had been there last night, trying to load up on painkillers. But I was so lucky—I was stopped after taking the first Roxicodone when I had my sights set on three more up my nose.

I wondered if my Higher Power was still watching my back. I had no desire to snort anything, which made no sense. How could addiction be pounding on my door last night and now I felt cured? Or, was it just leaving me alone?

I brushed and then swished the toothpaste out of my mouth. I closed the cabinet with the Roxicodone on the shelf. I wanted pancakes, not pills.

In the kitchen, Mom was busy making breakfast. Her hair was up and she was wearing a housecoat spattered with flowers and butterflies. It must have been as old as I was.

"Buddy, will you serve the orange juice for all of us?" I looked at the table, set with the good plates, silverware, and placemats. There was a lighted candle in the center. It was what I would call a fancy breakfast. Although the whole family was usually home on a Sunday morning, it was rare that all of us ate together.

I started drinking my juice before the pancakes arrived. My father was watching the morning news on television and complaining about Washington politicians.

Mom put the platter of pancakes on the table. "Sit down, everybody. It's time to eat."

Dad stuck a fork in two of the pancakes, but Mom stopped him.

"Before we eat, I want us to bow our heads and join hands. It's time we got a little closer as a family." After last night's hug, I wasn't surprised and sat quietly.

"You lead us in prayer," Mom said.

I looked up to see who she was speaking to. She squeezed my hand.

"Go ahead, Buddy. Say something we can all relate to, something nice and spiritual."

It was time to put my Higher Power up to another test. Was He even listening?

"Start with gratitude," He whispered. I could tell that nobody else heard a thing.

"Okay, here goes. We should all be grateful that we're together to share this meal." As I was searching for more to say, I felt Mom's grip tighten. "You're doing fine," she said, keeping her eyes closed and head bowed.

"I put everybody through a rough month, including myself. Not only am I going to fully recover, I'm changing my attitude. You're all going to see a happier me from now on."

"Amen," Mom said, and we broke the circle of hands. "That was wonderful, honey. Now dig in."

My brother made whipped cream faces on his pancakes and my father continued to rant about the political situation. Mom shot him a hard glare. "Okay. I'm done. No more politics."

"This is the way we should eat from now on," Mom offered. "Families who eat together and pray together have less drug addiction. This is a perfect time to start, don't you think?" Mom looked at me with a hopeful smile.

I could swear my Higher Power jabbed me in the side, reminding me to just keep my smart remarks to myself. Very politely, I answered, "Sure, Mom.

Let's give it a try, at least on weekends. I feel closer to each one of you already."

I really wanted some of those words to be true, but I couldn't believe they were coming out of my mouth. It would take some practice to be comfortable with the whole "pleasant conversation" thing.

When breakfast was over, the rest of my family settled into their regular Sunday routine: Dad returned to the couch and more CNN, Junior went next door to play catch, and Mom washed the dishes.

"Sweetie, what's on your schedule today?"

I was tempted to say, *Getting you to stop saying Sweetie, Dear, and Honey*, but I knew better.

"I'm going to hang around in my room and read or listen to music or write in my notebook. I'm waiting for Joe's call. He's taking me to my first NA meeting today."

"That's right. My son is going to his first NA meeting. Do you want me to go with you?"

I couldn't think of anything I'd like less. "That would look too much like elementary school, Mom. I can handle this. My friend will look after me. He knows what to do."

"I know. And I trust him. It's just that there are going to be drug addicts there. Some of them may have been criminals, the kind with tattoos and motorcycles, and they might not be nice to you. I'm concerned. I want this to be a good experience."

I rose up from my chair and turned toward the stairs.

"Mom, I don't care who goes to NA or what they look like. If we have addiction in common, then I'll fit in. Brenda wasn't the easiest person to get along with, but eventually we had a breakthrough and now we like each other. I'll bet the same thing can happen with anybody at those meetings. You'll see."

"I'm sure you're right. Just be careful. Don't try to make friends with everybody."

"I'll be upstairs if you need me." I took off for my room.

CHAPTER 41

Phone Calls and Messages

Once in my room, I unplugged my cell phone from the charger and listened to two messages.

"Hey, Bro. I've got some news for you. I'm not with Sidney any more. She cleaned me out. I used it on drugs and gifts for her. She kept promising to make out with me. Then she dumped me once she found out I was broke. I feel like the dumbest fool who never got kissed. I had fun with the pills, but I'm not buying on credit like you did. I heard about those two guys she sent to rough you up. Some kind of Ninja nurse took them out. You are one lucky dude. Catch you later. Jeffrey out."

I expected the next message to be Jeffrey's follow-up call. As I listened, I felt an involuntary shiver pass through my body. Sidney's voice always started like the first bite of a southern peach: sweet and juicy.

"Hello, Babycakes. Welcome home. Sorry I couldn't be there to hold the banner and lead a parade of cheerleaders. After all you've been through, you deserve the very best. Two of my men weren't so fortunate. They aren't on my payroll anymore, either. But you still owe me, so when you least expect it, your hand may end up in a meat grinder. But you can prevent all that with just five hundred dollars. That includes a finder's fee for my new agent. Call me."

I saved the message. But who should listen to it? My parents? The cops? An attorney? Nobody? I wished I had Brenda protecting me here at home. But I had to consider other options. Should I do nothing and wait to see if Sidney really meant it? That was probably a bad idea. She had a pit-bull mentality. I decided to tell my parents and ask for the extra hundred; Mom's cookie jar had plenty to spare. But I was going to demand that the transaction be civilized. I didn't want some knuckle-dragging gorilla to burst into my house and put anyone's life in jeopardy. I was a paying customer and I deserved some measure of respect.

My mom walked by with an armful of towels and I called out to her.

"What's up?" She paused at the door and noticed my concerned look.

"I just listened to a message from Sidney—the girl who sold me the pills on credit, the one who sent those guys to break my fingers."

"You're kidding. I thought you were done with all of that. You said the nurse took care of everything."

"Yes, but the debt still stands and it grew a little bit larger."

"You mean she wants more money?"

"Precisely."

"How much more?"

"Five hundred all together. And then we'll be free."

"This is highway robbery!" Her foot came down on the word *robbery* and I flinched.

"I'm sorry, Mom, but let's not mess with Sidney. We have to play by her rules or the price is going to go higher."

Mom just grunted. "What do we do next?"

"I'll call her. I don't want her to send someone else to collect the money. She has to come by herself."

"Let me know what she says. I'll be glad when this is over." Her troubled look made me feel guilty for getting myself addicted. I wanted her to stop worrying.

"Mom, all I need is the money. Leave the rest up to me."

Mom didn't leave the room, though. She just stood there, looking at my poster of Einstein and his wild, unruly hair.

"I wonder what the smartest man on earth thinks about? Maybe how stupid the rest of us are?"

"Geniuses have more important things to think about," I said.

She kept studying the poster. "Well, I'm no genius, but I sure wish I could write that Sidney one nasty letter."

"Mom!"

"Only kidding. When you come downstairs, five hundred dollars will be on the kitchen table in an envelope."

I nodded in acknowledgment, then I waved her out of the room saying I had things to do. After she walked out, I hit the redial next to Sidney's phone number; the Georgia Peach answered after three rings.

"I had a feeling you would call. There's a certain erotic vibration I get when the subject is money. I never get tired of it. So, did your mommy spank you hard for being naughty and make you promise not to play with girls like me? Or did she take money out of your college fund to teach you a lesson?"

"I have the money," I said. "It's yours. Just come here alone to pick it up. The sooner, the better."

"I think I'll bring Vinnie with me. He's my new enforcer and he does enjoy straightening out troubled boys like you ever so much—especially those who wreck beautiful cars, like mine was."

After a moment of silence, Sidney's voice erupted from the speaker with a powerful vengeance.

"Don't mess this up or I'll give Vinnie the green light to rearrange your anatomy. Be outside with the cash in one hour. I don't ring doorbells." She ended the call without saying anything more.

Part of me wanted to give her the money and end this. Another part wanted to stand up for myself. She definitely had the advantage. She might have looked like a prom queen, but she had Grim Reaper in her blood. She was dangerous, and more kids were going to snort their way into hospital beds or coffins.

I decided to give Jeff a call. I suppose it was because he had partied with pills and it was only a matter of time before he had enough money to do it again. Maybe he could be rescued.

"Hey, Man, what gives? You back home scarfing down chocolate chip cookies? How's the busted leg? Still got those pins holding you together with that whatchamacallit? Can't wait to see you, Bro. Do you have a date with any nurses yet? I heard that nurses . . ."

I broke in to keep him from going another twenty minutes.

"Jeff. Shut it down and listen, will you?"

"What gives?"

"Sidney called me. Today's payday. In one hour, to be exact. And she's bringing some guy named Vinnie. Did you ever see him around when you were with her?"

"Yeah, the last time I saw her, yesterday. That's when I brought her some Victoria's Secret nighties."

"That's the slinky stuff." I had taken more than a casual glance at Mom's catalogs.

"And expensive, too," Jeff replied.

"Why'd you do it if you guys were breaking up?"

"We were never going out. I was just another sucker with money. Man, she made me believe I was going to get lucky. Now it's over. I don't even want drugs anymore. I spent all my money with nothing to show for it."

I knew how Sidney's heartless vanity could crush a man's ego.

"Forget about it, Jeff. She's bad to the bone."

"She's worse than that, Buddy. She tried to tempt me into a deal for more Oxy 80s. I listened to her offer because, let's face it, they are good when you get all you want. But she crossed the line with me, Man."

"What do you mean?" I asked, hearing the unmistakable resentment in his voice and knowing his loyalty to me.

"She said, 'If you want one of these, there's one little thing you have to do.'"

"What was that?"

"To make an example of you. But I wouldn't do it. That's why I left you the message."

My stomach got queasy at the thought of something getting broken.

"So how did you leave it with her?" I asked.

"I said we're finished. I told her that you and I were best friends and I was going to warn you. So I grabbed the box of nighties and started to bolt, but she snapped her fingers and this guy came out of nowhere. She called him Vinnie.

"He's a bad dude, Man. I don't mean to scare you, but he could make his mother want to take her name off the birth certificate. He had a toothpick in his mouth and was smoking a cigarette at the same time. He looked Italian, but not the good kind. He took the box of nighties right out of my hand, then told me to scram."

"Did he hurt you?"

"No. But on the way to my car, I heard him tell Sidney, 'The pleasure will be all mine.' I think he was talking about you. Anyway, I just wanted you to know that this might be a good time to carry a baseball bat. Seriously. Do whatever it takes to make peace with Sidney and soon."

I considered myself warned. She was on her way with someone who liked to hurt people. I needed to check in with my Higher Power and get ready. I wanted to give Sidney the money and be done with her. Did I really need protection? My mother and father were home and I hoped that was enough security standing by. I kept reminding myself to keep it simple as I was searching for ideas.

The answer came as I looked at my talisman on the nightstand—the gift from Brenda, who had saved me from harm's way. I knew I needed to hold it, to be silent, and to listen. I felt that it was another way to contact my Higher Power. So far He had surprised, amazed, and humbled me. I may not have been given what I wanted or expected, but I always received something I needed. I wondered if any reasonable request could be denied.

As I tossed the meteorite into the air over and over again, I noticed how heavy it was for its size. I let my mind wander to things I'd previously had no interest in, like the expression *be in the moment*. That very moment, I didn't feel good. There was potential for a lot more trouble, as well as the possibility Sidney would take the money, make some rude and crude remarks, and drive off. But that was only a probability, not a certainty. The only certainty was right *now*.

I began thinking about the notion of *now*. I found it interesting, because it's always *now* and can't be anything else. Yesterdays, tomorrows, and any other time don't exist in reality. There's only *now*, constantly *now*. That meant the notion and measurement of time was created by man for convenience. Yet, how convenient is it to worry about something that might happen in the future, which doesn't even exist and never will? What a total waste of *now*.

I found that mental exercise interesting, but not very practical as Sidney's visit was approaching. My peculiar way of thinking wasn't going to make Vinnie a gentleman or get Sidney to accept payment on my debt or even stop her from selling drugs to vulnerable teenagers.

I shook my head, hoping to clear my mind, to figure out how to keep from getting hurt by Vinnie. But I kept returning to the idea of *now*. Not knowing why, I just let my mind play around with it some more. Suppose I was injured enough to die. What would happen to the real me? My spirit. My existence. My life force. Once my body can't live any longer, is that the end of me, too? I decided to believe that I would go on, somehow. And since it was always *now*, *me* would always be an eternal *me*, only without the arms and legs and other parts. Clever. Thinking about being endless was way off the beaten path for my mind. Then, it occurred to me that my Higher Power was behind all of these thoughts. Maybe there was something serious about this after all. But how was it going to keep Vinnie and Sidney from violating my right to remain in one piece?

I suddenly remembered that it was time to get the money. Vinnie and Sidney were on their way. My mission was to stay alive by paying off my drug dealer while keeping all my fingers and toes. I glanced at my watch and realized that time was running out. Interesting how I couldn't say *now* was running out.

I went downstairs, picked up the envelope, and headed for the front door. I wanted to do this by myself, so I was careful not to let my parents hear me. I assumed my Higher Power was along for the ride and I had a lucky-charm meteor in my front pocket. I hoped the money would be all that really mattered to Sidney. I would turn it over and be off the hook in time to make that first NA meeting.

CHAPTER 42

All Types of Messages

As I opened the front door, someone slapped my face and pulled me outside. Vinnie had me in his grip. My feet were dangling off the ground; my crutches were dropped in the house. The door shut and it all happened faster than the time it took to wet my pants.

Vinnie didn't look like a Vinnie. He looked more like a lineman for the Green Bay Packers. Sidney looked royally po'd. "I told you I don't ring doorbells. Did you think I was kidding?" She signaled Vinnie to put me down. It was a hard landing. I felt a jolt of pain in my broken leg. My back ached.

"What's all this?" Vinnie was amused. "Looks like some kind of brace here." He grabbed the padded aluminum cross bar, just below my collar bone, and gave it a jarring tug. I restrained myself from any show of pain.

"And that looks like it might hurt."

I felt defenseless as he eyed the pins and fixator and whet his sadistic appetite.

"He's a scrawny dink, Sidney. I bet he's a little tender, you want me to rough him up a bit?" Vinnie looked a little too eager for my comfort level. "If he tries to scream for his parents, I can do something really quick. He'll just pass out. It's the neatest thing."

The darkening stain from urine was growing slowly and I hoped they wouldn't notice. Somehow, I found a way to keep my bladder from emptying completely.

I flinched when Sidney raised her hand again, only this time she lightly stroked my face and said, "I love a man with pimples. Maybe someday, when these all dry up, your face will be rugged-looking, like Humphrey Bogart. Now there's a man for you. Did you bring the money?"

I hadn't uttered a sound yet. Everything had happened so fast. My Higher Power must have known what was going down, so why was I still on the verge of getting something broken?

"Yes," I answered, trying to hide my fear. "I have the money. It's in my pocket—all five hundred dollars. Take it and leave."

"I think he's a little too bossy, don't you?" Sidney smiled at Vinnie.

A hand that felt as big as the bucket on a backhoe put a clench on my crotch. I saw stars. Vinnie quickly let go of me and made a sound of disgust. "He wet himself. It's all over my hand."

Sidney said, "If you can't handle it, maybe you should find another way to make a living. Get the money, will you? This is already taking too long."

Vinnie took the envelope and handed it to Sidney. She removed the bills and quickly fanned out the twenties. She crumpled the envelope and instructed Vinnie to force my mouth open.

"You need more fiber in your diet," she said, stuffing the wad of paper in my mouth; I started to gag.

Sidney glanced at the pee stain and then looked me up and down.

"You are pathetic. Even if I hurt you, no one outside this house is going to care. You are nothing, a nobody. While you were in the hospital, I knew you were fighting for your life on that machine. At school, the biggest news was about my Sebring being totaled. Your coma didn't matter to anybody. The world wouldn't miss a beat without you. You're expendable, a nonessential. I'm irreplaceable and everybody knows it. If I told Vinnie to take you out, your parents would be the only ones who'd show up at your funeral. And they aren't even out here to save you. If you ever bother me again, I'll make sure the pieces are too small to be found."

I tried to remove the envelope, but Vinnie pinned my arms to my sides, and I was helpless.

Sidney walked toward her car. Even as scared as I was, I had to be honest: from behind she looked awesome, her hips swaying from side to side.

She must have felt my charged-up hormones staring at her backside, because she stopped abruptly and spun around. "I told you this day would come. It's payback time for my Sebring—that I'll never see again."

She was filled with contempt as she gave Vinnie the final order. "Do what you want, but make sure it's enough to keep his dirty eyes off of me from now on."

Her last words were tossed over her shoulder as she resumed walking. "Hurry up. I have a nail appointment."

Vinnie just stood there, apparently trying to decide how to hurt me. An amazing idea flashed through my mind. Then . . . BAM! I used my head like a battering ram and bashed it into his nose. I heard bone and cartilage crumble and watched a gush of blood spurt out each nostril. His nose wasn't a nose anymore: it was flattened and angulated sharply to the right.

He let go of me. I took the envelope out of my mouth as I watched his knees buckle. His head reared back and both hands groped to find his collapsed nose. He was in agony. Blood and Italian curse words spilled out of his mouth. I'd reduced him to a schoolyard bully complaining about a lucky sucker punch from the skinny kid.

I heard Sidney yell, "Step on it, I'm never late for my nails." Vinnie turned toward her at the sound of her voice; once she saw all the blood drenching his shirt, Sidney got into the car and took off. I opened the door and went back inside the house, leaving Vinnie frantically dialing his cell phone.

I could feel the effects of adrenaline slowly wearing off and I caught my breath. That was such an unexpected rush. I didn't feel so scrawny any more. I'd trusted my instinct and used my hard head perfectly. Vinnie was at least temporarily out of commission and Sidney had her money. Once again, I was taken care of. I'm sure I had my Higher Power to thank, but why had He cut it so close? I was almost toast . . . or was I?

I picked up my crutches on the other side of the closed, bolted door and stopped in the living room where my parents were watching a movie. At least, that's what Mom was doing; Dad was asleep.

In the past ten minutes, I had grown and changed once again and I wondered if it showed. "Sidney was here," I announced, making sure to stand behind the couch and keep my wet pants out of view.

"That was fast," Mom greeted me. "Did everything go okay?"

It surprised me that she hadn't heard Vinnie carrying on in Italian. "No problem. She took the money and left."

"That's nice. I hope this is finally over with."

"I made sure of that."

"Good. Do you want to watch the rest of this with me? It's about a ten-year-old boy whose mom is dying of cancer and he's trying to make her final days really special. It's so sad."

"I think I'll pass. I'm going up to my room for a while. Call me for lunch."

I made my way to the upstairs bathroom and checked for injuries. There was only a slightly swollen red spot in the center of my forehead. My mom hadn't even noticed it.

I opened the medicine cabinet to intentionally look at the Roxys. The day before, I'd failed the test and couldn't resist taking a pill. This time, I wanted see if my temptation was gone. Was my Higher Power on duty? There was only one way to know.

I snatched the bottle and heard the pills rattle like a snake's tail. It was a hypnotic sound. I began to unscrew the lid.

"Are you at it again?" Frustration and annoyance saturated every word.

The voice was loud enough to make me duck my head as though preparing to be swatted. I promptly screwed the lid back on and instantly felt like I had been caught red-handed.

"Let's go over a few things, shall we? Addiction isn't going to leave you alone just because I'm around. It may not be wise for me to bail you out of every jam you're in. Getting everything you want is no way to teach gratitude. So don't be surprised if I let you sink a little deeper in the quick sand. Don't worry, I'll always be there to show you the way out, but you've got to do the work. Otherwise, you'll never learn that pills aren't worth the risk you're taking when you pry that lid off."

I hated being lectured to, but I knew He was trying to teach me something valuable.

"You should have left that bottle in the cabinet," He said. "It's time you realize that pills will just empty your wallet and leave you desperate for more. Isn't that blatantly obvious to you by now?"

Having a Higher Power on duty was what I'd asked for. He was right. The trouble I had gotten into with pills hadn't crossed my mind. Nearly losing my life clearly wasn't enough to scare me away from doing it all over again. Now I was being saved one more time. I put the bottle back on the shelf and shut the cabinet door.

I had learned another lesson in addiction recovery: Stay away from the product and the people who have it, sell it, or use it. That was probably going to include a lot of kids at school. What was I supposed to do when pills were everywhere and easily available? How did anyone stay sober? I knew I didn't really know enough about addiction.

I headed back to my room and fired up the computer; I was going to visit the Narcotics Anonymous website but I clicked on Wikipedia first. I knew everything there would be condensed and I could learn a lot in a hurry. I could check out NA.org later, if I still needed to.

> NA is a worldwide fellowship with 50,000 weekly meetings in 130 countries. It's a twelve-step program of recovery for drug addiction modeled on Alcoholics Anonymous. It's nonprofit and open to all people for whom drugs have become a major problem. The only requirement for membership is a desire to stop using.
>
> The members meet and help each other stay clean, which means complete abstinence from all mood and mind altering substances. Membership is free. Narcotics Anonymous has no opinion on outside issues including politics, science, and medicine. It doesn't even promote itself. Members are attracted through public information and outreach. Narcotics Anonymous carries its message to hospitals and institutions such as treatment centers and jails.
>
> (http://en.wikipedia.org/wiki/Narcotics_Anonymous)

I learned that addiction is a progressive disease with no known cure, and it affects every addict's life in a physical, mental, emotional, and spiritual way. The disease of addiction can be arrested and recovery is possible through an understanding and application of the twelve-step program.

What a relief, I thought. *The monkey will stay off my back and sit in the banana tree where it belongs.* I wanted to learn and understand the Twelve Steps. I read everything at the site and felt I had a good grasp of the NA fundamentals. I figured that mastering recovery should soon follow. I asked my Higher Power if He agreed. A prolonged silence was followed by a big belly laugh.

"You can't be serious," He said.

I was aggravated. "Why did you laugh? What more is there to know about addiction and sobriety?"

"You think skimming through a few pages on Wikipedia about addiction is all you need to be sober?"

"I don't see why not."

"You didn't even go to NA.org, where you could have found thousands of pages on the subject."

"Precisely," I said. "I know enough."

"You don't know jack about recovery, my friend."

"I beg to differ. Go ahead and quiz me. I bet I can get most of the answers right."

Another belly laugh. "You are something else. You never cease to amaze me. For a kid who called himself a loser nerd, you sure are cocky today."

"Okay, This is what I remember. Recovery involves abstinence, meetings, literature, sponsorship, the steps, helping others, spirituality, and service. Once I do all of that, my addiction will be arrested. Case closed."

"You may as well order your recovery at a drive-through window. Speed is not the answer here. Listen, a few minutes ago you were dangerously close to pulling out a Roxy and snorting it. Now, you want me to believe that you're ready to master recovery in one giant leap after just browsing on Wikipedia?"

"Why not?"

"It doesn't work that way and I don't have all day to argue with you. You may have enough brain power between your ears, but information does not equal experience, nor does it yield results. Just because you know the recipe doesn't mean that you're going to bake a great-tasting cake. More likely, your concoction will be as appetizing as sawdust with frosting on top; it may look good, but you can't eat it. What you just learned on the Internet probably won't keep you away from a pill."

I couldn't believe I was having this conversation with my Higher Power. Why wasn't He helping me out? I didn't need this aggravation. "Do you think dumping on me is going to keep me away from pills? I checked out the reputable website, learned what I could, and gave it my best shot. Since you plan on hanging around, is it too much to ask for a little more assistance here?"

"I accept. Maybe you're teachable after all. Let's start with some basic training."

"Okay, tell me what you know; I don't have forever."

"Wrong. You have more than that. Now shut up and listen."

I wasn't going to get anywhere in this argument. He clearly had the upper hand, so I conceded and held my tongue.

"First of all, you aren't going to be instantly transformed into recovery. You're going to grow into it. You may have a few spurts here and there, but for the most part, it will be slow, steady, and deliberate. Recovery means change. Change is continuous, gradual, and sometimes hardly noticeable. It happens with every breath, every thought, and certainly, with every action."

"Come on, then. Let's get going." I was impatient to be "in recovery."

"You'll have to wait."

"For what? Aren't you the Master of All Creation? The Knower of the Unknown? The Seer of the Unseen? The Listener of the Unspoken? And whatever else you call yourself?"

"If you're looking for buttons to push, you won't find any. I'm unflappable when I want to be. I'm not going to constantly be a superstar just because I can. Sometimes, persuasive nudging is more interesting . . . and a lot more amusing."

Why doesn't He just show me the short cuts? I thought. He knows them all. Why is He making me take the long way?

"I suggest you pay attention. The messages will arrive on my schedule. If you miss one, I'll give you another chance. I never give up. You may not always realize who the messengers are. They will come in all shapes and sizes. It's easier if you try to find something of me in everyone you meet, because I am everyone you meet. You'll hear me speaking through them if you shut up and listen. Remember, you can't learn a thing when you're the one doing the talking."

"I suppose that doesn't apply to you, does it?"

"Good one, Sport. And I like you just as much. But I've got some business to attend to."

"And I don't."

"See you later, Buddy. I'll be rooting for you." It felt like He was gone. But

I wasn't going to be fooled. Of course He was still there. He was everywhere, all at once, and that was just too wild. But, bottom line, the Big Guy was speaking directly to me. Someday, I hoped to know why I had been chosen.

Now, I had to wait for a messenger, which could be anybody. I didn't want to miss a single message. Each one could be crucial for my recovery. I really needed to pay attention to everything.

My cell phone rang and vibrated at the same time. I flipped it open and answered it.

"Welcome home, my friend. How goes it?" It was Joe, my new recovery pal. I lit up with a big grin.

"I was hoping you'd call, Joe. How have you been?"

"Taking it one day at a time. Staying clean and enjoying the ride. What about you, Buddy?"

I was ready for this *Aha!* moment. My sponsor was going to be messenger number one, my teacher of the day.

I immediately wanted to impress him as the best student he would ever have, so I tossed out a few NA slogans.

"Joe, get a load of these: First things first. Live and let live. Let go and let God. Keep coming back. It works if you work it. Turn it over. Take what you can use and leave the rest."

He was silent. "How was that?" I finally asked.

"You sound like you've either been to a hundred NA meetings in the last twenty-four hours or you memorized a bunch of slogans from a website. I'm guessing you haven't got a clue what you just said."

"Not yet. That's where you come in. I'm getting ready for tonight's meeting. I want to make sure I fit right in so you'll be proud of me."

"Buddy, you're too much, Man."

As soon as I heard that, I realized how useless the slogans I'd found at cyberrecovery.net were when I didn't really know what they meant. "I want to be more like you, Joe, but I must have sounded more like an NA nerd. Sorry about that."

"That's okay. I was just a little speechless for a moment. Listen, Buddy, nobody has to try that hard on their first day. It's going to be fun watching you grow. So don't worry if the words don't mean much. They will in time. For now, just keep it simple. Remember, you nearly lost your life trying to get high and the next time you snort, eat, or shoot another drug, you might never stop. A loaded gun pointed at your head would probably be a faster way to shorten your misery, drugs will only prolong it. Now, if you want to stay away from pills, you're ready to take Step One."

I was able to follow along easily. I had memorized all the Twelve Steps from Wikipedia, just in case he asked me

"I read about Step One, so correct me if I'm wrong. Does being powerless over drugs mean that I won't want to stop once I get started?"

"Yup."

"That no matter how much I take, it will never be enough?"

"Precisely."

Joe was boosting my confidence, giving me a chance to figure it out for myself. This type of give and take made him a great teacher. "What about the second part of Step One?"

"You mean, how did drugs make my life unmanageable?"

"Right."

"Easy. Just look at the brace holding my spine together and the hardware connected to my shin bone."

"That's a start," Joe encouraged.

"You know what I mean, Joe: that whole catastrophe, smashing into the tanker and all the trouble it brought me."

"That's all there is to it. You just have to admit that it's true: being addicted to drugs made all of that possible. Ain't it swell?"

"Hell, no!"

"I was only kidding. Don't sweat it. I'll take you through the Steps and you'll see how great recovery can be. Just keep reviewing what you told me, because it is a critically important part of your foundation. Make sure you get it right or you won't be able to go on to the next step. You don't need to go any deeper; you've already struck gold. Take your few nuggets and be satisfied."

It was hard to imagine that one year ago, this same person was being hunted down by drug dealers. Now, he was helping me understand the basics about Step One. I needed that. I needed him. I sent a silent thank-you to my Higher Power for sending Joe, a great messenger.

"Buddy, you got quiet all of a sudden."

"Sorry, Joe, just thinking to myself how much I appreciate all you've done for me."

"You're welcome, Sport. Someone did this for me and now it's my turn to help you. My break's over now, so I have to go. I'll pick you up at five. And don't worry. You'll do good."

"Thanks a lot."

After Joe hung up, I sat on the edge of my bed and thought about what had just happened. A college student—someone handsome, athletic and intelligent who was probably going to make a major contribution to the human race someday—had called me. We were both addicts and, at one time, losers. Now we were friends. He had one year away from drugs and a lot more experience knowing how to stay sober. He had been shown the way, and now he wanted me to follow him.

He was unselfish and willing to give his attention to me as though I really mattered, as though I was somebody. This college kid was willing to let me be who I was and show me a way to improve on that. There was no pressure, just guidance. I think he was nudging me gently, the way Higher Power talked about. It felt good and I wanted more.

I got the notebook out to write a paragraph or two.

> *Dear Higher Power,*
>
> *I am writing to thank you for the messenger and the message. Send as many as you like. It would be better to miss a few than to not have enough to get the job done. I suppose you could say I am a work in progress.*
>
> *I foolishly tried to impress Joe by spouting slogans as though I created them. When he poked a little fun at me, I didn't feel embarrassed or ashamed. I actually felt a closeness, like he was my big brother, and he smiled at my attempts to be more like him.*
>
> *I feel loved by Joe. It's weird to be saying that. But I really want to learn about it. I think I can understand the love I feel from my family. That tender hug with my mother convinced me of that. So, why would Joe want to love a misfit like me? Isn't being friendly and helpful good enough? I know that love is so much more, and I am sorely lacking in experience. I have a feeling the answers are in my heart, but I am not exactly sure how to get at them.*
>
> *I am so grateful for what I have already been taught about addiction and recovery. It seems like I've learned so much in just a few days. I have taken Step One, and I can feel the beginning of a solid foundation, something I can depend on for the rest of the Steps. I can see myself taking each Step and moving further away from ever taking another pill to get high. I want to be spiritually strong and prepared for whatever addiction can throw at me.*

As I closed the notebook, I felt a tightness release from around my heart. I didn't even know it was there until it just let go. It felt so liberating and fantastic that I wanted to tell somebody, but not just anybody. I dialed the hospital.

CHAPTER 43

Love Someone as Much as You Know How

I asked for the nursing station on the orthopedic floor.

"Ortho unit." Brenda's familiar voice filled my ear. She was my superhero, saving the day in white scrubs, her snakes ready to strike the evil-doers. In my heart, she was beautiful and I wanted to use my ability to love and bring us closer.

"Hello, Brenda. I'm so glad you answered. It's me . . ."

"Buddy! Hey, Big Fella, I was just thinking about you and I got my wish. How are you doing?"

Before I even answered, a smile took over my face. It amused me to think that a few days ago, Brenda wanted to exterminate all teenage drug addicts; I was going to be her next victim. She was constantly rattling my cage with belittling insults. And now we were becoming friends. "I called because I'm doing pretty good and I miss you."

"Aren't you sweet? I miss you, too. How are the leg and your back?"

"Swell. I bet I could walk without crutches. I'm wearing the back brace like I'm supposed to. But I know it's going to heal up fine. I want to get moving."

"Take it easy, Superman. Don't do anything crazy."

"Speaking of crazy: Sidney, my drug dealer, came to the house today. We agreed to pay up and get it over with."

"Smart move. Don't mess with those people." Brenda clicked her tongue in sympathy.

"She brought a guy named Vinnie. He was fixin' to hurt me."

"Did he look like a six-foot-four, two-hundred-and-fifty-pound George Clooney?"

"Exactly. He scared the you-know-what out of me and I dribbled a little down my leg."

"He has that effect on people. He was in the joint when I was a nurse there. He was a bad boy. Did he try anything? I know where to find him if he did."

"No. But I bet he wished he had."

"What do you mean?"

"Sidney took the money and told Vinnie to finish me off."

"Yeah, so then what?"

"I clobbered him with my head and smashed his nose like it was a pumpkin. Blood poured out like water from a faucet."

"No way! You did that to him?"

"His nose was caved in. He stood there stunned and then the gushing blood must have made him panic. Sidney peeled out in her car and left him there hemorrhaging. I went in the house, so I assume he got a ride. My forehead's got a nice little bruise on it. I bet you're really proud of me, aren't you?"

"You're not a wimpy kid anymore? I heard if you stand up to Vinnie, you can find his weakness. Now we know it's his nose. Way to go, Hammerhead."

"I have to give you the credit."

"Me? Why is that?"

"I had the talisman in my pocket. It was like having you there to save my life."

"Well, what do you know?" Brenda chuckled. "I actually felt a shooting pain in my forehead today. Five seconds later, it was gone. Imagine that: we've got a connection."

"Does that mean what I think it means?"

"Heck if I know. If you get in any more trouble, we'll find out soon enough. And I wouldn't worry about Vinnie. He's a shamed man now. He'll pack up and leave."

It was good to have someone like Brenda to share personal details of my life with. I admired her strength and, perhaps through the talisman, she had passed some on to me. I wanted to stay on the phone with her, even have her make fun of me in her own special way. That's how our friendship was being built: on the lighter side. That was our kind of love.

"Do you think we could get together?" I asked hopefully. "I really think you're cool. When I'm around you, I feel more like the self I want to be."

"And what exactly is that: handsome?"

"No, even better, comfortable in my own skin."

I looked at the poster of Einstein posing for the camera as a silly buffoon, sticking his tongue out. He was still a genius who was just being playful. It was my turn now and Brenda was making it easier for me. Brenda moved on to her favorite topic, the gym.

"If you really want to be comfortable in your own skin, you need some beef under the blanket."

I laughed, but I didn't know what she meant.

"You've got to put some meat on your bones, Boy. You're a scarecrow. Don't sweat it. I'll turn you into a gym rat: you'll be doing curls and squats and flies. Just heal up and get that hardware off your body and I'll take you to my place."

"Me, pumping iron?"

"Don't worry. I'll go easy on you . . . not." We both laughed. Mine was nervous, hers sounded delightfully devilish.

"Seriously, Kid, we've got to do something about those spaghetti arms. So, buy some work-out gloves. And don't show up at the gym with a headband or shorts with stripes. You do and I'll pretend I don't know you . . . then I'll squeeze your pimples with tweezers.

Brenda was smacking me around with her heart of gold and I loved it. She might become the best big sister a kid could ever have, one with muscles, brains, and nothing to fear.

"I can't wait for everything to heal. I was hoping to see you sooner. How about pizza or video games? Anything to keep me out of my shell I spent so many years hiding in."

"Sure, Kid. I'll think of something. How about going to watch an Ultimate Fighting Championship? Those guys are the toughest competitors in the world of sports. There is no giving up when they go at it. The winner is always the one who wouldn't quit. I'd give anything to train with them. Imagine making money by punching, kicking, and twisting people into human pretzels."

I was not surprised by her fiendish attraction to such a blood sport. I had seen commercials for those cage matches. "Okay. I'll go."

"I'll get the tickets and call you. It's my treat. You buy the hot dogs and drinks. I have to run. The nursing supervisor is walking down the hall with that clipboard. Give me your cell number real quick."

I hung up the phone and felt the smile on my face grow. It was almost too good to be true. I had made friends with a college jock with NA credentials and a power-lifting nurse with tattoos who liked hand-to-hand combat in a cage.

After my conversation with Brenda, I headed downstairs for lunch. I found Mom tasting the chicken soup she'd made. She had all the grace and charm of Martha Stewart and, as I watched her, I realized how pretty she was. Why hadn't I noticed that before?

"Hi, Buddy. I made your favorite. Sit down—it's ready to serve."

"Can I help?" I asked.

"No, just relax and enjoy. It feels good having you home, now that everything's better between us."

I felt the same way as I watched her ladle soup into each bowl with tender loving care.

She called Dad and Junior to the table. Junior arrived with his glove and baseball.

"Junior, did you wash your hands?" Mom asked.

He looked at them. "They're okay. I didn't get them dirty."

"Wash them anyway," she said. "And use soap."

Junior obeyed her with a smile, something I never did. Mom finished filling all the bowls and sat down, giving all of us a final inspection.

"Daddy, will you do the honor this time? Say something nice before we start this splendid meal." He put his spoon down and gave Mom a look that said he'd feel less tortured if she'd asked him to dance or sing.

Mom folded her hands and cleared her throat as a command for everyone to follow suit. She bowed her head and everyone copied her. Dad's knuckles turned white from nervously interlocking them together.

"Here goes nothing," he said as he let out a deep sigh. "We are gathered here to eat this food that my wife made, and it smells good. We are grateful for her ability to cook. Uhhh . . . we are also happy to have our son home and wish him a speedy recovery. Uhhh . . . I can't think of anything else to say, except 'let's eat.' Amen."

"That was nice, dear. A little bit short, but thoughtful. How's the soup everyone?"

Our mouths were full and all we could say was "Mmmmmm."

Mom looked pleased. She turned to me and asked, "What have you been doing this morning? Anything interesting?"

"I talked to Joe. He's coming to pick me up at five for the NA meeting."

"He's a nice boy. I like him."

"He's going to show me around and teach me what I need to know."

I wondered if the time was right to tell them about my plans to get together with Brenda. As spectacular as she was to me, she was probably more like a charging rhino to my parents. I needed to prepare them.

"I also called that nurse who saved me from those two guys. You know, Brenda, the one with the snake tattoos."

"Why would you want to do that?" Mom looked concerned. "Did she ask you to call her?"

I had to go easy here, so I asked Higher Power for a little help . . . and then it came to me: there was nothing to hide or be ashamed of. Brenda was simply another person who wanted to be my friend, and friends were a rarity in my life.

"No, she didn't ask me to call. It was my idea. I have lots of new ideas since I got in the crash. I wanted to thank her for being a good nurse. But I also want to see her again. I think she's neat."

Mom and Dad both stopped eating. To me, their silence and stares meant rejection. I'm sure they didn't want me to be mixed up with an older woman.

Dad was the first to speak. "Isn't this nurse too old to be hanging around with a kid like you? Doesn't she have any adult friends?"

"Of course she has adult friends," I answered, trying not to be flippant, "and I want to be one of them. Except for Jeff, I haven't had any friends. I decided that it's time to be with nice people like Joe and Wendy. They treat me like I'm normal and Brenda will too, so you'd better get used to it."

Mom said, "That's all well and good, Sweetie, but I think you'd better reconsider Brenda. She's got tattoos of snakes and looks like she's training for the World's Strongest Woman contest. She's not right for you. I don't want you spending time with her."

I wanted them to understand that we had already bonded, that we were able to see the simple beauty the other possessed, without flaws or defects. We saw nothing to judge and we just enjoyed talking to each other.

Instead, I said, "I don't see why I can't have adults as friends. I'm going to an NA meeting tonight. There are going to be adults there. Some of them might be bikers and ex-cons. There are probably going to be a lot of tattoos at those meetings, too, and I'm going to be looking at them. I doubt very much if that will turn me toward a life of crime. Brenda is an exceptional person. I'm sure she has plenty of good virtues besides being a great nurse. I think she'll be good for me. She's the kind of person you can trust."

Mom looked at Dad, and they shrugged.

"Son, you have grown up pretty darn fast," Dad said. "I think we should meet this woman in our home. If she's anything like you say, then I'm okay with it."

Mom didn't look quite as certain. "Of course, you're right. We have been treating you like a child, and a bad one at that. Up to now, I was certain drugs would rule your life or kill you. Now you've started fresh and things are looking up. If you want to make good, clean, healthy friends, I support that. Age shouldn't matter. Granted, she is a bit extreme but that's just me looking at the window dressing. I'm sure she has fine, upstanding qualities. We should meet her up close and personal. You can't be too careful these days."

I reached into my pocket and massaged the talisman. My parents were being so cooperative and encouraging. My Higher Power was really taking care of business here. I hardly had to do anything except be honest and make sure of that for now. I left out any mention of cage fighting.

My parents were growing and changing along with me. I knew enough to be patient with them. When tender new shoots start poking out of the ground, they don't grow any faster when you pull on them. Live and let live. Wasn't that one of the NA slogans? It made sense to me now.

When lunch was finished, Mom headed to the kitchen to wash the dishes. I walked over to where she stood at the sink, kissed her on the cheek and said, "Thanks for a terrific lunch." It sounded corny to me, but being able to show my mom that I no longer took her for granted was also part of the new me.

She scooped a handful of suds and blew them right into my face. I nudged her out of the way, scooped my own helping of suds, and returned the favor. Mom laughed, then took a deep breath. She hugged me as though she was trying to gobble me up like a little child.

"I'm just so happy and I think it's because of you. I am so proud of you. You really are different. I can't get over how nice you are. I sure hope it lasts. I feel spoiled."

I realized how much we had denied each other the essentials of kindness and love. It felt good to be able to express my feelings and it was coming more naturally. I planned to make this change in myself a permanent one and I planned to use this ability on as many people as I could. No longer would I deny kindness and love to anyone who needed it. It was easy enough to do and I'm sure it would also bring great joy. I could see that the greatest gift of all was the honor and privilege of giving to others.

CHAPTER 44

Loosening Up with Jeffrey

As I crutched my way back to the stairs, there was a loud banging on the front door.

"I know you're in there. Open up. It's your son I want. You have five seconds."

My heart was pounding as my parents both rushed into the front hallway. Dad mouthed "Who's out there?"

"Is it him?" Mom whispered. I knew she meant Vinnie.

The voice grew louder and more insistent. "I'm losing my patience." The door rattled as a fist pounded on the other side.

I looked out the peephole and an eyeball looked back.

"Boo!" Jeffrey stepped back so I could see his face and then grinned. "Scared ya, didn't I?"

It took me a few seconds to stop hyperventilating. Then I opened the door and began to yell at him.

"Don't ever do that again! I thought you were Vinnie."

"Let me in, Bro. I gotta use your bathroom." Jeff bounded past me through the door. "You thought I was Vinnie coming to get you. You should have seen the look on your face, Man. It was hysterical."

"Not to me. Vinnie almost took me out. I was lucky to get rid of him."

I looked at my parents, who were still standing frozen behind me. I realized I was going to have to explain what had happened when Vinnie came to collect the money.

"What happened out there today?" Mom interjected. "Did this Vinnie person try to hurt you? Is he on his way back? Should we be calling the police? I don't want any more trouble."

Jeff answered, "Don't you worry about your son. He took care of Vinnie. Busted his nose and made him bleed enough to go to the emergency room. They had to pack it. He was a screamer."

"How do you know so much?" I asked again. "I thought you broke it off with Sidney."

"I didn't get the intel from her. I know a guy who pushes people around on stretchers in the hospital. He said it looked like they shoved ten yards of gauze up his nose. They took him to surgery after that."

Mom looked at me quizzically and asked, "What did you do to this man?"

"Sidney took the money," I answered, "and told Vinnie to make me pay for trashing her car. Before he could hurt me, I let him have it. A powerful rush of courage came over me and my head did the rest." I proudly pointed to my forehead.

"I butted him in the nose and cracked it open like a hollow walnut. And it felt good."

"You used your head to break his nose? Are you all right?"

"Never felt better. I could do it again if I had to. Maybe my days of being pushed around and dumped on are over."

Jeff had returned from the bathroom. "People are going to hear about this. Nobody's messing with you again."

My mom looked confused. "Wait a minute. One day, you're my shy, stay-at-home son. Now you've put someone in the hospital who came here to hurt you? That is not the way to settle our differences. Are you expecting anyone else to show up and endanger our family?"

My father waved his hand in the direction of the living room, signaling a family meeting was to take place. Jeff joined us without waiting for an invitation.

"I love that coconut-scented hand lotion in your bathroom. It absorbs nicely. You should get some shaved curls of soap and put them in a dish . . . hey, cookies!" Jeff had spotted the chocolate chip cookies on the coffee table. The nonstop talking ceased.

Dad spoke in a lowered voice so I would listen up and take him seriously. "You know me, Son; I'm not one to do much talking, but this is serious business. Today some Vinnie person showed up and we had no idea you were out there with him. It was one thing to pay off your drug-using debt. It's a whole lot different when somebody gets injured. Is there anything else we need to know about you and your associates?" The last word sounded sarcastic.

I didn't want to shoot my mouth off and get into more trouble. I slowed the conversation down with the excuse that I needed to use the bathroom. What I really needed to do was think.

I stood by the sink and remembered what my Higher Power had taught me: Complaining would always create emotional turbulence in my life, even when I felt justified. Acceptance was the only way to feel better.

"Pssst. Kid. I think this might be a good time for you to learn a thing or two." It was Higher Power, dropping in to teach me a lesson.

"You have been more of a challenge than I expected. Buddy, I want you to get to know the work of Eckhart Tolle. He wrote a book called *The Power of Now*. I helped him, of course, but he wrote about me using my other names:

Being, Presence, and Awareness. Since you haven't read his books, I need to speed things up and give you the short version."

"I'm ready when you are, but what about my parents? They're waiting for me." I said.

"Don't worry about them. We've got eternity to get this right. It will only seem to your parents like you've been gone a minute. Tell me how you feel about what your father just said."

"He insulted me and my integrity. He hurt my feelings and I'm mad about that."

"Did your father make you mad or did you choose to get mad?"

"It's his fault, not mine."

"Not really," Higher Power explained. "Nobody can create your feelings except you. You own them. Your father doesn't have the power to make you feel anything. It's your choice to feel any way you want."

"That never occurred to me, but it makes sense."

"Just for now, allow yourself to keep being mad. Don't try to push it away." I closed my eyes and pictured my dad as he asked me about my "associates." He had implied that despicable people were my preference.

Higher Power continued, "Feelings are not continuous. Have you noticed how they come and go, appear and disappear? They're kind of like clouds, harmlessly drifting by. Even a painful feeling won't last. The problem arises when you stuff them, cramming them into places where there is no room. If you're blaming someone else for how bad you feel, resentment builds and eventually you have thoughts of revenge. You believe that getting even is the only way to regain your peace of mind. Well, it isn't. That kind of stress will eventually make you sick in ways you can't imagine."

"Eloquent. Very eloquent." I mocked Him with applause. "Obviously, I'm not very good at letting go, so what do you want me to do next? My father's waiting for me to get back out there and say something."

"Trust me on this one. You're more ready than you think. I'll take you through it."

I returned to the living room where my parents were sitting on the couch talking to each other; they stopped as I sat down.

"Dad, I got connected with these so called 'associates,' courtesy of my addiction. I saw an opportunity to have some fun with drugs and I took it. If my life hadn't sucked so much, we wouldn't be having this conversation. Sidney had the pills and we made a deal. I had no idea she was dangerous enough to send someone to hurt me. But now it's over. I'm sorry this had to happen at our house. I promise you, it won't ever happen again."

My father took a deep breath. "No more bad guys showing up here, correct?" I shook my head.

Higher Power was right. I got through it and must have let go of something, because I actually felt better. Maybe this was a good time to tell them what I learned.

Jeffery finished the last cookie and headed for the kitchen. I sat down next to Mom and propped my broken leg on the coffee table. It felt good to stretch it out. By then, Jeff was rummaging through leftovers in the fridge.

"Anybody here know about Eckhart Tolle and *The Power of Now?*" I was sure that answer would be a very disinterested "no."

"I do." Mom spoke up enthusiastically. "I've seen him on PBS. He's a brilliant man, said some amazing things that really made a lot of sense. I think *The Power of Now* is one of his books. Why'd you bring him up?"

"I learned something today that left an impression."

"Like what?"

"Like feelings," I answered. "Did you know that we choose the way we feel? I didn't really understand that until now. I always thought that people made you feel a certain way. Well, if that's really the case, the person who made you mad chose that feeling, not you."

"Yeah, so?" Jeff chimed in.

"So, if the other person is responsible for making you mad, you can only stop feeling that way when that person gives you permission."

"Huh?"

"Precisely. It makes no sense. Of course, the other person didn't really make you mad. Imagine how ridiculous it would be, asking someone else how you're supposed to feel."

Dad leaned forward, looking troubled. "What's your point?"

"It's this: If you believe that someone else has the power to make you mad, only they can undo it. After all, they hold the power. If you believe that it's your choice to feel mad, then you don't need anyone's permission to stop feeling that way. You now have the power to let it go."

Dad smiled and said, "I think I get this."

"Of course you do. We all do. Feelings are nothing more than emotions that come and go, only it's time we realize that we have the control to create them or delete them. We don't have to feel stuck with them while we blame someone else for putting them there."

"And you just learned all this?" Mom asked. "From Eckhart Tolle?"

"Yeah. It's the coolest thing. We can have all the feelings we want. We made 'em. We own 'em. We can trash 'em and we can make some more."

"You think it's that easy?" Mom asked. "Or is it just that simple?"

"It's both," I said. "It's good for me to know that no matter what feelings I have, I can always let them go. That way, no feeling can actually hurt me. Come to think of it, nobody can actually hurt me, emotionally speaking."

Jeff came from the pantry with a bag of popped corn and walked around the living room inspecting all the framed family photos and other knickknacks. As long as he was eating, he was quiet.

"I remember something about Tolle that interested me," Mom offered. "He said everything is meant to be the way it is, or it wouldn't be that way. It sounds logical and makes sense, but a problem is a problem. I don't care if it's meant to be that way. I want it fixed."

"Let me take a stab at that." Jeff said, taking a small statue of an angel off the mantel. "It might surprise you that I know a thing or two about Tolle. My Mom wouldn't change the PBS channel, so I checked him out. He's a weird-looking dude. Has a scraggly beard and is kind of scrawny, like you, Buddy, only not as good-looking." Jeff crossed the room to take his can of soda off the tray that Mom had brought in earlier.

"So here's what I got out of it. When you're all upset over something bad that happened, you're really not in good shape to do the next right thing. That's what he called it, 'the next right thing.' You see, for every problem you have, there's always the next right thing to do about it."

Jeff looked and sounded intelligent. I was baffled. My parents looked almost spellbound. We had no idea Jeff was capable of this.

"And if you do enough right things, the problem should go away. That part I made up. In other words, once the problem's there, don't fight with it. Just accept it and do the next right thing. Because if you stress out over the problem, you probably won't be able to think of the next right thing to do. You might even think of the next wrong thing to do and either create another problem or create a bigger one than you have."

Dad walked into the kitchen while rubbing his temples. "I think you guys are overworking my brain," he said with a wry smile. "I need a couple of Tylenol for this headache."

"Sorry about that," Jeff said, taking a seat on the ottoman near the couch. He never looked so relaxed.

"I doubt if it's you, Jeff," Mom added. "It's more like CNN." Everyone laughed.

"All this talk about problems and stress; it seems like my life has been nothing but that for the past two weeks," Mom lamented. "Now that Tolle has become the hot topic here, it's reminding me of something he said. What I heard, I wanted to remember because I was sure I would use it in some practical way."

"What'd you hear?" Dad asked, grinning childishly. "A Tolle top secret?"

"Go ahead, laugh." Mom smiled back at him. "Tolle's no joke. He's known all over the world. People attend his seminars just to hear what I'm about to tell you."

"Come on, give it." Jeff was getting excited and started pacing the room. I wanted to know the secret, too. I knew this was going to be a Higher Power message without having to hear Him whisper the words.

"Tolle says, now is all we've got and will ever have. Yesterdays and tomorrows don't really exist. We talk as though our problems can be found somewhere in the past or somewhere in the future, but you can't go there to fix them. All the repair work has to be done in the Now."

I looked at Dad and Jeff; they were paying close attention. I was very interested, too.

Shaking her head, Mom said, "I can't tell you how much time I have wasted thinking about what happened the day before, just so I could make sure who to blame for my problems. I have replayed so many yesterdays and let myself get worked up with one complaint after another. Now I realize how tiresome that was and I have nothing to show for all the effort."

She was right. Tolle was right. Attempting to revisit the past was a worthless endeavor.

"So there I was, standing in my own personal moment of Now—a never-ending, continuous Now. And what did I do? Worry worry worry. About what?"

Here it comes, I thought. Worry about me, your son, the screw up.

"About something that doesn't exist. The future. Don't we all do it? I have worried myself sick believing the worst thing might happen if I didn't worry about it. It's crazy the things we do with our beautiful minds. What an absolute waste. My worrying changed nothing about the future. It only messed up a perfectly good opportunity to the do the right thing, NOW."

"Everybody worries," I offered. "You worried about me every day. I was probably closer to dead than alive. What were you supposed to do, ignore the truth and pretend that I was fine?" I didn't even know where I was going with those remarks.

"But I do." Higher Power was loud and clear in my head. "Watch this."

"He's got a valid point," Dad said.

Mom was up to the challenge. "I worried. Believe you me, I worried night and day. But that was a waste, looking back on it. Buddy was lying there being kept alive by a machine and a team of medical experts, not by my worrying. My worrying didn't heal a single thing on his body. It only made me so sick I couldn't eat or sleep. I could barely function; some days, all I could do was sit by his bed and cry. Now, does that sound like time well spent? I think not."

"I told you it would be worth it." Higher Power's tone was gloating. I guess he was entitled.

Jeff stopped pacing and grabbed some mixed nuts out of the bowl on the coffee table. "Right on," Jeff agreed, his words garbled by his crunching. "So what would you do differently if Buddy were back on the machine?"

There was silent anticipation as we waited for Mom's answer.

"I'd be grateful," Mom said triumphantly.

That was it? That's your nugget for the day? I thought.

"She's not done yet," Higher Power said.

"Granted, I'd look at Buddy lying there unconscious, injured and helplessly vulnerable." She paused again. "And then I'd thank God that he was my son, for better or worse. That I could love him and hate what he did. Most important, that he was alive, knowing every second of life was precious and blessed with the possibility of miracles."

"Wow," Jeff exuded. "That's a mother for you."

"She's my Mom and that's just the way I like her." I answered proudly. Our eyes met and Mom's were moist.

"Thanks, Honey. You're worth all of my gratitude. I'm not wasting any more *nows* on worry. What's done is over and can't be changed with tears or cross words. What's yet to come is meant to be a surprise. Why spoil it with fearful expectation? Just take it as it comes and make the best of it." She nuzzled me in a motherly way and I felt as though my future, with its unpredictability, was going to be bright, shiny, and new . . . naturally.

Jeff grabbed the empty nut bowl, licked the salt off his fingers, and headed back to the kitchen. I stood up, moving slowly and feeling stiff.

"I'm going to head upstairs. I want to take a break before I have to get ready for tonight's big NA meeting. It was great sitting here with you guys, pretending to be having a think-tank discussion on something so . . . out there. Here's my last thought on the subject."

Jeff walked back in the living room and perched on the ottoman. Mom and Dad looked like they were front and center for their son's piano recital, their faces filled with admiration.

Before I spoke I could feel my Higher Power preparing the words in my head. It felt like we were a team. He did the thinking and I did the talking.

"The power of *now* must have something to do with being present as your true inner self, being fully aware of what you really are instead of the labels you give yourself. This nonsense of always referring to myself as a pimple-faced, loser geek is ridiculous. I am so totally done with it."

"Thank goodness." Mom's relief was echoed by my dad's "Attaboy."

"It also seems logical to me that the entire power of the Universe must therefore reside in this precious *now*. And this power can create anything the mind can imagine. It can tirelessly operate this way, for eternity."

I saw Jeff looking like he was ready to raise a cheer. "Go for it, Bro."

I felt some kind of spiritual energy building inside me. "I know this sounds out of character, since I've been shy for so many years, but I actually want to make friends. Not only that, but I want to learn about love. Not just the romantic type of love, but the kind that can fill my life with joy, knowing that I belong here, just like everyone else."

The room was quiet again. Mom rose off the couch and beamed as she approached me.

"That's our son," she boasted. "Only winners talk like that."

She kissed me on the cheek and I headed for the stairs. I called goodbye to Jeff, who was already in the kitchen, scratching his head as he looked in the fridge one more time.

I stretched out on my bed and must have fallen asleep, because the next thing I knew, the clock showed several hours had passed. I looked at the poster of Einstein. His sparkling eyes and protruding tongue told a different story now. He looked so happy to be in my room with the new me.

I took a shower, then swabbed some antiseptic around the pin holes in my leg. I dressed, put a clean shirt over my back brace, and headed downstairs to the kitchen where Mom was removing a shepherd's pie from the oven. As she was setting the pan in the center of the kitchen table, the doorbell rang.

As I opened the door, Joe and Wendy charged in and embraced me.

"Hi, Buddy." Wendy lit up with a big smile. "You look great."

I beamed back at her. "Thanks. I *feel* great."

"How's your leg? Any trouble with the pins? Any pain?"

"No, I wish I could put my full weight on it, though. I'm sick of these crutches."

Wendy laughed and gave me one more hug.

"Ooo, I could just eat you up. You are so cute." Then she whispered in my ear, "Your skin is clearing up. I can't believe the difference since you left the hospital." She pecked my cheek, then said, "Oh, heck. You deserve a real one."

Wendy's kiss was as moist as watermelon and lasted just long enough to be unforgettable. My mom walked in and I'm not sure how much she saw; I tried to act as laid-back as if I had kissed girls before.

"Don't you two make a nice couple?"

We took a step back from each other and Mom closed in with a girlish grin. "Did I interrupt something?"

I felt my face turn bright red. "Hey, Mom, look who's here. It's Wendy and Joe."

"I wasn't expecting both of you," Mom said in acknowledgment. "Is the NA meeting still on?"

"I'm going with them," Wendy explained. "I wanted to be there when you get your first key tag, Buddy. Your parents are welcome."

Her brother held up a rainbow cluster of pear-shaped plastic key tags, all interconnected. "Get a load of these, my friend." He tossed me the collection of tags on their key rings. I knew from my reading that they were offered to everyone in NA who stayed sober.

"This white one is for newcomers. Each color represents a different length of clean time. On the back of each tag is a slogan. Read the white one for us."

I held the white one up. "It says 'One day at a time.'"

Mom looked over my shoulder as I shuffled through them. There were seven tags in the bunch. There was orange for thirty days, green for sixty days, red for ninety days, blue for six months, yellow for nine months. Joe told us that moon glow was the color for one year.

"This must mean you have really come a long way in your recovery," Mom commented. "I bet it wasn't easy. You must be proud of yourself."

Joe pulled his sister close with a sideways hug, mussing her hair with a quick spin of his hand. "The first month was the easiest, because I was sent off to rehab with thirty other addicts. I was too busy with group sessions and everything else to even think about doing drugs. It was a nice place out in the country and I was willing to do whatever I was told to get a handle on recovery."

I watched mom as she listened to Joe and I imagined what a big NA success she wanted me to be. She didn't know there was no competitive ladder to climb; there were only the simple Twelve Steps and colorful plastic key tags to celebrate the journey.

"Once I was discharged from rehab," Joe continued, "I had to return to the real world. That wasn't so easy. My parents were relieved, but still upset with me. I had stolen so much from them that I couldn't pay back. On top of that, I owed plenty of money to the drug dealers. That was a tough month. My parents didn't sleep. My father sat by the window with a shotgun more than once, watching cars drive by. I owed five grand and Dad did not want to part with it. But once I took him to a few NA meetings, he could see how serious I was about my sobriety. I did my ninety in ninety, got a sponsor and kept reading NA literature.

"What's ninety in ninety?" I asked.

Joe put his arm around my shoulder. "Meetings, meetings, meetings; the more the better. The dropout rate for newcomers is high and the statistics get worse every day you miss a meeting. Your goal is to make it day by day, but every month you stay clean makes it a little easier to add one more day to the list. I don't know what the statistics are, but if you can make it sober for ninety days, your chances of continuing improve considerably. So I'm going to make sure you go to ninety meetings in the first ninety days."

"You're on." I said with a fist bump. The cool thing to do.

"What about all that money you owed and the drug dealers?" Mom asked. "That's so dangerous."

"It's all paid," Joe said. "My dad came through with the money and I have settled my debt with him. Now I have money in the bank. No more five hundred dollar a week habit: the money goes toward my education. You're looking at someone who is extremely grateful." Joe's story was amazing and inspired me to strive for success in recovery. I wanted to make my parents proud. They had been disgraced enough.

"Being sober is never easy for me, but I am getting better at it," Joe continued. "I attend several different NA meetings and make sure to introduce myself to new people at each one. I ask for phone numbers in the fellowship—and I use them. The phone has been a lifeline for me. I've made calls asking for help and found the other person worse off than me. That's when you know you're doing a good thing.

"I also like doing service work for the fellowship. I've been elected as my home group's treasurer. I collect the donated money at each meeting, pay the rent, and buy the coffee and cookies. I keep us well supplied with pamphlets, books, bumper stickers, key tags, and medallions. Now that's a far cry from a lying, cheating, and good-for-nothing thief, wouldn't you say?"

Mom looked like she might burst into tears by the time Joe was done. She gave him a hug and my father shook his hand.

"Well done," he said. "I hope you can help our son to accomplish just as much."

"Wait a minute," Joe cautioned. "This isn't going to be a contest for your son. NA isn't a club you join for achievement and merit badges, like the Boy Scouts. I looked forward to getting each key tag, but only because they represent a commitment to stay sober. We both have an addiction. We may look like everyone else, but inside, we bear the mark. The party is over for us. It doesn't matter how unfair it seems that the other kids can get high. As far as I'm concerned, NA is our last shot and our only one. If we use pills again, we will surely end up in jail, a mental institution, or under a tombstone. What I intend to do for your son was done for me. I offer it to him free of charge. If I don't give it away, I don't get to keep what I've got."

Mom and Dad looked even more impressed. I admired Joe, too. If my life was at stake, a few colored key tags would not save the day. Staying sober: it wouldn't be easy. It couldn't be done without help. But it was worth everything I had to do to pull it off. My happiness depended on it.

Mom motioned toward the kitchen. "Dinner is served. We're having shepherd's pie tonight and you two are joining us."

"We'll have to eat and run," Joe said. "The meeting starts in one hour. I want to get there early and introduce Buddy around."

We ate quickly, enjoying small talk with my family. As soon as our plates were empty, we excused ourselves to leave for the meeting and, after exchanging hugs all around, Joe, Wendy, and I walked to Joe's car and got in.

CHAPTER 45

The First Meeting

Twenty minutes later we pulled into a church parking lot that was half filled with cars and five motorcycles, big ones. A group of people was standing outside. A cloud of cigarette smoke billowed above their heads. My stomach began to tighten because I was a stranger to all of this. As I stepped out of the car, everyone seemed to turn at once and stare. I put my head down and tried not to feel self-conscious about gimping along on crutches with pins sticking out of my leg and a brace that I strapped on outside of my T-shirt.

Joe put a reassuring hand on my shoulder. "It's okay, Buddy. These are brothers and sisters in recovery. They all felt the same way at their first meeting. We'll do this together, one step at a time."

Wendy walked beside me and said, "Keep your head up. Newcomers are always welcome. Come on."

We walked across the parking lot as a threesome. I remembered my Higher Power's voice telling me to find something of Him in all of these people. That would make things easier. I was surrounded in a few minutes as people approached to extend a friendly greeting. One man in particular appeared to have some seniority; as he walked toward me, everybody was suddenly quiet and respectful. He was obviously somebody important.

He was very short and had to look up at me. He had more age lines on his face than there were rivers on a map. His teeth were missing, and his lips had caved in. He kept flicking an unfiltered cigarette but didn't take a drag. His voice was raspy and corroded by years of smoke. "Sonny-boy," he said. "It looks like you're new around here and I hope you weren't thrown out of a moving car."

Joe tried to be inconspicuous when he nudged me. Perhaps this man was going to make even more tasteless remarks and I should prepare myself.

"At my age, I say and do pretty much what I damn well please. I hope you came to stay awhile. We can use some new blood."

I intended to listen to him carefully; I was pretty sure he was my next messenger.

"The only heroin I could get back in the day was Mexican tar; we called it Muck. It was gummy as hell, but that made no difference to me. I shot it in my arm every day. I didn't have the luxury of pills. I did it the hard way and I paid my dues."

He lit another cigarette then held it loosely in his lips and kept speaking.

"I had to keep my needles clean just to get the junk into my veins. Nowadays, all you have to do is crush a pill and snort it. It goes right to your brain. How easy is that? No wonder everybody's getting hooked. They don't need to shoot up anymore. In my day you needed a little skill to get high with a needle."

Here was an old-time, hardcore mainliner trying to inject humor into his message for me. I didn't think any of it was funny, but it was apparent some of the others thought he was charming. A crowd steadily grew as he continued sharing his memories with me.

"When I started shooting up tar, it felt like the Golden Girl was dancing in my blood. I thought I had veins to last me forever. No matter how good I was with a spike, I clogged up with phlebitis and did some skin-popping. A few times I was desperate and shot it right into the muscle. I had no choice; my veins were gone. That's when my arm turned to gangrene."

He rolled up the sleeve of his right arm and everybody shimmied in closer for a look. They'd probably all seen it before, but it was my first look at something extraordinary. Half of the old man's forearm was missing. He displayed the withered remains.

"This is what's left. My arm died slowly and painfully, right in front of my eyes. The infection took over and had to be cut away. The doc at the free clinic called it necrotizing fasciitis; I called it dumb-ass stupid. I watched him remove pieces of dead meat week after week. See that?" He pointed into a large crater that spanned the distance from the elbow to his wrist. "There's no bone on that side of my forearm—that had to be removed too. No antibiotics could save it. Eventually, the doc gave up and put a wad of maggots onto the dead meat. He said it was the last resort."

The crowd seemed to know this part was coming; they made squealing noises and watched me to see if I was grossed out.

"When those maggots got to grazing, I could feel them wiggling around. When they ate their way down to the good meat they stopped and just died off. After some skin grafts, what you see is what you get."

This time he wanted me to inspect his emaciated arm more closely. Where a hand used to be, the fingers had become curved, deformed and stiffened into a useless hook.

"It looks like a claw hand, but that's okay with me. It's better than a stump."

It was apparent that the crowd wanted to hear more. I realized he was used to dusting off his old material for newcomers. Although he was the center of attention, the performance was all for my benefit. His cigarette stayed in his mouth and a continuous curl of smoke orbited his right eye. It made him squint, but he never moved the cigarette or inhaled any smoke. The ash on the tip grew to an inch long before dropping off. He allowed the stub to burn down to the edge of his lip. He crushed the last quarter inch with his finger then lit a fresh one and the cycle repeated itself. His act was polished and he had more to say.

"That was fifty years ago, kid. Narcotics Anonymous was founded in 1953, but it fizzled and came back to life in the sixties. That's when I joined up. There wasn't much left of me. I'd been shooting Brown Sugar with every dime I got. But I liked to call it Black Pearl—that's dirty street talk for heroin which is also known as H, Charley, Horse and a bunch of others. One day somebody called me Little H on account of my smallness and it stuck ever since."

"I couldn't stay off the stuff even when my arm started rotting. The doc kept pleading with me and I guess it was my time. Like they say, when you're ready, you're ready. The day I started kicking it, a man named Clarence found me in the Bowery of New York City. If you coulda seen the alley I was curled up in, you would've called it the bowels of New York City."

His audience chuckled and I noticed the number of people had dwindled, but those left were very engrossed.

"My first week off junk was worse than hell. I would've preferred the devil jabbing me with a pitchfork for eternity. I owe my life to Clarence. He was a big mountain of a man. He talked like he was doing missionary work, always mentioning Jesus and praying over me. He lived in some rat hole place, but to me it was the Waldorf Astoria. Anyway, there I was dope-sick; sweating out every last drop I had. I was cramped up and puking. Whatever came out of my rear end was hotter than a flame thrower. Every bone in my body ached right into the marrow. My nerves were jumpy and I was constantly jerking with one muscle spasm after another. I shivered and shook with the worse chills I ever had and my skin was crawling and driving me nuts. Clarence prayed for it to stop, and I wished I was dead. That man never left my side. As soon as I could eat and walk, he brought me to an NA meeting and got me started. I never saw him again after that. I like to think of him as an angel sent to do this good deed and move on. I'm taking the time to tell you this in honor of him."

The story the crowd had gathered to hear must have been over because they all dispersed. Little H gave me his undivided attention. His voice was firm, with a singleness of purpose.

"Listen up, Kid. This is the part you need. The other stuff was entertainment."

He dropped his cigarette and coughed to clear his throat. He motioned me to lower my ear closer to him. As I did, I felt even more special, because I knew he was about to share a nugget of wisdom, a gift for my youth and inexperience.

He said, "I don't care how you got here. Everything you need to fight the dragon is right through those doors and it's free—but you have to ask. No one's going to shove it down your throat. If you want it, there's enough experience, strength, and hope to keep you on the path. Find the winners and follow their lead, advice, and suggestions. Every mistake has already been made by one of us and the solution to go with it. Don't try to figure anything out on your own; it's already been done for you. Unless you're asking for help or showing gratitude, keep your mouth shut and listen up. You get twenty-four hours a day, just like the rest of us. Don't waste it. Recovery is a full time job and nothing is more important. Get through all Twelve Steps, and you own the Book of Life. You can have it all if you want it that bad—just stay sober and keep dancing to the right music."

I felt lucky to have this private time with him and I thanked him for it.

As he walked slowly toward the meeting room, everyone along his path respectfully acknowledged him. They obviously admired his seniority and I imagined that many of them began their journey listening to him, as I did, on their very first day in NA. Joe tapped me on the shoulder to get my attention.

"He's quite a guy. A year ago he had the same conversation with me. It worked. Now it's your turn. You'll always remember this day. There're more where he came from and they're in that room. Let's go in and get a seat up front," Joe suggested. "My sponsor should be here."

Wendy walked ahead and disappeared in a group of women about her age. Some looked like they had seen too many difficult days and others looked a little too sexy, in low-cut tops and too much jewelry. I remembered that labels were limiting and I recognized that they all gathered to support each other equally with recovery in mind. NA was a place where spiritual intentions meant everything and appearances were just packaging.

The NA room was a large space with a podium and microphone at the front and more than twenty round tables, each one with six chairs around it. A long table in the back was covered with books, pamphlets, flyers, and bumper stickers. A coffee pot sat on a counter along with three types of cookies on paper plates. As I looked around, I saw people laughing and talking in small groups and everyone seemed to be greeting each other by shaking hands or hugging. They all looked healthy and happy; it was not what I had expected.

Like the women, the men tended to congregate together. Some looked like forty-something bikers and had colorful tattoos. Their smiles displayed missing teeth and their midsections were overgrown. They kidded around with each other, but I imagined that they also took the Twelve Steps of recovery very seriously. I looked forward to discovering which ones were the winners I should follow and learn from.

Joe pointed out his sponsor to me as we approached the group where he was chatting with a man who had a long gray ponytail, a tear-drop tattoo, and something unmentionable written across his knuckles. In contrast, Joe's sponsor, who stood over six feet tall, looked like he'd just come from a photo shoot for *GQ Magazine*. He was handsome, with a full mane of silver hair, khaki slacks, Topsider shoes, and an embroidered golf shirt that read *Pebble Beach*. He looked like he could be worth millions, but his friendly smile made him easily approachable. I wondered how he ended up at NA; it was hard to believe that he'd ever abused drugs.

"Buddy, this is Mark. He's my dear friend and sponsor. Don't be fooled by the clothes, he buys off the discount rack, too."

Mark, who I thought of from then on as Silver Fox, shook my hand vigorously and invited us to sit down beside him.

"Welcome, Buddy. Joe told me you were coming tonight. I understand this is your first meeting. You must be as nervous as you are excited. Just sit back, relax, and take it all in. You are among friends. We all want the same thing and we qualify to be here. Don't be put off by the difference in the way we look— on the inside, we all need some repair work."

Joe put his arm around my shoulder. I felt the knot in my stomach start to loosen, but I was hoping Joe's sponsor would keep talking.

"Mark, we've got a few more minutes, do you mind telling Buddy a bit of your story?"

"Sure thing." His gentle laugh put me more at ease. "I've done this a few times, haven't I? Well, Buddy, my life fell apart ten years ago. I was a cocky know-it-all. I wanted to be CEO, CFO, and pretty much every O you could hang a corporate title on. I was making deals and getting big bonuses. A lot of investors were counting their millions off the sweat of my hundred-hour work week. It was exhilarating and I wanted more."

I was quickly impressed with him. He was a winner to latch on to. My Higher Power must have arranged this, just for me.

"Before I made it to the top, I was grinding it out and waiting my turn. I had to prove myself, because only the exceptional ones move on. I read every *How to Succeed* book I could find and I had all the right affirmations written on a stack of three-by-five cards. I had a vision board for my vision board. I was making a respectable income, but multimillionaire sounded a whole lot better.

He had done everything right . . . so how did his wheels come off the track? He looked great and he sounded great, too. I wanted to do the same thing with my life. I was going to get his business card and pay attention.

Mark continued, "So there I was, getting closer to the top, but it wasn't happening fast enough. The competition was stiff and I started pulling all-nighters. More days than not, I was dead on my feet, with nothing left in the tank. One day, in my hotel room after just two hours of sleep, I was in no condition to give a big presentation. My assistant offered me a Lortab and said it would give me a shot of energy and that I'd be mentally sharper and become chief executive material.

"I was desperate, but not stupid and irresponsible. I had my suspicions that this was going to be some kind of speed pill that would have me wired and out of control. He assured me that my mind would have effortless clarity, that I was going to impress my bosses and put myself on the short list for the number-one spot. I already had the goods—I just needed the energy to pull it off. What I learned next sealed the deal. He told me he was supplying the top brass of the organization with the same drug. If I took one, it would only level the playing field. I took the damn thing and my rocket was launched."

I was glued to Mark's every word. What a fascinating story. I had never thought about the extent to which the giants of corporate America were functioning under the influence of dope. I wanted to know how far Mark was able to get ahead while taking pain pills. Then I paused and asked myself, *Why is that even important?* I saw how easy it was to stray off the recovery path.

Silver Fox continued. "That one little pill woke me up and I knocked it out of the park at the meeting. After that, they asked for even more and I delivered. I had the pills and the brains. The things I accomplished were not humanly possible, but nobody questioned them. I was promoted and written up in magazines as a rising star. Every project I managed was a spectacular success. Contracts were pouring in and I was in demand. I was given every perk and gift you can imagine: from a Mercedes S-Class to penthouse living, even the Gulfstream IV company jet. The best-looking women were willing to do anything to be with me. It was ridiculous, but I wanted more and I knew how to get it. I had connections and plenty of dirt on my competition, just in case. I was untouchable and invincible. All I needed was my brilliant mind, enough hours in one day, and the magic pills."

I was in the company of someone who made it to the top as a corporate superstar. I didn't care if it was good for my recovery or not: I was impressed. He had done it all and had been it all. I could only take credit for raising a blue-ribbon crop of pimples, smashing a hitman's face, and colliding with a tanker truck in a drugged-out stupor. I had no business sitting next to him. I heard some old loser tapes starting to play again in my head.

Higher Power spoke up. "Stop comparing yourself to his Wall Street portfolio. You will always come up short. He's got a lot more to offer than stock market tips. Spiritual recovery does not accept MasterCard or Visa. You have to pay with the pain in your heart, like he did."

Silver Fox put his arm around the back of my chair. He still seemed to be genuinely interested in me and showed no signs of being conceited. So far, he was just a nice guy with an incredible story.

"If you've been crushing and snorting pills, you know what happened to me. I was more than willing to pay the price for fame and fortune. At first, my assistant warned me. After all, he knew how hard I was pushing for promotions. He was happy to accept the recognition and rewards that he received as a result of my hard work. He was my opiate manager, in a manner of speaking. He picked the drugs, from Lortabs all the way to Roxicodone and OxyContin. We both knew that my habit was going to grow and without them I was going to lose, because the competition was going to stomp all over anyone who showed any weakness."

He was talking about Roxicodone like it was a fuel that drove him into the winner's circle. We both took the same drug, for the same reasons. I wanted to fit in at school and Roxicodone was my chance to pull that off.

"I didn't care how many I had to swallow, snort, or inject. Nobody was going to catch me, even if I had to take pills by the handful. And that is exactly what happened. Have you ever taken forty Roxy 30s in one day? I did. Most days I only needed twenty-five. I'd get up, snort five Roxys, shower, shave, snort five more Roxys for breakfast, then mow down anyone who couldn't keep up or get out of the way. I ignored everything that was once near and dear to me, including my wife, my three children, and my health and fitness. Hell, I even gave up golf, because every minute mattered and there were too few of them. When you're running on thin ice, it's too dangerous to stop."

I could tell where the story was going and I wanted to hear it all. I wanted the details of how he lost it and got it all back, only sober this time. I wanted to make sure the Twelve Steps were not synonymous with a clean, boring, mediocre life. I had to know how a teenager could find recovery appealing. Silver Fox and Joe were converts and I wanted to be sure that playing by the twelve-step rules was better than getting high.

Silver Fox said, "Kid, I have to save some for later. The Chairperson is about to start the meeting. It was nice talking to you. I look forward to helping

287

Jamie Smolen, MD

along the way. Make sure you get up when it's time for the newcomer key tag."

And with that he turned towards the front of the room and tuned me out.
At least he wants to help me and I like him.

Joe leaned over and whispered while the Chairperson was speaking. He told me that there was an opening introduction and a reading of the steps and traditions.

He did not need to prepare me for reciting the famous Serenity Prayer, which was like taking the Pledge of Allegiance in grade school. It sent a chill down my spine when everyone in the room spoke these words:

God grant me the serenity to accept the things I cannot change, the courage to change the things I can, and the wisdom to know the difference.

I had already read about the importance of the prayer. Bill Wilson, the cofounder of Alcoholics Anonymous, wrote in *AA Comes of Age* that in 1942 he had found the prayer written in a *New York Herald Tribune* obituary. Bill Wilson had five hundred copies of the prayer printed. As the voices in the room rhythmically recited the prayer in unison, I felt a sense of something far greater than the individuals in the room. It felt like my Higher Power had spread across the room, bonding all of us and protecting us at the same time.

After the introductory proceedings, the chairperson asked the guest speaker of the evening to come up to the podium. Joe told me the speakers often came from other groups to tell their stories about their years of using drugs, how they came to be a member of NA, and how their lives had been changed for the better as a result. I couldn't wait to hear what this speaker had to say.

CHAPTER 46

Messengers

The speaker was a woman with purple streaks in her jet-black hair. She had a ring piercing her lip and a ruby stud on the side of her nostril. Her eyes were rimmed with heavy mascara. Her T-shirt was covered with the names of bands, which made me wonder if she had been a rocker . . . and maybe she still was. I wondered if there was such a thing as sober concerts.

She looked nervous and self-conscious and avoided making eye contact with the audience.

"Hello, my name is Tanya and I am a grateful recovering addict."

The group responded in unison, "Hi, Tanya."

I had formed an unfair opinion of her. Two minutes into her presentation, I realized what a poor judge of character I was. I had no right to be so unkind. She was a messenger, too, and I needed to listen carefully.

She continued speaking and for thirty minutes Tanya told a story of growing up in a dysfunctional home, physical and sexual abuse, and experimenting with drugs, which eventually led to her drug addiction.

As I looked around the room, I could see the unanimous compassion for her; Tanya shared deeply personal and private material, yet there she was, holding nothing back from these strangers. I got the impression that she felt her secret was safe with the group and I remembered reading that in NA, confidentiality was guaranteed.

"My husband hurt his back at work and needed surgery. He was laid up for three months, but still got paid. He was in pain and took Lortabs. I knew about them, but never had more than a Darvocet after my babies. I was just lucky, I guess. Anyway, after a bad night of drinking, I couldn't get up. My head was splitting, and my husband told me to take one. It was like flipping a switch—I was up and running through the house, cleaning it like there was no tomorrow. I remember I was talking nonstop and my husband just laughed and said, that's Lortab for you."

I nodded. We had Lortabs in common. I fondly recalled the supercharged effect it had, shifting me into a higher gear for a few hours.

Tanya continued to describe how she took her husband's pain pills just to keep going every day; the pills were gone in less than a month. Once that happened, she was cranky and moody, and tried to blame it on PMS. I could see where this story was going and it was all too familiar.

She shared her journey from those first Lortabs to OxyContin and from taking a pill at home to finding a dealer, through stealing money from her husband's business to racking up ten thousand dollars' worth of debt. She cried during some of her story and someone brought up tissues and a bottle of water.

"Once my husband found out, I promised him that I would get off the pills and make it right. He was worried and upset, but he wanted to believe I could do it. I learned on the street that you can get off OxyContin if you take methadone. I took some, but I liked it too much.

"My husband managed to get the creditors to give us a break for a while. He saw that I was feeling better, so he assumed that I had detoxed and quit the pills. But I hadn't. I started pawning everything that I thought he wouldn't miss—I even sold my diamond engagement ring. When he noticed it was missing, he accused me of being on the pills again and then blew up. I have never seen him so mad. He found a medical detox for me. He brought me there the next day and told me that was my last chance. Either I quit or he wouldn't take me back."

Tanya continued telling her story and you could have heard a pin drop in that large room. She shared about her stay in detox, her first NA meeting, and the destructive force of her addiction on her marriage and her family.

"I would like to tell you that my first year in recovery has been great. It hasn't. My husband and I are still married—at times, just barely. We lost our house to foreclosure. He is now working two jobs just to pay off the credit cards and that may take years. I hurt him badly and he doesn't trust me very much yet. He drug tests me at home. He knows I go to NA and has even met my sponsor. But he realizes that addicts relapse more often than they stay sober. Even though I want our marriage to work in the worst way, I still have those moments when a pill is so damn tempting. When I see how upset my husband gets after the mess I got us in, I want to snort an 80 and forget about all this trouble. But I haven't used. Tonight is my one-year anniversary. I couldn't have made it this far if it wasn't for my devoted and understanding husband, my sponsor, the Twelve Steps, and the fellowship of NA. It works if you work it. Keep coming back. Thank you."

The group erupted in thunderous applause that turned into a standing ovation. Tanya put her face in her hands and wept. A man rushed up, took her into his arms, and gave her a powerful hug. He wiped away her tears and kissed her briefly on the mouth. I could read his lips saying, *Honey, I am so proud of you* and her response of *I love you so much*.

The chairperson got up and said, "This is a good time for a coffee break."

Several women gathered around the speaker and took turns hugging her and crying. I was a witness to the recovery process in action. There was no doubt in my mind that Tanya would make it and I wanted to make it, too. NA was the right place for me. My turn was coming.

During the break, Joe and Silver Fox teamed up for a chat and I decided to check out the plate of cookies.

"You're new here, aren't you?" I looked around to find the source of the voice that was high-pitched and strong, like a cheerleader's. The girl attached to the voice was about sixteen, but no more than eighteen. Her hair was short, brown, and straight. Her eyes were hazel with iridescent flecks of gold and her skin had known the ravages of a pimply past. The acne was gone, but the texture was rough in places. When she smiled, she displayed two perfect rows of sparkling teeth, the handiwork of an experienced orthodontist.

"Hi," I answered. "Yeah, I am new. This is my first meeting, ever. How are you?"

I wasn't shy, nerdy, or geeky. That deserved an attaboy from Higher Power.

"What happened to your leg?" The girl's cute smile faded a little.

"I'll give you the short version today. I was in a car wreck and totaled my body. You should have seen me three weeks ago. I was in a coma with busted ribs, a broken back, and a shattered leg. These pins hold it all together, thanks to this Home Depot fixator."

I was trying to be funny and she laughed.

"You're quite a guy, Mr. What-Do-You-Call-Yourself?"

"Buddy. My name is Buddy."

"Okay, Mr. Buddy. Will you be my buddy?"

She laughed again and this time she was even cuter. I laughed back.

"Amber. You can call me Amber."

I wanted everybody to go away and leave the two of us alone. Meeting her was better than all the Oxys and Roxys I had ever taken. I didn't want to wake up from this dream.

"Can I show you something," Amber asked.

"Sure. What?"

"These." She rolled up her long-sleeve T-shirt and showed me at least a dozen puncture marks in a row on the inside of her arm.

"I've been shooting up heroin for the past year. When I quit, I was so dope-sick I was crawling out of my skin. Now I'm on Suboxone. It's a miracle drug; I feel so good, like I'm normal again. I am so happy, I could hug someone. Do you mind?"

She wrapped both arms around me.

"Hey, what's this?" She was referring to my back brace.

My mind was still on her needle tracks. She was a hardcore addict who traded her life in for mainlining dope. I was quick to condemn her for being enormously brainless. How could she make such a dangerous choice, just to get high? I was fast to judge her, to label her a loser, and I wanted to walk away and avoid her. She could not possibly be one of the winners I wanted to listen to or follow. My brain was telling me to reject, discard, and delete her. But Higher Power paid me a visit with His voice of reason.

"Hey, Buddy. Sorry to disturb your insanity, but it's my job to push you out of the mud when you get stuck, and my friend, you are plenty stuck. First of all, where in the recovery rule book do you find permission to put this exquisite human creation on trial for addiction? Better yet, where do you get off denouncing this person because she found a way to get her dope fix into the brain faster than you could? Do you think a needle in her arm is any different that a straw up your nose? I think not, and it's about time you realize that."

I was reading Higher Power loud and clear. What was I thinking? Before I knew that she shot dope, I had a completely different opinion about her; in fact, she'd been verging on fantastic.

I had to show some respect. Amber came to an NA meeting to chalk up an hour of sobriety, and I was selfishly labeling her as more addicted and worse off than I was.

I rejoined the conversation and answered her question.

"That's just my back brace. If I remove it, I break in half."

She laughed again. "You crack me up. Are you always this funny?"

"Not really. Do you always find people this amusing?"

"As a matter of fact, I haven't laughed this hard in months. It just feels so good to be clean. What about you? Why are you here?"

"That's the other part of my story, the crazy part. I was snorting every Oxy and Roxy that wasn't nailed down. I wish I could say I simply liked to party too much, but that's not so. In all honesty, I've never even been to a party, but one day a Lortab changed my life. It wiped out a whole bunch of pain and put a smile on my face that didn't belong there. After that, I started snorting anything that could be crushed. It didn't take long for me to overdose—not once, but three times. I got so loaded that I rear-ended a tanker truck while doing a hundred miles per hour. After I came out of my coma, I got some pills and did it again, right in the hospital. You might call it lucky, but I know I'm blessed. This stuff called recovery is starting to grow on me. How do I look?"

"You look great, I wouldn't change a thing. As for me, I'm surprised you didn't bolt after seeing the way I butchered my arm." The sparkle in her eyes grew dimmer. "I better stop beating myself up. I worked hard for this good mood and I'm letting it slip away."

"You're right. I promise to be nice to me if you promise to be nice to you. Deal?"

"Deal. And if you can overlook the way I wasted a year of my life on heroin, I'll forget what you did in the hospital."

We both nodded and laughed again. The attraction between us wasn't romantic, but it felt good.

Our brief conversation was over; the chairperson brought the meeting back to order and Amber gave me a look that suggested we'd be seeing each other again soon.

Joe was called on to give out the key tags after the break. He seemed very comfortable in front of the crowd and began by saying, "Tonight I have requested the privilege to present the key tags, because I brought a new friend of mine to his first meeting. This key-tag ceremony is how we acknowledge and celebrate different amounts of sober time we've earned. If any of you are interested in our way of life, we would be happy to present you with a white key tag as a newcomer with twenty-four or more hours clean."

Nobody got up. Joe looked directly at me and waved the white tag as an incentive for me to walk over to get it. I was frozen in the chair; I knew I had the dumbest look on my face.

Silver Fox tapped me on the shoulder. "Hey, Man, this is the moment. Get up there."

Wendy hooked my elbow and stood me up. She handed me my crutches and said, "Come on, I'll go with you. You don't want to miss this. We all need a reason to celebrate. Tonight you are the newest hope we have and it's your duty to accept that. Now move it or you won't get another kiss from me, ever."

I started walking, with Wendy by my side. Once we reached Joe, he placed the white key tag in my hand, and the room came alive with applause. I lifted up the key tag and showed it to the group. The ovation grew louder.

Once the applause subsided and people were back in their seats, Joe put his arm around me.

"I would like to say a few words about this young man, our newest member. His name is Buddy."

"Hi, Buddy," the audience said in unison. It actually gave me goose bumps.

"I first met this fellow in the hospital," Joe continued. "I don't think he'll mind if I tell you that he died more than once at the hands of this disease. But for the grace of God, it could have been anyone of us in his place. The illness of addiction plays for keeps and cheats to win. Buddy here has pins in his leg and a broken back to prove it. He also had a collapsed lung, a ruptured spleen, and head trauma bad enough to keep him in a coma on a respirator for ten days. Compared to all the millions of addicts, he is one of the luckiest."

He paused and scanned the faces in the audience. I wondered if that was just for dramatic effect.

"He's one of the luckiest, because he made it here. And he can stay. He doesn't ever have to get another white key tag for the rest of his life if he doesn't want to. The relapses can be prevented if we help enough. That's our job. Who's up for it? Who's ready to show him the way with the Twelve Steps?"

The crowd in the room roared again.

Joe made a sweeping motion with his hands and turned to me. "They're waiting for you, Bro. All you have to do is keep coming back and be willing to do whatever it takes. We'll show you how, one day at a time."

Wendy gave me a congratulatory hug and led me back to my seat. As Joe continued handing out the rest of the key tags, Wendy leaned over and whispered to me.

"Your parents would have been so proud if they were here tonight. But now we are all your family, too. You mean so much to me and my brother. Together, there isn't anything we can't do."

She kissed my cheek and I felt dignified and worthy. I was no longer a geek with pain in my heart. I was filling up with love and my Higher Power had arranged it all.

My attention was grabbed by the most booming applause I had ever heard. Tanya was back in front of the room; she was crying and beaming as she received a one-year medallion. I looked forward to the day I'd have one of my own.

Tanya's sponsor, who had joined her when Tanya received the medallion, took the microphone and the crowd quieted and waited expectantly.

"I have known Tanya since day one," the sponsor began. "I remember when she walked into her first meeting; she was shaking, sick, and scared. That was a perfect way to start. She was as broken as you can get. She knew that she had pushed her marriage over the edge with lies and deceit. She was so filled with shame and self-hatred. There was no way to promise anything better than one sober day away from pills, if she was willing to do what she was told. I knew she was desperate. I told her to attend ninety meetings in ninety days and to read the Narcotics Anonymous textbook. She did both and never missed a phone call to me."

It was obvious how special their relationship had become. Her sponsor had taken Tanya's life into her hands and protected it while Tanya slowly healed. The sponsor continued to describe how Tanya had worked hard every single day to take advantage of everything the fellowship of NA had to offer. She talked about how Tanya had accepted full responsibility for her past, even though she made most of her mistakes while under the influence of drugs, and she was proud and grateful to be Tanya's sponsor. "Rarely have I been a witness to someone so extraordinary," she said in conclusion. "Tanya, I love you."

The sponsor gave Tanya the microphone and implored her to say a few more words.

Tonya smiled at the crowd. "Today is, by far, the best day of my life. I had no idea when I walked into my first meeting what was in store for me. I'm glad I didn't. I would have taken off and never come back. Recovery is no picnic and it's no party. It has been the most difficult thing I have ever done, but it has been worth every ounce of pain that it took to get me here. I have grown so much and discovered more about who I am. I can honestly say that I love myself now. I have forgiven myself for what I did to ruin my life and my marriage. I don't know what will happen in the months ahead, except one thing: I intend to continue to make sobriety my number one priority, because without it, I have no marriage and no hope. I may as well be dead. As long as I stay sober, everything is possible and happiness is guaranteed. For the newcomer tonight, Buddy, it works if you work it and it IS worth it. Keep coming. I love you all."

She stepped away from the mike and returned to her chair. Her husband greeted her with another hug that had *for better or worse* written all over it.

Once the applause died down, the chairperson announced the meeting was open for sharing.

A shrunken arm with a deformed claw hand poked into the air was immediately acknowledged by the chairperson. "Little H, you're next."

Little H stood up and the room was pin-drop silent.

"You all know me. I'm an old burned-out Bowery junkie."

"Hi, Little H," we all said.

He began telling a tale that meandered for a while and I wasn't sure where he was going with it. Then he got my attention.

"But there's one thing that hasn't changed since the old days. Addiction turns all of us into despicable losers. We have to be, so we can be rescued. We're not going to come in off the street, smelling sweet, and filled with virtue. No, no. We have to be rotten to the core and ready for the garbage truck. Then, and maybe only then, can we be plucked from our misery, cleaned up, and taken in by the most loving hands in humanity. Narcotics Anonymous has never and will never turn any of us away, no matter how bad we smell, look, or act."

That was more like it. His message was definitely no nonsense.

"NA is not looking for angels. But it's willing to make angels out of the worst sinners the world can create. Tonight you are all a witness to a miraculous healing that takes place whenever love conquers addiction. Don't you ever doubt it. Turn your life and will over to the care of this fellowship and just watch the stars come out and shine from the heavens above. We are in recovery and whatever we have lost to our addiction can be regained. Thank you Tanya, for being brave and facing the dragon without fear. This is just the beginning. Look how I turned out."

He modeled a toothless smile and pretended to slick his hair down after licking his fingers. He waved at everybody and sat down. I loved him already.

After several other people spoke up, the chairperson announced that it was time to close the meeting. He thanked Tanya for being the speaker and the group for allowing him to chair the meeting. He asked for volunteers to put the tables and chairs away and clean up the room. Everybody stood up and migrated to the outer edge of the room, forming a circle. Everyone interlocked with arms over shoulders, like a continuous hugging chain. Joe was on my left and Wendy was on my right. I wondered if someone was going to lead the group in something like a camp song. Instead, the group recited a prayer that seemed to unify us. I intended to memorize the prayer and join in at future meetings.

I felt the prayer was a pledge to answer the call from a fellow addict, day or night. It was a silent promise to rescue a soul in trouble. I was relieved to know that I could count on anyone in that room for help.

As the circle broke and the meeting came to an end, most people headed for the door. A crew quickly rearranged the room and in minutes the floor was cleared and ready for the next function. Joe, Wendy, and I were headed toward the parking lot when I heard Silver Fox's voice behind us.

"Let me borrow Buddy for a few minutes; we have some unfinished business."

Mark reached into his pocket and withdrew a business card.

"Buddy, you've taken one of the biggest steps ever by coming here. This is a scary place, because addiction can't win here. We've been following its instructions for so long that we assume that we and the addiction are one and the same—but we're not. Addiction is a disease, a medical condition with faulty wiring in the brain and software programmed for over-consumption at all cost. You've got what I've got. We're no different, except for the amount of time that we played the game. It took me a few years to lose it all. You ended up in the ICU after only a few days of using."

The longer he talked, the more comfortable I felt. It was a lot like getting to know and trust Dr. Stone.

Silver Fox continued, "I'll make this short. Here's my card. Use it. My home and cell numbers are included, along with my e-mail address. Stay in touch. Call me tomorrow, just to make sure I'm still alive. Give me your numbers and e-mail, because I am going to track you down if I don't hear from you. I'll tell you the rest of my story another day. For now, you might like to know I have gotten back everything that I lost and more—a lot more. I do not need all that I have. It's a gift that comes from delivering a valuable service to others. I have been paid well. When success was pounding on the door, I opened it and said yes and thank-you. But always remember, recovery first. There will be plenty of time to dig for treasure. Let's talk tomorrow."

He wrote down my e-mail address on another card, then dialed my cell phone number so he could add it to his address book. I did the same with his phone number before saying good-bye.

"I want to thank you for spending so much time with me tonight and telling me your story," I said as we shook hands. "It means a lot because, let's face it, I don't exactly look like I belong in your foursome at Pebble Beach. I feel like the biggest idiot for trashing my life with pills and all that craziness. Now I'm busted up and sitting at an NA meeting and I'm only sixteen. What does that tell you? You don't have to be nice to me, talk to me, and hang out or anything else. I can take the rejection, if you know what I mean."

He held up his hand and signaled me to stop talking.

"Buddy, I hope I only have to say this once, but I have a feeling it may take a few more times for you to get it. Big egos have the biggest pity parties, and you, my friend, have one of the biggest. I don't care about all the hang-ups you've got or the fact that you're used to identifying yourself as a loser. Those are poor excuses for not loving your true self. I know you have a way to go and I am willing to help out with the teaching. From now on, you better toss the feeling-sorry-for-yourself attitude. Decide if you want to accept what I have to offer. Rejecting it means you don't think you're worthy. I suggest you convince yourself that you are. It feels better and reduces your chances of relapse."

My Higher Power chose that same time to have a chat with me, too. "Pay attention to this man. I put the messages in his head. Pity is the addict's emotional plaything. It's a poisonous reaction to the way you think. If you want to feel your regrets, have at it. Just remember, your true authentic self is not created by the thoughts or feelings you have. They are only what you experience while living your life. Don't use them to determine who you really are. Feel them and then let them go."

I got a little heated up trying to listen to two sets of advice at the same time.

"Okay, I got it. Message received." I heard the impatience in my own voice.

Mark heard the abrupt remark and stopped speaking. I was answering back to Higher Power, but Silver Fox didn't know that. I had to think of something else to say.

"I'm sorry, Mark. I didn't mean to cut you off like that. I follow you loud and clear. You're right: I bet I have a nice big red ring in the exact shape of the pity pot I've been sitting on."

We both laughed. He shook my hand one last time; his grip was strong and masculine. He walked away and pointed the key fob at a 2012 silver Mercedes S65 AMG. He was rich, all right. Although his spiritual bank account impressed me the most, taking his car for a spin was right up there with it. Like he said, we don't reject the bonuses when they come as part of the recovery package.

I felt a tap on the shoulder from behind and heard Amber's merry voice.

"Hi, Buddy. I just want to say good-night and I hope that I see you again at a meeting. I'd like you to be here when I get the rest of my key tags. Take good care of yourself and get a sponsor as soon as you can."

She threw her arms around me for the briefest of hugs, then she took off through the parking lot. I yelled to her, "Thanks for introducing yourself. I'll be there for all your key tags."

When Amber was out of sight, I turned to look for Joe and Wendy. As I walked to where they stood chatting with Little H, I smiled to myself. This had been one heck of an evening . . . and I knew I'd found a new home.

CHAPTER 47

Debriefing

Joe asked what I thought about my first NA meeting as we drove back to my house.

"There's a lot to think about," I answered thoughtfully. "I had no idea that using pills could cause so many problems. Up until a few weeks ago, I never gave drugs a thought. But here I am with a story of my own and problems that were just as big or bigger. What amazed me was how much your life can change for the better, just by giving up drugs. At first, the pills were just for fun. I don't think anyone who starts out in that direction expects it to make matters worse, but it does. I should have known better. I should have stopped as soon as I got into trouble, but I didn't. It really blows my mind that addiction could do that to me."

Joe said, "That's addiction for you. Now, what part of the meeting did you like the most?"

"I'm not sure. I was really impressed by all that honesty. That's a powerful thing. What those people were willing to say about themselves was so personal. I thought it was too much; you know, too risky to let everybody in on your private business. But now, I can understand the reason for doing it. We can't ever forget that this disease ruins lives as long as it's active."

Joe kept glancing over at me and seemed genuinely interested in what I had to say, so I kept talking.

"Sharing your troubles makes it possible for someone to start caring about you. That's the medicine I think I need for healing. Even if your family rejects you, the fellowship won't. It's like getting a new family that will accept you with all your faults and never judge you. The love you get in recovery is probably the best way to stop the behaviors that turned the world against you in the first place. I like that part about NA a lot."

"Buddy, recovery is a journey that lasts a lifetime. You get to add to it or subtract from it every day. It requires a lot of different tools. Some of them you will be given. The others you will develop on your own. Learning how to use them takes years of practice. When you use them wisely, the results will be rewarding."

I wondered when he was going to let me in on some of those precious tools.

Joes seemed to know what I was thinking. "I have a few suggestions for you. Tonight before you go to bed, I want you to pray. Don't freak out over the word. It's not a religious thing I'm asking you to do. A prayer is a few words you put together. Start with your intentions and send them along as a request to your Higher Power for help. Keep it simple. Make sure you are thankful for the day of sobriety you have been given. Remember, a day away from pills is an unmerited gift. It's free for the asking and requires no payment, so thank your Higher Power for it."

I decided that praying was something I could do as long as it wasn't in church.

Joe had more to say. "When you wake up tomorrow, the first thing I want you to do is express your intentions for a sober day. Admit that you are powerless over your addiction and that your life had become out of control. Be humbly aware that your Higher Power has put it back on course. You want to include a conscious contact with your Higher Power throughout the day, so you can pay close attention to His guidance and appreciate His strength. Got that?"

I heard it all, but it didn't sit right with me. It sounded like my mommy signing me up for Little League soccer so I'd grow up big and strong like the rest of the boys. I had to say something.

"Listen, Joe. Is all of this really necessary? I went to a meeting. I got my newcomer key tag. I won't use pills, heroin, cocaine, pot, alcohol, or any other addictive substance for the rest of my natural-born life. Isn't that enough? I've got my work cut out for me trying to stop being a loser-geek. Is it really necessary to pray and do this conscious-contact thing with my Higher Power? I'm not sure I like Him, anyway. He's bossy like you and He runs his sarcastic mouth off."

I regretted the words as soon as they were out of my mouth; I let that cat out of the bag, didn't I? Now Joe knew I'd been dialoguing with my Higher Power. What would he think about that? He'd probably think I was crazy. I expected him to be upset or at least insulted, but instead, he smiled and laughed, just like the Fox.

"Buddy, you're trying way too hard to figure this all out and get one in the win column. I can see where you're going with this, so let's back off and make it even easier for you. How about this: Tonight, just say, 'Whoever is helping me out, thanks and keep it up, see you tomorrow.' And another thing: my Higher Power talks to me all the time. I talk back to him, too; it just feels better that way. I do it out loud as often as I can, when people aren't looking. And I don't consider myself to be a whack job. I'll call you tomorrow. Now get out of here before I change my mind about being your sponsor."

Wendy got out and walked me to the front door. As we walked, she leaned toward me conspiratorially.

"My brother really likes you. I was there when he met his sponsor. They had the same conversation. My brother wasn't told what he must do. He was told what he should do. He hated it and griped every day. If it wasn't about praying, it was about how many meetings to go to. Next, it was how much reading he was assigned from the Narcotics Anonymous book. I think the last big bitching he did was about writing out the fourth step. That can take weeks."

It was good to hear that Joe put up a struggle at the outset. He didn't like being told what to do any more than I did.

Wendy continued, "He completed all Twelve Steps and look at him now. He's going to be a good sponsor and ride you a bit hard. Don't tell him I told you how much of a whiner he was in the beginning. I think all addicts can make a career out of whining. Don't let it bother you. You'll outgrow it like he did. Follow his instructions. Remember, the addiction you have wants you to put up some resistance and complain. That's how it weakens you and picks you off with the temptation to use pills again. When you're praying tonight—and you will because I'm telling you to—just imagine your addiction getting all bent out of shape, then pray some more. Do it with a smile—just for me, your friend and helper."

I didn't want to give in that easily, but she hugged me, kissed me on the cheek, and trotted back to the car.

I walked into the house and headed straight for the living room, where Mom was watching TV and Dad was sprawled out asleep on the couch. Mom smiled proudly and I remembered how she used to do that when I brought home a drawing from school. She turned the volume down on the TV so we could talk.

"How did it go, Honey? Did you meet some nice people and make new friends? What did they look like? Were there any real drug addicts there? You know, the kind that lives on the street and . . ." She stopped abruptly as I interrupted her.

"Mom, you may not realize this, but I'm no different than anyone else with an addiction."

"Oh, Honey. Come on, now. You're not that bad. You live in a nice house, you have good parents, get good grades at school . . ."

"Mom, I thought you knew better. Addiction is a disease. It's not a lack of social graces and fine etiquette. It's a sickness of the brain. You don't become addicted because you weren't raised right. The people at this meeting were all good people. It turns out we did some bad things and some worse than others. There was nobody there who looked or acted more like an addict than the next person. We're all equals and we treat each other that way. You should try it."

As soon as I said that my Higher Power snarled in my ear.

"Hey, Buddy. Who do you think you're talking to? It's your mom, Pal, and she deserves better. You were at the meeting. You have the advantage of knowing how an addict feels in his or her own skin. She doesn't. She's innocent. Now cut her some slack and answer her questions with respect. We have a way to go, Amigo. It's a long cattle drive. Now, sweeten it up."

I could not run and I could not hide from Higher Power. All Knowing. All Seeing. Everywhere and Always. Why did I have to get a Higher Power like this? Why couldn't He be a lazy, good-for-nothing, generic brand? I was stuck with Him. He probably couldn't be fired or cast out by exorcism. There had to be a way to shut Him up, though, even if just for a little while.

"Mom, I'm sorry. I guess I'm tired. It's been a long day. You're right. As addicts, we're all the same and we're all different. Some of us are just getting started and have a big mess to clean up and others look more like upstanding citizens with great credentials. If someone showed up who is hurting and could use a shower, clean clothes, and a hot meal, I'm sure the group would arrange that with as much kindness as you'd find in any church. Fortunately, I am way ahead of the game, thanks to you and Dad."

What I said must have worked, because she gave me a tender look.

"I'm trying to understand what you're going through, but it's difficult," Mom said. "Overdoses, car crashes, broken bones, and hit men are not what I am accustomed to. It will take some time for me to get adjusted. You should try being as patient with me as I was with you. I want you to succeed and be as happy as you can be. You seem to have a real good start and two good friends who have a lot of experience and care about you. I'll catch on."

I could see that she wanted to be a better mom than ever before. I figured if I told her a few things about the meeting, she could know that I was in good hands.

"Mom, the meeting was great. There were at least seventy-five people there and I was given the royal treatment. I met a guy who was ancient and would probably turn into a fossil if he stopped moving for about five minutes, he's that old. He told some great stories about the old days when heroin was called Tar. I also met Joe's sponsor, a middle-aged man who lost a fortune and got it all back, thanks to recovery. Oh, yeah. A girl, a little older than me, introduced herself and she was very sweet and funny. I'd like to see her again. She was cute."

I took out my white key tag and dangled it in front of her.

"Know what this is?"

Mom took it out of my hand and gave me a big smile. Yes, she did know what it was and she looked impressed.

She read the inscription, *One day at a time,* and said, "Now you have one, too. Just like Joe's. What are you going to do with it? What are you supposed to do with it? Are you going to put keys on it? Who gave it to you?"

"Whoa, one question at a time," I said. "This is a big deal for me and for every addict. I hope this will be the only newcomer key tag I'll ever get. It was Joe's idea to give it to me. He told the group about me and what happened with the drugs and the car and my busted-up body. I'm going to collect them all and then get a medallion. A woman got one of those tonight for being clean for one year. She was crying and everybody clapped and hugged her."

"Was there anyone there we know?"

"Actually, I'm glad you asked that question. The anonymous part of the program is for our own protection. When we go to a closed meeting, we know that the members are not there to spy and tattle about who they saw and what they heard. So starting now, I intend to obey that rule. It's called a tradition. There are twelve of them and they are a set of principles that protect the fellowship from itself and any outsiders."

"You mean that you have to keep quiet about what goes on behind closed doors? Is this some kind of secret society? Do you have to take some kind of pledge and promise some code of silence?"

She was getting ridiculous again, and I wanted to set her straight, but I already knew that my Higher Power would slap me silly if I mouthed off. So, I told her a little bit about what I'd read of the traditions.

"Mom, NA meetings can be open or closed. The open ones allow the general public to attend, so there is nothing secret there. Our faces are available for anyone to see. Fortunately, nobody shows up without a legitimate reason and that is usually to accompany someone and offer support. The open meetings are speaker-type affairs where a guest will tell their addiction story, knowing that there may be people in the room who are not in recovery. The closed meetings probably serve to help the addict who's having trouble and needs to speak freely to the group about it. All meetings are important to an addict, but the closed meetings are serious business."

Mom seemed interested in learning about this, so I kept going.

"Now, about those traditions. I read that they were created many years ago by a committee of people who debated long and hard about what rules to abide by. The tradition system was established to protect NA from anyone's personal agenda that could weaken it or, worse, contaminate it with anything that destroys its primary purposes: the common welfare of the members, their personal recovery, and NA unity. NA has no government, only leaders who are trusted servants. The ultimate authority in NA is a loving God. NA stays away from opinions that could draw it into any public controversy. NA is fully self-supporting and only accepts internal donations from its members. I could go on, but I think you understand that its one purpose is to carry the message to the drug addict who still suffers, and there are plenty of them out there chasing the ultimate high."

I'd memorized that information before the meeting. I wanted to impress Joe and his sponsor with some trivia. I thought if I could recite the steps and the traditions, they might find something about me they liked. I didn't even get the chance, but I hadn't needed to impress them with trivia anyway; they accepted me for who I was.

Mom said, "Whatever you say, Honey. I'm just glad that you are taking NA seriously and I know you'll do well. Won't you?"

"Of course I will . . . but now, I'm ready to turn in," I said. "See you in the morning. You're the greatest mom a kid could ever have. I love you."

"I love you, too. I'll have breakfast ready when you get up. Sleep tight, and thanks for making me proud. Perhaps the reasons aren't what I would have chosen, but I am proud just the same. God bless you. And now, I could use a hug," she said.

"Me too." I put my arms around her, and our hug felt more mature. I knew I was one very lucky guy.

Once I was ready for bed and back in my room, I picked up the journal. It was time to start writing.

Dear Journal,

What an incredible day I had. It feels like it's been a year since I got up this morning. I think I lived more life today than ever before. By living, I don't mean just going through the motions. I accepted everything and rejected nothing. I actually enjoyed it all, even the parts that would have bothered me in the past.

I can see how and why I belong in this world. I was surprised that my Higher Power showed up so often. I suppose that's what teachers are for. I wonder if He'll ever learn any manners? I doubt it.

The NA meeting was the best part of my day. Little H tried to make tar heroin sound like a mouth-watering treat, but his arms told a different story. I'm sure painkiller addicts are more common today than heroin addicts, because pills are so easy to get.

I wonder how many pills are snorted relative to one human life going down the path of recovery? A thousand, ten thousand, a million? The amount must be unbelievable. To buy a thousand Roxys or Oxys would cost about fifteen thousand dollars. That could pay for a lot of college. So much money is wasted by addicts. Getting high is a very expensive hobby.

Now that I have made it through the doors of NA, I'm keeping my seat. Let someone else call the dope man and order up another dance with the devil. I know that my addiction is a permanent fixture. I'm taking it to the grave with me. Along the way, I intend to get all the help I need to keep it arrested so it will leave me alone.

I consider myself to be very lucky. I have been delivered out of the jaws of addiction. I still have a family who loves me and wants me around. There are millions who are dying from this condition. I met a couple of others tonight who were headed down the same path I was, but lucky for all of us, the fellowship of NA is there to help.

Do what we do and you can have what we have, is a slogan from NA, AA and probably all the twelve-step fellowships. But addicts are impatient, and maybe they don't want to work so hard to master the one thing that will guarantee protection from harm. I am sure the addict who is still using considers the sober life to be tedious and boring.

Even though I've only been to one NA meeting, I have already decided that I prefer recovery. I think I can enjoy that life style. It is far better than years of being miserable.

Pills brought to life a part of me that was long overdue for fun. I have to admit I found it indescribably thrilling, even though I was dangerously out of control. As much as I liked the ride, the crash got more of my attention. When I snorted OxyContin, I was caught between the front end of a freight train and a thick wall of concrete.

As bad as the physical collision was, I felt more like a loser than ever before. Since the accident, addiction has put me through a lot of trouble and hardship. But I found something still intact that addiction couldn't have or didn't want, my true self, the life within me. I want to enjoy living it and loving it. With the help of the Fellowship, my parents and new friends, I want to keep it that way. The real me belongs here.

I closed the journal and snuggled under the covers, turned out the light, and I slept better than I'd slept in months.

CHAPTER 48

Different

A metallic clicking sound roused me from a deep sleep, then I became aware of a tapping vibration in my left leg. It was an odd sensation, as though something tiny was walking up and down my shin with cowboy boots and spurs. I reached over, my eyes still closed, and touched a small warm body. It was my brother's.

I opened my eyes and said, "Hey, what's going on?"

He turned to look at me and smiled playfully. "I'm tightening your screws."

"What are you doing to my leg? Give me that." The sound of more metallic clicking was disconcerting and it just felt weird.

Junior was attempting to insert the head of a screwdriver into the fixator that was holding my broken leg together.

"I'm just trying to make sure it's nice and tight," he said. "You don't want this thing to come apart."

"It's fine the way it is. Now give me that."

He surrendered the screwdriver and I noticed that he had a few other items on the bed, including Allen wrenches and a Black and Decker power tool with enough attachments to take anything apart. He reached for that and pulled the trigger, making it rev up. My room sounded like an auto body shop. Junior's mechanical curiosity had caused him to dismantle a few things around the house . . . and most of them could not be reassembled. I didn't plan to add my fixator to that list.

"Ok, you win," he said. "I'll put the tools away. Mom told me to get you for breakfast. Do you want me to tighten anything up?"

"Sure, why don't release this leather strap on my brace, then pull it tighter and fasten it back down."

Junior tugged on the strap and it felt a little more snug when he was done.

"You know," Junior said, "This thing doesn't look like much. Are you sure you have a broken back? You don't look broken. What's a broken back anyway? I don't suppose you know. See you downstairs."

Typical kid: he lost interest even before he became interested. After going to the bathroom, I headed for the kitchen. I was thinking about how nice it would be if my Higher Power was called away on assignment. I welcomed the peace and quiet. An instant later, it occurred to me that He was always around.

He wasn't just a guest or a visitor, He was an occupant. He was all of me, but I was only a tiny amount of Him.

Mom was stacking up the pancakes as I walked into the kitchen. I parked my crutches against the counter and gave her a kiss. I was in a good mood and breakfast smelled wonderful. The aroma of coffee made it feel like a brand new day: fresh, clean, and still trouble-free. No problems came to mind for the first time in a long time. There was nothing to do but eat and relax.

As I dove into the pancakes that were dripping with syrup and melted butter, Mom surveyed her family around the table.

"You look like a happy bunch. Buddy, remember you have an appointment with Dr. Stone today. He'll be excited to hear all about your first NA meeting and the white key tag. Make sure you bring it with you. I think the appointment is at ten this morning, so don't dilly-dally after breakfast. I suppose he's probably going to be talking about recovery. I hope he notices how much you've changed. We have. By the way, Honey, what are you going to bring up?"

"I don't know," I said. "I'll just wait to see what he asks me."

"What if he asks you about us? What kind of parents we are. What would you tell him?"

I was on the spot. I had to be careful with my answer. Too much honesty could ruin the day.

"I would tell him that you're good parents."

"What about when you were growing up?" she asked.

I knew what she was getting at and I wasn't in the mood for dissecting this issue at the breakfast table. The day was starting out so nicely, I wanted to keep it that way. "Things were different then," I explained carefully. "You and I were different then."

"That's not an answer. He's going to want to know about what it was like growing up in this house, how we treated you, and whether or not it's our fault that you ended up like . . ."

She paused and looked uncomfortable.

"You mean, ended up getting hooked on drugs, don't you?" Before I could explain that it wasn't her fault, she choked back her tears and spoke in a quivering voice. I wanted to hear this. It just might help us heal.

"This is so hard for me to say. But it has bothered me ever since you were in that coma. When I was sitting there in the ICU, watching that machine inflate your lungs, I felt pretty helpless. There you were, my son, injured from head to toe and all I could do was watch. I had a lot to think about and I tried to figure out where I went wrong. I knew you were different as a little boy. It didn't take long for me to realize that you weren't going to be athletic or popular. And I could live with that. But when you grew up and we stopped talking to each other, I had no idea what was going on in your head. I thought I lost you. You became something and someone I did not recognize. When the drugs came into your life, I was caught completely off-guard. So I wondered, did I do this to you? Did you turn to drugs because I wasn't a good enough mother? Someone must know the answer. I figure Dr. Stone does."

I'm not sure if she wanted to accept full accountability for my mistakes or pass it off on me for choosing the path of destruction. How much was her fault and how much was my fault, even Dr. Stone wouldn't know. Nobody would. But she started all of this and I should finish it, and do it right. This was my mom and nothing could undo the past. I didn't want to see her get hurt anymore.

I stopped eating and gave her an answer.

"Mom, I have always been me, an original, right out of the box. I was never something that you could mold into your version of a beautiful child. I was already whole and complete. Believe it or not, I made more of my own choices than you can imagine. You may have tried to influence me by taking me to soccer practice. But you couldn't kick the ball for me. That was my own decision."

I had her full attention and I was hoping she would understand my explanation and let herself off the hook.

"You gave me everything a kid could want from a mom. Hugging and kissing was just not for me. It may be difficult for you to understand why I became a nerd, a geek, and overall loser. Believe it or not, it was my choice. I did not use you or anyone else as a role model. I am not sure how it came to be so natural for me."

Mom looked at me in a way I had never seen before. I think she was beginning to understand something that had always been a heartbreaking mystery to her.

I kept going. "As far the drugs are concerned, I'm human, too. I wanted to feel wild and free. The day came when a Lortab made that happen very easily. If I could have spent the rest of my life in that state of mind, I would have—it was that good. The bad part was taking too much. You know the rest."

Mom looked at me without saying anything. Then she pointed at my plate and said, "Your pancakes are getting cold."

"That can wait. This can't. I have a bit of a confession to make."

Mom turned pale. She looked at my father and I knew they were both thinking my confession probably meant I had relapsed and lied about it.

"I don't know how much the two of you believe in your own faith," I said. "But I have been getting some messages from mine. It even has its own voice. Now, don't get freaked out, thinking I'm crazy. I'm not. I have been communicating with what you might call a Higher Power. It's been going on pretty regularly for the past week. Recovering addicts have access to this power to help them resist drugs and do the right thing. I didn't know that my Higher Power would be such a talker. And He really seems to care a lot about me. He's always trying to help me out. Sometimes He says things that are mean and get me upset. I think it's His way of getting my attention, so I take Him seriously. Anyway, He told me yesterday that I am going to turn out all right. So you don't have to worry. I may not have gotten the best start in life, but it's going to get better, a whole lot better."

Mom got up from her chair and threw her arms around my neck. She was sobbing.

"Those were some of the nicest things you could have said. I just knew you were being touched by an angel. I could see it in your face. It shows all over.

Her question was directed to my father; when it came to spiritual matters, he usually preferred to remain silent and this time was no exception, so Mom moved on.

"If you have a Higher Power who talks to you, I say you should talk back. It's a miracle. You've got God drawing up the map, Jesus as your copilot, and the Holy Spirit as your chauffeur. What could be better?"

I couldn't let her make incorrect assumptions. My Higher Power was not charming, nor was he angelic—and neither was I.

"Okay, Mom. My Higher Power isn't your version of God or anyone else's. He's not quite the way I would like Him to be, but I'm getting used to it. He knows I can be a wise guy and He manages to get His messages across, loud and clear. I also wanted you to know that the past is already in the history books. We can't go back and change a word of it and I can accept that."

I wasn't sure if my mother was getting this straight. I think she would have preferred that I believe in God, right out of the Bible. She could relate more easily to that.

"I have chosen my own path, for better or worse. You were never at fault for my screw-ups. I take full responsibility. More important, I intend to make better choices from now on and I expect better outcomes because of them. My life is going to be something spectacular."

Before I finished the last sentence, Mom walked over to the stove and said, "You sound like you're brand-new all over. I'm so happy for you. I'm making you a fresh batch of pancakes to celebrate. It'll only take a minute."

While Mom cooked, we heard a knock on the front door and my brother sprinted to open it. He yelled back, "There's a nice guy you liked who was here yesterday. What do you want me to do?"

Everybody yelled back. "Let him in."

Joe strolled into the kitchen and walked over to where I was sitting. He patted me on the shoulder. "Hey, Buddy, great mom you've got here, piling up flapjacks. Mmmm, they smell so good. Do you mind?"

He snatched one of the cold pancakes off my plate, rolled it up, poured syrup on it and devoured it. "These are awesome. Mind if I have another?"

He was rolling up a second one when my mom told him, "Don't eat those. I'll have some hot ones done in a minute."

"Oh, I don't mind. I love cold pancakes. I can eat anything cold; spaghetti, pizza, you name it."

Joe took a seat while my mother served the hot pancakes. We kept eating and looking at each other, grinning like brothers with a big secret.

"This is a nice surprise, Joe," Mom chatted away. "What brings you over so early?"

"I have the day off. Thought I would help Buddy get his day started on the right track. It's something we do for each other in recovery. My sponsor came over to my place in the beginning. I think he was trying to catch me taking pills for breakfast, like I usually did. Instead, he caught me with a bowl of cereal. It was nice. We had coffee and got to know each other. So here I am."

The pancakes were gone and I finished the last gulp of orange juice. Joe asked me where my key tag was.

"It's upstairs in my bedroom. Why?"

"I figured as much. I want to teach you something important about key tags. On one hand they're cheap plastic with a metal ring. On the other, they can be lifesavers, if you want them to be."

He pulled out his most recent key tag.

"This stays with me at all times. I never leave the room without it. If I'm in the shower, it's near my shaving kit. When I'm asleep, it's near my alarm clock. It's in the pocket of each pair of pants I wear. It even goes for a jog with me. It's got the power to keep me sober. I was taught that when I have this baby in my hand, I will never have pills in the other. I can't snort a drug while this key tag is on duty, because I say so and I know so. So, go get yours . . . now!"

I paused too long and he said it again, this time with more intensity. "Addiction doesn't kid around, Buddy, and neither do I when it comes to sobriety. Now go get it."

My mom handed me the crutches and watched me hustle toward the stairs.

Then she turned toward Joe and I could hear her ask, "What's the hurry? He's not going to do any drugs any more. Can't this wait until after breakfast?"

"Of course he's going to be okay, because he's got a good sponsor and is doing what he's told, but we can't afford to cut our addiction any slack. Give it an inch and it will bust you wide open and eat your insides while your heart is still beating. We are no match for addiction. We need all the help we can get. The key tag can represent a protection from temptation, cravings, and stupidity. Addicts possess all three in generous quantities. The key tag gets rid of some of that. A Higher Power, a sponsor, the group, daily meetings, prayer, meditation and all the literature takes care of the rest. He's got a long way to go and a lot to learn. The key tag is a very important beginning. His life depends on it."

I returned with the key tag, holding it tightly, as though death would be the only way to pry it out of my hand.

"I've got it. That won't happen again," I said. "This is going to be my constant companion. Strange as it may seem, I actually feel better when it's in my hand. I feel stronger and safe. That was good advice."

Joe reached across the table and motioned for the key tag. He started rubbing it with his eyes closed; he appeared to be engaged in a solemn mystical ceremony.

When he was done, he said, "There. I've juiced up your key tag with my own spirit, wisdom, and experience. My sponsor did that for me. Make sure you have some other members do the same. That's one way that we pass it on. Wherever you go, I go with you, and so does everybody who has gone with me. We take care of each other. We have to or we die."

As Joe and I sat looking at the all-important white key tag, Mom—always the practical one—spoke up. "Honey, look at the time. You better get into the shower—pronto. We have to leave in half an hour."

"Joe, you want to take a ride with me to Dr. Stone's?"

"Sure. I can drive you over to his office, if that's all right with your mom."

She nodded yes and I headed up the stairs to get ready. Dr. Stone . . . I wasn't sure how I felt about seeing him again.

CHAPTER 49

Visiting Dr. Stone

I was back downstairs in twenty minutes. Mom walked us to the front door and inspected me for neatness.

"Give the secretary your insurance card. Here's a signed check. Just fill in the amount for the copay. Bring back your appointment card for the next visit. And remember; tell the doctor how you feel. How you really feel. He's a psychiatrist. That's his job. We're proud of you."

That's when she got mushy and started hugging and kissing me. I squirmed, which made Joe smile. Eventually we made it out of the house and took off in his Mustang.

Joe quickly turned off the CD that was playing and the two of us kept talking. Joe was quite a music lover and we exchanged some trivia about our favorite bands.

In no time at all Joe said, "Dr. Stone's office is just around the corner. He's a good man. Be straight with him and he'll do everything he can to help you make it. Are you ready for this? I hope you got some pee in the tank. You're going to be tested."

"Tested? As in drug tested?" I asked.

"It's routine. He wants to establish a record of proof that you're taking recovery seriously. It's a good idea. If you slip up, the best way to get back on the path is to pee dirty and learn your lesson. You'll hear addicts with good recovery say that they don't think they could make it back from a full-blown relapse. It's a reminder that some of us only get one shot at it."

"Don't worry. I want sobriety as much as you do, Joe. Whatever it takes, I want to learn and I want you to teach me."

A few minutes later, I walked into Dr. Stone's office. The first thing that struck me was how peaceful and quiet it was. The waiting room had large comfortable chairs with a Key West theme; the paintings on the wall depicted lush tropical vegetation, mangrove coves with cozy beach houses, and a sailboat moving slowly by.

Dr. Stone's assistant was friendly in a way that put me at ease while I got all the paper work done. I had to register and fill out questionnaires about depression, anxiety, and mood swings, as well as a five-page substance-use inventory. Dr. Stone was thorough, all right.

After that, I waited. Joe grabbed a *Sports Illustrated* and I thumbed through the latest *People* magazine. I could hear Dr. Stone's voice as he came down the hall and I glanced up to see him leading a crying woman toward the door. He had his arm around her and she was thanking him at the same time. I was cynical enough to think it was a pretty sweet deal to get paid while women cry on your shoulder, but I remembered that I had no business judging him or his patient like that. I decided my Higher Power was having a positive influence on me.

As soon as his previous patient was out the door, Dr. Stone greeted me warmly. "Hi, Buddy. It's nice to see you again. Hi, Joe, how are you?"

He walked over to Joe and they hugged. "Doc, take good care of a friend of mine," Joe replied. "Give him the special treatment."

Then he winked and the doctor smiled. I felt a bit out of the loop.

Dr. Stone walked down the hall and disappeared into a room on the right. Then I heard him call out, "Buddy, let's go."

I moved at top speed with crutches, fixator, and back brace in tow. "I'm coming," I called. "A broken man can only move so fast."

The doctor's office was spacious and roomy, the furniture strategically placed for professional intimacy. My eyes took a tour of the room: bookcases were crammed with psychiatry texts and I wished I could look at each title and thumb through the pages to see what he thought was so important.

"Buddy. See anything you like?"

"Yeah, I like to read when I get a chance. I haven't done much of that lately. For now, I get my fix on the Internet. Information overload."

The doctor sat behind a large desk with his hands folded, leaning back in a black leather swivel chair. He had a smile that would make Scrooge want to give up his fortune. No wonder that crying woman was so grateful. It just felt good to be around this man.

He said, "Buddy, how have you been? From the look on your face, I'd say you're still sober."

"That's right, Doc. I have something for you."

He watched me dig in my pocket and surface with the white key tag. His eyes lit up as he reached out to receive it from me.

"Wow, you got one. Cherish this gift, Buddy. It's a big deal." He inspected the front and back of the key tag before he squeezed it between the palms of both hands. Then he rubbed it with his fingers as though he were polishing tarnish off of it. He bowed his head and appeared to pray silently; ten seconds later he was back to being enthusiastically cheerful.

"Here you go, Buddy. That felt great. You now have me in your pocket as long you have this in your pocket. Together, addiction is no match for us. Can you feel that?" Dr. Stone asked.

He handed me the key tag. A very satisfying sensation began to flow into my body; I was invincible and indestructible. Was that recovery? I had waited a long time for those feelings. It was almost too good to be true.

"Feels pretty good, doesn't it?" Dr. Stone smiled at me across the desk. "Try explaining that to the Earth People. They can't feel it, because they aren't one of us."

"Earth People?" I questioned.

"Right. We're addicts. Earth People won't understand addiction. They can't finish a rum and coke before the ice melts in their glasses. They take narcotic pain medication as directed. If it doesn't hurt, the pills stay in the bottle. What's that all about?"

He's cool, I thought. I smiled back and nodded approvingly. I listened for more.

"Earth People don't get drunk, and they don't get high unless it's completely by accident. These folks can't party. They allow Lortabs to expire in the medicine cabinet. They keep alcohol in the house just in case somebody drops by on New Year's Eve. Earth People. Gotta love 'em," he said.

I asked, "What's the point of recovery—becoming Earth People?"

Dr. Stone's laughter was raucous before it ended in a cough and then a deep sigh.

"Listen, kid, you can't turn an addict into Earth People any more than you can turn a pickle back into a cucumber. You can act like Earth People, but that's as close as it gets. Everywhere you go, you're an addict. You can't afford the luxury of letting down your guard for a second or addiction will get you high and steal your wallet and your self-respect before you can blink. Don't ever forget that," he said.

I was confused; first, he was making fun of common ordinary folk, calling them Earth People just because they don't get messed up with drugs or booze. Then he wanted a twenty-four hour guard posted around our recovery to make sure addiction doesn't break in and steal a precious ounce of it. So I asked, "If we're not supposed to be sober Earth People, what are we supposed to be?"

He leaned across his desk. "We're supposed to be addicts in recovery. There's a big difference. And the difference is recovery. We aren't natural. We're unnatural and we have faulty malfunctioning equipment. Our brain, our neurocircuitry, and our DNA are making mistakes. We down an opioid pill and the amount of dopamine released is far in excess of what Earth People experience. We get high and reach for the pill bottle to shake out two more, while Earth People are content to sit down and enjoy the relief from pain."

I doubt he learned all of this from books. He must have been around a lot of addicts to possess so much knowledge and to be such a great teacher.

He continued, "After we take pills, we're verging on the orgasmic. When they wear off, we overshoot in the other direction. We feel worse than before we started. So what's the logical addictive course of action? Do it again, only more the next time. And so our story goes. More eventually feels like less. By then, it's too late. We're married to the junk and we can't get divorced."

I was following along. "Can't get divorced until . . ."

"Until we stop feeding the addiction. It feels terrible at first. That's all we know: pills, marijuana, coke, booze, heroin. The addiction screams bloody murder and drives us crazy until we give in. Recovery is what gives us the secret."

This I had to hear. "Secret? What secret?"

"The secret is learning how to say no to addiction and mean it. How to say no and not change your mind. How to say no and bear up to the pain, the cravings, the temptation, and the desire and still ignore the lies. Ignore the addicted voice in your head that promises you that next time, it's going to be different, better, and trouble free."

I had heard this before, but he explained it better.

He said, "That's the secret. It's in Step Two. It's called Being Restored to Sanity. Buddy, when you come to believe that a power greater than yourself can restore you to sanity, you have the secret. Addiction is a losing proposition. Sanity means that you have seen the light. You understand fully that any drug, in any form, is going to eventually blow you apart. Therefore, when addiction comes calling, you say 'no,' because it is the only logical answer to give. You must say 'no' with conviction, no matter what might be trying to persuade you to change your mind."

Dr. Stone picked up an inscribed medallion from his desk and handed it to me. It was red and rimmed with gold. I read the Roman numerals on the medallion: XXIII. Twenty-three years of sobriety for him. What an amazing accomplishment. There it was right on his desk, in full view for all to see. More important, it was a constant reminder that he owed his life and his recovery to a power that was as much inside of him as it was outside of him and he put it to good use every day.

"Doc, this is magnificent," I remarked as I handed the medallion back. "I would love to have one of these. What does it take, a whole year of sobriety to get one?" He nodded yes.

"I can't wait. But I suppose that's the whole point. One day at a time and eventually they add up. I'm here with my white key tag . . . whoopee. I know, I know. It's still the best thing I own and I will treasure it forever. It's just that it's going to take so long before I can be something better than what I am, and I'm in a hurry. I've been this way for too many years, and I'm tired of it."

Dr. Stone raised his hand like a traffic cop, signaling me to stop.

"Buddy, you're talking like an addict now. I want you to be aware of when your addict is sitting at the head of the board room and barking out orders. Right now, you are what we call an 'egotistical self-centered crybaby.' The best thing someone can do for you is to point it out. That was pointed out to me a few thousand times in my recovery. Get used to it. Someone is doing you a favor. If you're insulted, it's only because your addiction is reacting through your ego."

Egotistical crybaby. I hate those words.

He continued, "In time, you'll be able to distinguish between the recovering you and the addicted you. The recovering you will eventually be grateful to have someone catch you wearing your addict's thinking cap and yank it off your head. Then you can say, 'I did it again. It's amazing how cunning, baffling, and insidious that is.' Those are some of our favorite words by the way; don't worry, you'll hear them again, I assure you. But they're cool words and they should become part of your recovery vocabulary. In short, don't get offended when someone kicks your addiction in the you-know-what and tells it to buzz off and leave you alone. Remember, once we shine the light of recovery on our addiction, it's like throwing holy water on a vampire. It will sizzle and burn up right in front of you, at least for a while."

"Say, Doc. Do you mind if I rub this medallion a few times like you rubbed my key tag?"

The doctor extended the medallion as his smile broadened.

"Go ahead, my friend. Be my guest. I don't think anyone has rubbed that baby for a few weeks now. It could use a little TLC."

I closed my eyes and listened for the faceless voice, but my Higher Power didn't say anything. *Oh well*, I thought. *I'll just make up a prayer and be silent about it.*

"God, Higher Power, or whoever is responsible for putting this unbelievable man in my life: I thank you. As I sit here now, I feel so comfortable just being me and I would rather be exactly that and no one else. I know I have messed up with my addiction, but I ask you now to restore me to sanity so that I might hear and understand your message. Grant me the strength to follow your will for me. Keep me sober and ready to resist any temptation to use drugs. Take good care of this man so that he may help others. We need him. Amen."

I raised my head, open my eyes, and gazed at the medallion one last time. I rubbed it and hoped I was putting more power into the medallion, not taking some away.

I handed it back to him and said, "Doc, thanks for coming to the ICU when I was all busted up in the hospital. And thanks for getting me started. You have no idea how low my opinion of you was when we first met. To me, you were a mama's boy with hang-ups that would have stumped Sigmund Freud on his best day. Boy, was I wrong, and it ended up being me with the hang-ups about my mother from my childhood. I'm glad you focused on my addiction as the main problem. My deep-seated neuroses can stay buried for a little while longer, wouldn't you agree?"

Doctor Stone seemed to have a different smile for every type of remark or question. This time, he looked like a proud new father.

"Buddy, I like you. A lot. Something about you reminds me of myself when I was your age. I used to use big words just like you do, when I was a teenager. Mentioning that you have neuroses and hang-ups as a way to impress me is narcissistic, but in a good way. I used to read the dictionary and look up words that sounded sophisticated enough to get attention from adults. I made up sentences that I could interject into a daily conversation. My teachers thought it was a demonstration of my intellect. My friends laughed and called me a brown-noser and a suck-up. They were right, but the day came when those words paid off and helped me to advance myself professionally . . . and personally, too: some of the girls I dated were turned on by it."

The doc was full of surprises here. I had no idea he was going to tell me so much about himself. Now I didn't feel so bad about learning seldom-used vocabulary words, even if I only did so for my entertainment.

"About your so-called neuroses," Dr. Stone continued. "Those can stay buried for now. I am more interested in what moves you forward and what holds you back. We all have beliefs that accelerate and propel and others that jam on the brakes and stall the engine. When you learn about the ones that derail your caboose, you can deprogram them, because they don't serve you anymore. You can also amp up the ones that clear the way for change, growth, happiness, friendship, and love. You've got them all, just like the rest of us. Good recovery helps you to sort through the pile and delete the crap and polish the silver. Stay with me and I'll show you how. My pile of crap was big enough to become a landfill. I swear it's got its own zip code."

We both laughed as he took a drink of water from a tall clear plastic cup with a large B on the side. He must be a Red Sox fan. The desk held other odds and ends that caught my attention, including a large ammonite fossil next to his computer monitor. It was a perfect specimen of sea life that became mineralized eons ago and now held a collection of fossilized sharks' teeth, like a candy dish. Sitting on the edge of the shell perched a small, luminescent green frog. I couldn't resist picking up the frog and squeezing it, pulling its soft, rubbery legs and stretching them.

I was curious about the meaning behind the different collections, so I simply asked.

"Those are gifts from patients, my staff, and my gorgeous wife. Many of my patients love to hold the frog and pull on the legs, just as you're doing. It helps them stay focused while they're talking about their problems; the pulling is a way to act out their aggressions, frustrations, and inner tensions. I think the frog likes it. See that green turtle figurine? A patient brought it just to keep the frog company. As for the shark teeth: I am a collector and find it very relaxing to walk the beaches and pick them up. They're mostly the teeth from lemon and mako sharks."

I pointed to a framed photo on the bookcase. "Doc, I can see your wedding photo over there and I agree your wife is an absolutely beautiful woman. You're very lucky. I bet the statue of the man and woman hugging each other is from your wife."

He picked it up and cradled it fondly.

"It was an anniversary gift from her. The statue is powerful, because it's so generic. The subjects have no faces, yet you can tell that they are in love, adoring each other with affection, trust, and vulnerability. Being vulnerable means being free to share and express feelings, knowing they will be accepted and respected by the one you love. The statue also depicts the couple as partners with equality. Neither member is dominant nor inferior. They are obviously empowered while together, being stronger in union than the sum of their individuality. That's exactly how my wife and I have built our relationship."

It sounded to me like Dr. Stone was a happily married man. I was certain that both he and his wife worked on the relationship until they got it just the way they wanted.

"My wife is a brilliant woman with many talents and desirable traits that make her that much more attractive. I may be smart from a bit of book learning, but the success of our coupleship and my serenity and wisdom, come from mastering the art of happiness through the practice of gratitude and acceptance. Together we can have, be, and do anything we want and make it fun and interesting at the same time."

I was riveted by what he was telling me. He was there. He'd arrived at a place few even dream of. Yet, the doc had it and lived it. It was genuine. He was not acting. He was the real deal.

"Buddy, see that figurine over there, the swans?"

The doctor picked up the ceramic swans; I remembered swans mate for life. The pair faced each other, their necks curved gracefully to form the shape of a heart. Their bills touched in a tender kiss. Peeking out from beneath their bodies was a baby swan.

Doc said, "For me, the swans symbolize an endless romance for eternity. A good marriage is supposed to grow stronger over time, no matter what. Adversity can only bring a devoted couple closer. It could not possibly weaken them, because life's problems are only opportunities to demonstrate love. There is no alternative. Love is the way".

The doctor looked at his watch and clapped his hands.

"Our time has just blown by like a windy day. We have to break this up, my friend. I want to see you at group therapy tonight and every week. The whole gang is in recovery from opioids and most of them are in their twenties. You'll feel right at home. They're nice people. Joe will be there, too. I'll explain more about the meeting when you arrive. It's from six to seven-thirty."

I assured him I'd be there.

"And one more thing. You have to pee in a cup before you go today. I am screening for twelve drugs. If you can wait a few minutes, I'll check the results and give you the news. And Buddy, stick with Joe: he has a lot of recovery smarts. Remember, if you want quality sobriety you can create it in just ninety days by going to a meeting on each one."

As we left his office together, Dr. Stone squeezed the back of my neck like a coach who was putting me in the game, believing that I could deliver the winning touchdown. If he had this much faith in me, I knew all I had to do was have faith in myself, too. Silently, I thanked Higher Power again for bringing Dr. Stone into my life.

CHAPTER 50

Drug Testing

After I gave a specimen for my drug test, Dr. Stone called me back into his office to share the results. The cup had a temperature strip mounted on the side wall. Once the urine made contact with the strip, a green dot appeared next to the temperature, which would range from ninety-five to ninety-nine degrees Fahrenheit.

Dr. Stone explained the procedure to me. "I test for twelve drugs with this dip card." He held the card out for me to examine. It was made of plastic and had six prongs protruding from the bottom of the card. "These prongs are submerged into the urine, which is drawn up into the chambers just like any fluid traveling through a wick. Any drugs in the urine will react with the enzymes on the card and pink lines appear. You need two lines in each chamber to pass."

"What happens if you don't pass?"

"Then only one line appears and that's the moment of truth. When I show addicts the card with only one line, first I get some strange looks, then I either hear, 'you got me' or 'this test is wrong, I didn't do drugs.' Some get pretty irate and insist I run the test again."

"Is this test always right?"

"Nope. I admit there was one time when it was proven wrong by a test run at the lab. Usually, though, I nearly always get a delayed admission of guilt and then a face covered in shame." Dr. Stone brought out a tubular plastic container and removed a strip with several tiny squares. It was a quarter-inch wide and four inches long. He dipped it into the urine for about ten seconds. "This is the strip I use to catch the cheaters. I check for nitrites, pH, creatinine, and specific gravity."

"What for? To make sure it's really urine?"

"Right. For some kids, it's extremely important to stay in my program; usually it's to please their parents so they can keep a bedroom, the car, and spending money. The only problem is they want all of those and some Oxys, too. Beating the urine screen is therefore a requirement for them.

"I've been fooled before. When I was just beginning to test my patients, I had a few things to learn about being tricked. I had no idea there were so many ways to beat the test. There's a very lucrative market in helping drug addicts pass the test. The products are sold on the Internet and in head shops.

"The first time someone cheated on my office test, I had no idea that synthetic urine existed or that you could buy a heating agent to warm it up to body temperature. You can see there's a temperature gauge attached to the cup; when the urine is too hot or too cold, I detect it and confront the patient about it. One time, a kid with synthetic urine passed the test, but when I called his mom to tell her the good news, she was astounded, because he was reeking of pot the day before. The kid confessed to me the next day and explained how he bought a synthetic kit and tried to fool me. I got a lot smarter after that."

I had no idea that addicts went to so much trouble to pass a test. It made sense, though, because urine tests are now pretty standard for pre-employment.

"When I test in the office," Dr. Stone continued, "I want to catch those who bring in adulterants. Those chemicals change the urine so that the drugs are not detectable. I learned that people who try to beat the test will use liquid drain cleaner, vinegar, bleach, and chemicals you've probably never heard of. The other group of adulterants is for sale on the Internet.

"I am always amused when my patients go to great lengths to pass the test and make ridiculous mistakes. One girl handed me a cold sample. I dipped my finger in the urine and asked her to do the same. I know that sounds gross, but it's sterile and harmless. Anyway, she said, 'It feels warm to me.' I couldn't help laughing, and I said, 'If this is your urine, we should be attending your autopsy, because you should be dead.' She started to cry and told me that she peed in a cup right before she snorted a few Oxys; she wanted to bring in clean urine for the test. She kept it refrigerated for days so it wouldn't spoil. She simply didn't know that chilled urine would be a tip-off that she was cheating."

I thought that was a perfect example of how desperate we addicts are to keep one foot on the side of recovery and the other dabbling with the drugs that got us there in the first place. That's insanity . . . and I was proud of myself for recognizing it as such.

Dr. Stone was obviously having some fun exposing the foolhardy ways of his patients. He got a bit more excited as he continued, "And there have been more than a few other times when my patients have brought in zip-lock bags or condoms filled with someone else's urine. They spend extra time in the bathroom pouring it into the specimen cup and running it under hot tap water until they think it's the right temperature. It's usually too hot, above a hundred degrees. But even then, when I test it and it comes out positive for Oxy or pot, you should see the shocked look on their faces. 'That's not possible!' they exclaim. 'That was my friend's urine and he's clean.' What I've learned is that practically any friend of an addict is an addict and chances are they are dirty, too. God bless them."

Dr. Stone was on a roll now. He told me about addicts who were willing to pay people to give them a sample of urine if they thought they could get away with it and how drinking too much extra water to dilute the urine has sent people to the hospital.

"Did you know that when you dilute your blood like that, your sodium level can be low enough to cause delirium and require urgent medical attention? Your brain doesn't function very well without enough sodium." Dr. Stone looked at me thoughtfully. I was pretty sure he was giving me a warning.

"Who knew drinking too much water could become a medical emergency. And we crazy drug addicts are willing to jeopardize our lives just to pass a test so we can stay out there and keep using pills," I replied, shaking my head.

Dr. Stone was finally ready to go over my own test with me. "So here we are with your test. Everywhere you see two pink lines, you passed. Your urine pH is in proper range, the creatinine is in range, and no oxidants are detectable."

He handed me the dip card. It was about an inch and a half wide and three inches long. I saw all the abbreviations for the drugs tested and two pink lines in each chamber. It was indeed a proud moment.

Dr. Stone pointed his pen at each chamber as he read the headings. "MTD is methadone; OPI is opiates, like heroin, codeine, and morphine; AMP is amphetamines, like Adderal; OXY is Oxycodone; BZO is benzodiazepines, like Xanax, Ativan, and Klonopin; BAR is barbiturates, like Phenobarbital; COC is cocaine; MDMA is ecstasy; PPX is propoxyphene, also known as Darvon; MAMP is methamphetamine; and THC is marijuana."

"How'd I do?" I already knew, but I wanted to hear him say it.

"You're clean, Kid. Good job. Do you want to keep the dip card and bring it home to show your parents?"

"Sure. This is my first one. I want them to see it." I replied. "It's kind of like seeing an A on a report card to prove that you're really that smart."

"You should be proud of yourself. Make sure to sign and date the form indicating you passed."

We walked down the hallway to the front office. Dr. Stone stood behind a woman who was seated at the reception window. She hadn't been there when I arrived. He gently touched her shoulder and her smile widened.

"Buddy, this is my wife. She not only makes all of this possible for my patients, she makes me possible."

They exchanged glances and she maintained her professional etiquette with modesty. I could see that she was at least a few years younger than Dr. Stone and quite attractive. She immediately put me at ease with an expression of kindness and compassion.

"Hello, Buddy," she greeted me warmly. "It's nice to meet you. I hope you do well in recovery. You have the best doctor around. I should know, I made him that way," she chuckled and Dr. Stone joined in.

"I'm only kidding," she continued. "He's really pretty fantastic. Ask any of his patients. They brag about him more than I do. If you come to group tonight, you'll see what I mean."

Mrs. Stone explained the treatment contract and other necessities, such as billing and scheduling follow-up appointments. She really made me feel special, almost exceptional. I understood why Dr. Stone kept so many reminders of her on his desk. He acted as if she was the fuel that ignited his spirit and made his life worth living. What a gift.

As I took care of the paper work and the bill, she said goodbye to both Joe and me. Dr. Stone gave Joe another hug and they exchanged a smile and a handshake. Those two men looked to be carefree and genuinely happy. I wanted to learn their secret. Maybe I'd begin to learn that night at group.

We exchanged goodbyes, and Joe and I returned to his car. I clutched my key tag with pride and gratitude. "Way to go, Buddy," Joe teased. "How'd the doc like your key tag? Did he juice it up for you?"

"Not only that," I remarked, "He showed me his twenty-three year medallion."

"Now, that's one you want to touch."

"I did. I even said a little prayer and it felt good."

"Way to go. We do some weird stuff, but I swear it pays off."

I realized how infectious Joe's positive attitude was. I wanted to talk this over with him while we drove.

"I have to admit, this is the most I have laughed and smiled since the first grade." I glanced at Joe to gauge his reaction; he had a prideful, brotherly look on his face.

"Joe, I can't thank you enough for showing me just how much fun life can be, even when there are things about it that aren't fun at all. When I saw you and Doc in there kidding around, I realized I didn't think that was possible for me. I've never kidded around with anybody. But here we are, having a good time just talking about ordinary stuff. I'm so relaxed. I don't have a care in the world. I don't know why I ever did. Whatever you're doing, please keep it up."

Joe smiled. "Buddy, I'll bet right now you feel cleaner on the inside than ever before. You may still be holding on to a lot of shame, but we'll take care of that after steps five, six, and seven. Someday, your soul will stand up for inspection and you will feel worthy and proud to show it off."

I sat back in my seat and let my mind imagine all that he was saying as an actual reality: me being clean, proud, and shameless before the entire world.

"Your past doesn't have to haunt you, anymore," Joe continued. "I like to think of those unpleasant memories as nothing more than 'used to be's.' From now on, we're going after the 'wanna be's.' When a great chef is about to create a masterpiece dish, he is not the least bit concerned about the cake he put in the garbage because it wouldn't rise. The muffed-up cake has no bearing on what he puts in the oven later. That's exactly how being in the *now* works. Take us, for example. We're having a great time. Nothing else matters. When you feel this good, it's easy to focus on the next right thing to do. All of your energy goes into creating what you really want."

Joe was pretty wise. I wished I could drive around with him all day long and keep talking. It was like having a constant hunger for my favorite food and being able to get as much as I wanted to eat and never filling up. Was that possible in recovery? Could anyone ever get enough of the Twelve Steps? I wanted to remember everything he said, word for word.

He continued, "I like to use a big word now and then, too. This time, it's 'manifestation.' That word means the outward, visible expression of something. That's what you get when something comes into your life that wasn't there before. A few minutes ago we were laughing and now we're talking like scholars. Life keeps moving along like that. Every choice I make brings me an outcome. I've learned that it helps to get used to the results, one after another. If I complain about what I end up with, life keeps going anyway. It doesn't stop because I disapprove. Life is continuously creating something. And it can continuously create more for me to complain about if I'm not too careful. Do you see where this is going?"

"I'm glad you put it that way," I answered. "It's just so easy to see everything as right or wrong, good or bad. I'm going to try a little 'thank you very much,' 'cause what you get is what you got."

Joe rapped the steering wheel. "Yes! Acceptance, that's what I'm talking about. It's like playing by a new set of rules. In recovery, we can do practically anything once we accept what we can't do anything about."

"Serenity Prayer 101."

"Right on, Bro. Hey, we're at your place." Joe turned his car into the drive. "I'll come by to get you tonight for the meeting. Be ready at five-thirty again. You're a great kid. I think we make a terrific team. One day at a time."

He leaned over to give me a hug and a handshake. His smile was filled with love.

As Joe drove away with a wave, I thought about how he was just an average young man who sold his life for dope until sobriety saved him from himself. Now he was my friend and his brand of manly love was free for the taking. He probably didn't expect anything in return. Giving unselfishly was reward enough for him. I could see where it was a kind of fuel for his spirit that drove him forward from one moment to the next. I imagined his Higher Power was also on duty, helping out and never being taken for granted. I was slowly getting used to my Higher Power and from now on, we could talk about all the miracles we experienced in recovery; I expected there would be bunches of them.

CHAPTER 51

Finding Myself

I opened the front door and the aroma of hickory-smoked bacon surrounded me. Mom was in the kitchen preparing lunch. Her voice sang out, filled with love that picked up right where I left off with Joe.

"Honey, I'm in the kitchen making sandwiches. Come on in and tell me all about your visit with Dr. Stone."

Before I could even round the corner and take a strip of bacon off the platter, Mom launched the barrage. "How did it go? Were you nervous? Did he ask any questions about me or your father? Did you show him your key tag? Did he like it? Did you get drug tested? Did you pay the bill? Oh, please tell me you paid the bill."

She was obviously excited and her mouth was in overdrive. I had to wave a hand in front of her face before she stopped with the questions.

"Mom, I took care of the bill. Give me a chance and I'll fill you in on everything."

She added the last of the cooked bacon to the pile and started toasting bread for BLTs.

"Everything went great with the doc. We mostly talked about addiction. He's a dedicated man and he takes sobriety very seriously. He's got twenty-three years of his own."

"I didn't know he had that kind of experience," Mom replied.

"It's the good kind. He's easy to talk to and doesn't treat me like a patient. When I'm with him, I feel hopeful and I really want to do what's best for me."

"And we want that, too. That's why we sent you there."

"Well, I'm going because I want to from now on. Staying sober is a big deal. It's more than being drug-free. It's the key to taking advantage of what life offers. It's like walking through the door of opportunity. Being sober gives me a chance to take that first step once it opens."

"Mark my words, opportunity will keep knocking until you answer."

It amazed me that I could stand her corny remarks. Doc should have been here to see me in action. Acceptance and gratitude, I was working it.

My mom called Dad and Junior to the kitchen for lunch and, as they piled their plates high, Mom announced, "Everybody . . . Buddy saw Dr. Stone today. And I'm sure he can't wait to tell us about his drug test."

"I passed. I mean, my drug test was clean, nothing habit-forming in my system . . . and I intend to keep it that way. I'm proud of that, and so is Dr. Stone."

By the time I'd finished the sentence, Mom was totally focused on her BLT. My test results didn't impress anybody, so I decided to keep the drug-test dip card in my pocket. Dad and Junior were busy chewing and wiping escaped bits of mayonnaise from their faces.

I muttered sarcastically under my breath, "Earth People." The doc was right, they were different. I must not condemn the totally clueless. Loving them wasn't going to be as easy as loving Joe and Doc, but it could be done and sobriety would show me how.

Mom finally noticed the sandwich I'd constructed, even though she hadn't paid any attention to what I had just said about the drug testing.

"Why do you make your sandwich so big that you have to squish it to fit it in your mouth? Couldn't you just make two, instead of trying to pile it all into one? And did I hear you say you passed your drug test? That's nice. Keep it up. I know you can do it."

Judging from Mom's tone, I didn't think she really expected me to respond. She was just letting me know that she was receiving my broadcast but not necessarily watching the program.

My brother finished his sandwich first. His cheeks were shiny with grease from bacon fat. A few flakes of potato chip blew out of his mouth with his first question.

"Did you have to study really hard for your drug test?" He was deadly serious. "I learned in school to just say no. Drugs are for losers. Didn't you know that?"

Out of the mouths of children, I thought, *comes the wisdom I need to hear.* Or was I hearing another message from Higher Power? I wasn't sure if Junior was going to sit there long enough for me to answer. But I tried.

"The drug test I took and passed was a urine drug test. I had to pee in a cup and my doctor checked it to make sure that I didn't have any drugs in my system. This is not about school or classes. It's not a written test."

My brother fidgeted in his chair. "You had to put your wiener in a cup and pee? That's it. I'm done here. I'm never doing drugs and giving anybody my pee. No way, no how. Later, guys."

"What are you going to do for the rest of the day?" Mom asked, her eyes following Junior as he hurried out the door. "I hope you don't stay in your room. What a shame to waste such a beautiful day locked up there alone."

I'd been hearing that remark ever since I refused to put on a soccer uniform as a child. My room had been a sanctuary from Earth People. With a computer or books, I was connected with the outside world without having to be there in person. It was safe and convenient. I could come and go as I pleased on any Internet website. In the real world, I wasn't welcome anywhere. But my computer simply followed my commands, it was my servant, and I was its master. On the computer, I was never made fun of. Likewise, a book was never offended because it was being read by me, an ugly person. Going to my room was never a waste of time. And from now on, a beautiful day was something I was going to create inside my mind. It's not a weather report.

"Mom, you need to understand that I am learning pretty quickly about what's best for me. Granted, I jumped into the deep end with the drugs, but that's over and I have a good idea what to do with my life for today. I may not know about where I'm going tomorrow, but I can figure it out. What makes a day beautiful for you and most other people is a lot different than what makes my day beautiful."

She looked at me with pleading eyes. I could tell by her furrowed brow that she hoped I would change my mind and do it her way. I continued my explanation.

"When I go up to my room, I'm not alone. I am becoming my best friend. And besides, I'm never without my Higher Power. Together, we make a beautiful day, no matter where I go. So I'm always in good company and being up there is time well-spent."

I kissed her and gave her a different type of hug than ever before. I needed her to understand that I was no longer the insecure boy who was hiding from the judgmental, prying eyes of scornful peers. I had come face to face with my most formidable foe—addiction—whose sole purpose was to rule my mind, body, and soul. I couldn't beat it at its own game. But, I'd learned, if I didn't play the game, I couldn't lose. I wanted my mom to see my emerging strength of character. I needed her to know that I was taking charge of my own life and she should detach a little more. I was ready to fly. My injuries were mending rapidly and my Higher Power was directing the spiritual repair work at the same time. It didn't matter what reflection I saw in the mirror; it was not the real me. I was now capable of feeling a new kind of love that was simple, clean, and wholesome. Some people call it unconditional. I call it perfect.

With a smile and another kiss, I left the kitchen and headed back up to my room. Mom would figure this out, and when she did, the new me would be ready.

Upstairs in my room, Einstein was looking at me differently. He seemed to be daring me to throw a pie in his face, or do something else fun and outlandish.

I picked up the phone and dialed the hospital. A nurse whose voice I didn't recognize answered the phone.

"Hi, this is a former patient. I was just discharged. I'm the guy who was in a coma with a broken leg, broken back, broken ribs, chest tube, ruptured spleen . . ."

"Sure, I remember you. Buddy, right? We never met, but I heard some stories. What can I do for you? Did you want to speak to someone?"

"As a matter of fact, I do. Is there any chance my nurse is working today? I wanted to say hi and tell her how I was doing."

"Which one?"

I was tempted to say the one who could bend steel with her bare hands and toss bad guys like frisbees. "Her name's Brenda. Is she there?"

"No, she has the day off. I heard you became her pet project. There's always somebody here who she gets attached to."

"Do you have her number? I'd like to give her a call."

"I don't see any reason why not. She told us that if patients call, we can give it out. You were the one who took an overdose and drove your car into a truck, right? She'll definitely want to hear from you. You're still her favorite topic. Here's the number. . . ."

It was nice to know my guardian still had me on her A list. I dialed her number and smiled as I heard a voice like a waitress taking an order at a truck-stop diner.

"Whaddya want?"

"Hi, Brenda, it's me, Buddy."

"Hey, Sport, how you been? Funny, I was just thinking of you. You miss me smacking you around, don't you? I bet your mommy's turning you into marshmallow fluff. I better get over there and put a stop to it."

Rude, crude, and offensive, Brenda was just the way I liked her. That kind of rush felt better than snorting an 80 of Oxy. She was not Earth People. She was boundless and natural, with no impurities. She was good for me, bad for my addiction. Just the way I liked it.

"I'm really doing great," I said. "I've been to my first NA meeting, met a bunch of neat people there, picked up a white key tag, hung out with Joe and his sister, and went to Dr. Stone's office this morning. But life isn't the same without you."

"Say, you want to do something today?" Brenda offered. "Give me your address. I'll come over, say 'hi' to your folks, and we'll talk. Get them prepared so they don't get the wrong idea about me. I'm no kinky cradle robber. I wouldn't hesitate to bash your head in if you stepped out of line."

I had never thought about her sexually. Yet she was warning me as though I had. Sometimes, it was hard to tell if she was kidding around. No matter, since my interest in her didn't go beyond watching her do chin-ups at the gym.

My thoughts caused me to pause too long and Brenda grew impatient as she waited. "I don't have all day here. What's the address?"

I recited it and then said goodbye. In an hour, she'd be badgering and hassling me face-to-face. I couldn't wait.

I enjoyed Brenda's jabbing sarcasm. Somehow it filled me with feel-good chemicals. She might frighten all the other boys, but to me she felt as good as a leather slipper for a puppy to chew on. It wasn't romance or a physical attraction, it was better.

Brenda would probably be a good mentor and coach when it came time to prepare for the real thing—dates with girls my age and managing broken hearts. She may not look like the romantic type, but I bet she'd been around the softer side of the birds and the bees and could help me understand girls when the time came.

The morning's activities had taken a toll on my energy level, so I sprawled across my bed and closed my eyes. As I was about to fall asleep, I heard Higher Power's voice, loud and clear. Every time He dropped in, I realized that He was never gone, even when I thought He was. He was always watching, listening, and scheming. He knew what was on my mind—and that included Brenda.

"You're trying to sort out every teenager's biggest stumbling block. I've already done it for you. Love comes in all shapes and sizes. But you've already come to the correct conclusion that this nurse is not a dating match for you. So let's move on to what you are ready for. This woman isn't in love with you, but she *loves* you in a very healthy way. She is offering you her gift of inner beauty, something you are beginning to see and appreciate. I want you to accept it graciously. It's powerful enough to scrub the barnacles of self-loathing, embarrassment, and shame completely off your soul."

"Did you introduce Brenda into my life for the specific purpose of assisting in my recovery?"

"As a matter of fact, I did. And if I do say so myself, she's just what you need. She's one of my Earth Angels. I like 'em rough and ready to rumble. There's no mistaking her brand of love. I let her scare the crap out of you in the hospital, just to get your attention. Now she's ready to help you cultivate your own inner beauty. Imagine that, the two of you creating love out of hate. What an ironic twist of fate. Don't worry I'm not going to generate any sexual tension here, only polishing my sense of humor."

I had to hand it to my Higher Power. He may have arranged for that crash to yank my chain hard enough to jangle a few neurons loose in my brain, but the wake-up call was worth it. He was the Book of Love. And He was setting me up for success.

"Okay. I think I get it," I said. "Love is an essential ingredient for recovery. I suppose addiction hates Love and the more I've got, the better the protection plan."

"Actually, the saying is, 'The more love you create and give away, the more you get in return.' And yes, that's the best way to keep addiction off your doorstep. Crank up the love machine and watch the little devil squirm like a worm on a hot sidewalk."

This kind of teaching was a whole lot better than all of His snide remarks. Maybe He was finally getting a handle on what worked for me.

"Love is the strongest force in the Universe," Higher Power continued. "There is no match for it. You cannot act out with any form of addiction when your love is at full strength. Imagine trying to snort a pill when you have loving thoughts about yourself: Impossible. For that matter, you can't overeat, smoke, drink to excess, gamble, or engage in pornography when you care about what enters and leaves your body and mind."

Why couldn't something this simple be applied to everyone's problems?

"There's more," He said. "If you want to live in the present moment, then become aware of your existence."

"I don't know how to do that and you know it. Stop showing off and teach me something easier to grasp."

"Okay, have it your way. Do you know what mortality is?"

"Of course, I do. You're born, you live, you die."

"No, no, no. Is that all there is to life for you humans?"

He was picking on me again. I wanted to get Brenda to meet Higher Power and rough Him up for being a wise-ass.

"The essence of your existence is consciousness, knowing, and all possibility. When you are aware of living in the Now, you will become calm, serene, tranquil, and silent; no thoughts, no feelings. Just perfection."

"All right. This is starting to hurt my head. I don't think I can grasp all of this at once. Can we give it a rest for now?"

"I'm almost done," He said. "One of these days, I'll teach you how to disengage from the incessant and compulsive noise in your head and sink into the stillness."

I wanted to know and yet I didn't want to know. My life had become complicated enough; I wanted something simpler, more practical.

"When you give the present moment your fullest attention, no thought is required," Higher Power explained patiently. "When you are free from thought, even for a second or two, you are in the blissful silence. Everything that ever was or ever will be originates in silence. It sort of waits there until it's time to come forth. So when you go into a state of thoughtless silence, you're there where it all began. I get chills just thinking about it."

"I think it's break time for me," I said.

"You're not getting it, are you?"

"Does that mean you're breaking communication for a while?" *That would be just fine with me.*

"Silence is my bliss. It's time for you to try it. We don't need to talk, but you need to feel that I am present. When you do, my message will come right through. By the way, I am always monitoring your every move, which happens to be my every move. So you see, you are the same as me, only a much smaller version. But when you work with me, it's like getting the whole enchilada. And be nice to that nurse—she can tear a phone book in half with her teeth. Later, Buddy."

He was gone, but not gone. I was alone, but not alone. How was I supposed to get used to that? It was as though I had no privacy. Then again, nothing was possible without Him. So He was in on everything in the Universe.

For most of my life, I worried needlessly with my meager human thoughts. At times I was in a constant state of fear. My mind was like the surface of the ocean, with waves of terror, panic, and dread all chaotically producing only one thing: my tormented suffering. For years, I felt anxiety and humiliation just because my face was decorated with pimples. I created a slew of different labels for myself and ended up feeling worse.

Then Higher Power showed up and handed me a new script, telling me that I was part of one . . . big . . . everything. He called it consciousness. It's unimaginable and yet it's supposed to exist. I'm supposed to be able to tap into it and get it to make great things happen that are good for me. He told me that consciousness is silent, without any thought and if I could just be quiet long enough I could be part of it. And when I'm part of it—in silence—that's where I find peace and bliss and I wonder what else.

He said I should give the present moment my full attention, without thought. If that was the case then I could not use my own thoughts to understand it. Once I decided to think about it, I could not get any closer to it. It was like rowing harder on the surface of the ocean in a vain attempt to plunge into its depths where the silence existed. Instead, I must become quiet and thoughtless. If I attempted to connect with consciousness through more thought, I would never be able to experience any revelation.

Yet, I didn't know if I could do it.

CHAPTER 52

Recovery Angel

The ringing doorbell startled me. I had spent the past hour with Higher Power and hadn't prepared my parents to meet Brenda. I moved as fast as I could, but Junior charged the door yelling, "I'll get it!"

I heard the door open, then Junior shouting, "Yikes! It's a big woman with snakes on her arms. Do you want me to let her in?"

Mom and I reached the entryway at almost the same moment. Just inside the door, Brenda was flexing for Junior, making the tattooed snakes writhe as he stroked them playfully. She stopped when she saw me.

Mom looked at the scene in astonishment and commented, "This is an unexpected surprise."

Brenda stood up straight and towered over my mother. In a matter of seconds, I was engulfed in one of her monster hugs. My crutches fell to the floor as Brenda smothered me with affection. I was dazed by the force of Brenda's hug, but I could also feel the kind of Love that Higher Power mentioned.

She noticed the look on my mother's face and said, "He was supposed to tell you I was coming." Then she looked at me sternly and started to reprimand me: "Buddy, I told you . . ."

My mother quickly regained her composure. "That's okay. It's nice of you to come and visit Buddy. You took such good care of him while he was in the hospital. We can't thank you enough."

A warm feeling flooded through me as I thought about Brenda as my Earth Angel . . . actually, she was more like my Recovery Angel. As she turned away from me, I noticed the T-shirt she was wearing. Printed on the back was a saying that was just a perfect description of her: *Hard on the Outside, Soft on the Inside.*

Brenda saw me reading the T-shirt. "I found this shortly after you left the hospital. It reminded me of how things have changed for us. In the beginning, let's face it I didn't like you one bit. I told you that I hated teenage drug addicts. I never give them a break. They don't deserve it. But there was something about you that changed my mind. I had a feeling you would latch on to recovery if you met someone who made it. Joe helped and you did the rest. I'm very happy for you."

As she turned to show my mom the back of the T-shirt, I saw what was written on the front. It was even better. It said. *If You Want What I've Got, You'll Do What I Did . . . Pump Iron.* That shirt was totally Brenda.

Mom invited Brenda into the living room where my father sat on the couch watching television. He grumbled a quick hello and I could tell by the look on his face that he was in awe of her bodybuilder's physique. He respectfully moved over to make room on the couch.

"You look a lot more muscular without that nursing uniform. Is working out all you have time for when you're not at the hospital?" At least Dad was trying to be polite.

Junior jumped up next to Brenda. "Are you a man in a lady's body or a lady in a man's body?" He watched Brenda expectantly for the answer to his logical question. Mom and Dad both opened their mouths to say something.

"That's okay. Don't get upset," Brenda stopped them. "I'm asked that question all the time at the gym. The men want to know what drugs I'm taking because they're jealous. The women want to avoid the drugs I'm taking because they think they'll turn into men."

My parents looked at her and waited for her answer.

"I am more woman that any man can handle. I can out-work, out-exercise, out-muscle, and out-think any man I have ever met. So I guess I am the best of both. As far as drugs go, I am all natural. I love the sound of that word. There are no chemicals in me that don't belong there. The reason I'm so big must be genetic. Somewhere in my bloodline there was probably an Amazon woman who could plow a field, plant crops, haul water, chop timber, and cook a killer meal without breaking a sweat. I guess her genes got passed on to me."

Brenda could tell my parents were relieved by her answer, and she changed the subject. "I came to hang out with Buddy. He called me today to say 'hi' and tell me how he was doing. I'd like to see him do well, so I accepted the invitation to come and see you both again and take Buddy out, if you don't mind."

"Just exactly what did you have in mind?" I understood Mom's concern since she knew almost nothing about Brenda.

I suggested that Brenda and I would just go for an ice cream and Mom pondered that. I think she realized this nurse wasn't going to take advantage of her son or introduce him to any bad habits, except perhaps for protein power shakes and barbells.

"Okay, but be back in time for your NA meeting." She headed to the kitchen to retrieve her purse and give me some money.

Brenda followed her, saying, "I got this taken care of. It's my treat." They disappeared for a few minutes and I heard them chattering away. I was happy they were trying to get to know each other. When they returned from the kitchen, Mom walked us to the door and gave me a goodbye hug and kiss on the cheek.

"Be good now," she said. "This nice nurse is doing you a favor coming all the way over here to take you out." She sounded like I was going out with my aunt who was visiting from out-of-state and taking me to the mall for a toy. I just sighed.

Brenda walked ahead of me toward her truck and had the door open for me by the time I got there. The cab of her truck was high off the ground. She carefully lifted me in, then tossed the crutches in the back seat and got behind the wheel. We looked at each other and simultaneously gestured with a fist bump. "Here's to a great ride."

As the truck rolled away, Brenda offered, "This baby is all the man I need right now. It's a Ram Hemi. It rides high, monster big, and loaded with enough power to blow the doors off anything with doors. I usually travel solo, but today you get to ride shotgun. Just don't touch anything unless you got the spare parts. That is, unless I give you permission."

She gave me a cold, hard look, then punched my arm and laughed.

"Come on, Kid, lighten up, I've already eaten my fill of little boys today. You're safe."

I decided to play along, and I punched her in the upper arm. Her muscle felt like solid steel.

She snickered and said, "Is that the best you got? Come on, lay one on me."

I accepted the invitation to hit her as hard as I could. This time the sound was deeper and richer.

She said, "Okay, Bruiser, one more. See if you can ring the bell. Up to now, your sledgehammer is somewhere between wimpy and weakling."

On the final punch, I gritted my teeth and closed my eyes on impact, imagining that her arm was the incarnation of addiction. If I'd been giving a karate demonstration, I believe I would have broken a two-by-four in half. She shrugged her shoulder and rubbed the spot with her hand.

"Now that's what I'm talkin' about. You are a sissy boy no more."

That was her kind of love, each punch made me stronger. Perhaps it was her way to get me toughened up for the difficult road of recovery that lay ahead.

I imagined that as my Earth Angel, Brenda was my protector, trainer, and mentor. She had been sent to make me stronger from within. Her power was available to me just for the asking. I also realized that we were connected by something we had in common. Although I couldn't give it a name, it was all we needed for our brand of love, a love that could probably heal all my wounds and make it possible for me to love others as easily as myself. I could sense it was going to be at the core of my greater purpose in life. Why else would I be thinking about it so much?

When I came back from my thoughts, the most beautiful and melodic music I had ever heard was playing. Brenda was paying attention to the road and the music, but it seemed she had forgotten me. We had drifted off on different tangents. I'd been down some philosophical trail about the meaning and value of love, and she'd become lost in the hypnotic music. I was surprised. With all of her brawn, bulk, and bravado, I would have expected the music to be something metallic with loud, screeching lyrics about pain, suffering, and injustice. But what I heard was heaven-sent. It was sweet and enticing, like the voice of a mythical siren that lured sailors into an irresistible and sensual madness.

I was really blown away, because Brenda was listening to operatic music. To my untrained ear, it sounded like a young woman singing Italian.

"She sounds beautiful. What is it?" I asked.

The look on Brenda's face defied description. It was obvious that opera had cast a spell on my nurse. She was captivated and charmed into some mystical state, and her features had softened and were pleasing to the eye. How was that possible? Her hard edge was nowhere to be found. I was entranced by the spectacle in front of me and remained silent, thinking that any words would cause it to evaporate.

When the song was over, Brenda paused the CD to explain.

"That was Mimi. Can you tell she was falling in love and dying at that same time? She sang, 'When the thaw of spring comes, the first kiss in April is hers, like rosebuds in a vase, filling her life with a gentle perfume.'"

"I'm hooked by that music. You have to tell me about Mimi."

"I played you an aria from *La Bohème*, one of Puccini's finest operas. I'm not going to give you all the details about how I acquired a taste for this type of music. Let's just say that it soothes the savage beast in me. But don't get the wrong impression. There's plenty of room in my frenzied mind for head-banging rock music. But now and then, something feminine in me gets a craving, and certain operas do the trick. Right now, Puccini gives me the most satisfaction.

"So back to *La Bohème*. Mimi is a seamstress and this story takes place in Paris during the late nineteenth century. She's living in some cold, dingy flat and her candle has gone out. She heads to the next door neighbor's for a match to relight it. Guess what happens next?"

Brenda was my coach for the day and Higher Power told me that lessons would steadily arrive in my life when I least expected them and from messengers of all shapes and sizes. Now it was a body builder, a composer, and the seamstress from Paris.

"Time's up," she said. "Mimi knocks on Rodolfo's door for the match. Actually, his aria comes before hers in the opera. I'm going to play it for you now. Just close your eyes and imagine two young people on Christmas Eve in Paris. Both of them are poor, barely getting by. I'll give you a little lead-in. Rudolfo is a starving poet. He lives with three other equally starving guys who are all trying to scrape by, but now he's alone with Mimi as they meet for the first time. After getting a match, she's on her way out the door and realizes that she has dropped her key to the apartment. They get down on the floor to feel around and search for it. And then it happens. They touch hands. Hers is cold and that is when the aria starts. You'll hear him sing, 'Che gelida manina. Se la lasci riscaldar,' which means, 'how cold your little hand is, will you let me warm it for you?'"

I was sitting in a truck with a muscle-bound giant of a woman who not only knew the storyline of the opera, but her Italian sounded flawless (at least it did to my inexperienced ears). What was such a gift doing in a person who defied all the conventions of femininity? And then it dawned on me that I had my gifts, too. Brenda was pointing at them, inviting me to look and take notice.

Brenda started the music again and I listened as goose bumps raised on my arms. I was dying to know what Rodolfo was saying to Mimi. I closed my eyes and imagined that Brenda was singing to me. Her voice was pure love, only the two of us would never kiss. That was not why she was here. She was awakening my soul to receive the new seeds of my life, the seeds that would grow into a confident manhood with purpose.

I caught Brenda wiping away tears and then heard the slightest sniffle.

"They're in love now," she explained as the aria came to an end. "It's unbreakable."

She pulled into a gas station parking lot and put the gear in park. Then she proceeded to explain the story of *La Bohème,* and it was all palpable: the music, the lyrics, the story about two lovers, and now I wanted to know how it all ended.

"I won't spill all the beans about the story, except to say that Mimi gets a little too flirtatious with another man and splits up with Rodolfo. Because Mimi is sick, you can see where this is going. The ending you must find out for yourself. Buy the music, at least the excerpts that include the ending, and have the libretto there with you to follow along. I can warn you now that you will feel something you never knew existed in any part of your body or mind. It will swallow all of your pain and bring you a peaceful understanding of your inner being. After that, you won't waste any more time on things that are unimportant. The meaning of life and how to take full advantage of it will be readily apparent. One last thing: be prepared to cry like a baby."

Brenda let her last words settle for effect, then she switched CDs, and blazing hot molten metal music began to roar out of the speakers, making the subwoofer grumble and growl like a junkyard dog. She clenched her fists and pumped them, inflating her forearms until they rippled with waves of muscular contractions. She turned her head, swiveling it with dexterity, and shouted, "Now, let's rock!"

CHAPTER 53

Spiritual Ink

I was pleased to know that Brenda was not limited to one musical dimension. She could hold her own with a convoy of truckers as easily as a maestro from the Met. She had a multitude of ways to experience herself and I realized that whether street smart or scholarly, hardcore or PG-rated, evening gown or blue jeans, they were all still Brenda. And I was no exception. I was just beginning to explore my other dimensions and I expected to discover many of them.

"Kid, I have a treat in store for you." Brenda's voice sounded youthfully mischievous.

I looked out the window in front of us. Up ahead was a blue neon sign that read, "Missing Inks."

I started to object, because I knew I'd be in major trouble with my mom if I came home with a tattoo, but Brenda stopped me.

"It's cool, Buddy—your mom and I talked about it and she's okay with you getting a tattoo. Remember when I followed her into the kitchen at your house? I told her I wanted to bring you here to get some special reminder of the new you, and I got her to agree to it. See, here's the permission slip she signed." Brenda waved a piece of paper in front of me and I decided this was one adventure I was ready to have.

The place was a small building, more like a bungalow, painted pitch-black with blood-red trim around the windows. It had a Halloween feel to it. There were three motorcycles parked out front, each one decked out with highly polished chrome and serpents, skulls, and naked women airbrushed onto the gas tanks. She parked the truck and flexed her biceps until they looked like mountains rising out of the ground.

"How would you like to have one of these?" The snake tattoos danced as she pumped more blood through her meaty arms.

Before I could answer, Brenda had my door open and was coaxing me out of the truck. Inside, all the customers were in various states of undress, depending on where they were being tattooed. Each one looked up as we entered the shop and I could imagine their thoughts about how mismatched Brenda and I were as a couple. Brenda's walk became a swagger that telegraphed the message, "Don't mess with me unless you want to be embarrassed in front of your buddies." But then she strutted over and greeted each one with fist bumps and high fives. They laughed together and I felt safe. I wondered if they were in NA, too, but I knew I shouldn't ask.

"Fellas, I want you to meet a good friend of mine—Buddy. He's a bit beat up, but you should see the other guy: he's in a wheelchair. I'm his trainer now and he's a work in progress. A little puny with some bad skin, but he's got potential. I think he'll grow when I finally get him off the crutches and into the gym. Heck, Max over there was a bit scrawny when I met him ten years ago. A few tattoos and a lot of barbecue really filled him out nicely. Are you still weight-training, Max, or are ya goin' soft?"

Max lifted his head off the table as the artist working on him continued the tapestry he was creating on Max's back.

"I took the winter off from heavy training, but I'm hitting it hard again. Give me a month and I'll be so ripped my mama won't recognize me. What did ya bring the kid in here for, a Mickey Mouse tattoo to go with his Goofy face?"

Brenda bristled at that remark. She walked over to the table Max was on, lifted his ankle off the table, and twisted it until its owner loudly objected.

"I don't mind you jerking me around like that, but he's my guest and I would strongly advise you to show him respect. He has friends in low places, if you get my meaning."

She gave his ankle another hard twist that made Max wince and his friends cringe.

"Okay, enough!" Max conceded. "I'm sorry, Kid. I didn't know that special rules applied to you."

She released his ankle and I decided it was time to say something while the balance of power was in my favor.

"Max, you're right. I don't need any special rules. If you want to rank on my face, be my guest. There's nothing you could say that would embarrass or shame me. You might call me ugly, but it's only my opinion that matters. Your words can't hurt. I wouldn't want to walk into your fist, but a stupid mouth like yours can only mean that your mind isn't far behind. I bet you stayed back so many grades in school that a bigger desk had to be ordered."

Max launched his body off the table and cursed.

"Wait a minute. I don't have to take your crap while you hide behind Brenda."

I walked up to him, stood almost nose to nose, parked my hand in his and said, "Now we're even."

I gave him a sinister smile followed by a wink.

He gave me a bone-crushing handshake and laughed like a drunken pirate.

"Kid, you're all right. You got what it takes. If you ever get a bike, we can show you around. If you want a tattoo, you came to the right place. Your lady-friend over there likes the pain. Do you like pain?"

Brenda and I looked at each other. She said, "It's time to step up to the plate and get inked. You're in good hands here. Let's talk over what you want and where you want it."

A few million thoughts zipped through my head, mostly about pain . . . but then I thought, *What pain? Getting a tattoo was nothing compared to wrecking a car in a drugged-up blackout.* I decided to go for it. It was my skin. A little bit of ink would be liberating. Brenda called me over to search the catalog of artwork.

I didn't even have to look; I knew exactly what I wanted. "I want a seagle."

Brenda laughed and commented, "A seagull? That's one dumb bird."

"I'm referring to Jonathan Livingston Seagull, a character in a book. And he isn't dumb."

"I know that book," Brenda answered. "That's the brave bird who leaves the pack, breaks tradition, and soars while his friends and family watch in disbelief."

"Exactly. He realizes his one true purpose, to soar like an eagle while still being a seagull. He's a seagle and I am too. I want one right here." I pointed to the place where my heart beats. "That's the spot."

One of the bikers got up from the chair and studied the new tattoo on his arm. It was a little girl in a bonnet holding a kitten in a basket filled with flowers. The tattoo artist looked it over one last time.

"Say 'hi' to Sissy when you get home. I hope she likes it."

The artist approached me and said, "You're next, kid. What do you have in mind?"

I described what the seagle looked like and he made several sketches until I approved. I removed my shirt and Brenda helped undo the back brace. The artist did a double take.

He asked, "What's that rig for? You got a busted spine, too? What did you guys do, fall down a flight of stairs while you were fightin'?"

"Something like that," I said.

I sat down cautiously in the chair, making sure to keep my back straight. The artist transferred the final sketch onto my chest. He told me to relax, but I gripped the armrest waiting for the buzzing noise to start and the needle to begin piercing.

First he outlined the tattoo in black ink using a single-needle gun. The needle protruded from the barrel a mere 1/16th of an inch and caused a stinging sensation, which I didn't mind. The worst part came when he fit the eight-needle grouping into the gun for colorizing. That was when I started counting the minutes until it was finally over.

Brenda hovered around like a mother hen. She kept tilting her head from side to side, watching the tattoo come to life and admiring it as a work of art.

Finally I heard, "We're done, you can get up now."

She walked me over to the mirror and we both examined it. The seagle was breaking through a cloud; it was from the scene in the book where he was commanding the sky to yield to his strength and ability to swoop, soar, and maneuver like a fighter jet. The horizon was below, with a white-capped ocean of dark blue. The eyes of the seagle captured the liberation and freedom of the bird—and my own.

Brenda patted me on the back and said, "For your first one, that's a killer tattoo. It says it all. Earth People can't fly like eagles. They quack like ducks. The eagle is a majestic bird and you are just as magnificent. More important, nobody has to agree with that except you."

I felt better hearing her confidence in me. The ink was permanent and I wanted the change in me to be the same.

"Recovery means change and that takes guts," Brenda continued. "You need to change everything about yourself that addiction finds appetizing. You want to become so spiritually enlightened that your addiction will go to sleep from sheer boredom. We, however, will find that very exciting and quite pleasing. For us, being spiritual has nothing to do with artistic preferences. You can be just as spiritual listening to the music of 36 Crazy Fists as you can with Verdi's *Don Carlos*. It's not about how you get to the garden, it's all about how you spend your time there."

It was pretty apparent that Brenda was my messenger for today; she was really laying it on thick. It was a good lesson for me.

"Remember, Buddy, growth is meant to be effortless. It's a process that follows the path of least resistance. It cannot be accelerated by force. That also applies to your opportunity to change. Your Higher Power will guide you and assist you through the change and He will provide everything you need and give you the best possible results. You merely have to ask, believe, and trust. Make sure you get out of your own way so you can receive the gift."

Brenda paid for my gift, my new tattoo, and by the time she returned, I had my shirt on.

I insisted on getting into Brenda's truck without any assistance. She obliged and it was worth the effort required to show her I could do it.

She started the truck and ran the air conditioner to cool off the cab, then let the engine idle.

"I have been asking myself today, from the moment that you called me, what exactly is my purpose here? What am I supposed to do with this scrawny kid who managed to score some drugs and cause a load of trouble in a short time? Where do I fit in? I've never felt any calling to help someone like you. I could have just as easily written you off as another creep with a greasy face. In the hospital, I wanted to hurt you, but something stopped me. And I'm glad it did.

"Something inside of me changed and I don't know exactly what or why," Brenda mused. "But I'm stuck with the change and I'm stuck with you. So I suggest that we figure out where we go from here."

I decided to offer my take on it. "Today I learned so much being with you. You taught me about love by showing me how beautiful you are inside. I had no idea how important inner beauty was and now I can see how much stronger I am because of it. You have instilled confidence in me. Thanks to you, I know about beauty through music. I have a tattoo that represents the inspiration to be myself, no matter how I continue to evolve and grow. I have courage now, and a determination to use it wisely. I might not know how to use it yet, but I'd like you to be there when I do."

She blinked back tears as she inspected me from head to toe.

"Buddy, I have developed my muscles and my mind while living on a social fringe with very few others to keep me company. I have become so strong that I can walk comfortably to any destination and I always feel I belong there. I always remain true to my own self. I either deliver a hug or crush a bone. The innocent get protected and the bad guys taste my brand of justice. It's my code and I'll live and die by it."

I could sense that Brenda knew my limitations and she wanted to share the benefit of her experience with me. As my instructor, she wanted to put me on the accelerated training program. I had catching up to do. I couldn't imagine Brenda ever being a loser, but there must have been a lot in her past that she'd had to overcome and she wanted me to do the same, only faster. I said, "If you're willing to take me on, let the games begin."

She reached over with her right hand and smacked me on the back of my head.

"Okay, Buddy. Let's seal the deal with an ice cream."

We pulled up to a Friendly's Restaurant and each ordered sundaes decked out with Reese's Pieces, M&M's, and crumbled-up Heath Bars, Oreos, and Milky Ways, and topped with hot fudge, whipped cream, walnuts, and a cherry. They each weighed a pound or more. We ate like two little kids.

Finally, our bowls scraped clean, Brenda announced, "That's enough excitement for one day. I'm taking you home."

On the drive back, she was humming to herself. I was content to listen to what I guessed was more Puccini. As Brenda pulled in to the driveway, my lesson continued.

"Okay, Kid, listen up, this is important. Very few people know my story and I like to keep it that way, so don't ask me. If you need to know something, I'll tell you. I prefer that you stay in shut-up mode as much as possible. That way I can think of what I want to teach you next and not be interrupted. I'm new at this, so I don't have any lesson plans, but I do have some ideas. Let's get together once a week like this and see how it goes. If you can't work your problems out with your sponsor or Dr. Stone, call me. I'll give it my best shot."

I was thrilled to hear Brenda agree to be one of my mentors.

"When I'm not around," she said, "keep swinging at what life is throwing at you. I'm a good coach, but you have to find out for yourself what works and what blows up in your face. The game is never over, so screw the idea of winning and losing. If you can hear the music playing, then keep dancing. When I say dance, I mean dance."

Brenda got out of the truck and walked over to my side, stood there, and waited. Once I had both feet on the ground, she punched me again in the arm, a bit harder than before. I clenched my fist to punch back but stopped in mid-swing. It wasn't about hitting, it was about loving. She may have been a puncher, but I wasn't. I had become a hugger. I lowered my arm and wrapped it around her. My other arm joined it. We stood there for a minute in silence, just hugging and enjoying the wonderful feeling.

Brenda spoke first. "Buddy, I had one hell of a time with you today. You make it easy for me to be the way I like to be: sometimes gritty and other times pretty. I thank you for that. You took some big steps today, brave ones, too. I'm proud of you and glad to be your friend." She broke our hug, stepped back, and looked into my eyes, her expression serious.

"From now on, only think about becoming what you want to be. Nothing else matters. Everyone in your life is either going to assist you or hurt you. Wisdom is nothing more than being smart enough to sort them out and get rid of what I call the *setbacks*. Those who help, I call the *bonuses*. In time, I will teach you how to turn a *setback* into a *bonus*. Okay, you've had enough for one day. Give your Snake Lady a hug and go find Puccini."

That hug was mixed with friendship and love. She squeezed hard and tight like one of those compactors that will crush a car into a small cube of metal. I answered back with a caress and she loosened up. Before we broke the hug, each of us took turns patting the other gently on the back.

Brenda finished up by messing my hair with both hands and turning me toward the house with a whack on my rear end. "Get out of here, before I take you home and make you my pet."

As I walked away, I was overwhelmed by my feelings; I wondered if that was because I really hadn't felt those feelings before. I turned to wave at her, and as I did, her window rolled down, an arm extended like the boom on a crane, and a snake waved back. I smiled and turned to walk inside.

CHAPTER 54

Heaven Is Being Perfect

Back in the house, I headed straight toward the aroma of homemade beef stew that was coming from the kitchen. The air was filled with the fragrance of carrots, celery, turnip, green beans, and potatoes. My mom saw me walk into the kitchen and her face lit up.

"Hi, Sweetheart, how was your afternoon? Did you have fun with your nurse friend? She does take a little getting used to, with all those muscles and tattoos, I mean. Ewww, I just hate tattoos. How anyone can do that to their body is beyond me."

"Brenda and I had a great time together. I think she's awesome and I like her tattoos."

"Just the same, she may regret is someday."

"I personally think her tattoos are more than just some cosmetic decoration. The heart and soul of that woman lives on her skin as well as in every cell of her body. Those tattoos were well thought out, like a painted masterpiece that you could never get tired of, no matter how often you look at it. I bet when she has grandchildren, she'll take them to get tattoos, and she'll share some of her valuable lessons about life and living. Kids need to grow up without fear and shame."

"Well, would you ever get a tattoo?"

It was cringe time. Buddy the Seagle was flying around on my chest and soaring skyward in my heart and mind. Was I going to cover up and lie or lift my shirt and show her how I had changed for the better?

I reached down to grab the bottom of my shirt and began to pull it up. Mom watched me carefully.

"Do you remember a few years back, when my face started to break out and nothing seemed to help clear up the pimples?"

"Of course I do. I took you to several doctors and we tried every concoction on the market. I felt so bad for you. You felt like the ugliest kid on the planet and my heart was aching. Whenever I brought up the topic you just ran away and hid. By then our relationship was so strained that I didn't dare try to comfort you. I felt useless. But I did try one other thing: I gave you that book about Jonathan Livingston Seagull. I even pointed out passages you should pay special attention to. I recall reading some of them to you, just in case you didn't get the message. Let me find the book, and I'll show you."

I flashed back to Mom reading to me and teaching me about this special seagull who wanted to impress his flock with his ability to fly at a tremendous speed. His talent only brought their scorn. He was ostracized and detested by the flock, leaving him no alternative but to leave. I had related to Jonathan, not because I wanted to impress anybody, but because I wanted to be left alone and ignored. Instead, my classmates ridiculed and despised me. Any hope of ever fitting in was extinguished. I left behind any chance of ever being happy.

Mom returned and stood next to me with the short story. She thumbed through the pages and stopped.

"Here's the part I always wanted you to read carefully. It's a quote from Chiang, the wise old seagull who was approaching death. He told Jonathan that . . . well, let me read it. 'Heaven is not a place and it is not a time. Heaven is being perfect.' Do you remember that?"

Of course I did. That was my favorite part, too, when I was younger and thought that believing in myself would make others like me.

"I wanted you to learn that you were already perfect and unlimited. You were already touching heaven. You didn't need to get rid of the pimples for that to happen. Do you remember what Jonathan decided to do after he left as the outcast?"

"I haven't forgotten. He learned so much about the meaning of kindness that he returned to the flock to give flying lessons. That required him to accept their opinions of him and to love them anyway. When you suspend judgment of anyone or anything, you have no limitations to overcoming adversity. As the flock flew higher and faster, they learned the meaning of freedom and the true nature of their Being. If they wanted, they could master the sky instead and transcend beyond being seagulls."

My mother beamed. "You got the message. I knew you would. Now, I hope you can live it, too."

And with that invitation, I lifted my shirt and inflated my lungs to make my chest expand like the horizon for my seagle. "Meet the new me. This is Buddy Seagle, spelled s-e-a-g-l-e. He soars without limitation and is not afraid to be misunderstood or disliked. He's free and filled with everything you wanted me to learn from that book. I couldn't be happier that you brought it up. No accident there. Just perfect timing."

My mother stood with eyes and mouth wide open. "Oh, my God. Buddy, what have you done? Is that real?"

She reached and touched the tattoo gently and then started to rub it and looked at her finger tips to see if any of it came off. "Oh, my. It's real. Oh, my. When I told Brenda I was okay with you getting a tattoo, I thought she meant a little butterfly on your shoulder or something. This isn't at all what I expected."

"Mom. Hold on a minute. Maybe you ought to reread that book you're holding. It's all in there and you were the one who introduced me to it. The tattoo is just ink on my skin. But what I had to become in order to get the tattoo was well worth it. When I said meet the new me, I meant it. I am so different now. You played an important role in making that happen. I am thankful and proud of this little guy flying around over my heart. Take a good look at it and you'll see a colorful picture of a bird in the clouds. Then take a good look at me and tell me what you see."

She leaned over for a closer inspection of the tattoo and then peered deeply into my eyes. Her eyes softened and filled with tears, then she threw her arms around me and embraced me like someone who had been kidnapped and returned home safely.

"You're right. The change in you is so obvious now. You've grown up before my eyes. I don't know how, but it's real and I am so happy for you. As for your tattoo, it's cute, and I'm glad you have it. Did Brenda supervise while you were getting it?"

I answered, "Yup. She made sure it was safe and sterile. But the tattoo was my choice and my decision. There was no pressure. I knew I was ready. I have thought about Jonathan Livingston Seagull and his story for a long time. I am grateful to you for that. When I return to school tomorrow, people will notice the change, but not because I want them to: It's because there will be nothing from my past to spoil living in the present. Even my remaining pimples are just that, pimples. I'm saying goodbye to them."

Our hug ended and Mom broke away. She looked at me sternly and said, "This tattoo is fine, but it's much bigger than I expected. It's a nice one . . . but I forbid you to get more until you're eighteen."

We both laughed as she held up the book and said, "I'd better read this again."

After dinner, I returned upstairs to get ready for my first group meeting at Dr. Stone's office. After brushing my teeth and making my hair look presentable, I had thirty minutes before Joe arrived. I decided to take off the cumbersome back brace and stretch out on the bed.

I pulled off the T-shirt and took another look at Buddy Seagle. I thought about how Chiang, the elder seagull in *Jonathan Livingston Seagull*, traveled instantly to any time and place simply by wanting to, as long as he believed that his true nature lived everywhere at once across space and time. I touched the tattoo and imagined being a traveler capable of disappearing and reappearing anywhere in a flash. What a cool thing to be able to do.

As I lay comfortably stretched out on my bed, Higher Power made His presence known without uttering a word. I just knew it was Him.

"Okay, what did I do now?" I asked. "It can't be the tattoo. Everybody's got one. If you had a body, you'd have one, too."

"Hello, Buddy. V'entrar con voi pur ora ed i miei sogni usati, ed i bei sogni miei tosto si dileguar!"

"If you're trying to impress me with your Italian, it's not working. Brenda sounded better. And at least I can see her when she talks to me."

"I came here to speak a little Puccini. I just gave you some of Rodolfo's lines from *La Bohème*. Do you want to know what he was saying to Mimi?"

He was starting to grate on me. I knew we were inseparable and that nothing in my life was possible without Him, but sometimes I just didn't like His attitude and this was one of those times. "Tell me, oh wise one who knows all." I couldn't hold back my sarcasm.

"Listen, Buddy, don't get smart with me. I can either help you win the lottery or make sure you keep picking the wrong numbers."

I took a deep breath and thought of the lessons Jonathan Livingston Seagull had learned. I could either make fun of the Master or I could learn His secrets of the Universe. I didn't think the Master really cared. I was now beginning to see that He created rules for the ultimate game of life. There was never going to be a winner, because the game would never end and neither would eternity. And that's the way He designed it. Nobody would get to have all the toys, boats, cars, or money. They were playthings, pieces on the game board that shifted from one owner to the next. I tried to convince myself that I had just learned something valuable, but it gave me no satisfaction.

"You know," He said, "I don't have to hang out with you. Using a voice to communicate with you is something I have done with only a privileged few. Billions more have lived out their lives without hearing a word from me. I thought you might be ready to take advantage and appreciate it. But you're like fine wine before the due date: you're just grape juice."

"Hey, wait a minute," I objected. "I didn't ask for you to show up."

"Yes, you did."

"When?"

"When you decided that drugs could make you feel better than your own natural ability, I stepped in."

"Why?"

"Because it's not true. We discussed it and you agreed. I also made sure that your life was saved after three overdoses. I brought recovery into your life through NA. I introduced you to Maestro Puccini with the help of one of my favorite nurses, who happens to also have a heart the size of a bus and a brain to match. You voluntarily came on board with me when you realized that growing up a loser was just the start you needed to prepare you for the greatest lesson of all."

"What lesson?" I asked. I was getting fired up and more disagreeable. I wanted to stay that way, but I didn't know why. What had happened to change my attitude? I had gotten along with Him well enough and felt like I had grown up and faced the responsibility of becoming sober. Why this? I was miserable again, just like the old me.

"I'll be brief. And by the way, I don't take this personally. I just act that way so you can be more comfortable around me. If I acted supernatural all the time you probably wouldn't listen to a word I said."

"What's your point?"

"Sorry about that. You, my fine young fellow, are going through what all addicts go through. This early in recovery, you can't be expected to remain happy like Joe. You don't have the experience or the gift of creating as much happiness as he has."

"What are you talking about? Of course, I can be happy. Why do you say I can't?"

"I said you've simply run out of it, that's all. You're a little cranky now. Remember, this, too, shall pass. And by the way, once you're happy again, that, too, shall pass as well."

"Then why am I trying so hard, if I can't make anything last? What good is getting sober? At least with pills, I was sure to be happy for a while."

"There you go, thinking like an addict all over again."

"Why don't you get lost and leave me alone."

"You know, that's not such a bad idea. It's worked before with tougher cases than you. Maybe I'll let you sit there with your addiction and stew for a while. I'll be back when I think you're ready for another lesson. I'm wasting my words on you now. But don't hurry on my account. I can wait an eternity. Can you?"

The silence after He left was so vast that my breathing and heartbeat sounded like a roaring jet engine inside my body. I sat up on the bed and studied the Einstein poster. I wanted to throw something at him for mocking me with his tongue. He had it made. His life was over and his achievements had already altered the course of history. He was famous and I wasn't. He didn't have to worry about going back to school with the same geeky face and reputation. He could just relax and enjoy the admiration of humanity. I still had to earn mine and my Higher Power, the ultimate source of everything, had just cut me out of the will. The feeling was very familiar; it was the ultimate pity party all over again, but I couldn't stop myself from having it.

My Higher Power had been my best chance at the brass ring, for finding a decent, respectable purpose for existing. Now, He was going to hunker down and ignore me for being what? An addict? Heck, I had spent so much time locked up in shyness that it felt good to sass Him back. It was better than agreeing with everything He said. If He wanted to play the game that way, He could stay away forever for all I cared. But He was too self-absorbed, uncompromising, conceited, stubborn, unyielding, and just plain spoiled.

I realized that my description of Him sounded exactly like me. He was right. My addictive thinking had taken over, but I couldn't see it until now.

I looked at the clock; I needed to hurry to get ready for Joe. I didn't feel good about what just happened. I wasn't sure how to deal with Higher Power and I didn't believe He knew exactly how to deal with me.

I was already downstairs by the time I heard Joe's car drive up. I opened the front door and headed toward his car before he could turn off the engine.

"How was your day, Buddy?" Joe greeted me as I carefully got into the car. "You look a little frazzled."

"You got that right. So much has happened since I last saw you." I wondered if I should share with Joe that my Higher Power had become a royal pain, coming and going as he pleased. Should I tell Joe that my Higher Power was a real piece of work and I didn't know how to get along with Him? I wanted to know how he managed with his Higher Power. I decided to tell him how I felt.

"Joe, you're right. I'm beyond frazzled. I've copped a real bad attitude, an angry one at that."

"At what? Or who?"

"This is touchy for me to talk about, because He's new in my life and I don't understand Him. When He came along, I was all ears. I was ready to believe that He saved my life and was going to help make it better and a lot happier. But we don't see eye to eye."

"Who are you talking about, Doc Stone?"

"No. I thought you'd get it right off the bat."

Joe slapped his knee and grinned. "I should have known better."

"You know who it is?"

"Sure. I've got one, too, and He doesn't always have a sense of humor."

I felt better already. I wasn't the only one.

"He's a wise guy, right? And He's an arrogant know-it-all, smug and conceited."

"Well, I wouldn't go that far in the negative column about my sponsor, and I didn't know you felt that way about me."

"This isn't about you!" I exclaimed, surprised that Joe had jumped to the wrong conclusion. "I think you're terrific. It's about my Higher Power. Don't you have one? I thought we all did."

Joe down-shifted and pulled into a convenience-store parking lot. He had a serious look on his face.

"You're supposed to design your own Higher Power," he said. "It's a customized make and model. There's no two of a kind. What did you do, make Count Dracula your Higher Power?"

He snickered, then quickly regrouped when he saw the look on my face.

"Joe. I didn't have a choice. Mine just showed up and starting lecturing me. Doesn't yours?"

Joe paused, closing his eyes.

"Buddy. My Higher Power doesn't say a word to me. Are you telling me that yours does?"

"Clear as your voice," I said. "It's a guy, too. A loud guy. I feel like I've got Darth Vader in my head bossing me around."

Joe tapped on the steering wheel. "So what is He saying that's so bad?"

"There isn't anything bad. He's really pretty smart. He can go on and on about life, existence, recovery, and a bunch of metaphysical stuff. I think He wants to help me with all His messages and special lessons. But today we sort of let each other have it. He got mad at me and I got mad at Him. It was childish how I poked fun at Him. Sometimes He deserved it, but sometimes I think He was trying to be nice. I couldn't help it. The guy is in my head all the time. I know He's there, but He only talks to me when He's good and ready. I don't have any say in the matter. Sometimes I would rather be left alone. I'm all wound up over this and I'm not even thinking about letting any of it go yet. I think I might be ready to do something important with all of it. I just don't know what."

"Do you mean to tell me that God Himself is talking out loud to you?"

I wasn't sure Joe would stay in the car with me if I told him the truth, but I had to tell somebody who had an addiction and could understand.

"Yeah. And I talk back. Only, today we had a fight and He took off and said He wouldn't return until I was ready. That pissed me off."

"That's it. There's nothing more?"

I was frustrated. Didn't Joe realize how big a deal this was to me?

"Joe, the last thing He said to me was, 'You came on board with me when you realized that growing up as a loser was just the start you needed to learn the greatest lesson of all.' Then I asked, 'What lesson?' and He basically said that my addiction had taken over my thinking. He made sure I knew that I was misbehaving like one as well. Obviously, I wasn't happy anymore and He made it a point to rub it in that you were better at creating happiness than I was. And do you know why?"

"Why?"

"Just because you have a year of sobriety and I'm a beginner. I've already run out what I had and He claims I can't make anymore. Where does He get off talking like that?"

At least Joe was still in the car, taking all of this in. I couldn't tell if he was buying any of it, though. I continued my explanation.

"Today, before He left, He said, 'I'll be back. If you're ever ready. Don't hurry on my account. I can wait an eternity. Can you?' After that, there was dead silence. Like something big and important was missing from my life, which I suppose was Him. Now I don't know what to do. What does He want from me? What do you think?"

Joe said, "Give me a minute. Let's see what we've got here. A talking Higher Power is spending time with you and you're complaining. Are you crazy?" The tone of his voice was a mix of excitement and exasperation. "Millions of addicts ask for God's will to be known . . . but we don't hear a voice in our heads. We ask for knowledge of His will with as much humility as we can, because we know how big our egos are. We pray for guidance and ask for forgiveness and try to be nice to our fellows . . . and you mean to tell me that you can chat with the Big Guy?"

I had not realized how unbelievable that was to comprehend and accept. "Well, He's not there all the time. It's not like I can summon Him whenever I feel like it. He just drops in unannounced and He can be weird and pushy."

"And you let that bother you? I suppose you would; you've only been sober a few days. Your pink cloud has evaporated."

"Pink cloud? That doesn't sound like a recovery term."

"It isn't. It's a phase we all go through. The pink cloud follows you around once you decide that you're going to clean up your act and go straight. It feels good just believing that you're done with drugs. You can almost get high on the feeling that it's over, no more chasing pills with money you don't have. Then you want to be everybody's friend in recovery, one big happy family. You can't wait to get to your next NA meeting and talk about how wonderful it is to be sober."

"What's wrong with that? I wanted to do the same thing."

"Only your pink cloud isn't there right now. You're frustrated, annoyed, irritable, and agitated, and you can't bring that happy face back, can you?"

"No, I can't."

"Well, neither could I. When I lost the pink cloud, reality had set in for me. I was sober all right, but my world still had plenty of unfixed problems and I couldn't use pills or heroin to chase them away. I had to face them and it didn't feel good. Now it's your turn. Only you had your Higher Power ringside and you sent him away. Now your addiction is making you mad, but you haven't had a pill to deal with it."

"And I don't want one. Higher Power's not here, or at least He's not in the mood for talking, but you are. You tell me what to do. You've done it and it worked. You're happy. I'm not, but I want to be—and without a pill."

"I've got a few things to say about your Higher Power first. This is the opportunity of a lifetime. You don't have to wait until your last breath to meet the guy. He's breaking all the rules and showing up now, way ahead of schedule. Can't you work with Him? He can't be all that bad. He's making all this happen, just in case you forgot."

Joe stretched his arms out to make an all-inclusive gesture. I got the message.

"You may be a little young to know this, but talking to God is the exception, not the rule," Joe explained carefully. "He must have picked you for a damn good reason. I suggest you find out what that is and work with Him. You may not think you're anyone special, but you must be a little more than just another loser taking up space and consuming the earth's resources. I suggest you humble yourself and find out why you're receiving the audio version of His message. If you take Him more seriously, the world might take you more seriously."

Joe had a point. Higher Power wouldn't start talking unless He had something pretty important to say. "So I should just shut and listen, shouldn't I?"

"And be grateful, too. You've been chosen to receive this incredible, unmerited gift of recovery. Don't blow it," Joe answered. "As for being happy without the pink cloud; gratitude will lead you back to the path. An excellent way to start is to simply say 'Thank you for this.' Which means, your Higher Power didn't screw up, because 'Happiness isn't getting what you want, it's wanting what you get.' I read that in Neale Donald Walsch's book *Happier Than God.*"

Joe did have the answer and now I knew how valuable and precious the gift was that I received. And I was offered even more than that. If I was given another chance, I decided I'd accept it. No matter what He asked of me I wasn't going to turn Him down. I needed His advice, His guidance and His Love if I was going to be happy again without pills. It was time to send a message to Him. I knew He would get it.

CHAPTER 55

My Name Is George Oliver Danbury

Joe stared at me while I was lost in thought. "Do you have some weird medical condition that I should know about? You look like you go into a trance while I just sit here and wait. I feel like I'm all alone when that happens."

I had been caught again. "Oh, that," I said. "It's nothing. I just get so caught up in my own thoughts that I forget to cut loose and rejoin the broadcast. It feels like I'm only gone for a second or two. But I suppose it's a little longer."

"Longer? Geez, Louise. You look like a robot after someone hit the pause button. I even moved my hand right in front of your face for about ten seconds and kept saying your name. You were checked out. You didn't blink. You didn't flinch. I didn't even know if you were breathing. Do your parents know about this? Are you taking some medication for it?"

"Hey, come on, Joe. I just go to a deeper level where there's no disturbance in the flow. You ought to try it."

"No, thanks. I'll stay right here where I can keep my eyes on what's going on. You, however, just scared the crap out me. You looked epileptic or catatonic or something. You aren't a whack job, are you?"

Joe began to laugh as he said "whack job." He pretended to be me, staring at nothing but air. He looked so funny that I couldn't help laughing, too. Our laughter continued as each of us made funnier faces until we were out of breath, coughing and holding our sides. Joe really liked me, I thought. No, he really loved me, I could tell. The feeling was unmistakable. Did my Higher Power arrange this or was He still avoiding me?

Joe put the car in gear and drove out of the parking lot and back onto the main drag. With the last morsel of a smile he said, "Bro, don't do that to me again, okay? I got all spooked out."

"Sorry, Man," I said. "My folks are used to it—they just wait it out. You'll get used to it. Who knows, one of these times I may come back with a brilliant idea like something to change the world and put money in my pocket. Wouldn't you want to be there for a moment like that?"

Joe pushed the accelerator and replied, "Enough already. I want to get you to Dr. Stone's so I can introduce you around before the meeting gets started."

As we pulled into the parking lot, I saw four men standing outside Dr. Stone's office, smoking and talking among themselves. Joe and I got out of his car and walked toward them.

"Hi, Guys, what's up?" Joe greeted the group. "I want all of you to meet Buddy. He's a new friend of mine and I want to make sure he feels welcome."

Each man greeted me with a handshake. I met Mike, Tom, Bill, and Stuart. The consensus was that I would like the meeting.

These men, who all appeared to be in their mid-twenties and early thirties, seemed like blue-collar types, hardworking, perhaps married with kids. Their hands were a bit callused and each one needed either a shave or a haircut. They smiled and seemed friendly and they seemed to have a genuine interest in each other's well–being. They were obviously a tight-knit group. I didn't feel that I was being stared at or judged in any way for my skinny, homely, nerdy features or my acne.

The office door opened and Dr. Stone poked his head out. "Gentlemen, I intend to make your evening the best you have ever experienced. I invite you to join me so our meeting can commence."

They laughed at him as they put their cigarettes out. The doctor greeted each one of us as we walked in. To my surprise, there were already eight other people seated in the lobby, both men and women, between the ages of twenty to fifty-five or so. I tried not to feel too self-conscious as they checked me out while I hobbled on crutches across the room. I heard Mrs. Stone's voice from behind the sliding glass partition of the business office.

"Hi, Buddy. Glad you made it. Have a good meeting."

Dr. Stone rolled a huge, black leather executive chair up to the front of the room. He sat down, snapped open a can of soda, and took a generous swig. The buzz in the room quieted down.

When he had everyone's attention, Dr. Stone began the meeting. "Once again, I am surrounded by beautiful people who are all in admirable pursuit of the coveted gift of recovery. I'd like to welcome Buddy to join us on this journey, a journey that is worth all the blood, sweat, and tears it costs."

He looked at me and said, "Buddy, the following is my introduction to what this group is all about. The others have all heard it, but as usual, they can't wait to hear it again, since I do it so well."

Everybody laughed with approval. It was pretty obvious to me as I looked around the room that these people thought the world of Dr. Stone and were thirsty for the knowledge and wisdom that he shared.

"Buddy," he continued, "This is a recovery group, which means that we all have the same thing in common: We all walked the plank with addiction and went overboard. Some of us had bigger train wrecks than others, but all of us have had enough. We all want two important things: one, we all want to abstain from the substances that pushed us into the hole; and two, we want to learn how to enjoy life naturally, meaning drug-free and alcohol-free. Some of us are a little further along than others when it comes to mastering the art of being happy without a drug, but we share the common responsibility of helping each other move along the path."

As Dr. Stone continued talking, I understood that while this was his flock of followers, he also included himself as an equal brother in the continuing pursuit of recovery. With over twenty years of experience to draw on for teaching and guidance, Dr. Stone had a level of knowledge this group obviously wanted to learn from. It was good to be reminded that living a drug-free and happy life was the reason I was here.

Dr. Stone continued. "There are many ways to move along that path in a sober direction. Every way that works is the right way. Some of us find it necessary to attend Narcotics Anonymous meetings for spiritual fellowship and an opportunity to learn and grow from the Twelve Steps. Some of us find prayer and meditation extremely helpful. All of us will tell you that this group is very powerful and assists us greatly in resisting any temptation to go back to pills. The group will share that they are rewarded for their effort in the books they read, and how they use family life to remain grateful."

I noticed that the group was riveted on each word. Was it respect or his charisma? I wasn't sure. I was caught up in the flow of his words and how devoted he was to the cause that brought them all together, and that group now included me.

"This is a talking group, which means that we share our lives. We are comfortable enough to open up privately and personally so that we can get to know each other intimately. It is not a group just to hear me speak. I expect all of you to interact. As issues come up, I emphasize points of interest and illustrate a recovery lesson that we can discuss further. Discussion is the responsibility of the group and this group is one of my best. Buddy, you are in for a treat."

Just then the room seemed to take a deep collective breath. They were united and listened intently and seriously. I was convinced that they had learned how to care about one another, even if they couldn't fix whoever might be hurting the most in any given moment. An act of kindness like that was fundamental to unconditional love. Someday, I was going to need plenty of that and coming here would be just the place to get a generous helping.

"This is also a confidentiality group," Dr. Stone continued. "We need to make sure that privacy is protected and speaking freely is honored and encouraged." Heads nodded in agreement.

"We like to acknowledge lengths of sober time in this group. Medallions are presented for one month, three months, six months, and one year. These coins represent a monumental effort to become drug-free and ask for another day of that." Dr. Stone held up a brass medallion with inscriptions on the front and back. Eyes in the crowd, full of admiration and reverence, were fixed on the coin. Everyone there knew the value of what was before them and each one wanted a full set of those to mark their time in sobriety.

"Before these medallions are awarded, we circulate them around and each of us rubs some mojo into them and says a few memorable words. The purpose of this ceremony is to establish a stronger protection against addiction, which would like nothing more than to cause our relapse and end our happiness. These medallions need to be in our possession at all times. They symbolize a very potent power. I believe that with medallion in hand, it is not possible to mess up with drugs. Of all the patients I have treated, not a single one has ever slipped up while the medallion was in his or her possession."

While he spoke, everyone with a medallion took it out and began to rub it. It struck me as something solemn and appreciative. The medallions then disappeared into pockets, wallets, and purses.

"The other medallion we award at this meeting honors the courage to tell your life story of addiction. I call it the Step One story, because it breaks the ice of secrecy and releases some shame. After at least one month of attendance, you will be eligible to share your story with the group. You can freely and openly tell us how drugs and alcohol came into your life and took it over until nothing mattered more than getting the next fix. We are reminded, through this process, that we all have an obligation to accept, comfort, and offer assistance to everyone who wants to try our way of life."

I was getting excited, because I wanted to tell my story to the group one day. I also wanted to be far enough along in my recovery to offer assistance and feel like I was contributing in some way.

"During the story, we make sure to also include something about ourselves to be proud of. There's more to us than a life of disappointment and failure. We need to keep holding our heads high. Addiction is no match as long as we stand as one. No pill can violate the sanctity of this room. The group goes with you when the meeting is over and continues to offer protection and strength as long as you believe. The medallion you receive for the Step One story is loaded with faith, praise, and glory. It is adorned with an engraving of praying hands and represents the group's most sacred plea that we are always together with an invincible spirit.

Okay, group, let's get this started. Joe, why don't you say a few words, then Buddy can talk about how we met at the hospital. Everybody be brief, please, because we have Alan giving his Step One story tonight, and we will need plenty of time for that."

Everyone readjusted in their chairs as Joe got ready to address the group.

"Hi, everybody. I'm Joe and I'm an addict. I've been coming to this group for almost a year now. I have pretty much the same story as most of us. I started out with Lortabs and loved 'em. I graduated very quickly to snorting Roxys and Oxys. I hit the wall when I ran out of money and couldn't get enough pills to keep me out of withdrawal. After detox and rehab, I found the good doctor here and signed up for his program. I heard it was the best around, and it's true. This group has given me my life back, and I am very grateful. Buddy, I want you to know that these people will do anything for your recovery. They're the finest people I know and I love them all. You came to the right place."

The rest of the group followed suit and they all said the same thing about addiction. They loved pills for the energy and thought they hit the jackpot until they couldn't get high anymore and couldn't avoid withdrawal.

What they said about Dr. Stone was heartfelt and sincere. Unanimously, their message was, "Listen to Dr. Stone. He will never steer you wrong. The man knows what he's talking about. He's been there. Trust him. He's good." As each person spoke, he or she looked right at me, as though passing on a secret to be cherished and valued for its ability to dramatically change lives.

Then it was my turn to address the group. What a moment.

I sat up as straight as I could. I looked around the room and was surprised that I was able to make eye contact and not shy away. I felt a little sweaty and nervous, but I knew I could do this. I had to.

"First of all," I said. "Thank you very much, Dr. Stone, for inviting me to join your group. Thank you, Joe, for bringing me here and the rest of you for the warm welcome."

As I looked over the faces of the people watching me, I felt their kindness soothe my nerves.

"My story is different. One look at me, and the word handsome is not going to register as a thought. Homely, gawky, scrawny, pimple-faced nerd are more like what you are thinking. Am I not right? But you don't have to answer. You're fine people. I'm the one with the insecure hang-ups."

Just then, Joe put his arm around my shoulder and pulled me toward him in a brotherly hug that felt so good. Our eyes met and he whispered with some affection, "Buddy, go easy on yourself. There's no cross here with a hammer and nails. You're among friends. This room is filled with love. I suggest you soak some of that up."

I took a deep breath and relaxed my clenched fists.

"I'm sorry for that. Let me start over. My name is George Oliver Danbury, and I am a drug addict of the worst kind. I prefer that you call me Buddy. I say I'm a drug addict of the worst kind, because I didn't start with marijuana and alcohol and graduate to pills. I didn't get slowly hooked on pills after a few too many parties. I took my first Lortab and, within days, I overdosed on Roxicodone, OxyContin and Xanax, and I collided with a tanker truck doing a hundred miles per hour."

There were a few gasps from the group, but most of the faces remained expressionless. Maybe they were shocked. Maybe they had heard this kind of story before and nothing surprised them when it came to drugs and the dangerous things people do.

"I was lucky enough to make it to the hospital so I could be operated on and hooked up to life support. By the time I woke up, I had been in a coma for ten days with a broken back, broken leg, ruptured spleen, and a collapsed lung. The back brace and my bionic fixator are the last reminders of this horrible tragedy. It's been about one month since I snorted my first pill. I have been in the addiction business for a very short time. I guess I didn't have to play with dynamite very long before it exploded my life and a few others who were standing too close, like my parents."

Joe held his hand out for a fist bump. It was a gesture that represented so much meaning. I felt initiated to a special status. Yes, I was a novice to this group, but I had become a member of the herd, which qualified me for its full protection from all predators. I could feel the acceptance and love in the room. I was just like all the others; I had found a place to fit in.

Dr. Stone swiveled his chair and faced me before speaking.

"Buddy, the fun part of this group is that I'm in charge, which means I can interrupt any time I want."

A few chuckles broke the spell. "At this point, I get to ask a few questions that might help us understand you and your addiction a little bit better.

"Buddy, you had literally come to a bone-crushing end on the road of getting high. What you experienced, I believe, was the most dramatically painful wakeup call of anyone I have ever met who survived. And yet, you arranged for your drug dealer to come to the hospital to deliver opiates within days of waking up from the coma. You managed to snort enough OxyContin to cause a cardiac arrest. Thanks to the Rapid Response Team, you are still above ground."

After a pause, Dr. Stone asked, "Did you ever, even for a split second, mentally challenge the impulse to get high? What I mean is, was there any warning from your brain telling you that snorting OxyContin after waking up from a coma might be a bad idea?"

The room was silent and everyone sat very still. I wondered if they were thinking that for them it would have been a bad idea, so why wasn't it for me? All eyes were on me, waiting for my answer.

I thought carefully about how to answer before I spoke. "No. For me there was no hesitation. It was full steam ahead and get high again. By that time, I had no life to look forward to. The sixteen years that had passed were nothing worth remembering. I felt ugly, useless, and ashamed for causing my family so much grief. I didn't care if I died. I knew I wasn't going to really enjoy getting high, but it was less painful than facing another day with a broken back, a splintered leg skewered with pins, and a personality that was dull and boring."

I looked out over the faces in the room and saw painful winces and looks of disbelief. But there was no way anybody could know how it really felt to be me: ugly Buddy.

Dr. Stone, however, was unfazed. "Buddy, why did you want to join this group?"

"I'm not sure," I answered. "A few things have happened in the past week that amazed me beyond comprehension. For starters, I really want to live now. I don't want my past to haunt me anymore. It's no longer important for me to blame anyone, including myself, for the way things turned out. People have taught me that I am headed in the right direction and I've learned that is a lot more important than where I have been. Those same people have treated me with so much kindness. Nothing else explains why I feel so good in such a short time. The most important reason I am here is because you convinced me I could have a better life if I learned to be happy without drugs. Joe has volunteered to be my sponsor and teach me how to do that." I looked out over the group and saw many smiles. I think the group approved of my explanation.

"I have also become acquainted with a Higher Power who happens to be pushy and weird, but also sneaky and smart. The guy literally talks to me, live, just like I'm hearing His voice. He seems to be working really hard to enlighten me and prepare me for some kind of mission."

The room started to buzz. The doctor waved a hand and got their attention and they quieted down.

I continued my story. "I'm told that a talking Higher Power is unheard of, but I assure you, I'm not crazy. So I assume it's miraculous, just like me surviving that crash and coming out of a coma without any brain damage. I'd decided that I'd better listen carefully and be a bit more willing to see what His intentions are. I need to stay open-minded. This is all happening so fast. I can get frustrated and confused and, at times, a little short-tempered. I'll keep you posted on what He says to me. Maybe you guys can figure it out."

There was a low murmur in the room. Doctor Stone propped his fingers in the form of a steeple and remained silent. He seemed deep in thought, although I wondered if perhaps he wanted the group to chat among themselves for a while.

Finally, he said, "Buddy, you're right. A talking Higher Power is rare indeed and we welcome the inside scoop on your conversations with Him. No matter what it took to get you here, I am sure we are all grateful that it happened and the experience brought you to us. We're all looking forward to your contribution to the group. Welcome."

Everyone in the room started to applaud and someone shouted out, "You can do it. One day at a time."

I felt so good that I wanted to get up and hug each one of them. Once again, I was sitting there without an ugly thought on my mind and a lot of hope in my heart.

CHAPTER 56

Alan's Story

Alan appeared to be in his early forties. He cracked his knuckles and cleared his throat, looking confident and eager to begin his story. From Dr. Stone's description, I got a sense that the Step One story was an ice-breaking rite of passage for anyone in recovery and a symbolic crossing of a spiritual threshold.

"I grew up around these parts and had a great childhood," Alan began. "My father worked hard in his repair shop fixing cars and Mom stayed home baking everything that smelled great in the oven. I had my parents all to myself and got pretty spoiled. My dad and I did everything together. We were always boating, fishing, hunting, customizing cars, and playing sports. I was good at baseball and football. I had a room full of trophies, and good grades to match. I hung out with kids who liked to party on the weekends. My father liked to have a beer in his hand pretty much all the time. Occasionally, he'd get drunk and stupid, but never nasty. My mom was the straight one, going to church and praying with her Bible. Both of them wanted me to go to college."

Alan was a confident speaker. He was clean-cut and handsome, with dark facial stubble. He had a broad chest and thick forearms. He looked comfortable up there and the group seemed to really like him.

"When I started drinking, it was fun and easy. I didn't get into any trouble, I never threw up, and the next day I was always the one who got over any hangover the fastest. I loved alcohol and it was a great way to unwind and let loose. I was serious about school and sports, but on weekends I pounded them down—shots and beers—and nobody could out-drink me. Puking and passing out was the price they paid for trying to keep up.

"I never made it to college. By my senior year, I was out of shape and didn't go out for sports. My parents and coaches were upset and disappointed, because they knew I had scholarship talent, but I liked being drunk more than studying, so my grades fell off and I quit school. I went to work fixing cars. Big deal." He shook his head and let it hang down.

I looked around the room at faces that mirrored Alan's disappointment in himself. People sat back in their chairs. They were empathetic; addiction had taken another hostage and stolen his chances for a bright future.

"My only shining moments came from a routine of crowd-pleasing raunchy jokes at a local watering hole. My success there was nothing compared to the touchdown cheers that made me so proud in high school. At the bar, the only scoring I did was when I got lucky hitting on anything with shaved legs and cleavage. I thought I was handsome and irresistible. But alcohol reduced me to making lame flirtatious attempts to pick women up for sex. I shot my mouth off and insulted just about everyone except those who were too drunk to care. I went home empty-handed, unless I paid for it.

"Before I would leave the bar, I liked to finish the night off with what I called the grand finale. I would shout out to the bartender to set up a row of doubles to include my best friends, Mr. Jack Daniels, Mr. Jim Beam, Master Jägermeister, and some expensive exotic vodka. I made a big production of knocking back each one, hoping to impress what I thought was an envious crowd of spectators. I expected some chick would change her mind and hook up with me just because I could drink fast and hard. That never happened. The girls only hung around as long as I was buying them rounds. The grand finale was all over in a few minutes. Then I bowed to my audience and staggered off to my car. One time, they applauded me for my drinking skills. Sadly, I actually felt admired and important. I was just a drunken fool with no scruples."

The room became very quiet, and everyone I looked at had the same expression on his or her face. They knew what was coming next, as though Alan's foot was perched on the edge of a very slippery slope.

"As time went on, I wanted to stay awake, drink, and party all night, so I'd spice up that routine by adding lines of cocaine to the mix. It wasn't much longer before pain pills were included."

There were murmurs in the crowd as people identified with the first time they took a Lortab or Roxicodone. I know I did.

"For me, opiates eliminated the need to get so drunk. That took care of the hangovers, but I was still being rejected by women. I made new friends called dealers, and I was so happy that I named my two Jack Russell terriers 'Roxy' and 'Oxy.' Getting high was never so easy. I could stay home and snort one pill after another. It was neat and convenient. I was in heaven. I also realized I had no use for women—not because I didn't want them, but because I couldn't do anything, even if I'd had the opportunity."

I heard a few chuckles as Alan made a face.

"Eventually, snorting pills became a boring and very costly routine. Fifteen to twenty pills a day emptied my bank account in a hurry. I tried taking fewer pills and was shocked when I went into withdrawal for the first time. Within hours, I discovered new ways for my body to hurt. My intestines felt like they were being twisted and wrung out with nausea, cramps, and diarrhea. Then I would sweat like a river was pouring out of my skin, and my bones ached right into the marrow."

Several people in the room rubbed their arms and touched their stomachs, as though they were flashing back to the nightmare of opioid withdrawal. Alan was doing a good job of describing the downward spiral of addiction and reminding them that they were only one pill away from re-experiencing that misery.

"You'd think that I might have been ready to get help and quit, but no . . . all I wanted was to get high, faster and cheaper. So in walks Mr. Heroin in the little plastic baggie. I learned how to cook it, tie off a vein, hit it perfectly with a needle, and get lit up. In no time, I had my kit and filled my life with one rush after another. I loved it and went up in a flash . . . bam, bam, bam."

People were startled and then began to laugh at the Chef Emeril impression. Alan dropped his head, closed his eyelids halfway, and nodded several times in an amusing and true-to-life imitation of a heroin high.

"For those of you who haven't had the pleasure . . . heroin promises very little high and provides a whole lot of pinpoint pupils, blurred vision, and arms and legs heavier than dead weight. You move slower than a snail crawling through thick sludge, while your mouth is so dry that saliva is a delicacy. You have to scratch every square inch of your skin or go insane from itching. The first time I did heroin, I heaved my guts into my lap. I cleaned it off and shot up again."

The mention of vomit stirred someone enough to moan, "Gross."

"Before heroin was done with me," Alan continued, "I had a few problems that I hadn't anticipated."

A voice in the room called out, "I got pneumonia." Another one said, "My arm got infected with abscesses."

"Precisely," Alan said. "Heroin sucked the life out of my body. I shrank down to nothing. I couldn't be bothered with food. I was hospitalized over and over again. I'd go in with a fever, sickly and weak, and feeling like reheated death. I'd get detoxed with methadone and fed a bunch of antibiotics. Each time I'd bounce back. The doctors told me what to expect if I kept it up."

I felt better knowing that I wasn't the only fool in the room who kept going when the light had turned red.

"I would leave the hospital and say, 'never again.' I was clean, and my health was rebounding. It felt good. I was working and even getting back into shape. And then . . . I just had to have something. I tried a few beers, a little pot, and even a few pills, but it wasn't the same. I wanted to be back on the needle, but at the same time, I didn't want to. It was crazy. I would go over and over it in my head, trying to talk myself out of it. I would remember how sick I was in the hospital, weighing 130 pounds with yellow, pasty skin from hepatitis. And the pain. My liver was swollen and stretched like a water balloon and hurt like it was being punched over and over again. That still wasn't enough to stop me. I wanted to get high, no matter what price I had to pay."

I knew the insanity he was referring to. I couldn't wait to hear how he overcame it and ended up here.

"The last time I got high, I hit the jackpot. I infected my heart. It's called endocarditis, which means bacteria were growing on the inside of my heart. That spread to one of the valves, which got chewed up and put me into heart failure. My lungs filled up with fluid and I was drowning on the inside. I couldn't get any air and needed a breathing machine to inflate my lungs until I could get an artificial heart valve to save my life. Not bad, huh?"

No one in the room looked shocked by Alan's story.

"Well," Alan said. "There's obviously a happier side to this story. After weeks of antibiotics and a new heart valve, I checked myself into rehab. I was lucky that I had good insurance and parents who saved their money for a moment like this. It was unbelievable how they were willing to give me one more chance that I didn't deserve.

"I was in for a rude awakening, though. Rehab wasn't what I expected, and it certainly wasn't what I wanted. It was tedious. There were long hours of lectures, groups, and homework. We were brought to NA meetings and we were expected to learn about the steps. I couldn't stand it. I wanted some dope so I could coast through. I had connections and figured I could get a delivery. Instead, a miracle happened.

"I met someone at a meeting who told my story, almost word for word. There was one major difference, though: he had AIDS. He still looked okay, but he told me about the time bomb that was ticking in his body and all the medications he had to depend on to keep it from going off and ending his life. He wanted to live so badly and there I was, trying to get my dealer to smuggle some drugs in for me. What a wake-up call."

I was even more captivated now and, by the expressions on the faces around me, so were the rest of the people there. Alan was a great teacher, and scattered throughout his story were the keys to recovery.

And then I heard Him again. My Higher Power was back. "Listen to this guy. Believe that it's Me you're listening to and trust the message. You need this more than you'll ever know."

I didn't question Higher Power's message and I didn't give off any sign that I had been visited by Him. I simply sat perched on the edge of my chair and continued to search for something meaningful in Alan's words. That had become my priority.

"This man I met in rehab introduced me to his reason for living. His wife had divorced him, but he still had a job, a place to live, a mother who loved him, and a twelve-year-old daughter who adored him. I learned that addiction didn't stop him from being a nice guy. He was about to graduate from the rehab program and was working the Twelve Steps. He had been praying and turning his life over to a Higher Power. This was all new and strange to me. I decided to suspend all criticism and judgment and just listen with an open mind. After the week we spent together, I was a changed man."

Several of the people who were sitting behind me began whispering about their own miraculous turning points.

"I felt a burden lifted from my heart that enabled me to clearly understand that I was a sick man," Alan continued, his voice repentant. "Addiction might have been something that existed in my genetic code, but there was a way to be safe from its lies and false promises. The insanity that once compelled me to feed drugs to this monster had been exposed for what it was. I was taught that only a power greater than me could protect and guide me to becoming drug free and sober. I was shown the few simple things I had to do each day to make that happen and I have kept them up ever since. I was referred to Dr. Stone for my aftercare, and I've been coming here for about six weeks now.

"I can't begin to tell you how much I have learned from him. He taught me that addicts are still lovable. I am no longer ashamed of what I did or why I did it. I am focused on today and how to get well. Dr. Stone inspires and motivates me to say the magic words, 'Thank-you for this gift.' He explained to me that everything exists the way it is simply because it is the way it is. My saying thank-you indicates that I accept life as it comes and spares myself the suffering that comes from complaining, because that's not the way I want my life to be. When I refuse to say 'Thank-you for this gift,' I am basically telling my Higher Power that He got it wrong and made a mistake, which I know is not true. Saying thank-you keeps me humble, yet empowers me do the next right thing. Dr. Stone has given me a lot of tools to help me do the next right thing to guarantee a successful life. These tools are now my way of living."

He looked at his watch and said, "I see my time is up. I want to thank you for the privilege of allowing me to share my experience, strength, and hope with you. Perhaps someone in this room has heard what they needed to bring them into the light. We need each other on this journey. We cannot do this alone. Addiction is no match when two or more of us share the Power that brought us together. Thank you."

The room went silent and all eyes turned toward Dr. Stone, anticipating his remarks and feedback. I wanted to applaud Alan, but I waited to see what happened next.

Dr. Stone unfolded his hands, uncrossed his legs, and leaned toward Alan. "Alan, you have taken advantage of every opportunity presented to you since you met your friend in rehab. I am impressed with your sober intentions as you've expressed them to me privately and here in group. As you know, they don't exist by themselves, they have to be created by you. You have to be the one who decides that you want this way of life. You have to ask for strength to say 'no' to heroin and mean it. You have to choose the people who are safest to be around. You have to show up for this meeting every week, pay attention, and extract all the sober energy in this room and put it into your mind and heart. You have done that and more."

I could understand why Dr. Stone and his message meant so much to these people. It was motivating and powerful, yet basic. Don't use, do ask for help, and go to his group and NA. He kept saying the same thing over and over again, but in a way that made it sound profound each time he said it.

He continued, "When I look at you, Alan, I see a bright light of possibility without any limitation. I do not see addiction lurking in the shadows, ready to pounce on you and drive you over the cliff into devastation and despair. You are free, natural, and gifted, and we are the joyful recipients of your experience, strength, and hope. For me, this beats getting high anytime. There is no way a pill could ever make this better. And that is the miracle I was promised when I put down the booze twenty-three years ago. You have it now and we are a witness to it. Everyone in this room is eligible for what you have. The supply is inexhaustible."

I felt a euphoria that I suspected was felt by everyone who listened to Dr. Stone that night. I was learning more about why I was there with that fine man and the amazing collection of people. All of them were addicted, yet they produced a healing energy so potent, I swore it could cure anything the human soul could be afflicted with: shame, guilt, anger, discouragement, depression, anxiety, and hopelessness. The group was a powerful generator of kindness, compassion, friendship, and love. And it was all free for the asking and taking. I wanted everything they had to offer.

CHAPTER 57

The Medallion Ceremony

Even though I had been present when Tanya was given her medallion at my first NA meeting, I very impressed with the way Dr. Stone's group went about it. The symbolism of the ceremony not only made it special, but made it a crucial, spiritual part of the recovery process. Dr. Stone explained it better.

"Alan, it's time for everyone here to honor you with love and words as they pass the medallion around. Listen and take all of this in, because it will remain with you as you leave today to live in a world where addiction is looking for a way to make friends with you again.

"Before I hand this over to the group, I want to tell you the story about the praying hands that are depicted on the medallion. They're actually world renowned. They are the hands of Albert Dürer, the brother of the famous renaissance artist, Albrecht Dürer. These two brothers wanted to go to art school, but only one could go at a time, so they tossed a coin to see who would go first. Albrecht won the toss and the privilege of attending the Nuremburg Academy to become an artist. The brothers made a pact: the loser would labor in the mines for four years to pay the expenses of that education."

"Albrecht was exceptionally talented and, after graduation, his works brought impressive commissions. When it was his brother's turn to attend the Academy, Albert's hands had been so brutally smashed and broken in the mines that they were too arthritic to take up a paint brush or even draw. Albert declined the offer to have Albrecht replace him in the mines. So Albrecht created a painting as his brother posed with his gnarled hands in a praying position. Many households today have this work of art hanging somewhere. It is regarded as the ultimate sacrifice and graphically illustrates the meaning of 'No one ever makes it alone.'"

As Dr. Stone let his words sink in, I thought about how alone I had felt. Even at school, amongst a crowd of classmates, if I wasn't being picked on I felt like an outcast. The word saddened me, because I had retreated to my bedroom where I spent so many years conditioning myself, finding ways to turn the Internet into an artificial companion and believing that I was actually happy. Now I wondered if I ever was. Those days were over. I was going to be in good company from now on, including my own.

Dr. Stone then handed the medallion off to the woman on his right. She took it and immediately turned it over and looked at the inscription and design. She smiled at Alan and said, "My name is Karen, and I am an addict. Alan, I want to thank you for telling a very compelling story. You did an awesome job. I could feel myself remembering when having to buy pills consumed my day and drained me of everything I worked so hard for. It's great to see you making a comeback. This medallion should make it safer and maybe a little bit easier, too. It's nice having you in the group."

The medallion traveled from person to person. Each one studied it with curiosity and admiration as though it were a rare coin. Their words to Alan were heartfelt, sincere, and spoken with great care. Alan appeared to be inhaling each word, inflating his self-esteem as the medallion passed around the circle.

I was the last one to receive the medallion. I looked at the praying hands and remembered the sacrifice that was made hundreds of years ago by the Dürer brothers. Somehow that story seemed to make this room a hospitable place for me. I didn't feel like a geek in this gathering; I felt like an equal.

I looked directly at Alan and said, "My name is Buddy. I am drug addicted and grateful to be accepted by this group and I will gladly accept any help with my recovery. Alan, that was unbelievable. We're unbelievable. After what I did, I'm not supposed to be here, yet I am. You beat the odds, too, with an infected valve that needed open-heart surgery. Now you're an example of what miracles can happen when you decide to stop the madness and accept help. I can't think of two better instances where the expression *you can't do it alone* applies. Even if I could do it alone, I would rather not try. Being here with all of you has taught me that. The best results come from combining my strength with yours and tapping into it. Alan, your message is what more of us need to hear, so please keep it up. And thanks."

I began to hand Alan the medallion, but Dr. Stone reached over to intercept it.

"Not yet," he said. "I have to take my turn with the mojo."

I sensed something extraordinary was about to happen. Dr. Stone held the medallion up as a reverent symbol that bestowed immunity from relapse upon its owner.

"Alan, I've been given a lot of medallions over the past twenty-three years. They have all been cherished, because each one signified what I was becoming, not what I had been. Year by year, as the anniversary number on the medallion got bigger, I made damn sure I not only felt better but had proof that my life, mind, and spirit were improved. I steadily upgraded myself into a better version of me. No matter how much I loved my wife, I was capable of loving her more. No matter how much I knew about psychiatry and addiction, I could learn more. No matter how much I cared about my patients, I could find a way to be kinder and willing to do more for them.

"Immunity from relapse has given me the freedom to use my energy and talent for these worthy pursuits, which have become my higher purpose. The principles of recovery exist for a very good reason: they are to be applied to life as a means to solve problems and create the conditions for which all that you desire may find its way toward you. The bonus here is that my addiction has become, for all practical purposes, dormant. It no longer bothers me. I am not blatantly aware of its existence, like most of you are. Oh, don't get me wrong. I know it's there, in subtle ways that I don't have time to explain today. And I am always on the alert for any sneaky way it can influence my life. And it has been, thankfully, caught many times and harmlessly disposed of."

I had no idea that was even possible. Addiction becoming sort of dormant. It made sense that for someone to stay sober and involved with their true purpose, addiction had to be neutralized to some extent. I wanted to know a lot more about that.

Dr. Stone continued, "This medallion is a symbol of us. Carry it with you at all times. Make sure it's in your pocket, next to your shaving kit or on your bedside table. Where it goes, we go, too. We are there in spirit and will not only protect you, but our voices will be with you and guide you along the path."

Everyone in the group was eating this up. Dr. Stone was our spiritual leader and every word was a perfect fit for the total message. To delete one word would only diminish its value and meaning.

"Alan, you have earned this medallion. The early days of recovery may be a gift, but it is often said that we wish you all the pain you need to grow. I know there has been no shortage of pain in your life. Take advantage of it and prove that pain is the ladder upon which you climb out of the hole of suffering. Every step is worth it."

Dr. Stone turned slightly toward the group and continued, "At this time, it is my pleasure and honor to award you with this medallion for sharing your story and pledging to do what it takes to add another sober day to your life. As you do, the world is a better place because you are here. Now let's applaud and start the hugging."

Everyone in the room stood in unison. The sounds of clapping hands and cheerful accolades filled the room. Dr. Stone was the first to embrace Alan. Then he was surrounded by the other members of the group, each one waiting his or her turn to pay him a tribute with smiles, tears, back slapping, and other celebratory gestures. Alan's thanks poured out to each person.

I wanted to be the last to congratulate Alan and wish him a future of fantastic success. As I stepped close, Dr. Stone stepped in front of me and took Alan into the hall, leaving me alone to wait. I figured the doc wanted to say something more private. Unexpectedly, I heard the all too familiar voice of Higher Power: He was back again.

"Did you get that?" He asked.

He was loud and I turned to see if anyone else had heard him, then realized no one else could.

"Well?" He asked impatiently. "Did you pay attention, or did I waste my time on you?"

He was talking to me as doc and Alan were standing close by. What was I supposed to do, go to the restroom or outside the building to answer Him?

He spoke up again, "Okay, I get the idea: the silent treatment. I don't really care. Mind reading is fun. Don't worry, I'll follow every thought you have, so you don't have to bother saying a word."

I stood there and stayed calm. I had the good fortune of having Him back. I intended to honor that privilege and not squander the encounter with sarcasm and complaints. My Higher Power was persistent and rambunctious, but now I understood that He had a reason, that was how He got through to me. I spoke to Him through my thoughts.

"I'm receiving Your message, but I don't know what You want from me. I think I am beginning to understand a little more about how You operate. Alan turned his life over to You and You spoke through him. It's hard for me to think about You when he's doing the talking. I am willing to believe that You're behind the scene creating the message, but does he know it?"

He said to me. "No, he has no clue about what I'm really up to. He did say a prayer quietly to himself before he started his story."

"What prayer was that?"

"'God, help me to say the words that are in keeping with Your will for me. Choose whoever needs to receive this message.' Now how's that for surrender?"

"You mean, You chose the words he used for the story tonight?"

"In a manner of speaking, yes. But they sounded like his and no one else's. He is simply learning a new language and I'm teaching him. He can't see me or hear me, but everyone he comes in contact with gets a message, courtesy of me. And I am recruiting you for that job. You are my pick for teacher but with a bit of a twist. I get to talk your ear off. The others don't have that privilege. However, I won't bother you ever again if you say 'no.' I give everyone a chance to say 'no.' They've all said 'yes' so far, and I have been doing this for a long, long time."

Dr. Stone and Alan broke from their private exchange and started in my direction.

"Buddy, I brought Alan back so the two of you could get better acquainted. I think he has a lot to offer you." Dr. Stone turned and walked into the office to see his wife, and I heard her say, "What a great group tonight. I am so proud of Alan," before he closed the door.

"I really enjoyed your story," I greeted Alan as I shook his hand.

"Nice to meet you, Buddy," he answered, his eyes bright. "I'm glad you decided to join us. We need new recruits. Just in the past month I've met a lot of new people at group. Most of them didn't return—addiction is that powerful. You get a glimpse of recovery, then it snatches you away. I hope you get to stay."

"I do, too. I should, because I came with Joe. He's my sponsor."

Alan said, "He's good people, a winner, in fact. Get close to him. He can teach you a lot."

"I hear that word 'teacher' a lot," I said. "I'm curious about who the teachers are and how you become one."

His response was lighthearted laughter. "It's not a job you apply for. It just happens when you're ready. We all have a message. Recovery happens when that message helps someone change for the better. Teachers have various levels of experience and share that freely with everyone. Some are more devoted to teaching than others and become sponsors and speakers. No matter what, we all want to believe that a Higher Power is behind the scenes directing the whole thing. That way, we don't have to be in charge."

Here was my chance. He mentioned a Higher Power behind the scenes; maybe we had even more in common.

"Does your Higher Power ever talk to you?" I asked hesitantly.

"Of course, all the time." He spoke confidently and I scrutinized him carefully.

"Out loud?"

Just as I said that, my tongue felt like it had been tied in a knot and I couldn't speak. What was my Higher Power up to? Why did He have to do that over one lousy question? I thought He was throwing his weight around way too much.

Alan was unfazed by the question, and appeared to ponder it. Finally, he asked, "Do you mind if I give you a hug?"

I obliged without saying a word. I still couldn't talk.

Alan embraced me with a strength that felt firm and secure. He spoke directly into my ear.

"Buddy, I'm not God, but I am a representative of His gift that influences my mind. I think God thoughts. If I didn't, I'd be in the company of my addiction and that would be a disaster. So I'm pretty sure He's right here with us now and He's choosing these words for me." Alan's squeeze got a little tighter.

"I love you," he said with a tiny crack in his voice. "You are more than a teenager who fooled around with a few too many pills. Judging from the pins in your leg and the brace on your back, I would bet you fooled around with way too many pills and got your ass handed to you in the hospital. We have a lot in common. Perhaps that's why we're hugging each other right now. I'm pretty comfortable, how about you?"

"Mmm hmm."

"Thought so. Now for the clincher. We need each other. Every time I get the chance to hold someone in my arms like this, I get stronger. I am more certain that God is an operating force for good in my life and that brings me peace and joy. Now that I have been saved with a new heart valve and a clean bill of health, I'm not going to waste it. I suggest that whatever message you get from God, especially if He's talking up a storm in your head, you listen and follow through. That way, you will always be going in the right direction. Life is too short to go the wrong way, even for a day. Got it?"

My voice returned just as he released the hug. He stared at my face for any signs of confusion or misunderstanding.

"Alan, thanks for holding me in your arms like that. I was trying to imagine that it was Him, My Higher Power, God. I think He was using you to get closer to me. He told me that He wants me to become a teacher. That baffled me, so I didn't say yes immediately, because I didn't get it. Well, I do now. I think I'm ready, thanks to you. I'm not sure what I'll teach or who I'll teach, but if it's anything like what you just did, then I'm game. You've got this light inside of you and I want it, too. You seem to understand what the world expects of you and you're ready to deliver. You look like you're happy to be alive and sober."

Alan put his hands on the top of my shoulders and gently jostled me.

"Kid, I couldn't have said it any better. As a matter of fact, you said it better than I've ever heard it. You got your wish. You're a teacher and that proves that beginners like us may be worth listening to. We get the same twenty-four hours to be sober as Dr. Stone gets. It makes no difference how many days, weeks, or years have been accumulated. That merely adds up to experience. Yesterday's sobriety is done and over with. Today is all that matters. Nobody gets any more than that, because once it's tomorrow, it's today all over again."

Alan shook my hand with both of his. They felt strong enough to mix cement.

"I have to get moving," he said. "I go to an NA meeting at 8:00 PM tonight and I have to fly to make it on time. You take care of yourself and I'll see you next week. Maybe we can hit a meeting together with Joe."

As he walked away, he waved at the doc and his wife through the sliding window at the reception area. They both signaled him with their love and good wishes for a great week.

I looked around the office and saw Dr. Stone with his wife, looking like the ideal pair. I could see Joe outside on the sidewalk chatting with three other group members, joking and teasing each other in good, clean fun. And then there was me, feeling like I fit in perfectly, and I knew who to thank for that. Just then I heard a voice from within.

"You're welcome, Buddy . . . my friend."

I smiled and, at that moment in time, I did not need anything else. Nothing could have made it any better. I felt like I was at home in my own skin, a winner at last.

On my way out of the office, Dr. Stone walked over extending his hand for a shake.

"Buddy, you did really well for your first group. Everybody likes you just the way you are. I hope to see you next week. It gets better each time, because we naturally get a little closer each time. When you take us with you in your heart, the world will be a friendlier place and you'll see welcome signs everywhere you go."

"Doc, you're amazing," I said, a big smile on my face. "Everything you say makes sense. I've been told by my Higher Power to become a teacher. I can see I have a way to go compared to you. But if it's my destiny, I will learn how. I'm psyched."

"Buddy," he replied, "teaching is something I take seriously and receive my greatest reward from. I believe you have the gift and can be one of the best. You'll have to come out of your shell and become the message you deliver. You'll have to ignore what other people think of you and focus on something far more important. Once that happens, people will always want more of you. The pimples won't matter. As a matter of fact, they won't even be noticed, because you won't draw attention to them anymore."

Once again, he was teaching and I was astounded. He had the gift and I was being called into service without experience. That was going to prove to be interesting. I decided to stop doubting the possibility and accept the probability that it would happen when I was prepared and ready. Trust was going to be necessary if my Higher Power was going to intervene and groom me for the job. I decided that if I was going all the way with recovery, I might as well go all the way with any service that I was called upon to deliver. It might be as rewarding as it would be interesting. Me, the primordial geek who evolved into a supreme nerd and outcast, being selected to be a messenger, while still decorated with a few leftover pimples. Who was going to listen? Whoever He wanted.

Joe opened the office door and caught me in one of my famous trances. "Hey, Doc, did Buddy go into the twilight zone on you, too?" He leaned over and nudged me hard enough to tip me a little off balance.

"Come on, Pal, snap out of it, we've got to move it. Say goodbye to the doc and his wife."

I blinked several times quickly and returned to complete awareness. Doc looked puzzled and shrugged.

"I don't know what just happened," he offered, "and maybe I don't want to know. Take care, Buddy, see you next week. Joe, bring him to a meeting every day. Treat him like your kid brother."

I decided to have a little fun with Dr. Stone. "I didn't blank out just then. My Higher Power pulled me away for a meeting. I never know when He will come calling or why. I just answer the command and follow instructions."

Dr. Stone was caught off guard by that remark and laughed nervously. He looked perplexed as I walked out the door. I loved it.

CHAPTER 58

Love Will Set Me Free

Joe throttled the Mustang and made it roar impressively as he drove out of the parking lot. He sang a few bars of a hit song while tapping out some percussion on the steering wheel.

Within a mile, he stopped singing and said, "I think you can tell why that group is so important to my recovery. Week after week, I meet with the same people and we really get into it. We share the most personal stuff and don't hold anything back. This is one of the best ways to grow. It will do you a lot of good."

"I know it will," I replied, watching the road ahead. "I could feel the power in that room. It's one thing to know it exists after hearing so many people talk about it. It's another thing to have it move right through you. It's intense, but I'm not afraid of it. I think it's a helping force. I would expect miracles to happen when it's around and I hope to feel it again."

Joe downshifted and pulled into the driveway at my house.

"You catch on real fast, kid. What you felt in that room was pretty spectacular. That force field can completely surround you. I felt it when I was doing my fifth step. It was like the heavens opened up, cleansing my soul and filling me with gratitude. It was the purest love I had ever felt. At the same time, the Fox and I both cried during the longest hug of our lives. While we were embracing, I felt a sense of peace and perfection, as though we completed each other. It had to be a God thing. That's what went right through you tonight. Man, that give me the chills. You are definitely blessed and chosen for something special. Be ready, because when it happens, it's going to be big and beautiful."

I thought about that for a few minutes before I replied. "I think I'm beginning to get this spirituality stuff, Joe. I know my Higher Power can be a bit rude and crude when He's talking to me. A little courtesy would be nice. But now I realize this power has the ability to change lives through the experience of love. I think that love is the ultimate. It has to be what I need more of if I'm going to dump this geeky nerd complex once and for all. Love is the answer. Love will set me free. Love will let people see the real me, a me that can be caring and kind. A me that has no shame and no fear. A me that will know where I am welcome and enjoy being there."

Joe sounded astonished. "Can you hear yourself talk? Pal, you're bending my mind here. What you're saying is way too advanced for a beginner. You're not making this up, either—this is legit. Your Higher Power has really got you dialed in. It's unbelievable."

I got out of the car and crutched over to his side, where he was waiting for me with a gentle but firm hug. As we hugged, I put my head on his shoulder. I felt like a cub, protected but not pampered. I was beginning to understand how much we meant to each other.

As the hug ended, Joe said, "Thanks for allowing me to show you what kind of friend I can be. I promise you, I will never be anything else. In time you will learn to accept what I have to offer and look forward to it. You deserve it. We both do. What do you say?"

"Joe, I have to admit this is all strange and unfamiliar, but in a nice way. I can get used to it. It must be awkward for you to hug a weird-looking guy like me."

And then I felt it, like the sting from a slap on my face. There was no voice this time. It definitely got my attention and suddenly I had more to say.

"Joe, I have to correct myself. There's nothing weird about me or the way I look. My personality isn't even odd, it's just interesting—actually, fascinating. You're going to enjoy getting to know me. I know a lot of things, neat things. You're in for a real treat as my friend. I want you to know that you can count on me. It would be a privilege and an honor to help you in any way I can."

Joe's expression changed from confused to one of pure joy.

"Buddy, if I hadn't heard you say it, I wouldn't have believed it. You just took one of the biggest leaps I have ever witnessed in recovery. You shed some old, useless baggage; it was like dead skin peeling off a snake. I'm glad to see you giving up that attitude about your appearance. Way to go. If you keep this up, we'll have to ask the doc to write a book about you. People need to know that this really happens and when you least expect it. Now, get out of here before you turn into something else that your mama won't recognize." As Joe drove away and I waved, I realized a miracle had happened. My exterior appearance had become a reflection of my inside. Wholeness had arrived and the nightmare was over. It felt like anything was possible for me. There were no limitations. I was the same, yet so different. Would anyone else notice? Did I want them to?

What about school? How would the other kids see me? As the geek or as Joe's friend? Now I realized it wasn't the pimples that caused the jeers, it was my fear of having pimples. People didn't push me around because I was weird, they pushed me around because I convinced them that being weird deserved bad treatment. Now what? Tomorrow it was back to school and I was going to find out. Tomorrow, the real me would show up, accepting the present moment without resistance. Tomorrow, there was not going to be any suffering. There might be pain, but that would never hurt me, not while my Higher Power was around. Tomorrow, I was going to take Him for a test drive right down the hallway at school and watch the miracles come out."

Inside the house, I responded to a grumbling stomach and headed for the chocolate chip cookies and ice-cold milk. Dad was barely awake on the couch while Comedy Central streamed through the room. Mom was reading in the den.

She called out, "Is that you, Honey?"

I could feel her sweetness in every cookie, each one packed with extra chocolate morsels. They were fresh today. Mom was all about giving. Interesting how I'd started noticing these things.

I walked by the den and said, "Hi, Mom, how's the book?"

"It's just another trashy romance novel," she replied with a smile. "How was the meeting?"

"I enjoyed the group. Everybody welcomed me and I felt right at home in no time, but it was different than going to NA. Tonight was speaker night. Someone told his story and received a medallion to mark the special occasion. It was pretty neat. I had no idea that a medallion could mean so much. It's supposed to be powerful enough to protect you from using drugs. They really made a big deal out of it. I can buy into that. Joe and I hit it off really well. I think he's going to make a great friend."

My mom closed the book on her index finger to mark the page. She took off her reading glasses and turned toward me with a look of approval.

"Sweetheart, I am very proud of you. I didn't think you would take recovery seriously. I am pleasantly surprised and more important, I'm impressed. You've changed a lot since you came home from the hospital. You're more grown-up. It's like you have some kind of wisdom you're tuned in to or like a voice in your head that gives you good advice that you listen to and follow. I can't explain it any other way. I'm certainly not responsible for this change in you. Whatever you're doing, you have my permission to keep it up."

She laughed, and we both knew how silly and unnecessary her last remark was.

She continued, "You know it's been a month since your accident. Tomorrow you return to school. Everybody will know about the wreck, but no one knows what really happened to your soul except your dad, me and you. That's kind of neat, because you've changed so much. I know it hasn't been easy for you at school. The kids can just be mean and nasty. But somehow things are going to be different. I'm not sure how, but I would love to be there when they see what I see. Boy, will they ever be surprised!"

"Mom, I finally understand what I did to create such a miserable life for myself. It all makes sense. I was an awkward kid with a grotesque face. Everybody noticed how terrified I was to be that way. I made myself an irresistible target for every kid who was looking for someone to make fun of. But that's over. I've got this new attitude, thanks to Joe and Dr. Stone. They taught me about self-acceptance."

Mom was very eager and interrupted me before I could finish.

"Thank goodness, I don't have to listen to you talk about your pathetic face one more time. I would rather hear about this new attitude you're going to take to school with you."

She was right. I had worked into such a bad habit of putting myself down. "Mom, the point is that now I accept everything about myself that I had been rejecting and frightened of. I hated my physical appearance, but no longer. Joe, Brenda, Dr. Stone, and the others don't mind the way I look. They hug me like I'm handsome. There is no ugliness when we're together. I hated being treated like I was a mutant laboratory reject. Call it nerd, geek, gawky, ungainly, graceless, or plain old weird. I'm still like that and Joe can see it. But when he makes fun of me, he's harmless and just goofing off. It's his way of telling me how much he cares. And that makes me feel strong, strong enough to withstand anything that could happen at school tomorrow, even the worst wise-ass who might try to insult me.

"I can accept being the way I am, because Joe can accept the way I am. He has taught me that I can keep walking when the world is busy being cruel and immature. My Higher Power is going to walk right beside me. So what could possibly go wrong?"

"Absolutely nothing!" Mom exclaimed. I felt the passionate certainty in her voice. My Higher Power was back again.

Mom threw her book aside without any concern about marking the page, stood up, and gathered me in her arms. Without another word, but with love written all over her face, she let me go with a kiss good-night. As I walked out of the den and up the stairs to my room, she stood at the bottom and watched. I could feel her watching me with admiration and respect. I didn't look back; I just kept moving, climbing up and away from the discarded life of a loser.

Back in my room for the night, I stretched out my broken leg on the bed for a few minutes. Then I headed to the bathroom. As I stepped into the room, I removed the brace and my shirt. The reflection of Buddy Seagle flying free, fast, and easy greeted me. Tomorrow he was going to be with me at school.

He was courageous and I intended to feed off of that unbreakable determination. I imagined walking out of the house with inner peace and wholeness and how that was going to represent all the change I needed to make it through the entire day. I was pretty excited and ready. I didn't need another day to prepare.

I fell asleep quickly. As daylight approached, I felt as though I was suspended somewhere between consciousness and another world. Brenda was there and the air became spicy, tangy, and pungent.

"Buddy, listen to me," she said. "Decide now who's going to show up at school tomorrow. Since you're not a dink anymore, there's no need to act like one—or you'll be treated like one. If it's Buddy Seagle, you will own the ground you walk on. If it's the scrawny geek, you'll get stomped. The students will think about you as you think of yourself. Choose wisely."

The voice I heard next was young and athletic. It was Joe.

"Buddy, you do pick the strangest ways to use your mind. My dreams aren't so creative. I'm usually hitting homeruns or scoring touchdowns. Your thoughts have their own energy. When you're walking down the hall at school, feel the emotion that you want to share with your classmates and they will be drawn to it.

"I became friends with your inner self, not your face. Your appearance is not who you are, it's just something to look at. What you feel when people look at you will determine whether you suffer or dignify yourself. Stop feeling ugly and others will be attracted to the beauty that shines through. Choose wisely."

Joe's message stayed with me. There was nothing to fear at school tomorrow as long as the feeling was right. And what feeling should that be?

Dr. Stone's voice answered my question. "Buddy, there is no such thing as a wrong feeling. However, you can choose the feelings you prefer. You have already mastered feeling depressed, defeated, abandoned, rejected, dissatisfied, tortured, and tormented. What about a few new ones like open, receptive, willing, and flexible?"

I frowned and asked, "Why did you pick those?

"Good question," the doctor replied. "Tomorrow, you need to have the willingness to walk among the other students without hesitation. You should be constantly letting go of what you see, and move on. Up to now, you have experienced life-long pain without knowing that joy can flow through you at the same time. Be receptive to that. You expect everybody to mock, tease, and ridicule you. If you desire to be accepted, you must be the first one to adapt. Being flexible will allow you to appreciate the other students with a feeling of compassion and friendly consideration. In return, you will receive the gift of belonging, which will warm you with well-being. In other words, send kindness out from your heart and more will flow in from those who feel it. Don't be afraid. They have hearts, too. And their hearts don't see ugly. Choose wisely."

As I drifted along in the dream, I figured out that "choose wisely" were the final words of each visitation and must mean something important. But what about the gift of belonging? How would that ever happen at school? I had never belonged there before.

The next voice was angelic and melodic, like musical notes. It belonged to Mom.

"Honey," she said. "I love you. There aren't enough cookies in the world to show you how much you mean to me. I know now that you belong in my heart and I welcome you to be there. You belong everywhere you go. At school tomorrow, make room in your heart for the other students and the favor will be returned. There is no better feeling. Trust me. Choose wisely."

I asked my last question, hoping He would hear me. "What do you mean by choose wisely?"

"You have been given the gift of awareness," came the powerful voice, "and tomorrow you will be able to understand people better than ever before. You have the inner guidance to choose wisely from now on."

One last voice coaxed, "Wake up, it's time for school."

The voice sounded familiar and soothing. I felt fingers in my hair. Mom was caressing me, something she hadn't done for years. It felt great. As I opened my eyes, she smiled brightly and said, "I'll have pancakes ready as soon as you get downstairs." With a last pat to my shoulder, she stood up and walked toward the door, then disappeared around the corner. I could hear her softly humming as she walked down the hallway. She was happy.

As I got up to face my first day back at school, I thought carefully about the dream and the messages I was supposed to be getting from it. I guessed that being able to choose wisely meant that my life was in my own hands and it was up to me to enjoy it or let addiction have it back. It was my choice.

In the bathroom, as I got ready for the day, I thought about school and gave myself a pep talk. I told myself I would get through the day somehow. I replayed the past month of my life: the overdoses, the accident, and all the people who crossed my path for good or evil. It had been an amazing journey that made me stronger, smarter, and wiser. I was definitely an upgraded version of myself, and I liked that.

Back in my bedroom, I cleaned around the pin holes of my fixator, put my back brace on, and got dressed. I took one last look at myself in the mirror before going downstairs for breakfast. By no means was I handsome, but the ugliness was gone. People either liked what they saw or they didn't—but no one was going to make friends with my face. They were going to get acquainted with me. And I intended to be worth knowing.

I glanced at Einstein as I left my room. His hair was unruly and looked electrified. With his tongue sticking out, he looked childish and idiotic. But now I knew he wasn't as ridiculous as he appeared. His appearance didn't matter and he knew it. I believed he was saying, "Don't take life so seriously. It will be over with soon enough and you'll regret not dancing to all the great music. Let go, be silly, and laugh at yourself."

I joined Junior and Dad at the kitchen table. We'd done this a million times before, but today was different. It was time to leave the safety of the nest. Flying school was over. Today was my first day at school as someone I had never been before.

My father put down his coffee and newspaper and said, "Son, you're not the boy we brought home from the hospital. You're a lot better than that and don't forget it—no matter what happens today. Keep your head up and you'll do fine."

Mom stood by the door with my backpack and did a final inspection. Once she was satisfied with my appearance, she said, "Today's a big day and I'm all excited for you. I believe in you now and I love you very much. Once the kids at school get a chance to find out who you really are, they'll either leave you alone or want to make friends with you. I'm sorry you have to go through this, but it's up to you now."

Her hug was tender and she kissed my forehead as she fought back tears. She held both my hands and looked at my face. I could tell that she did not see the pimples or anything else that was unattractive.

"I don't know how I failed to see what has become so obvious to me now. I'm sorry. I didn't know what I was missing." Mom's expression was filled with love for her son. We smiled at each other, and I felt grown up.

"Mom, I can take it from here. Whatever I need, I already have. See you after school." I closed the door softly behind me.

CHAPTER 59

Hearts Don't See Ugly

My walk to the bus was slow and deliberate. I was putting some weight on my leg, but I wasn't quite ready to leave my crutches behind. The back brace was well hidden by an oversized shirt. The fixator on my leg was going to get the most stares. It was hi-tech creepy, just what kids like to make faces at.

I kept my head down, as always, and a large shadow appeared beneath my feet. I looked up at a huge oak tree and was jolted by something. Thoughts were beginning to pour into my head, but they were fragmented and didn't make much sense. At the same time I became aware of a radically different feeling that I never had on my way to the bus. It was a feeling of being okay.

That encouraged me to pick my head up and look straight at my classmates. There they were, the kids who had stared, scoffed, and poked fun at me in the past. I froze and stopped fifty feet short of the bus stop and waited. I was always the last one to get on the bus. Fear was already gripping my heart.

I was surprised by a strange impulse to keep walking, so I followed it. My fear began to build, but as soon as I hesitated, an inner voice said, "Keep moving." I realized that it wasn't my Higher Power doing the talking. It was me. I was giving the directions.

Once again, I looked at the students. They were checking me out and I dreaded getting any closer. Then I heard my inner voice again. "If what you are seeing brings fear into your heart, letting go can replace it with love and joy."

It didn't mean anything at first. I thought it might have been a lesson from my Higher Power or maybe it was from Dr. Stone or Joe. As I thought about it, the feeling of being okay gradually returned. I started again toward the bus stop. As I got closer, I noticed the other kids talking out of the corner of their mouths. My inner voice spoke up again: "Don't label. Don't judge. If you want to be accepted, you have to start first. Appreciate them with kindness and you will belong."

Suddenly, my feet stopped moving. I was frozen on the spot. I looked at the kids, and the whispering halted. They were waiting for my next move.

The inner voice got louder and kept coaching me. "Send kindness out and more will come back. They have hearts, too. And their hearts don't see ugly."

At that moment, I knew what I had to do if I was going to be okay. A sense of calmness came over me. I lifted my right hand off the handle of the crutch and began to wave. I forced myself to smile. "Hi, Everybody," I said with confidence. "If you missed me, I'm back. If you didn't even know I was gone, I've got an unbelievable story to tell you."

The silence continued. They all looked like deer in the headlights, stalled in the middle of the road. Up until now, all they had ever seen was how unapproachable I was. They had never heard a kind word from me and I had never heard a kind word from them.

As I started to move forward, their eyes remained glued to mine. Intuitively, I felt these young people didn't want to despise or reject me. They were probably curious and wanted to know what happened to me. What was the next kindest thing to do? Tell them about the crash, the broken body parts, and anything else that kids find gruesomely exciting. I was not going to be afraid and appear unapproachable. I wanted to give them a chance. I wanted to give *me* a chance.

Suddenly, I lost my balance and started to stagger.

The staggering lead to stumbling and, as I tried to catch myself, I fell. My arms were outstretched, preparing to break my collision with the ground. The crash was not graceful. The palms of my hands stung from skidding along the sidewalk. My nose hit hard and was instantly swollen and throbbing. I'd landed facedown and I hesitated to move. I thought I might be broken again.

Two sneakered feet appeared next to my head. A sympathetic female voice asked, "Are you all right? Let me help you." Then she knelt down and began to gently assist as I turned over onto my back. When our eyes met, there was concern in hers, and I hoped she could see the gratitude in mine.

"Thanks," I said sincerely. "I'm so clumsy with these crutches. Can you give me a hand?"

My smile returned as soon as I realized that there were no serious injuries. My swollen nose was no big deal. At the worst, I'd have a couple of raccoon eyes the next day as they turned black and blue.

The girl smiled back, then called her friends over. Her voice was filled with relief. Then she said the nicest words anyone from school had ever spoken to me.

"Let's take it easy and go slow. You've been hurt enough already, we don't want to hurt you anymore. Right, Guys?"

Three of her friends had joined her and they nodded in agreement. As four sets of hands began to grab hold and help me off the ground, what I heard next was even more surprising.

"Relax, we've got you."

"Just let us do all the work."

"On three, we'll lift you up.

As I felt all the hands carefully hoist me off the ground, I noticed them matching my smile. It was as though "ugly" and "pimples" had been deleted from their vocabulary and prejudice was unknown to them. It was as though Joe, Wendy, Doc, my mom, and Brenda were in the hearts and minds of these kids who were all pulling for me.

Just a month ago, those same students were taking a sadistic pleasure in making fun of everything I hated about myself. They were replicas of me, carrying out my thoughts of insecurity and self-loathing. Now they were demonstrating a genuine act of kindness. Stumbling and falling were more like a leap of faith into the waiting arms of my schoolmates. This was what belonging felt like.

I stood and quickly checked the straps of my back brace. I tapped the fixator to make sure the pins were rigidly in place. I leaned on my crutches after exhaling a deep breath. Everybody was watching me and finally someone spoke up.

"Well, are you okay or do we need to call 911?"

There was real confusion about my condition and they looked worried. That meant one thing: They weren't pretending. At that moment, they seemed to actually care about me. That was as close to belonging as I had ever felt.

I decided to test the limits. While I touched my swollen, scraped, and bloodied nose, I quipped, "I don't mind taking a fall for you guys, but the next time you invite me over to play crash-test dummy, at least bring some Band-Aids and an ice pack."

Everyone laughed nervously and they began to jostle me around in the friendliest way. It was like an initiation. I was no longer an outcast. I was vulnerable and needed them, and they needed my kindness for their hearts. I saw beauty everywhere I looked. Ugly was nowhere to be found. The loser was gone and forgotten. They helped me off the ground because it was the right thing to do under the circumstances. The Maker's Love was the power that brought us all together and let the miracle occur.

The girl who had first helped me stood directly in front of me and asked, "You're Buddy, aren't you?"

"Yes," I answered.

"You were in that bad accident a month ago, right?"

I pointed at the pins in my leg. "Right."

"We were wondering what happened to you. Nobody knew for sure."

"I was in quite a wreck, with an assortment of broken body parts."

She looked embarrassed. "I want you to know that you've always been a mystery to us. I'll be the first to admit I wasn't polite. Actually, it must have seemed to you like we were . . ."

"Cruel," I said. The word jumped out of my mouth, because it was too painful to keep it locked up any longer.

"Exactly," she agreed. "There was no excuse for that behavior and I want to apologize. Ignorance is no reason to be nasty. I don't know if you'll ever forgive me, but I sure would like to start over. You seem like a pretty nice guy."

Other voices chimed in with, "We're sorry," and "Me, too."

My kindness toward them was paying off. I was receiving the kind of guidance that I could put to good use, and it was time for me to be humble.

"I want to thank all of you for coming over to help, but mostly for being honest and open-minded. I have a bit of a confession to make and that will probably take every ounce of courage I have."

Every one of them looked serious and focused.

"I'm not exactly a Brad Pitt look-alike. It was my fault for feeling like a total reject before any of you had a chance to treat me that way."

They were silent, and I wondered if I was doing the right thing.

One of the guys in the group stepped forward. He was tall, handsome, and athletic, my polar opposite.

He said, "Buddy, if that's the worst of it, I don't have a problem with you. You see, I'm barely getting Ds in my easiest subjects and I hear you are as brilliant as Einstein. Your zits don't bother me. Not getting a scholarship to play football bothers me. Do you think we could work something out here?"

He wrapped a long arm around my shoulders and pulled me in tight. "With your brains and my body, we can go places."

That loosened everyone up. They all started laughing and gave me pats on the back.

When the bus honked, everyone grabbed their book bags. A very pretty girl who was holding mine asked if I needed any more help.

"No, thanks, I'm okay now."

"I'll save you a seat," she called back as she hurried to board.

The rest of the group was already getting on board. The guys were pushing and shoving as always and the girls watched with amusement and practiced nonchalance. As I carefully climbed the step, a voice called out from an open window, "Come on, Buddy, move it along or take another day off from school." It was the football player and he was smiling the whole time. It felt good to have my chain yanked in a nice way.

Once I was inside, I saw a girl patting the cushion of a front-row seat, inviting me to sit beside her. She smiled at me as I sat down, then took her cell phone out and began texting.

At that moment, it occurred to me that I had finally done it. Everything I was taught in the past week literally came true, right before my eyes. It was unbelievable, yet I should have expected it, because I was prepared. I owed so much to so many for making it possible. I decided it was best to sit back and take it all in and feel grateful. The scrawny, pimple-faced, geeky nerd was only a creation of my mind that came to life when I was convinced it was the truth. An act of love canceled that mistake and brought me new friends.

And what about Him?

My inner voice said, "Who, me?"

And I muttered under my breath, "No . . . Him. Where is He when I want to say thanks?"

"I'm still here. Where did you think I went, to a Higher Power convention?"

Laughter bounded through my head like an echo. My inner voice was Him all the time.

"Better get used to it, Kid. This is just the beginning of something truly amazing. Trust me, you won't want to miss it. Because I am you and you are Me and we are the One. Don't you get it? You never were a loser. You've always been perfect, whole, and complete. Like Me."

Just then, my new bus partner said, "I don't know where you just went with your mind, but I bet it was someplace smart. Anyway, you're kind of cute when you do that."

And then she giggled and went right back to texting.

I smiled. I was finally comfortable with my own skin.

EPILOGUE

Joe and I pulled into the parking lot at Dr. Stone's office. Half of the group was outside smoking and consuming high-powered energy drinks, the newest way to get a sober fix with caffeine, taurine, and sugar. Joe reached into his pocket and pulled something out. He kept it concealed in his hand.

"Buddy," he said. "Tonight's the night, isn't it? You get to tell your Step One story. Are you ready?"

I was ready, all right. I had been through the toughest three months of my life and I was proud to be sober. My leg and back had healed perfectly and I was walking with barely a limp. I had done ninety Narcotics Anonymous meetings since leaving the hospital. I had made quite a bit of newcomer progress in addiction recovery. I took out the red key tag I received at last night's NA meeting.

"Joe, when I got started in sobriety, I had no idea what was in store for me. I thought giving up pills would be more than enough. I can understand now why that was just the beginning. Tonight I want to tell the group what it was like growing up as someone who wished he had never been born. Being a geek isn't so bad as long as you like what you've become. But I hated every minute of my life, because I hated me. Thanks to you, Dr. Stone, and the group, I don't feel that way anymore."

"You'd better not," Joe said. "All of us, including your parents, worked long and hard to break you out of that habit. I'm glad those days are over."

"I guess I'm ready, then."

Joe opened his hand and I saw what he was holding.

"Before we go in, I want you to know that I'm giving you my Praying Hands medallion. It's done me a lot of good. It's time you take care of it, and it will take care of you. Okay?"

"Thanks, Joe. Of course I will."

We looked at each other and I could read in his eyes the emotion that he was feeling in his heart.

"I love you, my friend," he said. "I mean that. You have brought so much joy into my life. As weird as you are, I wouldn't have it any other way. We're perfect together. You're the first person I have ever sponsored and I'm still learning." He sniffled a bit and wiped a tear from the corner of his eye.

"I have become closer to you than anyone I know," I said. "I trust you with my life and I value our friendship as much as I will value that medallion and my sobriety. I will honor it forever. Now, let's go before they start without us."

We took our seats as Dr. Stone was giving his traditional introduction. We all welcomed Marci, the newcomer to the group, then he turned the meeting over to me. I was eager to get started.

"Hi, everybody. Tonight I am telling my Step One story. I have to admit I've been rehearsing it, because I want to get it right. I waited this long because I wanted to be sure I had changed enough and was totally ready. For me this is an honor and privilege that I take very seriously. My name is Buddy and if it wasn't for all of you, I would be a very bitter, lonely, unhappy kid. Instead I am a grateful recovering addict.

"When I was growing up, my parents tried to be good to me and I hated it. Eventually, I hated myself even more. Then I got lost in a world of my own pain. Pills never took the pain away. In a very short time, they were responsible for so much wreckage that it has taken me nearly three months to recover from it. That's what brought me here. I want to tell you how I got addicted so fast and why I didn't need months or years of it before I could be rescued. However, I would like to start from the beginning and not leave out anything important. So here goes. . . ."

After I finished my story, Dr. Stone held up Joe's Praying Hands medallion for everyone to see.

"This young man is not supposed to be here tonight. The odds were not in his favor. He should not have survived three overdoses and a crash so serious that he was in a coma for ten days. Yet here he is without any physical problems. To me, that's a miracle. These miracles can't be bought. They can't be earned. They are gifts that are unexplainable. Why he was chosen is unknown to me. Why any of us have been chosen is a mystery. But now that we have been, it's up to us to use it wisely. So Buddy, I ask you, are you willing to preserve and protect this gift? How much will you do each day to keep the gift of sobriety? I don't have that answer. But I do recommend that you do more than enough and not take any chances. Because every day you are sober, the world is a better place for all of us. When you use pills, you're a burden. When you're drug-free, you're a blessing. And I would rather have you become what you are meant to be, which so far has been something incredible. Congratulations on your first three months of sobriety."

The group remained silent as he stood up and hugged me before giving me the medallion.

As we embraced, I said, "Doc, you have been the blessing in my life. Thanks for believing in me and making all of this possible."

The rest of the group applauded, then took turns greeting me with hugs and words of congratulations and encouragement. It felt great.

After the meeting was over and everyone else was gone, Joe took Dr. Stone aside. I told Joe I'd meet him at the car. The air was breezy and cooling off as the sun went down. I stood alone and kept rubbing the medallion with my thumb. I found it hard to believe that only ninety days had gone by, it seemed more like a year.

I was a sixteen-year-old opioid addict. Pills that were meant to be fun nearly put me in a casket. A truckload of painkillers still wouldn't have been enough for me—I always needed more. There was only one explanation for that, I was hooked. It no longer mattered how I got that way. It only mattered how I was going to stay sober.

A voice from within caught my attention.

"We only have to do it one day at a time."

I smiled, because I heard His voice and mine together as friends. He had been me all along, only bigger . . . He was much bigger.

ACKNOWLEDGMENTS

I owe thanks to many people whose influence inspired, supported, and encouraged me over the years. Without them, this book would not be.

To my wife JoAnn, who encouraged me to write this book and pour all of my passion for the subject of addiction onto every page. For the past twenty years she has faithfully stood by me wherever the practice of addiction medicine brought me, all the time nurturing my patients with acts of kindness to instill hope and faith that one day they too could be restored to happy, productive, and prosperous lives. She confidently believes that the readers of this book will know how much my heart has chosen the words, and their authenticity can lead many onto the path of recovery, a path where the first crucial steps to healing can be taken by the addict as well as their families and friends. JoAnn has made the ultimate sacrifice, a willingness to allow me to devote nearly all of my very little free time for the past two years of my life as I created this book. She did this with patience, understanding, and unwavering love.

To my dedicated office staff. Thank you for your contribution to all of the daily challenges we manage as a team. Because of all that you have done for me and our patients, this book was made possible and is now one more extremely important way for us to help them.

To my parents, Fred and Jane Smolen, who profoundly deserve so much credit for providing me with an excellent start in life and all the tools I needed to remain successful. I apologize for all the pain and suffering they had to endure because of how I acted under the influence of my addiction. I hope that offering my sobriety, my work with addicts, and this book in some way makes up for their loss and heartbreak.

To my brother Robin Smolen and my sister Susan Smolen, two of the kindest, most gentle, and giving souls on the planet, I thank you for always loving me, no matter how far I strayed, and welcoming me back whenever I returned. Thank you for taking care of our parents and making so many of their years worthwhile and comfortable.

To my three children, Jay, Ryan, and Kelly, I love you and miss you very much. I hope and pray that one day your hearts will soften and we can become a family again. Until then, I thank you for the best years a dad could ever hope for, raising three wonderful children for as long as it lasted.

To my stepchildren, Sean and Nicole Trites, who love me generously and are with me each day to fill my life with joy, hugs, and I love you's. Thank you for honoring me with respect and admiration that has made me feel fatherly.

This book was possible because of my successful journey on the path of recovery from alcoholism. Without all the teachers and teachings along that path, I would have perished like so many who were not fortunate enough to become ready to choose a sober life. I am grateful that Alcoholics Anonymous with its Twelve Steps was available for me to attend daily meetings. There are thousands of other alcoholics who shared some aspect of my life as I attended thousands of AA meetings. I am thankful for their willingness to show me the way.

AA also prepared my sponsor and trusted friend, Jim Fenimore, now with over forty years of sobriety, to guide me through troubled and difficult times. He supplied me with friendship and love and helped me to overcome depression and regain my self-esteem and confidence. He convinced me that I could and should return to the practice of medicine. He saw to it that I remained sober as I met every challenge and rebuilt my life successfully back to prosperity, abundance, good health, and happiness.

During the first ten years of my sobriety in AA, I was helped by the experience, strength, and wisdom of Mark McEnerney, David Dorian, Ted Newhook, and many others who were close companions on my journey and hopefully remember our time together.

A special thank you to Ted Newhook, who was there when I was down to my last dollar and eagerly gave me my first job cleaning carpets after I regrettably closed my medical practice because of severe depression. Being out of work was extremely humbling for me, and Ted was there to help me off my knees. He was also my best man when I married JoAnn.

To Dr. Andrew Reinfurt, who was my personal physician, exceptional friend, and spiritual advisor. He included me in his beautiful family and shared his faith-based beliefs that gave me hope.

To Jim Ganley, an author and personal trainer who spent many productive years with me at Smolen Clinic when I was practicing sports medicine and orthopedics. He has made the biggest contribution during many years of my professional success in the '80s and '90s. He read the first draft of my manuscript and sent it to Janet Brennan, who liked it and became my publisher.

I also owe a great deal to the world-renowned transformational leaders whose writings I have been depending on for thirty years, most notably Jack Canfield and the Breakthrough to Success (BTS) meetings I attended. Jack inspired me to create a vision of success that included this book and much more. Michelle O'Connell is credited for becoming my Canfield Coach during the first draft of the manuscript, reading every word and planting the belief in my mind that it would turn out to be great.

I also joined a BTS Mastermind group that included Dave Dyall, Jennie Dyall, Ralf and Cornia Holzapfel, Betty Crossman, and John Smith. Since August 2008, this supportive group has joined me on a conference call every three weeks to hear updates on the progress with the book. They've contributed their encouragement and eagerly anticipated its completion and release. Special thanks to Dave Dyall, who also read the entire manuscript as I submitted the newest pages each day. He cheered for me to keep writing and was my devoted fan.

To David Klement for spending nearly three years of Saturday mornings with me over breakfast, kindling a friendship that has become wholesome, warm, and personal. Our sharing has become progressively more private and cleansing, something I found useful to unclutter my mind and stay on the task of my mission and purpose for starting and completing the book.

To Martha Brown, MD, a colleague in addiction psychiatry with impressive credentials who has been my mentor since 2001 when I began my Fellowship in Addiction Psychiatry at the University of South Florida. She has been instrumental in the advancement of my career in all the right directions.

To Janet and Art Brennan, husband and wife partners at Casa de Snapdragon, who have been willing to take on this project. Publishing a work of fiction on the topic of addiction is something new to them. They believed that my personal triumph over addiction and my experience with its treatment prepared me to write a compelling story.

To Candace Johnson for the ingenious line editing of my manuscript. After meeting me and JoAnn, she was inspired to work with me to deliver a cleaned-up manuscript that I would be proud of. She gave her heart and soul to this endeavor and always cheerfully motivated me with the brightest, most positive optimism. The fact that she came into our lives is a reflection of the incredible power we all have to shape our destinies . . . if we just believe.

To Ryan for reading the manuscript and helping me to accurately describe the experience Buddy had getting high on opioids. To Jake for his work on the cover and the photography. To Jared for helping to create the cover.

And finally, to all of my patients with the condition of addiction who have struggled to remain on the sober path: your stories both humble and inspire us to always strive to do the next right thing. That is the only way to get to where you want to go in recovery and it's worth it, every single step . . . even the painful ones.

ABOUT THE AUTHOR

Jamie Smolen, MD, a former orthopedic surgeon and sports-medicine physician, became a psychiatrist to help others recover their mental health as he had overcome major depression. His proudest and most challenging achievement is his sobriety from alcoholism for more than twenty years; he has been sober since February 26, 1991. He now specializes in the treatment of addictions as his most important purpose and mission in life.

Born and raised in Ludlow, MA, the youngest of three children, Jamie enjoyed a traditional 1950s family life. His interest in choosing orthopedic surgery as his first career stemmed from the multiple sports-related injuries he sustained in high school. Jamie entered the pre-medical program offered at St. Anselm College, in Manchester, NH, graduating in 1971 with a bachelor's degree in biology.

He attended Georgetown University Medical School, was married, and graduated in 1975. He completed a surgical internship at the University of Vermont in 1976 and moved to Worcester where he trained in orthopedic surgery at the University of Massachusetts. By then, Jamie's alcoholism had become pervasive and adversely affected his marriage. A highly skilled surgeon who was still operating with precision and dexterity, he was in a state of denial that all alcoholics encounter, and he did not seek help.

In 1980 he set up his private practice of orthopedics in Manchester, New Hampshire, while alcoholism continued to take an extensive toll on his marriage and professional career. Because of alcohol, he regrettably gave up his one true passion—orthopedic surgery—and adjusted his career to include sports medicine. Finally, in 1986, Jamie became sober for the first time.

His medical practice grew and he became a pioneer in the field of physical rehabilitation, shortening recovery time and restoring injured athletes to peak conditioning. He became a team physician to the local high schools and colleges. He took an avid interest in positive psychology, applying it to his patients who were in pain and suffering from depression.

He aggressively pursued a successful and fulfilling life of fitness and spiritual well-being until 1991. Devastated by the death of his mother, Jamie relapsed with alcohol, which had a long-lasting and detrimental impact on his life.

On February 26, 1991, he joined Alcoholics Anonymous. Applying their recovery principles to his life, Jamie learned an entirely new way of living. As he gained sober experience, he invested nearly all of his time working with other alcoholics; this became his next passion. By that time a father of three, Jamie's troubled marriage finally ended in divorce, which led to a career-ending major depression. He closed his practice in 1994 to devote himself to his own personal recovery from depression.

During years of individual counseling and psychiatric treatment, Jamie began to rebuild his life. He met and married a woman who would become his strongest supporter and devoted partner.

Jamie established a new career, utilizing his medical expertise by consulting with multiple law firms, doing case reviews for several years. But his true passion—working with alcoholics—eventually awakened the possibility of returning to the practice of medicine. He was accepted into residency training at Boston University in 1998 at the age of forty-eight. After four more years, he completed fellowship training at the University of South Florida in Tampa, becoming an addiction psychiatrist. Jamie set up his private practice in Bradenton, Florida in 2002, and also worked at Manatee Memorial Hospital at the Center for Behavioral Health. He became board certified in psychiatry with special qualification in addiction psychiatry.

At the time of this book's publication, Jamie has been happily married for fifteen years and credits his wife with helping him establish and manage the daily operations of his very successful practice. He also enjoys a close relationship with his two stepchildren. Jamie devotes a large part of his practice to the treatment of opioid dependence, which afflicts millions through the abuse of pain pills. The alarming rise in deaths from accidental drug overdoses prompted him to write this book in hopes of bringing desperately needed attention to this epidemic and to encourage addicts to seek treatment.

Recent Releases from Casa de Snapdragon

Adventures of a Substitute Teacher
Tim Kreiter
ISBN: 9780984568178
Genre: Humor/General

Tim Kreiter gives readers a glimpse of the often amusing, frequently hilarious, and always entertaining happenings inside contemporary classrooms. These real life adventures are seen through the eyes of one who loves children, filtered through the imagination of one who relishes humor, and illustrated by the itchy fingers of one who enjoys cartooning. A thoroughly delightful read!

They don't make memories like that anymore ...
Katrina K Guarascio
ISBN: 9781937240004
Genre: Poetry

Katrina Guarascio explores the "slap and kick" of love, memory and destiny. These lyrical poems travel the complex and passionate journey between the "I" and "you,"—evoking the self, lover, friend, family member as well as river, flower, ocean and cloud. In these poems, the poet-speaker looks for and finds herself in the interweaving world. These poems embrace a large and personal universe that vibrates "between skin and bone," reverberating with song.

A Thousand Doors
Matt Pasca
ISBN: 9780984568161
Genre: Poetry

Matt Pasca's poems maneuver deftly between the seemingly simple and mundane details of the world around us and the sublime world we often miss in the myopia of our pain. Published by JB Stillwater Publishing (a subsidiary of Casa de Snapdragon LLC)

Visit us at http://www.casadesnapdragon.com for more information on these and many other fine books.